Shakespeare: The Tragedies

Related titles from the same publishers

Shakespeare: The Tragedies

JOHN RUSSELL BROWN

palgrave

First published 2001 by
PALGRAVE
Houndmills, Basingstoke, Hampshire RG21 6XS and
175 Fifth Avenue, New York, N.Y. 10010
Companies and representatives throughout the world

PALGRAVE is the new global academic imprint of
St. Martin's Press LLC Scholarly and Reference Division and
Palgrave Publishers Ltd (formerly Macmillan Press Ltd).

ISBN 0–333–58956–4 hardback
ISBN 0–333–58957–2 paperback

This book is printed on paper suitable for recycling and
made from fully managed and sustained forest sources.

A catalogue record for this book is available
from the British Library.

Library of Congress Cataloging-in-Publication Data
Brown, John Russell.
    Shakespeare : the tragedies / John Russell Brown.
        p. cm.
    Includes bibliographical references and index.
    ISBN 0–333–58956–4 (cloth)
        1. Shakespeare, William, 1564–1616 — Tragedies. 2. Tragedy. I. Title.

PR2983.B76 2000
822.3'3—dc21   00-041498

10   9   8   7   6   5   4   3   2   1
10 09 08 07 06 05 04 03 02 01

Printed in China

Contents

List of Illustrations

Preface

The purpose of this book is to share my reading of the plays and show what experiences they can offer to audiences. In doing so, I tell the story of Shakespeare's pursuit of new forms for his tragedies, in structure, dialogue, and focus of attention.

Inevitably, I am indebted to a great company of people whom I cannot acknowledge and thank individually. Other writers on my subject are so numerous and so aware of each other that no one could keep track of each influence; only for specific and factual discoveries have I been able to indicate sources. I am also indebted to many students, colleagues, and friends, especially those at the Universities of Sussex and Michigan where I have taught in recent years, and at Middlesex University where I teach at present. These influences are still more difficult to identify because there is no permanent evidence for the continual rephrasings and appropriations that happen from day to day. Indebtedness to actors and others with whom I have worked in the theatre is the most difficult of all to re-collect in any detail because this experience underlies everything I can write about the plays. I hope that some of my associates in theatres and universities will recognize themselves as helpful presences in these pages and will accept this necessarily unspecific but hearty thanks.

My considerable debts to editors of individual plays I can gratefully acknowledge. Particular use was made of the Arden editions for *Titus Andronicus* (1995) by Jonathan Bate, *Richard the Third* (1981) by Antony Hammond, *Richard the Second* (1956) by Peter Ure, *Romeo and Juliet* (1980) by Brian Gibbons, *Othello* (1996) by E. A. J. Honigmann, and *King Lear* (1997) by R. A. Foakes; of the Oxford editions for *Julius Caesar* (1984) by Arthur Humphreys, *Macbeth* (1990) by Nicholas Brooke, and *Coriolanus* (1994) by R. B. Parker; and of the New Cambridge edition for *Antony and Cleopatra* (1990) by David Bevington. In chapters considering individual plays, quotations and references are from these editions, although I have occasionally modified punctuation and some presentational details for the benefit of the immediate context. For *Hamlet* I made use of both G. R. Hibbard's Oxford edition (1987) and Harold Jenkins's Arden (1982); quotations and references are from the more complete Arden text. To make cross-references consistent and more accessible, all other quotations and references are to the one-volume edition of the complete works edited by Peter Alexander (London: Collins, 1951).

While none of this book has appeared in print before, Chapter 3 uses, with permission, some passages reworked from a lecture in *Proceedings of the British Academy*, 87 (1995), and passages from articles that appeared in *Connotations*, II:1 and 3 are reworked in the chapters on *Hamlet*. Two friends and earlier colleagues, R. A. Foakes and A. K. Thorlby, read an earlier draft and I have benefited greatly from their comments and suggestions. I am most grateful for this generous and painstaking help.

Progress at the hands of the publishers and my own involvement in writing have both been greatly assisted by the generous support and careful advice of Margaret Bartley. Additionally, by her means, I have enjoyed the comradeship of Graham Holderness and Kieran Ryan, authors of two parallel but independent books on the histories and comedies; in a series of convivial lunches, the four of us have been able to benefit from each other's views on how best to serve our readers in presenting these plays. While preparing for publication, I have also been ably assisted by Beverley Tarquini and Felicity Noble. Later, during copy-editing and production, Valery Rose has, once again, been most attentive and helpful.

JOHN RUSSELL BROWN
Court Lodge, Hooe

1

A Theatre for Tragedy

In England for a few decades around the year 1600, audiences crowded to see tragedies that ended in violence and disaster. Death came in many forms but always brought the revaluation of a life, as an individual was separated from his or her fellows and endured some kind of trial or confrontation. Tragedies were usually named after these central characters, and audiences invited to judge their ultimate resources of thought and feeling. In words taken from John Webster's *The White Devil* of 1612, it was thought that:

> . . . affliction
> Expresseth virtue, fully, whether true,
> Or else adulterate. (I.i.49–51)

Death brought a final truth-telling.

Perhaps tragedies were so popular because they offered audiences the opportunity to assume the role of an all-seeing assessor not unlike the God whose judgements were otherwise reported by authoritative clerics, often in fierce disagreement with each other. As they watched a fellow human being suffer, they were invited to act as judge of his or her intrinsic worth. Near the end of Shakespeare's *Tragedy of Julius Caesar*, men are likened to horses valued for their ability to confront danger and pain:

> There are no tricks in plain and simple faith;
> But hollow men, like horses hot at hand,

1

> Make gallant show and promise of their mettle;
> But when they should endure the bloody spur,
> They fall their crests, and like deceitful jades
> Sink in the trial.   (IV.ii.22–7)

Towards the end of *Hamlet*, the hero tries to share his own sense of a 'bloody spur' that is about to probe to his very heart: 'thou wouldst not think how ill all's here about my heart' (V.ii.202–8). He moves through the play as if seeking an ultimate judgement on himself, rounding on Guildenstern who tries to 'sound' him and 'pluck the heart out of [his] mystery', considering what is 'nobler' in the mind, what is 'rightly to be great', and to what 'base uses' even the greatest heroes must return (III.i.57; IV.iv.53; V.i.197–210). In later tragedies, the true and tested nature of their heroes is the subject of active interrogation. In the first Act, King Lear asks: 'Who is it that can tell me who I am?' (I.iv.229) and this question persists in different forms to the very end. Near his last moments, Othello asks: 'Who can control his fate?' and 'Where should Othello go?' (V.ii.268 and 274). Rather than asking questions, Macbeth realizes that he no longer responds as he did: 'I have almost forgot the taste of fears . . . ' (V.v.9). The later tragedies are more speculative and their questions involve other persons: 'O mother, mother! / What have you done?' in *Coriolanus* (V.iii.185–6) and 'Think you there was or might be such a man / As this I dreamt of?' in *Antony and Cleopatra* (V.ii.93–4).

This probing of a personal mystery is one reason why Shakespeare's tragedies are still performed today. We are interested in the hero's inner consciousness at least as keenly as we await the satisfaction of barbarous revenge, overthrow of a tyrant, or consequence of love or lust. *Hamlet, Lear, Othello*, and *Macbeth* remain the most performed and studied plays in the history of theatre despite portraying societies and dynasties long dead and debating political, moral, and philosophical themes in terms that are no longer current. Many people see these plays time and again because they raised questions about human nature that were new and even revolutionary in their own times and today, in the words of Søren Kierkegaard, offer entrance to that 'midnight hour when all men must unmask'.

Yet this is not all. The unfolding of these stories grips attention as well as their outcome for the heroes. As Samuel Johnson noted in his *Preface* to the plays (1765):

> Others please us by particular speeches, but he always makes us anxious for the event, and has perhaps excelled all but Homer in securing the first purpose of a writer, by exciting restless and unquenchable curiosity and compelling him that reads his work to read it through.

And that is only half of the matter: besides working on a reader's curiosity, the very shape of the action can spell-bind an audience. As Friedrich Nietzsche wrote of Greek tragedies in *The Birth of Tragedy* (1870–1):

> The structure of the scenes and the concrete images convey a deeper wisdom than the poet was able to put into words and concepts. The same may be claimed for Shakespeare, whose Hamlet speaks more superficially than he acts, so that interpretation of *Hamlet* [has] to be based on a deeper investigation of the whole texture of the play.

In Shakespeare's tragedies, the alternation of scenes provides a succession of very different visual images. A crowded stage may be followed by one that is almost empty. Sometimes a ceremony or ritual, an argument or debate, that involves many figures in meaningful relationships, will give way to a face-to-face encounter between two persons, a chase or fight, a series of entries and departures, or a free-for-all of almost chaotic activity. A stage property, such as throne, grave, altar, or weapon, can focus attention on a particular action or give indisputable symbolic value and be followed by snatches of improvised business that give little rest to the eye or allusive speech that unsettles earlier perceptions. Such variations of action and 'concrete images', functioning in conjunction with story and plot, strongly affect the experience offered to an audience and, as a consequence, these tragedies have appealed to audiences across almost every barrier of language, culture, and politics. They have been adapted to other styles of theatre production, reworked as opera, dance, musical theatre, film, television, and radio, and inspired prose fictions, poetry, and even burlesque and comic strips. Their stories, structure, and spectacle can carry the plays and if we wish to understand what they offer to audiences, in addition to the sense and suggestions of the words and the minds of their heroes, we must also take account of the ever-changing interest of their stories and all that happens on the stage.

Methods of study developed for literary texts will not entirely serve. In 1931, in a letter on language, Antonin Artaud, actor, director, and visionary, emphasized the physical and sensuous quality of Shakespeare's tragedies:

> . . . if we are clearly so incapable today of giving an idea of Aeschylus, Sophocles, Shakespeare that is worthy of them, it is probably because we have lost the sense of their theater's physics. It is because the directly human and active aspect of their way of speaking and moving, their whole scenic rhythm, escapes us. An aspect that ought to have as much if not more importance than the admirable dissection of their heroes' psychology.

Once attention is given to their 'active' elements, the achievement of Shakespeare's tragedies cannot be explained solely in terms of the inner resources of their leading characters. In performance, they require a whole company of actors, a 'fellowship of players', as Hamlet calls them, who can 'let fly' at an entire play and bring every part of it to life. The presence of up to twenty or more actors is responsible for the 'traffic' of the stage that the Prologue to *Romeo and Juliet* introduces and which, in all the tragedies, brings families, kingdoms, or warring factions before our sight. The demands of nation, race, sexuality, intelligence, supernatural influences, ambition, and poverty are all made evident to our senses by the action and 'scenic rhythm' of entire plays.

The effect of what happens on stage depends on how an audience responds. In an Elizabethan theatre, where spectators were close to the actors and in the same light, a rapport between them could sometimes be very close, at other times antagonistic, puzzled, or encouraging; occasionally, both watchers and watched might be of the same mind and experience similar feelings. The conclusion of a performance could be a shared triumph or disaster, both parties elated or wearied after collusion in continuous and varied effort. Then the experience would be similar to that at the end of a hard-fought game: the goals scored are important, but so is the whole process which resulted in them, the quality of the game. If our study concentrates on what the tragic heroes say and do, we will some-times miss where the action is and fail to explain what happens to an audience and its changing view of the drama.

Attention to the words of a few leading characters is, however, by far the easiest way of studying these plays and, until recently, this approach was almost universal. The pattern was firmly established by Andrew Bradley in his *Shakespearean Tragedy* of 1904. Head and shoulders above his contemporaries, he traced the various conflicts between good and evil, the crises in the minds of the principal char-acters, their recognition of fate or the supernatural, but all these ele-ments were judged of less importance than the intellectual 'greatness' of the tragic heroes. Shakespeare's tragedies were about individuals who compel our respect because of their hidden reserves of power: being born to greatness, they achieve even greater greatness. Bradley belonged to a world in which many people believed that one strong-minded man could set the world to rights and he presented Shakespeare's 'tragic vision' in support of that assumption. He defined this greatness in many ways: strength of 'will', 'life', 'glory', 'magnificence', 'magnitude'. While recognizing the growing weak-ness of Lear, he still held his ground:

> we feel also that everything external has become nothingness to him, and that what remains is 'the thing itself', the soul in its bare great-ness.

Critics following Bradley were slow to question his basic assump-tion that the intellectual spirit or 'character' of their heroes is the dominant feature and greatest achievement of the tragedies although they define what these are according to different views of exceptional human experience. For example, John Bayley's *Shakespeare and Tragedy* (1981) offers an alienated hero:

Shakespeare's instinct, in a tragic setting, seems always to be at work through characters who in one way or another are unsuited to the action, its conventions, its atmosphere. Their natures in fact declare themselves through this unsuitability: it is by this means we get to know them and to feel intimate with them.

But in common with Bradley, Bayley has no doubt that the 'mind' of the protagonist is the principal achievement of a tragedy:

The usurpation by the mind of both practical action and purposeful idea in tragedy . . . is the most important feature of Shakespeare's relations with the tragic form.

The study which is now beginning is different from either of these predecessors by making its object of attention the whole achievement of each play in continuous performance before an audience. Bertolt Brecht, dramatist, performer, director, and theorist, was one of the earliest to insist on this width of critical focus. In *The Messingkauf Dialogues* (1939–42), writing of the tragedies from several points of view, he recognized their political, historical, and social implications and interest:

The Dramaturg.	What about tragedy in Shakespeare?
The Philosopher.	He takes a tragic view of the decline of feudalism. . . . [His tragic heroes] are all living in a new world and are smashed by it.
The Actor.	That explanation might spoil the plays for a lot of people.
The Philosopher.	But how could there be anything more complex, fascinating and important than the decline of great ruling classes?

Without making such deductions, Harley Granville Barker was another dramatist, performer, and director who, as a critic, insisted on a similar width of attention. His series of *Prefaces* to individual plays (1927–47) give as much attention to dramatic structure and on-stage action as to the consciousness of the tragic heroes. For this critic, the tragedies were complex mechanisms that show what he called a 'world' or 'life', as well as individual characters and a story: *Hamlet* he saw as a play for an 'age of doubt' while, in *King Lear*, he identified a 'capricious cruelty' as the 'main tragic truth about life'.

A similar concern with what happens in the full scope of the tragedies is found in advertisements written for their original title-pages. The first quarto edition of *Richard III* (1597), for example, is not recommended for its psychological revelations:

> *The Tragedy of King Richard the Third, containing his treacherous plots against his brother Clarence, the pitiful murder of his innocent nephews, his tyrannical usurpation, with the whole course of his detested life and most deserved death.*

This anonymous critic emphasizes the events presented on stage during the action, not the mind or 'soul' of the hero. So does the Prologue to *Romeo and Juliet*, which introduces two households obsessed with 'ancient grudge' and 'new mutiny' and then refers to the deaths of hero and heroine as the means of bringing peace to the city-state. It also speaks of the actors who hope to stage the show to the satisfaction of their audience.

These tragedies are dominated by their central characters but in performance an entire theatre company goes on trial as they enact the events of their stories before an audience in a sequence of 'concrete actions' that speak to the senses as well as an intellectual understanding. Besides giving attention to the words that are spoken and what can be sensed of the 'mind' of the heroes, the plays must be considered in terms of all that happens on stage in an active and interactive operation. At once two difficulties arise. First, performance varies greatly according to who the actors are, how they have trained and developed, and what they have chosen or have been directed to do. Where and when the play is performed, and in what form of theatre building, will also affect what an audience experiences. This study makes no attempt to be inclusive or prescriptive in these matters but, to avoid being lost among many and contradictory details, gives prime attention to stage effects that are specifically required by the text, those tasks that must inevitably face any actor. To give a greater sense of actual performances, occasional notice is paid to different ways of performing a crucial moment or the achievement of a particularly effective actor.

The second and still greater difficulty is to understand the plays from an audience's point of view, because all audiences are different and seldom are they consciously aware of how they are reacting; still less are they unanimous in reponse. Special attention is given to changing visual patterns, expectations raised by the on-going story, and exchanges of lead, pauses, and developments in the dialogue: these affect response as much as what can be read on a printed page. But in the absence of any theory that can analyse all possible reactions to a play, or deal in detail with how the words of a text are received at any one moment, the account that follows is undertaken from the point of view of 'an audience', not any specific one or, still less, all audiences. The phrase 'an audience' should be taken to refer the author's own experience as an audience member: trying to follow this reaction, however limited and uncertain it may be, is preferable to ignoring how a play is received and the effect that has on the experience that it offers. Where the passage of time has most clearly altered the probable responses of audiences, an attempt has been made to consider the reaction of Elizabethan or Jacobean audiences; Chapter 3 is especially concerned with this.

Actors and audiences, specific stages and theatre buildings, historical events and changing cultures, all influence what the tragedies become in performance and this study brings what it can of all this to its assessment of their individual achievements. The intention is to give an impression of a marvellous, complex, and meaningful life arising on stage before us and engaging our imaginations so that the 'structure of the scenes and the concrete images' will do their work together with the words of the text, and something of the 'directly human and active aspect' of Shakespeare's imagination may be better understood.

2

Titus Andronicus: Shakespeare's First Tragedy

Shakespeare wrote his first tragedy as if he were surrounded with possibilities and wanted to test all of them. In the course of *Titus Andronicus*, an audience's attention is shifted from one kind of play to another as the tragedy breaks usual bounds, changes tack, surprises or introduces complications not at all necessary for the narrative. Creating an appropriate form for this tragedy – its presentation and manipulation of an audience – seems to have taken precedence over a clear structure or the telling of a story, as if how the action is perceived was more important than the creation of a tragic hero. After an early success, the play was considered both unreadable and unplayable but in the second half of the twentieth century it was once more vindicated on the stage and critics began to take pains with what had seemed to be blunders or mere contrivances. Today the skill with which it was written is generally recognized and each distinct element of its make-up, including those that seem overwrought or irrelevant, can now be judged to be the work of an amazingly gifted and ambitious young man.

Opening Challenges

Titus Andronicus begins by raising political questions: who will have power in Rome and attempt to govern the armed and divided crowd

9

that fills the stage? These issues are posed inescapably and yet all is
not clear because the rival claims are not adequately explained and
are left unanswered. Tribunes and Senators enter on an upper level,
wearing signs of their office and announced by trumpets, but they
say nothing at first. Two sons of a deceased emperor enter from
opposite doors, each with their armed supporters and '*drums and
colours*', Saturninus pleading an elder son's right of inheritance and
Bassianus asserting unspecified moral grounds for opposing this.
Action is imminent when one side is urged to plead for right 'with
your swords', the other to 'fight for freedom'. The effect is likely to
be chaotic since the small-part actors, with door-keepers and stage-
keepers to add to their numbers, have no guidance about how they
should respond. An audience is left to make its own choice between
the two parties until a Tribune announces that the Senators have
already decided that the next emperor should be Titus Andronicus,
not a member of the royal house but a conquering hero who has
defended Rome against the barbarous Goths. Even now there is no
formal debate: the rival sons dismiss their followers and leave the
stage by a central opening that represents the gates of the Senate
House. While they agree to pursue their claims 'in peace and hum-
bleness', their words sound forced and unyielding.

Still an audience has no clear guidance what to think. Titus is
called 'the good Andronicus, . . . surnamed the Pius' but, returning
from war five times in the last ten years, he has slain the most noble
of his prisoners as 'sacrifice of expiation' (ll. 35–8). This reference
attracted attention from the printer or editor of a second quarto
edition of 1600 who deleted it, either as an unacceptable excuse for
a barbarous action or as an anticipation of what will happen some
hundred lines later. The situation is further complicated when
Bassianus addresses the Tribune's spokesman as Marcus Andronicus,
a brother of Titus likely to benefit from his elevation. Bassianus also
acknowledges himself to be emotionally tied to Lavinia, daughter of
Titus, so that his own self-interest must also be involved. And still
who ought to succeed remains an open question: should it be the
former emperor's eldest son or his younger and morally assertive
one, or the much older outsider with an impressive military record?
As soon as the two young rivals appear above with the Tribunes,

Titus is announced, drums and trumpets sounding together now to draw all eyes to his entrance.

Years later, Shakespeare was to introduce *King Lear* in much the same abrupt and puzzling way. Again an audience is challenged to choose between three claimants, but here the old king is still alive and in undisputed charge. The opening of *Romeo and Juliet* also has similarities with *Titus*, as two households are pitched violently against each other without any good reason being given. In almost the first words of *Richard II*, Mowbray and Bolingbroke are openly at odds with each other. The start of *Titus* is more uncertain and challenging than any of these in that no one with authority takes charge and all the rivals have powerful supporters; dramatic focus is divided and uncertain.

At this point, a stage direction introduces a new tone and tempo by calling for a processional entry so long and varied that it must draw on the entire strength of an acting company. The supporters of Saturninus and Bassianus have left the stage just in time to change costumes and make a quick return through another door to swell the long line of captive Goths, victorious Romans, and the bearers of an unspecified number of coffins that contain the bodies of Titus's sons slain in battle. The lengthy stage direction, appearing in the first edition of 1594 that was probably printed from a manuscript in Shakespeare's own hand, specifies twelve persons taking part, plus *'others, as many as can be'*. Variety and numbers ensure a strong and lengthy visual impression and yet, when Titus addresses the assembled Romans, an audience may soon realize that he is deeply troubled. A tomb is opened and, solemnly, he orders his sons' dead bodies to be placed inside:

> There greet in silence, as the dead are wont,
> And sleep in peace, slain in your country's wars.
> O sacred receptacle of my joys,
> Sweet cell of virtue and nobility,
> How many sons hast thou of mine in store
> That thou wilt never render to me more!
>
> (I.i.93–8)

Any hesitation is soon over as Lucius, Titus's eldest surviving son, asks formally for

> . . . the proudest prisoner of the Goths
> That we may hew his limbs and on a pile
> *Ad manes fratrum* sacrifice his flesh . . .

Titus accepts this as a matter of course:

> I give him you, the noblest that survives,
> The eldest son of this distressed queen.   (ll. 99–106)

Once more, the play seems underwritten, for how is this received? Tamora, Queen of the Goths, is the only person given words of protest. Perhaps all the other Goths, in panic or distress, are unable to make a sound while the Romans accept the decision in silent superiority. Alternatively, in line with the opening of the play, a more active, unscripted, and disruptive response may arise from the two opposing sides.

Although weeping, the captive queen has the self-command to call on the 'gracious conqueror' to consider that her sons are soldiers like his own:

> O, if to fight for king and commonweal
> Were piety in thine, it is in these.

For an audience, her plea may sound unanswerable:

> Wilt thou draw near the nature of the gods?
> Draw near them then in being merciful.
> Sweet mercy is nobility's true badge:
> Thrice noble Titus, spare my first-born son.   (ll. 107–23)

More than this, the killing of prisoners was against the rules of war, but here, shockingly, Titus is unaffected and, as his sons leave the stage to 'hew' the victim's limbs, Tamora gives a fuller voice against his inhumanity and pious self-justification: 'O cruel, irreligious piety!' she cries and Chiron, one of her two remaining sons, takes up the charge: 'Was never Scythia half so barbarous!' When Demetrius, her other son, calls for a 'sharp revenge' to 'quit the bloody wrongs', he announces, unmistakably, that this tragedy will deal with the rights and wrongs of war, ambition and submission, mercy and justice, as well as with the good government of a city-state. Romans are more barbarous than the 'barbarous Goths' against whom they have fought long and 'weary wars' (I.i.28) and, as if no more could be said, the funeral ceremonies continue until 'smoke like incense doth perfume' the air on stage and in the theatre (ll. 147–8). But then, after prayers for his sons' 'peace and honour' in the security of their tomb (ll. 154–9), another surprise follows when Lavinia, Titus's daughter, enters and is greeted as 'This cordial of mine age to glad my heart.' Now an audience may sense that Rome, in its ruthless pursuit of victory and virtue, is not without some tenderness

Shakespeare followed no single source for this picture of Rome, but brought together features from several distinct eras in the empire's rise and fall as if he wanted to show the worst possible corruptions of whatever origin. Titus himself is shown in starkly different poses, leaving actor and audience to make what continuous sense they can of his role, his desire for 'peace' as well as for virtue and revenge. All happens with such an onrush of incident that the impact is inescapable, even though there is little opportunity for sustained reflection. Elizabethans, however, may have responded more readily than us because the conflicting issues raised would have been of immediate concern. They knew that the old Queen of England had no publicly acknowledged heir and that an older generation throughout the land was often at odds with the 'new men' whose fortunes came from commerce and self-betterment, not from inheritance and guardianship. When *Titus Andronicus* was first performed, it must have seemed to some Englishmen that nothing could prevent future disaster and that everyone had to manage for themselves as their peace was also threatened by 'changes and mishaps, . . . treason, . . . envy, . . . drugs, . . . storms, . . . noise' (I.i.155–8). The grotesque and horrible fantasy of the Rome that Shakespeare called into life might have seemed not so very far from the circumstances of its audiences' own daily lives. At this time, some Christians fought and tortured each other in defence of their own beliefs. Even today, the wider political issues may catch and hold an audience's attention: at this stage of the play, they are more clearly and boldly presented than what Hamlet was to call the 'conscience' of its tragic hero.

More surprises are still to come in the lengthy first scene. On grounds of being too old, Titus refuses to stand as favoured candidate for emperor and champions Saturninus who is openly antagonistic to him; the people, both patricians and plebleians, accept his recommendation with no further debate. Saturninus then names Lavinia as his empress, at which change of fortune she is unaccountably silent. An aside follows in which he reveals his attraction to Tamora before openly promising to advance her fortunes. Asked what she thinks, Lavinia says that she is not displeased. The next act of Saturninus is to set free all the prisoners, in a moment undoing a major achievement of the wars recently concluded with great loss of life. After being silent during all these reversals of fortune, Bassianus at last speaks out to claim Lavinia as his own bride by prior agreement and another unexpected sequence of events speedily follows. Bassianus is supported by Marcus Andronicus and by Lucius, Lavinia's brother, but Titus calls them all traitors and summons the emperor's guard. When another son, Mutius, draws his sword to help them escape and Saturninus does nothing to stop them, Titus sets out to bring Bassianus and Lavinia back and, when opposed by his own son, kills the 'villain boy' without a further thought (I.i.295). Saturninus, now on the upper stage, rejects these efforts to retrieve Lavinia:

> No, Titus, no, the emperor needs her not,
> Nor her, nor thee, nor any of thy stock.   (I.i.304–5)

At this point in the dizzying sequence, Titus loses the initiative. After a cry of disbelief, he falls silent: the high-wrought drama, having brought disappointment, suffering, and revaluation, operates now at a deeper level of feeling; all he says is 'These words are razors to my wounded heart' (l. 319). Only when he is alone, in the first soliloquy of the play, does Titus voice his bewilderment:

> I am not bid to wait upon this bride.
> Titus, when wert thou wont to walk alone,
> Dishonoured thus and challengèd of wrongs?   (I.i.343–5)

After many fantastic surprises and reversals, simple words bring an intense focus on the tragic hero: feelings are raw and, in comparison to what has come before, completely understandable. The pace slows up as Marcus urges his brother:

> O Titus, see! O see what thou hast done!
> In a bad quarrel slain a virtuous son. (ll. 345–6)

The three remaining sons kneel with their uncle and beg Titus to reconsider and, at length, he agrees that Mutius can be buried in the family tomb and accepts his own helplessness: 'Well, bury him, and bury me the next' (I.i.391).

The rest of the first movement of the play (Act I in modern editions; I.i. and II.i in earlier ones) has yet another pace and style, as the focus shifts yet again and narrative momentum slackens. With bravado and sour humour, Saturninus and Bassianus taunt each other about their respective brides. Titus and his sons are reconciled to the new emperor, but only after Tamora has publicly interceded for them and privately told Saturninus to bide his time since she will 'find a day to massacre them all' (l. 455). Titus then invites everyone to hunt with him the following day and the stage empties except for one person, Aaron the Moor. He has stood by watching all that has happened and now, in the 'high-astounding' style that Marlowe had recently made popular with his *Tamburlaine the Great* (c. 1587), he reveals that he is Tamora's lover and that, by her means, he will 'mount aloft' in triumph. His twenty-five lines are sufficient to wrench an audience's expectations aside and hold attention for a witty, resourceful, and unscrupulous outsider. And still the first movement of the play is not over: Chiron and Demetrius re-enter and Aaron prevents them from falling out over the attractions of Lavinia:

> Why, are ye mad? Or know ye not in Rome
> How furious and impatient they be,
> And cannot brook competitors in love? (I.i.574–6)

He suggests that they both rape her in the woods and the two young men agree that 'some certain snatch or so / Would serve [their] turns' (ll. 595–6). Demetrius cries out that, right or wrong, he will go through hell to 'cool this heat'; the idea is taken from Seneca's tragedy, *Hippolytus*, which he quotes in Latin to confirm the debt: '*Per Stygia, per manes vehor.*'

In these concluding movements of its long opening sequence, the tragedy is no longer a moral 'show', in which the issues are politics, public service, and virtue. Now asides, soliloquies, intrigue, and savage comedy are the staples and at issue are personal ambition and sexual desire. Titus had talked about treason, envy, damned drugs, and storms and, now, much of this, together with stupidity, cunning, and unbridled appetite, is about to be brought to the stage. Pursuit of sexual satisfaction and exercise of political power were to come together repeatedly in Shakespeare's later plays, notably *Troilus and Cressida* and *Antony and Cleopatra*, but this early treatment is distinctive in its sudden clashes, lively and lurid humour, and freedom from usual protocols and restraints. The servant Aaron presides as ringmaster for two headlong and avid lechers. An audience is not so much puzzled and challenged now; it is likely to laugh and wait for the narrative's development. And still, after more than six hundred lines, it can hardly know the workings of the tragic hero's mind.

Variety of Influence and Impact

The quotation from Seneca points a new direction and strong moral intention. His forceful rhetoric and gruesome stories were imitated by Elizabethan dramatists who wished to write about overwhelming passions and frustrations. Later audiences have found this aspect of *Titus Andronicus* the hardest to accept; not only the fixation on extreme experiences but also the verbal extravagance and nightmarish exaggeration. Seneca, as Polonius was to say, could easily become 'too heavy' (*Hamlet*, II.ii.395) and more especially in English translations. In Jasper Heywood's version of *The Tragedy of Thyestes*, a Fury warns an audience what to expect:

Let brother dread the brother's wrath, and father fear the son,
And eke the son his parents' power; let babes be murdered ill,
But worse begot! Her spouse betrapp'd to treason's train to kill,
Let hateful wife await, and let them bear through seas their war,
Let bloodshed lie the lands about and every field afar!

In Shakespeare's time, this laboured style was new and thrilling, giving expression to feelings and fears that were otherwise unspeakable. Driven by his passions, the hero of this tragedy is said to become as a bloodhound in the hunt, his face deformed and loathsome, his hands like 'clinching claws'; the gods are afraid to look at him. Yet for all their sensationalism, the Elizabethan translators claimed a moral purpose: *The Tragedy of Oedipus* was said to be:

. . . unto all posterities, a dreadful example of God's horrible vengeance for sin. Such like terrors as these requireth this our present age, wherein Vice hath chiefest place and Virtue, put to flight, lies as an abject, languishing in great extremity.

Sanctioned by its classic status, Senecan tragedy encouraged a vivid protest against injustice and abuse of power in 'our present age'.

When all theatre performances were censored, Seneca provided a useful precedent and Shakespeare might naturally summon Seneca to mind when he wished to alert his audience to outrage, injustice, and the pain of estranged families. Difficulties in our response to the exaggerations are lessened by the crude and denigrating humour by which Shakespeare lightened what is 'heavy' and kept an audience aware of deception and stupidity. Moreover, in this early play, he avoided the Senecan ghosts and personifications that had been made popular by Thomas Kyd, six years his senior, in *The Spanish Tragedy* of 1590, the entire action of which is overseen and commented upon by Revenge and the Ghost of Andrea. As we shall see, Shakespeare also offset the 'hellish' events and outsized passions with a contrasting simplicity.

The second and fourth Acts of *Titus* also show the influence of Ovid. Details of the rape and mutilation of Lavinia were taken from the story of Philomela and Tereus in the *Metamorphoses* and more generally influential were the poet's detailed expressions of feeling and his similes and metaphors taken from the natural world. Shakespeare used Arthur Golding's translation in which enough remained to attract him to the manner, as well as the matter, of these narrative poems: when Tereus holds Philomela captive he never takes his eyes off her and 'skips' in eagerness, catching hold of her like an eagle seizing a hare to carry off to its nest; taking her to 'forgrowen' woods, she is like a 'wounded lamb' shaken in the teeth of a wolf. Visualized detail is often both grotesque and horrific in effect; for example, when Philomela's tongue is cut out:

> the stump whereon it hung
> Did patter still; the tip fell down and, quivering on the ground
> As though it had murmured, it made a certain sound;
> And as an adder's tail cut off doth skip a while, even so
> The tip of Philomela's tongue did wriggle to and fro,
> And nearer to her mistressward in dying still did go.

Shakespeare attempted nothing comparable but echoes of Ovid's fantasy and detailed sensationalism can be heard when the play insists that its audience views the consequences of inhumanity.

The second Act moves more swiftly than the first but, with the help of Seneca and Ovid, no less forcefully. After competitive baying and trumpeting at the beginning of the hunt, and with only a few persons on stage, entries and exits are both frequent and quick. As Aaron manipulates everyone with great efficiency, he leaves himself sufficient time to share his intentions and pleasures with the theatre audience, but the shocking pressure of events continues relentlessly. On his instructions, Chiron and Demetrius take Lavinia off stage to rape her and then to cut off her hands and cut out her tongue; they then kill Bassianus and incriminate the sons of Titus in the murder by means of a 'fatal-plotted scroll' and a bag of gold (II.ii.47). Meanwhile Aaron receives Tamora's advances and so gains an accomplice.

Grotesque and sardonic humour runs throughout the scene. When two sons of Titus, Quintus and Martius, are tricked by Aaron so that they fall into the pit where the gold is hidden, one boy pulls the other after him with a touch of slap-stick comedy. Lavinia joins

Bassianus in 'saucy' rudeness to Tamora about her 'goodly gift of horning' and 'swart Cimmerian' lover (II.ii.55–87). Demetrius derides Lavinia's 'quaint hope' that marriage to Bassianus would allow her to brave the 'mightiness' of Tamora (ll. 124–6). Chiron mocks his victim for supposing he might prove 'a bastard' by pitying her (l. 148). Tamora, knowing all that has happened, feigns a wonder that in performance will almost certainly raise laughter by its mock simplicity:

> What are they in this pit? O wondrous thing!
> How easily murder is discovered. (ll.286–7)

A further element towards the close of these hunting episodes are echoes of some of the most dramatic moments in the earlier Act. First, Lavinia pleads for her own death, in much the same way as Tamora had pleaded to Titus for the life of her son Alarbus; only the echo is not exact in that Tamora taunts her suppliant by reminding her that 'fierce Andronicus would not relent' and Lavinia becomes a 'fond woman' so clinging to Tamora that she is curtly told to 'Let me go!' (ll. 165, 172). Not long after this, when his sons are denounced as the murderers of Bassianus, Titus himself begs on his knees for permission to bail them. When Saturninus refuses, Tamora consoles him with unconcealed sarcasm that is a reminder of his treatment of her:

> Andronicus, I will entreat the king;
> Fear not thy sons, they shall do well enough.

To this, he can respond only by calling Lucius to leave with him as the scene ends.

Following these bruising and extraordinary events, a short scene follows with Lavinia at its centre, in great pain, unable to speak, and scarcely able to move. Proud of what they have done, Demetrius and Chiron taunt her gleefully:

> *Demetrius.* So, now go tell, and if thy tongue can speak,
> Who 'twas that cut thy tongue and ravished thee.
> *Chiron.* Write down thy mind, bewray thy meaning so,
> And if thy stumps will let thee, play the scribe.

They leave laughing together:

> Chiron.   And 'twere my cause, I should go hang myself.
> Demetrius.   If thou hadst hands to help thee knit the cord.
>
> (II.iii.1–10)

Horns are heard from off stage and Marcus, the tribune and brother of Titus, enters from hunting. As Lavina tries to run away, he recognizes who she is, calls after her, and slowly realizes the full horror of what has happened. His long speech has often been criticized as undramatic and artificial, a useless amplification of what is all too apparent, but by its means Shakespeare has held an audience's attention for what is abhorrent, almost incredible, and impossible to stage adequately:

> Speak, gentle niece, what stern ungentle hands
> Hath lopped and hewed and made thy body bare
> Of her two branches, those sweet ornaments
> Whose circling shadows kings have sought to sleep in
> And might not gain so great a happiness
> As half thy love. Why dost not speak to me?
>   [*Lavinia opens her mouth.*]
> Alas, a crimson river of warm blood,
> Like to a bubbling fountain stirred with wind,
> Doth rise and fall between thy rosèd lips,
> Coming and going with thy honey breath. . . .
>
> (II.iii.16ff.)

As Lavinia holds the visual focus, the obviously contrived words identify what is present for all to see and so lead an audience to think carefully through every aspect of her condition, even as it responds instinctively and emotionally to the appalling spectacle. In its context, the speech can seem to be entirely true to the helpless and yet totally involved observer of the horror. Of course, in no way is it a 'true' representation of such a situation; rather, its words provide a frame or outline of complicated signs in which the individual imaginations of actor and audience can find their own sense of reality. So acted and received, it is like skilful music: harmonious, climactic, and able to shatter ordinary expectations and feelings.

The Affective Centre

Shakespeare took great risks in writing his first tragedy and it is no wonder that it has been criticized adversely as irrational and book-ishly imitative or, alternatively, as a blatant crowd-pleaser for times less civilized than the present. With Act III, however, a new concen-tration on the hero's predicament is sustained through a number of appalling events so that here even adverse critics have recognized a sensitivity to isolation and suffering and found traces of later and 'greater' tragedies. Besides, Titus now shows courage, endurance, and honesty, virtues that are more suited to usual notions of a tragic hero.

Nevertheless, commentary will stumble before the text of this central and unrelenting scene with its highly wrought imagery, per-sistent puns, writhing rhythms, varying focus, clashes of mood, laboured rhetoric, incisive wit, and unexpected silences. Two con-trasted passages in which Titus describes himself in relation to the sea will probably leave the strongest impression from a reading of the text. After Lucius has been banished for seeking to release his brothers from execution for the murder of Bassianus, and after Marcus has brought the mutilated Lavinia to him, Titus sees himself as one who must

> stand . . . upon a rock,
> Environed with a wilderness of sea,
> Who marks the waxing tide grow wave by wave,
> Expecting ever when some envious surge
> Will in his brinish bowels swallow him. (III.i.94–8)

Later, after he has cut off his own hand as the price the emperor has put on his sons' freedom, and with Lavinia kneeling beside him helplessly, he no longer stands on firm ground, but has become like the sea itself; he cries out:

> I am the sea. Hark how her sighs doth blow.
> She is the weeping welkin, I the earth.
> Then must my sea be moved with her sighs,
> Then must my earth with her continual tears
> Become a deluge overflowed and drowned. . . (ll. 220–30)

In performance, when an actor speaks these words and takes upon himself all that they imply, in his body and emotions as well as in his mind, he will enact a huge change, a transformation of himself that can rouse an audience's imagination to follow.

The text gives the actor no respite. After the first image of the sea, Titus lists his miseries and then becomes so abruptly and crudely practical that he might almost be making a joke:

> Thou hast no hands to wipe away thy tears,
> Nor tongue to tell me who hath martyred thee.   (ll. 107–8)

Only a few lines later, he is suddenly delicate in apprehension:

> When I did name her brothers, then fresh tears
> Stood on her cheeks, as doth the honey-dew
> Upon a gathered lily almost withered.   (ll. 112–4)

After he becomes like the sea itself, a carefully spoken Messenger brings back his hand, which has been cut off to release his two sons, and, with it, he also brings their two heads. At first, Titus is silent at this cruel betrayal of trust, saying nothing while Marcus and Lucius express outrage and compassion and the speechless Lavinia kisses the two severed and bloody heads. When Titus does speak, he has only a single, half-crazy line: 'When will this fearful slumber have an end?' (l. 253). Urged to express his grief, he utters only 'Ha, ha, ha!' (l. 265), a laugh that in performance can be wild and obsessed or so private that it is scarcely heard. Only after this puzzling and dangerous moment does Titus speak at length and take back control of the scene:

> *Marcus.* Why dost thou laugh? It fits not with this hour.
> *Titus.*   Why? I have not another tear to shed.
>   Besides, this sorrow is an enemy
>   And would usurp upon my watery eyes
>   And make them blind with tributary tears,
>   Then which way shall I find Revenge's cave?   (ll. 266–71)

From this point on, Titus is no longer reserved but full of energy, decisive and active; inexpressible suffering has been overtaken by an unhesitating desire for revenge.

Some emblematic actions are so clear and provocative that they may prove the most accessible part of the scene. For the original audiences who could send nothing by mail, someone in need had to seek out persons of power, and then stand or kneel before them to hand-deliver a petition or attempt to speak. People with some influence might send their servants at first, but many in an audience at the Rose Theatre of London where *Titus* was first performed would have tried to catch the attention of 'great ones' and would recognize the need for Titus to plead desperately for his sons as they are led to execution. Some would know what it was like to be passed by in silence, as happens to Titus when he '*lieth down, and the Judges pass by him*' (S.D., l. 11), and they would understand why he weeps and madly pleads to the stones of the street (III.i.16–22). Physical actions on stage and experience from everyday life are both potent here as everything ordinary is left far behind and Titus's suffering escalates into painful and terrible madness.

Strong physical actions come one after another in this scene, especially on entrances when the time taken to reach centre stage holds the new figure in focus: Lucius '*with his weapon drawn*', Marcus leading the raped Lavinia (a sight that Titus cannot take in at once so that Lucius responds well before his father), 'Aaron *the Moor alone*', Lucius and Marcus returning too late to stop Aaron cutting off Titus's hand, the Messenger '*with two heads and a hand*'. On several occasions, kneeling and weeping are clearly required by the text: 'Gentle Lavinia, let me kiss thy lips' (l. 121) implies a gruesome action whether Titus does actually kiss her blood-stained mouth or she refuses to allow it; their physical encounter here gives a shocking impact to a father's familiar impulse.

With feelings of ever-greater intensity, both silence and physical actions carry an increasing proportion of the load. At the end of this central scene, all the remaining Andronici stand round as Titus takes charge again and is more decisive than ever. Thoughts of revenge have transformed him:

> Come let me see what task I have to do.

> You heavy people, circle me about,
> That I may turn me to each one of you
> And swear unto my soul to right your wrongs.   (ll. 276–9)

In this formal grouping, a vow is taken in silence and then follows extraordinary and dispersed activity:

> The vow is made. Come, brother, take a head,
> And in this hand the other will I bear.
> And, Lavinia, thou shalt be employed:
> Bear thou my hand, sweet wench, between thy teeth.
> As for thee, boy, go get thee from my sight:
> Thou art an exile and thou must not stay;
> Hie to the Goths and raise an army there,
> And if ye love me, as I think you do,
> Let's kiss and part, for we have much to do.   (ll. 280–8)

In the mind's eye during a reading of the text, it is hard to see all the ugly and, necessarily, clumsy actions these instructions involve. How reluctantly or avidly do they all respond? Probably Titus has picked up one head before Marcus takes the other. Holding it in his one remaining hand, he cannot pass his severed hand to Lavinia, so she must kneel to put her face down to the ground and take it between her teeth. The first edition of the play adds an extrametrical 'in these Armes' after 'thou shalt be employed', which may reproduce a correction added to the manuscript because the other instruction had proved too difficult to manage; but it is only a degree easier to pick up a severed hand with two painful and bleeding stumps than with a mouth. With careful modern stage-management, the severed hand will be in the same place at every performance but, in more improvisational Elizabethan performances, Lavinia may have to search around the stage for this lifeless object before she can kneel to take it in her teeth. Turning to Lucius immediately after instructing Lavinia, Titus gives him no opportunity for speech: the only remaining son must approach the father who is holding a brother's bloody head in his one remaining hand and take his leave with a kiss. 'For we have much to do' indicates that Titus keeps up a brisk pace throughout all this hideous and, probably, clumsy business.

The two preceding Acts help to make this scene appear stylistically acceptable and even natural. Persistent punning, comic asides, extravagant passions and devious actions, formality and tender instincts, quick-changing moods and rapid surprises, a physicality whereby the drama becomes a 'show' of striking visual presentations that speak directly to the eye and are repeated and modified as the story advances, together with a recurrent and helpless silence: all these elements have already been present in the play before being used again here for the sustained presentation of Titus's suffering. Here, they can hold open his intense pain and grief like wounds prepared for a surgeon's attention; and they mark the beginning of his desperation, determination to revenge, and near madness. The extraordinary variety and daring of this play's dramatic idiom is not the result of casual and youthful experiment or the flexing of muscle, but a concerted attempt to write a tragedy that probes horrendous suffering and displays inhuman actions, as later tragedies will continue to do.

At the conclusion of this long scene, the physical necessities of performance ensure that dramatic focus is widened. As the family moves off stage without saying a single word, the grotesque procession is watched by young Lucius, who vows to be revenged and so, once again, a double focus has been contrived in which suffering is visually evident while words speak, with renewed energy, of retaliatory destruction. Saturninus and his empress will be made to 'Beg at the gates' of the city, promises Lucius (l. 299): dramatic interest is political as well as personal, and what is individual is related to the story of an entire family at odds with those responsible for justice, a situation that will be more powerfully presented in later tragedies.

The Process of Revenge

After such an exhausting scene, relief was necessary if an audience was to stay with the play and this is achieved with yet another change of dramatic form. Titus is withdrawn from attention for much of the time and has no direct contact with his opponents until the very last scenes; what he does until then fails to advance the

action. It is Marcus who shows Lavinia how to tell the story of her
double rape so that the audience watches her painful writing in the
sand and has to wait for Titus to learn the bare facts that it already
knows. When he does understand her message, his only response is
to quote Seneca in Latin, the two verse-lines saying nothing of what
he will do, only that he can scarcely believe that the powerful
heavens are so slow to take notice of human crimes. He does send
bizarre and allusive messages to his opponents, each accompanied
with some weapon or, finally, two doves, but it is hard to see how
useful these will be – indeed they could be counterproductive by
warning that he intends to revenge. Until he has killed Tamora, the
extent of the revenge he has planned is not revealed and perhaps not
even then, since he does nothing to prevent Saturninus killing him
with a single blow and it is left to Lucius to kill Saturninus who, in
many respects, was Titus's principal enemy.

In Acts IV and V, Titus often seems to be merely illustrating how
great grief turns a sufferer mad. Little is surprising in this; as the boy
Lucius says at the start of Act IV,

> . . . I have heard my grandsire say full oft
> Extremity of griefs would make men mad.   (IV.i.18–19)

However grief also makes Titus blind, as he explains to Tamora:

> we worldly men
> Have miserable, mad, mistaking eyes.   (V.i.65–6)

From this blindness derives what tension arises from Titus's slow
progress towards his killing of Chiron and Demetrius in order to feed
them to their mother at a feast and then to kill her. How much does
he see and know, and what does he plan? When Tamora visits him
dressed as Revenge to get him to invite Lucius to a feast, it is only after
she has left her two sons as hostages that an audience can be sure that
he has seen through her deception and, perhaps, feigned a mad blindness to mock and deceive her. When he kills Lavinia before enacting
his revenge, he invokes the precedent of Virginius but adds that he has
'Killed her for whom my tears have made me blind' (V.iii.48).

Feigned or real madness, blindness, and apparently indecisive action do not readily yield compelling drama and it sometimes seems that Shakespeare intended to create a main character who progressively reveals more of himself and has failed to do so. When Titus answers Tamora's visit, he speaks as someone deep in his own thoughts but does not say what these are:

Who doth molest my contemplation?
Is it your trick to make me ope the door,
That so my sad decrees may fly away
And all my study be to no effect?   (V.ii.9–12)

It may be that Shakespeare intentionally blurred the focus on Titus in order that an audience, once again, makes up its own mind and to accentuate other matters that he held to be more important.

That Shakespeare or the players became uneasy with how little the audience knew of Titus by the end of the play may explain the presence in the Folio edition of 1623 of a new scene added to the end of Act III. In this, the Andronici sit together at a meal and Titus suggests that Lavinia should kill herself, knowing very well that she could not do so without her hands. In the midst of this crazed talk and the weeping of young Lucius, Titus's grandson, Marcus, stabs at a fly that has alighted on one of the dishes. The dramatic purpose of this unexpected action becomes clear when Titus rebukes him:

How if that fly had a father and a mother?
How would he hang his slender gilded wings
And buzz lamenting doings in the air.
Poor harmless fly,
That with his pretty buzzing melody
Came here to make us merry, and thou hast killed him.   (III.ii.61–6)

This incident is often emphasized in modern productions because it is the only occasion when Titus seems capable of sympathetic feelings and sees beyond a cruel act to its consequences. Yet this expression of sympathy can be performed as a craziness that Titus consciously assumes to hide or to forget his own grief. When Marcus says that the black fly had reminded him of Aaron, Titus says at

once that he has 'done a charitable deed' (l. 71) and belabours the
dead fly himself, striking at it as if it were both Aaron and the
empress. He goes off with Lavinia and the boy, saying that he fears
his eyes 'begin to dazzle' (l. 86) and, once more, his thoughts are
hidden from an audience.

Much of Shakespeare's invention in the last two Acts brings
the audience's attention to other characters who have previously
been overshadowed by the protagonist. Each is given a story, but the
most dramatic of them concerns Aaron. First, with Chiron and
Demetrius, he learns that Titus knows they have raped and mutilated Lavinia and then, with immediate decisiveness, he defends his
own infant child to whom Tamora has given birth and now sends to
him with instructions to kill the black evidence of their relationship;
instead he kills the nurse who brought the child, mocking her pain
with: '"Wheak, Wheak!" – so cries a pig prepared to the spit'
(IV.ii.148). Aaron dominates this scene, starting with an extended
aside to the audience and then bending everyone to his purposes and
making his own point of view evident in bold and witty speech. He
leaves Tamora's two sons to do as he has ordered but is next seen as a
prisoner who is brought to Lucius as he is preparing an army of
Goths to march on Rome and revenge his father. Lucius gives orders
that Aaron should watch as his baby is killed and then be hung as an
'incarnate devil' (V.i.40). When Aaron offers to tell secrets to save
the child, his courage and primary concern for his child are made
clear in ways that cannot fail to hold attention.

Lucius is presented in a far more confusing way. He is loyal to his
own father but threatens Aaron's defenceless child:

>   that he may see it sprawl:
> A sight to vex the father's soul withal.   (ll. 51–2)

He calls his home 'great Rome' (V.i.2) but leads an army of Rome's
enemies against the city, promising them 'treble satisfaction' in
revenge (V.i.5–8). Tamora is shown taking initiative away from her
husband–emperor and confident that she can deceive and trap Titus.
A new focus of attention is a nameless clown who is going to the tribunes with a gift of two doves to plead for justice on his uncle's

behalf, as Titus had earlier tried to plead for his sons. Titus redirects him to the court where Saturninus also redirects him: 'Go, take him away and hang him presently!' Dramatic focus narrows and the bemused victim catches at an audience's sympathy: 'Hanged, by' Lady? Then I have brought up a neck to a fair end' (IV.iv.48).

In the last two scenes, Titus is once more the dominating figure, at first mysteriously and then, with Chiron and Demetrius bound and gagged, lethally. First he recounts their crimes and tells them that he intends to feed them to their mother; then he slits their throats while Lavinia holds a bowl between her stumps to catch the blood. 'Come, come, be everyone officious', says Titus, while nothing is said or done to stop the horror. He concludes with crazed mockery:

> So, now bring them in, for I'll play the cook,
> And see them ready against their mother comes.   (V.ii.204–5)

Single-minded and efficient in words and actions, Titus has been given nothing with which to gain an audience's sympathy, no hesitation or compassion, almost without either passion or feeling.

Other preparations for the concluding scene follow immediately: Aaron enters under guard and Lucius confronts Saturninus and Tamora. The emperor's 'What, hath the firmament more suns than one?' (l. 17) neatly questions where power lies and then Marcus introduces the main business with words that momentarily give a vision of Rome at peace:

> The feast is ready which the careful Titus
> Hath ordained to an honourable end,
> For peace, for love, for league and good to Rome,
> Please you therefore, draw nigh and take your places.   (ll.21–4)

The old and 'noble' hero of Rome then enters dressed humbly like a cook – or, perhaps, comically, even clownishly, so – and is accompanied by a veiled Lavinia. So an audience is prepared for the cannibal-banquet but, when Titus starts by slaying Lavinia, the play takes a decisive direction that will almost certainly outstrip what has been

expected. The eating of human flesh in a 'pastry' and the rest of the
killings all follow rapidly, with none of the principals speaking more
than a few words. No death-speeches and no careful judgements are
offered, the text not even calling for a single cry from those who are
murdered. The entire scene is chaotic and in some danger of
becoming unmanageably comic, rather than solemn and frightening.
As the whole stage erupts into action, Titus has no words with which
to declare his purpose or show any access of understanding; he may
well be momentarily lost to view. When everything has subsided, it
is Marcus who addresses his fellow countrymen:

> You sad-faced men, people and sons of Rome,
> By uproars severed, as a flight of fowl
> Scattered by winds and high tempestuous gusts,
> O let me teach you how to knit again
> This scattered corn into one mutual sheaf,
> These broken limbs again into one body.   (ll.66–71)

Again Marcus is spokesman for peace, but he can achieve little and
soon confesses himself unable to say more. Lucius who has entered
Rome at the head of an enemy army is left to proclaim publicly
what has happened and to be hailed as Rome's 'gracious governor'
(l. 145).

The new emperor's first act is to arrange for homage to be paid his
father. One by one, Lucius, Marcus and Lucius's son kiss the 'pale
cold lips' and weep on the 'bloodstained face' (ll. 152–3). These
long-drawn-out actions have been given far more prominence than
the violent and sudden killings that have preceded them.
Shakespeare has brought his first tragedy to rest in an expression of
affection and reverence for its crazed and blinded hero and, at the
same time, in memories of other repeated acts of kneeling, more
especially of the slow and grotesque kisses that had marked the end
of Act III, scene i, in which Titus had suffered so terribly and continuously. These are all elements of the play, together with the first
spectacle of the mutilated Lavinia, that draw directly upon the audience's sense-reactions, carrying a huge weight of feeling and a recognition of helplessness. This may seem a strange conclusion for a

verbally ambitious and violent tragedy but, with hindsight, we can see that this choice, like the almost incoherent madness and 'blindness' of Titus, looks ahead to *King Lear* and its concluding call to obey 'the weight of this sad time' (V.iii.313).

To complete the play and counterstate these last dutiful actions, Shakespeare kept the silent entry of Aaron *'under guard'*. Lucius is totally remorseless:

> Set him breast-deep in earth and famish him;
> There let him stand and rave and cry for food.

Quite specifically he forbids pity under threat of death:

> If anyone relieves or pities him,
> For the offence he dies. This is our doom ...   (ll. 178–81)

Tamora's body he orders to be treated like a common criminal, and thrown out of the city 'for beasts and birds to prey' (ll. 194–9). The audience may well expect no less from Lucius, who had shown callous cruelty towards Alarbus in the first scene of the play, but one last surprise follows. Aaron does not kneel for pity as others have done, and his wrath and fury cannot be silenced. In a last speech, he repents none of his evil deeds but wishes he had committed ten thousand worse. He vows:

> If one good deed in all my life I did
> I do repent it from my very soul.   (ll. 188–9)

The Most Lamentable Roman Tragedy of Titus Andronicus is clearly, as the title of early editions indicates, about its hero and his suffering but, especially in the opening and concluding Acts, it is also concerned with a 'gored state' (*Lear*, V.iii.320) in all the outrage, cunning, cruelty, and absurdity of what has been shown. Inventing his own plot and its context, Shakespeare set himself on a course that was to lead forward to tragedies that cannot be summed up in their heroes, however exceptional and 'great' they may be and however actual their sufferings are made for an audience. *Titus*

Andronicus is, perhaps, a harsher play than many that followed in giving so little hope that the world presented might ever know lasting peace. Shakespeare's complex and popular first tragedy leaves an audience burdened with a sense that efforts that attempted to bring peace and honour to society and some achievement to individual and family lives have led to little but the continuation of tyranny and uncertainty.

3

Popular Tragedies and their Audiences

Besides Shakespeare's *Titus Andronicus*, other notable successes in the years 1587 to 1594 were Thomas Kyd's *Spanish Tragedy*, Christopher Marlowe's *Tamburlaine*, *Jew of Malta*, and *Doctor Faustus*, and the anonymous *Arden of Faversham*. These plays were frequently performed, published, and reprinted; phrases from Kyd and Marlowe entered common usage, their heroes became proverbial. What Shakespeare's tragedies offer their audiences may be seen more clearly as part of this unexpected and unprecedented surge in popularity.

Violence

Terrifying and unnatural acts were prime ingredients. Tragedy, a character in the Induction to *A Warning for Fair Women* (1598), gave a run-down of what an audience might expect:

> . . . some damned tyrant, to obtain a crown,
> Stabs, hangs, imprisons, smothers, cutteth throats,
> And then a Chorus too comes howling in,
> And tells us of the worrying of a cat,
> Then of a filthy whining ghost,
> Lapt in some foul sheet or a leather pelch,
> Comes screaming like a pig half-sticked
> And cries *Vindicta*, revenge, revenge.

Stephen Gosson, a critic who held all playgoing to be sinful, was sure that

> The argument of Tragedies is wrath, cruelty, incest, injury, murder either violent by sword or voluntary by poison.
>
> > (*Plays Confuted in Five Actions*, 1582)

Horatio's summary of the 'argument' of Shakespeare's *Hamlet* (1600–1) supports Gosson's contention by speaking:

> Of carnal, bloody, and unnatural acts;
> Of accidental judgments, casual slaughters;
> Of deaths put on by cunning and forc'd cause;
> And, in this upshot, purposes mistook
> Fall'n on th' inventors' heads.   (V.ii.372–7)

Hamlet and other plays of its time were tragedies of blood in a triple sense, involving 'carnal' passions, family ties, and blood-spilling.

The taste for violence was not only popular. When Shakespeare's Hamlet welcomes the players to Elsinore he calls for a 'passionate speech' and remembers one he 'chiefly loved' from 'an excellent play' that was performed 'not above once' because it pleased too few people. The speech was Aeneas' tale to Dido, and 'thereabout of it especially where he speaks of Priam's slaughter'. Recounting one of the worst atrocities of the sack of Troy, an eyewitness re-creates the horror when Pyrrhus, son of Achilles, is:

> total gules, horridly tricked
> With blood of fathers, mothers, daughters, sons . . .
> And thus o'ersizèd with coagulate gore,
> With eyes like carbuncles, the hellish Pyrrhus
> Old grandsire Priam seeks.   (II.ii.451ff.)

The young warrior hesitates before killing the old and defenceless king but then he 'goes to work'. A few years earlier, writing of the same moment in his *Dido, Queen of Carthage*, Christopher Marlowe had added that a trembling Priam had prayed for mercy and:

Not mov'd at all, but smiling at his tears,
This butcher, whilst his hands were yet held up,
Treading upon his breast, struck off his hands.   (II.i.240–2)

This Pyrrhus did not pause, but soon was swinging a 'howling' Hecuba through 'the empty air' and ripping the old man open 'from the navel to the throat at once'. Shakespeare's player continues with his speech but hesitates, begins again, and then comes to a shuddering halt, his face ashen; he weeps and can say no more. Hamlet, however, has not heard enough and promises to hear him out later, in private.

Without staging the violent act, theatre could make an audience weep for Hecuba, sharing the sensations of those who had witnessed the horror. But not content with words alone, Elizabethan playwrights also called for defenceless men, women, and children to be murdered on stage in full sight of an audience. Shakespeare, who was called 'gentle' by those who knew him, had an old man tied up and his eyes torn out, a woman slowly smothered to death and another savagely stabbed, two young men held still as their throats are slit, and an innocent poet torn limb from limb. When he did not actually stage a brutal act, he could force his audience to witness its results, as with the rape and mutilation of Lavinia. Whereas Marlowe's Aeneas told of the heartless murder of Priam years after the event, Shakespeare's Macbeth, with blood still warm on his hands, speaks of what it was like to slaughter Duncan in his sleep, and does so for an audience which has just shared that quiet and horrendous moment with Lady Macbeth, at only a little distance from the helpless victim.

It used to be said that the bloodletting so common in Elizabethan and Jacobean tragedies was a regrettable reflection of an age more primitive than ours, when men went about the streets fully armed; vagrants and disbanded soldiers terrified ordinary persons; bearbaiting was a popular sport; and corporal punishment, in homes, schools, or public places, would often be physically brutal and degrading. Now, however, we have come to recognize a day-by-day violence in our own time and sensational entertainment is no longer out of fashion. Now we read in newspapers of real-life arrests, tortures, bombings, murders, and 'casual slaughters' and witness them daily on television without any means of stemming the horrors. We feel to some extent implicated and understand how a dramatist can feel morally obligated to bring violence on stage and not deflect attention from the most sensational events. Our world engenders violence and a theatre which does not deal with it cannot engage with what most troubles us.

Shakespeare did not abandon the sensationalism of *Titus* or that of the more lurid episodes in the three parts of *Henry the Sixth*, written a little earlier. Rather, he pursued his interest in violence and developed the use of it. Naked and undisguised, it is present on stage in later tragedies, especially those that are commonly regarded as the furthest reaches of his imagination, *Hamlet*, *Macbeth*, *Othello*, and *King Lear*. Rather than glossing over violence in Shakespeare's plays, passing quickly by and looking in another direction, we should pay close attention to their depiction of cruelty, pain, and unspeakable horror. We must recognize that a terrible atrocity has often been placed close to the centre of a play's action so that it draws the leading characters into irreversible changes and affects the final outcome as much as any fine speeches and sensitive feelings.

Even when no violence is shown on stage, it is often present in words. An extreme and well-known example is Lady Macbeth's:

> I have given suck, and know
> How tender 'tis to love the babe that milks me –
> I would, while it was smiling in my face,
> Have pluck'd my nipple from his boneless gums,
> And dash'd the brains out. . . .   (I.vii.54–8)

The pain involved in visualizing such a brutal infanticide does not release a reader or an actor from giving an imaginary reality to this boast, as he or she would, more easily, bring the 'rooky woods' or a guttering candle to the mind's eye later in the play. Both text and stage directions will often require physical responses that push the acting towards sensationalism: how should Hamlet 'lug the guts' of Polonius from his mother's closet, how should he handle himself when he says he 'could drink hot blood' (III.iv.212; III.ii.380)?

Even when we see a performance, we may not experience the violence required by the text because action is seldom raw and ugly on our stages. Peter Brook's production of *Titus Andronicus* in 1955 represented Lavinia's torture by substituting elegant red ribbons for stage blood. The last appalling scenes were rehearsed repeatedly and the text cut progressively until performances were no longer plagued by the nervous laughter which their crazed brutality had provoked in early rehearsals. Today's directors and designers follow suit and seldom allow a play by Shakespeare to be crude or harrowing or to be so inhuman as to risk laughter or disbelief. Violent scenes are rehearsed with care until they become disciplined and safe, coherently designed, carefully modulated in tone, balanced in form, fluently ingenious in movement. When blood is spilt, it does so under strict control. Designers make sure that lights are dimmed or so tricked out with strobe effects that an audience cannot see anything for long, and has difficulty in following what is actually happening. Sound effects crescendo, obliterating the individual cries of pain, or one particular cry is chosen to be isolated and exaggerated. Shakespeare's violence can be reduced to part of a scenic effect which generalizes the particular and takes eyes and ears away from appalling facts and intense suffering.

At the height of his career, Shakespeare was still seeking new ways to deal with violence, as if he had not yet probed far enough into its nature and consequences. Over the years, he came to distrust the ability of words to do this work. In the third part of *Henry the Sixth*, when Rutland's tutor is dragged off stage, the 'innocent child' opens his terrified eyes and immediately addresses his assassin:

> So looks the pent-up lion o'er the wretch
> That trembles under his devouring paws;
> And so he walks, insulting o'er his prey,
> And so he comes, to rend his limbs asunder . . . (I.iii.12ff.)

The boy goes on to beg for his life, for time to pray, or to be given a reason for his death. He reminds his killer that he has a son who might also be threatened with death. After receiving the death-blow, he quotes Ovid's *Heroides*, as his tutor might have taught him. So violence is made apparent by words, one step at a time, but in *Macbeth*, written years later, a similar horror is staged without verbal embellishment to detract from its brutality. The young son of Macduff says nothing when a messenger tells his mother to flee 'with your little ones' (IV.ii.68). When the murderers enter, he seconds his mother's defiance recklessly, with 'Thou liest, thou shag-eared villain!' but when one of them turns on him, with 'What you egg? / Young fry of treachery!' the boy is silent until after he has been struck he cries, 'He has killed me, mother. / Run away, I pray you.' According to the Folio's stage-direction, the mother then leaves the stage crying 'Murder!' and probably carrying other 'little ones' with her so that only inchoate cries are heard from off-stage as they also are killed. What an audience sees is the one child lying dead, a small mutilated corpse which will lie there until some stagehand, saying nothing, drags it away. Years earlier, in *Henry the Sixth*, the last focus had been controlled by the exultant words of Clifford directing attention away from the victim to his blood-covered sword: now nothing mitigates the horror.

In *King Lear*, written around 1605–6, violence and prolonged suffering, in one form or another, run throughout the play, in the king's resistance to the buffeting storm, the blinding of Gloucester carried out with savage precision, the poisoning of Regan suffered until its pain becomes unbearable and she leaves precipitately. By the end of the play, the accumulated weight of all this pain presses down upon actors and audience.

Popular Morality

In one respect, present-day readers and audiences may be less ready to view atrocities as Shakespeare presents them because they can see less cause to do so than his contemporaries. In his day, accounts of violence would be familiar to everyone who, in accordance with their legal duty, heard the Scriptures read aloud in church or attended sermons about the suffering of martyrs. Copies of *Foxe's Book of Martyrs* were made publicly available in churches and colleges; Sir Francis Drake took a copy around the world with him for recreation and kept himself from being bored by colouring its pictures. In this frequently reprinted book anyone might read scrupulous accounts of suffering as, for example, the death at the stake of John Hooper for whom, because of a great wind, three successive fires had to be lit so that he suffered continuously for three quarters of an hour:

> . . . when he was black in the mouth, and his tongue so swollen that he could not speak, yet his lips went [on moving] until they were shrunk to the gums; and he knocked his breast with his hand until one of his arms fell off, and then knocked still with the other, while the fat, water, and blood dropped out at his fingers' ends.

The comment that follows made this story palatable:

> And he now reigneth, I doubt not, as a blessed martyr in the joys of heaven prepared for the faithful in Christ before the foundations of the world; for whose constancy all Christians are bound to praise God.

Such horrors as this were also memorialized in impressive paintings which worshipers could contemplate (see Plate 1).

Elizabethan tragedies are not about Christian martyrs – matters of state and religion were forbidden on the stage – but they were written in a theatrical tradition that had developed from earlier mystery plays that had presented, with whatever realism could be managed, various kinds of death, torture, and suffering as demonstrations of Christian faith and the power of God's love for his people. Audiences at these highly popular plays, that were performed until the last decades of the sixteenth century, saw actors who were people like themselves enact the violent killing by Cain of his brother Abel, the scourging and crucifixion of Christ, and the multiple sufferings of the damned. In the Massacre of Innocents, Herod's knights slaughtered one new-born baby after another, with slow pleasure or cruel mockery. Blood flows and the mothers roar, curse, lament, fight back, and cry for vengeance:

1   Titian's *Martyrdom of St Lawrence*, 1550–55

The suffering of violent punishment is depicted in this impressive and vivid painting for the greater glory of God and as an aid to devotion. Light from the heavens is given pride of place in the composition but most witnesses pay attention only to the victim. (*Dating from between 1550 and 1555, this painting belongs to the church of the Jesuits in Venice, by whose permission it is reproduced by courtesy of AKG, London.*)

> Alas, my bab, myn innocent,   my fleshly get! For sorow
> That God me derly sent,   of bales who may me borow?
> Thy body is all to-rent!   I cry, both euen and morow,
> Veniance for thi blod thus spent: 'out!' I cry, and 'horow!'

As they fall on the ground, the 'old trots' are told to get up, 'Or by Cokys dere bonys / I make you go wyghtly.' Scenes of appalling violence were acceptable as part of the whole story of God's dealing with mankind. An audience was shown how to react by various verbal signposts – such as the anachronistic reference to God's bones in this quotation – and by symbolic actions and stage-properties. Angels, devils, prophets, saints, and God himself were brought on stage, or above or below the stage, to watch, comment, or interact.

Elizabethan dramatists profited from this example. In Marlowe's *Faustus,* its hero sees 'Christ's blood' streaming in the firmament and Good and Bad Angels preside over the horror of his entry into hell. Shakespeare seems to imitate this at the end of *The Tragedy of Richard III*, but does not run so close to what the censor would allow: rather than angels, the Ghosts of those whom Richard has killed come on stage to curse him and then to bless his opponent, Richmond; as he goes to battle, Richmond calls on 'fair Saint George' and, after victory, on 'the Great God of Heaven' (V.iii.350; V.v.8). While such specifically Christian signposts are usually avoided, in their place political and moral representatives are used to mark the causes and consequences of violence, even though they can achieve nothing by their intervention. One such is the innocent country clown towards the end of *Titus Andronicus* (IV.iii). In *Romeo and Juliet*, the Apothecary marks the course that the hero is taking towards death and, in *Richard II*, a Groom from his stable. The pursuivant and priest in *Richard III*, who appear out of nowhere and for no clear cause, set a moral context by representing the rival claims of the world and of the church, as Hastings goes towards his death (see III.iii.97–113). Similar markers are the pious old man who encounters Ross and Macduff as they flee Macbeth's castle and prays that 'God's benison' go with them (II.iv. 40–1) or, in the same play, the presence off-stage of the holy King Edward of England who can cure 'wretched souls' with his touch, 'such sanctity hath heaven given his

hand' (IV.ii.141–5). *Hamlet* has numerous markers, though none of
them so clear in their influence on the audience's reception: the
Gravedigger who knows about death, Osric who is so 'spacious in
the possession of dirt' that it is 'a vice to know him', and Fortinbras
who stands for decisive action and military prowess. Horatio does
not make a similar unexpected and last-minute entry but, being a
man who in Hamlet's view 'is not passion's slave' (III.ii.61–72), he
helps the audience throughout the play to estimate the hero's contrasting progress. As Fortinbras and Horatio face each other over the
dead bodies in the last scene, they may be intended to mark two
contrasted courses the hero might have taken and so indicate some
cause for his suffering and the brutality that has taken possession of
the stage.

Violence was customarily associated with unequivocal moral judgements. As Alexander Neville expected his translation of Seneca's *Oedipus*
to be a warning to his countrymen (see above, p. 17), so Thomas
Heywood writing in defence of the popular theatres claimed that:

> If we present a Tragedy, we include the fatal and abominable ends of
> such as commit notorious murders, which is aggravated and acted
> with all the art that may be, to terrify men from the like abhorred
> practices. If we present a foreign History, the subject is so intended
> that, in the lives of Romans, Grecians or others, either the virtues of
> our Countrymen are extolled or their vices reproved, as thus, by the
> example of Caesar to stir soldiers to valor and magnanimity; by the
> fall of Pompey, that no man trust in his own strength; we present
> Alexander killing his friend in a rage to reprove rashness; Midas,
> choked with his gold, to tax covetousness; Nero, against tyranny;
> Sadanapalus, against luxury; Nynus, against ambition, with infinite
> others, by sundry instances, either animating men to noble attempts,
> or attacking the consciences of the spectators, finding themselves
> touched in presenting the vices of others.
>
> *(An Apology for Actors*, 1612)

This defence reads like special pleading, but a contemporary moral
and political relevance does often underlie scenes of extreme violence
on the Elizabethan stage, as at the beginning of *Titus Andronicus*,
even when the text did not explicitly direct attention to this.

Public Shows and Personal Responses

Other popular features help Shakespeare's tragedies of blood to reflect contemporary life. The 'Shows' that fill the stage several times during the course of a play's action, often without words but drawing on many actors and accompanied by music, are representations of events that many in their audiences would have witnessed (see Plate 2). When rulers of the state or church processed in public through a city, they drew crowds into the streets to stand and stare, and to comment among themselves. Walking or riding in the procession, the greatest persons in the land or local community might greet spectators with a wave of the hand or inclination of the head and be greeted in return with bows, curtseys, and cheers, or sometimes with curses, abuse, and, possibly, the throwing of missiles from the safety of a crowd's anonymity. Occasionally, a spectator might catch the monarch's eye and believe that he or she had been personally acknowledged.

Such events were closely observed by Shakespeare. In *All's Well That Ends Well*, four young women and an older widow watch a troop of soldiers pass and comment on their appearance until one in the procession 'has spied' them (III.v.72–89). In *Troilus and Cressida*, Pandarus and Cressida keep up a continuous commentary as the Trojan soldiers pass: 'If he see me', says Pandarus, 'you shall see him nod at me' (I.ii.186–90). The king in *Richard II* gives a vivid picture of Bolingbroke's 'courtship of the common people' as he processed through them on his way to banishment:

> How he did seem to dive into their hearts
> With humble and familiar courtesy;
> What reverence he did throw away on slaves,
> Wooing poor craftsmen with the craft of smiles.   (I.iv.24–36)

At the end of *Henry IV, Part Two*, Falstaff and his friends prepare to greet the royal procession of the new King Henry, 'putting all affairs else in oblivion, as if there were nothing else to be done but to see him' (V.v.26–7). In the tragedies, the entrance of Claudius and Gertrude on their marriage day, or of Macbeth and his lady newly

2   The Coronation procession of Edward VI

This eighteenth-century copy of a 1547 original shows an occasion for public display as the procession passes through the streets of London; its citizens crowd together for the rare view of their rulers and their retinue. (*Reproduced by kind permission of the Society of Antiquaries of London.*)

crowned, or Lear when he calls his daughters to speak of their love, are all similar occasions for an assembled court and servants to greet their monarch.

In present times, when public parades are no longer 'live' for most spectators, the effect of these shows in the theatre may well be lessened, but their real-life popularity in Shakespeare's day was depended upon and exploited by dramatists. Stage directions in

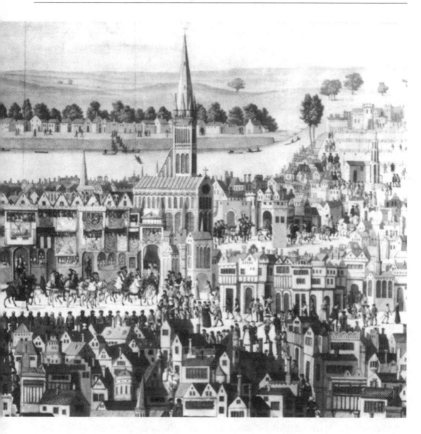

Thomas Lodge's *The Wounds of Civil War: the Tragedies of Marius and Scilla* (*c.* 1586–9; published 1594) give a taste of what might be done; for example:

> *Enter* Scilla *in triumph in his chair triumphant of gold, drawn by four Moors before the chariot; his colours, his crest, his captains, his prisoners:* Aracathius, *Mithridates' son,* Aristion, Archelaus, *bearing crowns of gold, and manacled. After the chariot, his soldiers' bands,* Basillus, Lucretius, Lucullus, *besides prisoners of divers nations, and sundry disguises.*

In our reading and staging of Shakespeare's plays, we should try to re-create something of this expansiveness and a similar invitation to stare and be curious. Processions were among the most life-like moments in a Shakespeare tragedy and should neither be dismissed as merely pompous nor staged with such efficiency that individual performances are scarcely observable and individual responses out of the question. They were moments when an audience around an open stage could feel included in the play and able to enter into direct relationship with its characters.

In performance, parades, processions, and other large-scale formalities were, to some degree, true and open meetings between actors and audience. Many of them had no fixed words to speak so that both parties could have their own thoughts and make their own responses. At the beginning of a play, its audience might not know how to respond and would therefore search for some sign of what is afoot – as at the start of the second scene in *Hamlet* – while towards the end they may have learnt so much that they would withdraw from any sharing – as, perhaps, at the beginning of the last scene of *Titus* – or be so eager to follow that they can scarcely wait for formalities to end – as in the last scene of *Hamlet*. Whatever the circumstance, whenever time is taken for a 'show', an audience can bring its own imaginations to work with what the actors display before them, as they scan the faces of the chief performers and speculate on what purpose or what secret each of them possesses.

Another form of public spectacle in Shakespeare's day was provided by mad persons. The Bedlam madhouse attracted visitors to see the wild and unpredictable antics of the inmates. The mad folk who were tolerated in ordinary society were often regarded with open-eyed curiosity. So it would have been in plays: mad-scenes were surprisingly common and offer opportunities to actors for surprise. They call for such active performances that they are not likely to be neglected in twentieth-century productions while their verbal originality and agility ensure that readers pay them close attention. Nevertheless, their effect will be changed and their importance diminished if they are not staged or imagined with a showmanship that exploits their strangeness and unpredictability.

For Elizabethan dramatists, these popular scenes were also useful in offering an escape from the strict dictates of the censor since anything said could be explained away as craziness. When the action of a tragedy involves revenge for crimes, madness often brings outspoken attacks on the processes of justice, such as Titus calling out to the stones because the tribunes will not hear him, or shooting arrows with messages attached into the court of Saturninus. The sheer impossibility of much that madmen say they do, or will do, is not only part of their craziness but also emphasizes the unreasonable nature of the injustice they are trying to oppose. Heironimo in Kyd's *Spanish Tragedy* (*c.* 1590) not only calls repeatedly for justice, but literally *runs* mad and attempts to dig into the 'bowels of the earth' with his dagger for a pickaxe (III.xii.71–5). To attack authority so openly in well-ordered, unambiguous words could not easily pass a censor watchful for any transgression of permitted freedoms. Hamlet does not take to madness solely because he is troubled in his mind and tormented by feelings he cannot fully control, but also because it allows him to express his horror at his mother's remarriage in front of the entire court and to sound out the king's secret purposes when face-to-face with him (see III.ii.104–30 and IV.iii.17–53).

Shakespeare used madness, in one form or another, in almost all his tragedies. Strange 'antics' drew attention and challenged audiences to understand what is meant, to piece together intended imperfections with their own thoughts. It was like setting a riddle. Lear commands:

> draw me a clothier's yard. Look, look, a mouse! Peace, peace; this piece of toasted cheese will do't. There's my gauntlet; I'll prove it on a giant. Bring up the brown bills. O, well flown, bird! i' the clout, i' the clout – hewgh! Give me the word. (IV.vi.87–92)

An audience will know what is a mouse, toasted cheese, gauntlet, bird, and 'the word', but few of its members would be able to follow Lear's disordered thoughts with any ease. Either a spectator must be content with very miscellaneous sights and sayings, making what sense can readily be made of it all, or must work hard to follow, interpret, guess, and sometimes fail to follow. In both cases, an audience will make what it can of the scene and each member will get involved with Lear's madness, half-creating it in his or her individual way. Lear speaks here of his realm as if it were England in the early

seventeenth century, not a much earlier kingdom in the history of
Britain, and he addresses imaginary people to whom his audience
might well put familiar faces: 'yond simp'ring dame . . . thou rascal
beadle . . . that whore'. More daringly, when he comments that
'robes and furr'd gown hide all' (IV.vi.160–6), he might address
actual individuals sitting in the best places of the auditorium. He
also speaks timeless truths so that they may have special immediacy
for anyone standing or sitting before him in the theatre:

> When we are born, we cry that we are come
> To this great stage of fools.   (ll. 183–4)

The Popular Appeal of Speech

Although this may seem intrinsically unlikely today, when contemporary plays make a virtue of being instantly recognizable as representations of everyday behaviour and speech, verbal dexterity and
rhetorical elaboration were also sources of tragedy's popularity.
Mythological and recondite references, figures of speech that take
time to fulfil their own complications, strange and sometimes clumsily ornate words are very different from ordinary speech, but they
all were used by Shakespeare and some of his contemporaries in
ways that their audiences could respond to readily.

The changing energies of Shakespeare's dialogue, what he called 'its
variation or quick change' (*Sonn.* 76), can effect a corresponding
transfer to the speaker's bearing, gestures, facial expressions, breathing,
and the very sound of speech. The iambic pentameter provided an
ongoing beat and could be varied endlessly with considerable subtlety.
Its harmonies called for spirited speaking and could command close
attention. 'When temp'red with Love's sighs', a poet's lines could
'ravish savage ears / And plant in tyrants mild humility' (*Love's
Labours Lost*, IV.iii.340–5). While numerous accounts have survived
showing that speeches might not be fully understood in Shakespeare's
time, quite as many point to the popular success of ornate language
and strong verse-patterns. The satirist Joseph Hall was mocking ignorant theatre-goers when he declared that if only an actor:

> . . . can with terms Italianate,
> Big-sounding sentences, and words of state,
> Fair patch me up his pure iambic verse,
> He ravishes the gazing scaffolders. (*Virgidemiarum II*, I.iii)

Some two years earlier Thomas Nashe inveighed against actors who neglected 'action' in order to 'embowel the clouds in a speech of comparison'. He had special scorn for

> the alchemists of eloquence who, mounted on the stage of arrogance, think to out-brave better pens with the swelling bombast of a bragging blank verse. (Preface to R. Greene, *Menaphon*)

How Shakespeare used language of great refinement and invented new words and usages with extraordinary brilliance and energy will often be the subject of later chapters. Here one further effect is particularly relevant. As already discussed with regard to Marcus's description of Lavinia (see p. 20), rhetorical elaboration proved useful for holding back dramatic action, slowing down the speed or restraining the uncertainty that are natural responses to horror or fear, or to quickening hope. As Marcus enumerates his response to the horror he sees, so Richard the Second will go from point to point as he resigns the crown:

> Your cares set up do not pluck my cares down.
> My care is loss of care, by old care done;
> Your care is gain of care, by new care won.
> The cares I give I have, though given away;
> They tend the crown, yet still with me they stay. (IV.i.195–9)

So Richard dwells in his thoughts, retuning the simplest of words until they express more fully the burdens on his mind. The device presents a complex situation in slow motion so that an audience may follow, one simple step at a time, bringing its own multiple, varied, and variable consciousnesses to share in the king's predicament. In one sense, the tragedy belongs to each and every person who follows its dialogue in their own imaginations; the fate of a king has a highly accumulative and popular appeal.

4

Richard the Third and *Richard the Second*: Historical Tragedies

Looking at all the available evidence, scholars are still unsure whether *Richard the Third* was first performed in 1590 or 1594, but it is hard to believe that it preceded *Titus Andronicus* of early 1594. Richard's domination of the stage for the first three hundred and twenty-five lines suggests that Shakespeare gained greater confidence in turning back from a fictitious Rome to deal with England's history that he had already treated in the three parts of *Henry the Sixth*. As Duke of Gloucester in those plays, the 'crook'd back' Richard had taken hold of his imagination and now he is made the centre of interest: the story of England and the two rival dynasties of York and Lancaster progresses steadily while this hero captures and taunts an audience's attention.

An Active Hero

Richard's abundant verbal invention, trenchant humour, and rapid control of mood give the impression of an active mind, its energy flickering and flaring, at one moment playful and, at the next, dangerous and cruel. In a long exchange with Lady Anne, Richard can turn her hatred into compliance and simultaneously recount much of their past history. Shakespeare had so mastered the expression of thought and feeling that he could now rely on a single agent to set his play in action.

The books he had read for source material would have set him on this course. For example, Edward Hall's chronicle *The Union of the Two Noble and Illustrate Families of Lancaster and York* (1546) followed Sir Thomas More's *History of Richard III* in portraying Richard as prime mover in all events, an obvious villain and also a fascinating man:

> he was close and secret, a deep dissimuler, lowly of countenance, arrogant of heart, outwardly familiar where he inwardly hated, not letting to kiss whom he thought to kill.

Christopher Marlowe may also have spurred Shakespeare forward. Born in the same year, this rival poet had already written *Tamburlaine the Great*, a two-part play dominated by a Scythian shepherd who became the tyrant–conqueror of the known world. While emulating Marlowe's phrasing, dramatic boldness, and narrative drive, Shakespeare capped this achievement by divesting his hero of the three supporting generals, Techelles, Usumcasane, and Theridamas, who are usually at hand in *Tamburlaine* to contrast with its hero and, where necessary, supply information, debate issues, and run errands. Unlike Tamburlaine, Richard starts the play alone in soliloquy, often acts alone, without accomplices, and, for much of the play, does almost entirely as he wishes.

Shakespeare's Richard is without precedent in Elizabethan plays except, briefly and more clumsily, his own Aaron the Moor. The Vice or Devil characters in early morality plays have his ability to deceive and to mock, but not his deep-seated compulsion or acuity of mind. Marlowe's Barabas in *The Jew of Malta* comes nearer, a villain–hero who shares with an audience a pleasure in his own abilities; neither he nor any other predecessor has Richard's finesse. With effortless sarcasm that scarcely disturbs a surface smoothness, he forces an issue:

> But, gentle Lady Anne,

> To leave this keen encounter of our wits,
> And fall something into a slower method: . . .   (I.ii.118–20)

A homespun proverb deals neatly with sensational and ambitious projects:

> But yet I run before my horse to market:
> Clarence still breathes, Edward still lives and reigns;
> When they are gone, then must I count my gains.   (I.i.160–2)

Having trapped Clarence, his brother, and sent him to death with a cheerful 'your imprisonment shall not be long', Richard brings an audience further into his confidence by mocking his own villainy:

> Simple, plain Clarence, I do love thee so
> That I will shortly send thy soul to Heaven –
> If Heaven will take the present at our hands.   (I.i.113–20)

A single word can lift a simple communication into veiled contempt and ridicule – 'And in good time, here comes the sweating lord' (III.i.24) – or allude to his own ruthlessness in battle as if it were a passing whim:

> Edward, her lord, whom I, some three months since,
> Stabb'd in my angry mood at Tewkesbury.   (I.ii.245–6)

Richard has been given an independent mind that fine-tunes the dialogue continually, for both actor and audience to enjoy.

Such small details are of crucial importance because, without this ever-present energy of mind, the tragedy would be too predictable as its story-line is driven all in one direction towards the hero's coronation and then staggers rapidly towards his defeat at the battle of Bosworth; any theatregoer used to tragedies of crime and retribution would expect no less. According to George Puttenham's *Art of English Poesy* (1589) tragedy was invented to show the consequences of tyrants seizing power:

> their infamous life and tyrannies were laid open to all the world, their

wickedness reproached, their follies and extreme insolencies derided, and their miserable ends painted out in plays and pageants, to show the mutability of Fortune and the just punishment of God in revenge of a vicious and evil life.

The inevitability of Richard's progress followed by his fall is heightened by the way entrances and other events, such as the death of Edward IV, are timed to fit in with his manipulations. The elimination of one adversary leaves another as the next target so that he seems to be caught within a series of murders that together function as a kind of net, each strand tied to others and making them inevitable. Were it not for Richard's cool wit, the tragedy would have been a routine display and condemnation of crimes but, with him in the ascendant, an audience cannot be bored or able to forget him for a single scene – as it could stop being concerned about Titus Andronicus.

As Richard drives the play forward and deals with king, queens, mothers, brothers, wives, more distant relatives, nobles, archbishops and bishops, the Lord Mayor and citizens of London, servants, hired assassins, a page, a scrivener, a disaffected gentleman, and several children, this hero-centred tragedy is also concerned, as *Titus Andronicus* had been, with the fate of families and an entire society. Queen Elizabeth sees:

> . . . the ruin of my House:
> The tiger now hath seiz'd the gentle hind;
> Insulting tyranny begins to jet
> Upon the innocent and aweless throne.
> Welcome destruction, blood, and massacre;
> I see, as in a map, the end of all.   (II.iv.49–54)

But Richard is not the only cause of this destruction; the 'grossness of this age' and 'the necessity and state of [the] times' (III.i.46; IV.iv.416) are blamed for failure to withstand his progress in tyranny. He is defeated and killed only when the young Earl of Richmond arrives from overseas to fight the tyrant and, in proclaiming peace, to insist on uniting the long-time warring factions of York and Lancaster in a new line of Tudor monarchs.

The Setting for Tragedy

The English setting allowed Shakespeare to raise moral and religious beliefs in conventional Christian terms. Death brings thoughts of heaven and hell, as to King Edward at the beginning of Act II:

> I every day expect an embassage
> From my Redeemer, to redeem me hence.   (ll. 3–4)

As death is met in different ways, the effect becomes far less assured and conventional. Lord Rivers prays to God as if making a bargain:

> Be satisfied, dear God, with our true blood,
> Which – as thou know'st – unjustly must be spilt.   (III.iii.22–3)

The Duke of Buckingham is more concerned with his own shame and wrong-doing than with redemption:

> That high All-seer which I dallied with
> Hath turn'd my feigned prayer on my head . . .   (V.i.20–1)

By no means all references to God demonstrate belief in His providence or redemptive power. On hearing of Clarence's death, Queen Elizabeth questions Christian providence bluntly: 'All-seeing heaven, what a world is this?' (l. 83). Many of them express little more than a desire that wrong should be punished. When Hastings, the Lord Chamberlain, remembers God as he goes to the block, he thinks mostly of human vanities and insecurities:

> O momentary grace of mortal men,
> Which we more hunt for than the grace of God,
> Who builds his hope in air of your good looks
> Lives like a drunken sailor on a mast,
> Ready with every nod to tumble down
> Into the fatal bowels of the deep.   (III.iv.96–101)

While such speeches mark out a Christian context of sin, redemption, and punishment, an audience cannot avoid seeing how variously and how belatedly these ideas come to mind when they can remedy nothing.

Shakespeare complicated this ideological context by drawing all the women together to act like a chorus to the tragedy, a helpless and repetitive one. Contradicting all the chronicles, he also kept Queen Margaret, widow of Henry VI, alive long enough to be present in the royal court for much of the story, at first at odds with the other women but later, in Act IV, scene iv, leading them in condemnation of the 'hell-hound' and 'carnal cur' (IV.iv.46–58) and teaching them how to curse. Her prayers to God ask only for the revenge for which she is 'hungry':

> Cancel his bond of life, dear God I pray,
> That I may live and say 'The dog is dead.'   (ll. 78–9)

When the Duchess of York, Richard's mother, asks 'Why should calamity be full of words?', the widowed Elizabeth answers:

> Let them have scope, though what they will impart
> Help nothing else, yet do they ease the heart.   (V.iv.126–31)

These female victims and witnesses call for Richard's punishment, but the complaints and prayers of this chorus stop none of the outrages and offer little in mitigation of suppression. Until Richmond enters in its very last scenes, belief in Christian providence and a sense of injustice offer little reassurance or trust in human justice.

Supernatural events may, however, play some small part in this tragedy, as they did not in *Titus Andronicus*. As early as Act I, scene ii, when Richard stops Lady Anne from accompanying the body of Henry VI to burial, the wounds of this murdered man are said to be visibly bleeding afresh in the presence of his murderer, in accordance with folk superstition. We cannot be sure if Shakespeare intended stage blood to be actually visible and freely flowing, but everyone on stage says that it does and so an audience will tend to believe as they do. Another supernatural happening may occur just before the last battle when the 'Ghosts' of Richard's victims enter and, one after another, curse him and bless Richmond. However, both Richmond and Richard say that these spectres are merely in their dreams, representing their own fears and hopes rather than being a supernatural intervention. Crime, retribution, and despair are their themes but nothing is said about faith in Christian providence or hope of redemption. Except for the clear lead towards a different future which is voiced by the inexperienced Richmond in the very last minutes – 'God, and our good cause, fight upon our side' (V.iii.241) – the England of this tragedy is a deeply wounded and helpless society, divided except in condemnation of crimes against human life committed by a politically successful and intellectually superior adventurer. A sense that peace should prevail or that God cares for mankind is much less clearly expressed.

The Tragedy in Performance

For all the bravura and resources of its huge central role, *The Tragedy of King Richard the Third* (to quote its title in the first Quarto edition of 1597) is, like *Titus Andronicus*, disturbing to watch. While a sense of political disaster is cumulative rather than shocking, the hero's solitary, 'crook'd backed' presence at the start of the play is immediately disturbing. Although Richard's deformity may or may not be seen at once, it is soon identified as a major motive for the ensuing action. In his view, it is an accident of birth:

> Cheated of feature by dissembling Nature,
> Deform'd, unfinish'd, sent before my time
> Into this breathing world scarce half made up –
> And that so lamely and unfashionable
> That dogs bark at me, as I halt by them. . . .

This is a fate he both accepts and overcomes:

> . . . since I cannot prove a lover
> To entertain these fair well-spoken days,
> I am determined to prove a villain
> And hate the idle pleasures of these days. (I.i.14–31)

While he may use his deformity as an excuse for what he wants to do, an audience can soon be in little doubt that he is both driven and tormented by some unappeasable need of his own.

While dominating the action, Richard is secretive and mysterious, suffering more than he admits. An audience hears that, from the time he makes Anne his wife, he is troubled nightly with dreams. Later, he grows more obviously uneasy, seeking assurance that his will has been done before he goes to bed. As battle draws near, he forgets to complete orders he gives, changes his mind, and strikes a servant. Before leading his army to fight, his dreams transform him before the eyes of the audience: 'Cold fearful drops stand on my trembling flesh' (V.iii.178). In many ways an assured and consistent hero, Richard is haunted by fear of failure; as if with an inner, irremovable compulsion, he pursues the crown and subsequently loses it.

Against this view, however, a few occasions suggest that other options were open and the inevitable course towards destruction might have been arrested. The first comes towards the end of Richard's wooing of Lady Anne. When he speaks of her beauty, '*She looks scornfully at him*' (I.ii.174, S.D.) and then, suddenly, he draws his sword and places its point towards his own breast. As he goes on to say that it was her 'heavenly face that set [him] on' to kill her husband, Anne '*falls the sword*' (l. 186, S.D.) and, without saying why, begins to change towards him. Richard quickly takes advantage of this lapse in hatred but, at the moment when Anne lets the sword fall and begins to trust him, it is just possible that he has truly been captivated by her beauty and, for that moment, is unsure how to proceed.

A very obvious occasion when the course of events is not inevitable comes immediately after Richard's off-stage coronation, a public occasion which draws particular attention from the audience on stage and in the auditorium (see pp. 43–6, above). He tells Buckingham that he is about to 'try if thou be current gold indeed' and talks of the princes imprisoned in the Tower. Buckingham insists that he does not understand what is being asked of him, requests time to consider, and leaves the stage. Richard says nothing in reply but, during his silence, Catesby observes, 'The King is

angry: see, he gnaws his lip.' When Richard does speak, his words
show that he had looked intently into Buckingham's face, noting his
'considerate eyes' (IV.ii.1–30). He now summons a nameless page to
his side and asks him to recommend someone who can be paid to
commit murder. Having his answer, he turns to Catesby with other
business, including the death of his wife, but shortly after speaks
aside:

> I am in
> So far in blood that sin will pluck on sin;
> Tear-falling pity dwells not in this eye.   (ll. 63–5)

He has recognized the possibility of pity. Tyrrel, whom the page has
introduced, enters immediately after this and accepts the task of
murdering the innocent young princes but this does not satisfy: as
all other talk stops, the king bends down and '*whispers in his ear*'
(l. 87, S.D.). This succession of impulsive physical reactions, hesitations, repetitions, reflections, questions, and inaudible words alerts
an audience to what cannot be said or is not thoroughly thought
out. They are the more effective because elsewhere in the play speech
yields to speech, full-laden lines of verse and strong action driving
forward together. Here, momentarily, Richard might seem about to
break the chain of events because he lacks the power or confidence
to proceed.

A third occasion when Richard will puzzle an audience is the long
encounter with Queen Elizabeth when he tries to win her daughter
as his new queen. In some ways, this wooing is a repetition of the
earlier one with Lady Anne, but its context is problematic for an
audience that has heard that, conveniently for Richard, Anne has
died in her bed without any cause being given. It is also more pres-
sured and repetitive. Richard must ask Elizabeth to forget so many
crimes he has commited against her family that the encounter is
lengthy and his eloquence more in assertion than argument; often
they answer one another one line at a time. When he seems to take
her irony for a straightforward proposition, the exchange stops,
rather than reaching any climax:

Elizabeth.	Shall I go win my daughter to thy will?
Richard.	And be a happy mother by the deed.
Elizabeth.	I go. Write to me very shortly,
	And you shall understand from me her mind.

(IV.iv.426–9)

When she has gone, rather abruptly, Richard calls her a 'Relenting fool, and shallow, changing woman!' (l. 431), a judgement which is completely wrong, as an audience will quickly learn: in fact, Elizabeth has deceived him throughout their talk, having already promised her daughter to Richmond. Richard has lost his power of perception and with it his hold over events: he is destroyed from within, by his own weakness, as well as by a woman he has under-estimated.

The wooing of Elizabeth for her daughter's hand in marriage is not necessary to the narrative and today many directors cut it entirely from their productions – in this long play, this long scene is easily dispensable. However, since the variations between the Folio and Quarto texts, which show the cuts made in early performances, do not affect this episode which is given at length in both versions, other scenes must have been thought less of a loss to the play. We can only suppose that Shakespeare wished to encourage an audience to take a probing interest in Richard by offering him once more to its attention and allowing the actor to choose how much, if anything, is seen of his insecurity.

Soon follows the most obvious moment when Richard is at a loss. His soliloquy on waking from his ghost-ridden dream is both indecisive and contradictory:

> Give me another horse! Bind up my wounds!
> Have mercy, Jesu! – Soft, I did but dream.
> O, coward conscience, how dost thou afflict me!

Struggling here to master his fears and prepare for battle, Richard has an opportunity to change his course of action by holding on to his prayer and recognizing the demands of his conscience:

> Perjury, perjury in the highest degree;

> Murder, stern murder, in the direst degree;
> All several sins, all us'd in each degree,
> Throng to the bar, crying all, 'Guilty, guilty!'

An actor will have to choose whether he could actually believe that God or man would 'have mercy' on him or if this is merely a passing reversion to the prayers of childhood. He continues:

> I shall despair. There is no creature loves me,
> And if I die, no soul will pity me.   (V.iii.178–202)

Are these words terrified, self-mocking or self-wounding, or impatient? Might they represent a total revaluation of his life that recognizes a longing to be loved?

The sight of Richard waking from his dream, accompanied by broken, violent, and contradictory words, is one of the most striking and memorable physical images in this play and has been frequently recorded in paintings and photographs (see Plate 3). Another follows when he enters alone during the last battle, calling out: 'A horse! A horse! My kingdom for a horse!' (V.iv.6). Catesby, still faithful to him, believes he wishes to escape (and Shakespeare's sources told how a light horse was brought to him for that very purpose), but that is not what he is seeking. Richard springs a last surprise on this faithful follower and, probably, on an audience:

> Slave! I have set my life upon a cast,
> And I will stand the hazard of the die.   (V.iv.9–10)

He leaves, sword in hand, seeking his enemies. At the end of this tragedy, the single figure of its hero stands out in bold and isolated theatricality, an image in great contrast to earlier and larger 'shows' when Richard had entered '*in pomp, crowned*' (IV.ii.0, S.D.) or at the head of his army in battle-order. The hero, on the field of battle, is another sight that stamps itself on the audience's mind, a figure not of despair, guilt, or loneliness as previously, but of defiant will and courage.

In many ways *The Tragedy of King Richard the Third* may be seen

3   William Hogarth's painting of Garrick's Richard the Third awaking from his dream

The elaborate robes, the crown, crucifix, and suspended light, together with the sword in hand, armour at the ready, and an army encampment in the distance, signify the nature of Richard's predicament; the outstretched posture and forward gaze indicate the uncertainty and violence of his feelings. David Garrick first performed this role at Drury Lane in 1742. (*The painting hangs in the Walker Gallery, Liverpool, and is reproduced by permission of the Board of Trustees of the National Museums and Galleries on Merseyside.*)

as a movement away from the exoticism, blatant horrors, and multiple plot of *Titus Andronicus*. Now a single plot gives a clear moral and political message by concentrating attention on a single hero in the setting of a country that is terrified by his progress and able to find no other response but condemnation. Beyond these changes, however, is a further development. At crucial moments the hero's thoughts and feelings are not defined by words or actions and, at the end, the actor's very being as Richard, what his imagination and performance has made of him, becomes what sustains the action and what the tragedy is about. A play that looks as if it is going to be very simple has more uncertain depths; the experience of seeing it can puzzle members of an audience long after they have left the theatre because the burden of understanding its central character – of recognizing what happens at the level of unconscious prompting – is shared between actor and audience: why does he 'stand the hazard of the die' and how firmly does he raise his sword?

At first such openness at the conclusion of a tragedy seems a strange refusal of a dramatist's task of bringing the tragic hero to some final achievement or apotheosis, some place of arrival, a verbal clarification of what he has stood for or what he has learnt. Instead of that, Shakespeare has trusted his actor to find what Richard has to do, and what he thinks and feels, and has invited his audiences to share that discovery with him. Instead of some idea or meaning, the play communicates something like a lived experience, intensified and extended by the actor's journey through the whole play and his ability to show the consequences that arise from his deepest and most instinctive being. Each new performance, he will be a new creation, according to how the entire company of actors have played their parts with him on that particular day. And an audience, all members of it, are left to understand the tragedy in their own terms, by responding as best they can and with whatever concerns they brought to the theatre with them that day. What seems like an empty hole, at the place where an interested reader might expect to find a secret revealed or an objective reached, is truly an opportunity for a shared creativity and the discovery of new meanings latent within the words and actions of the entire play. Already Shakespeare had found one of the staples of his art on which much of *Hamlet*, *Macbeth*, *Othello*, and *King Lear* will depend.

Two Kings in Opposition

The Tragedy of King Richard the Second was first published in a Quarto of 1597 but probably first performed in 1595, soon after both *Titus* and *Richard III*. It has a tighter and more complex structure but is considerably simpler in the demands it makes on a theatre company: there are no ghosts or fresh-bleeding corpse, no citizens, children, scrivener, pursuivant, priest, page, or half-convinced assassins. Curses, moral judgements, and hunger for revenge are much reduced and in their place clearer references to Christian redemption, providence, and holy sacraments, many in relation to Richard, the 'Lord's anointed', hallowed with holy balm. This new concentration of interest is in keeping with the play's narrative which depends almost wholly on the aggression of Henry Bolingbroke against his cousin, King Richard. These two face each other in two of the first three scenes and later at the head of their armies (III.iv) and in Westminster Hall where Richard resigns the crown in a formal act of Deposition (IV.i.154–318). In the last scene of all, Richard is brought in his coffin before the newly crowned Henry the Fourth.

The political context for this personal drama is complex and directly applicable to the political situation in which its early audiences lived. The first three Quarto editions omitted the crucial 'Deposition scene' which is evidence that the quasi-legal process of a crowned king's resignation in face of superior military force was considered likely to arouse rebellious thoughts at a time of growing political unrest in England; ideas that would lead, a few decades later, to civil war. In 1599, the players were paid to perform a play of *Richard II*, probably Shakespeare's, on the night before armed men paraded the streets of London in support of the attempted *coup d'état* of 1599, led by the Earl of Essex. Although this uprising was to prove an ignominious failure, recent scholarship has concluded that it was not only an expression of the earl's frustrated ambitions but also a symptom of discontent that was more general in England at that time, heightened in people's consciousness by continuing uncertainties about succession after the Queen's death. Elizabeth was ageing visibly and her actions growing more unpredictable and difficult to influence; in these circumstances, 'many soldiers, courtiers, and country gentlemen resented the domination of Robert Cecil and a small inner group at the centre of power' (*The Later Tudors*, p. 376).

While the tragedy's political issues are not elaborated, as in *Richard III*, with choruses of complaint and examples of treason's consequences, one scene does introduce a Gardener who speaks of his garden as a parable to show the need for strong government. His message is a harsh one: while 'some supportance' should be given to early-ripening fruit, a ruler should be ready to 'cut off the heads' of growths that 'look too lofty in our commonwealth' and 'root away' weeds that bring no 'profit' (III.iv.28–39). In effect, he condemns both Bolingbroke and Richard, one as an insurgent and the other as a 'wasteful king' who is not ruthless enough. Simply spoken but articulate, he introduces hard-headed ideas about maintaining good order and strict obedience to a monarch and yet, when he is face to face with Richard's 'poor queen', his belief in coercion is mitigated with pity for her tears; to prevent more suffering, he would be willing, he says, to lose his skill in gardening (ll. 102–7).

At the start, as in *Titus Andronicus*, an audience is not given the full truth of the situation. Both Bolingbroke and Mowbray seem to be voicing an impassioned truth as they protest their loyalty and yet, as Richard reminds them:

> one but flatters us,
> As well appeareth by the cause you come,
> Namely, to appeal each other of high treason . . .   (I.i.25–7)

Bolingbroke accuses Mowbray of killing the Duke of Gloucester, one of Richard's uncles, and Mowbray accuses Bolingbroke of slander. Nothing is resolved here but the appellants are called to trial by combat at Coventry and this provides the business of the third scene. Once there, however, the truth still does not become plain: without explaining his action, Richard stops the duel just as it is about to begin and banishes both young nobles from the land.

That Mowbray had arranged the killing of Gloucester at the king's request is the crucial fact that neither judicial process brings into the open, but an intervening scene makes it abundantly clear. In an episode that is in none of the play's sources, Bolingbroke's father, John of Gaunt, is visited by Gloucester's widow and begins by asserting that King Richard was responsible for Gloucester's murder, Mowbray acting as his agent in arranging it. Gaunt calls for patience and trust in God's providence, 'Since correction lieth in those hands / Which made the fault' (I.ii.8), advice which the aged and ailing

Duchess cannot accept. She replies in terms reminiscent of Senecan tragedy and Shakespeare's earlier plays:

> Finds brotherhood in thee no sharper spur?
> Hath love in thy old blood no living fire?   (ll. 9–10)

Gaunt is proposing despair, she says, and not patience:

> In suff'ring thus thy brother to be slaught'red,
> Thou showest the naked pathway to thy life,
> Teaching stern murder how to butcher thee.
> That which in mean men we intitle patience
> Is pale cold cowardice in noble breasts.   (ll. 29–34)

Realizing that 'with her companion, grief, [she] must end her life' (l. 55), she breaks down and weeps and the scene moves still further from the stark imprecations of *Richard III*. She stumbles in her speech, forgets what she was going to say, and, no sooner than she has asked that the king's other uncle, the Duke of York, should visit her at home, she changes her mind:

> Alack, and what shall good old York there see
> But empty lodgings and unfurnish'd walls,
> Unpeopled offices, untrodden stones,
> And what hear there for welcome but my groans?
> Therefore commend me; let him not come there
> To seek out sorrow that dwells everywhere.   (ll. 66–71)

Although this scene is often cut from modern productions because it does not affect the main narrative and the Duchess plays no further part in the action, it is thematically of great significance. When a physically weakened Duchess is played with full emotional power, she disrupts the narrative by drawing attention to undisguised feeling and undeniable signs of her loneliness and grief. By revealing the deceptions of the king, Bolingbroke, Mowbray, and the otherwise persuasive and impressive John of Gaunt, from now on an audience has been alerted to question what everyone says and does, and what they avoid saying or doing. What does Mowbray 'know' about

Bolingbroke that the king will come to 'rue'? Why does Richard lessen the sentence on Bolingbroke once Mowbray has left? Such questions continue in subsequent scenes and concern the king himself. Is he so flippant when he learns that his uncle Gaunt is seriously ill because he will soon be rid of a powerful opponent or because he wants to take money from his 'coffers . . . for these Irish wars?' How just is criticism of his 'light vanity' and love of 'praises . . . Lascivious metres, . . . [and] report of fashions' (II.i.17–39)? Shakespeare seems to have heightened such uncertainties deliberately: his sources in the *Chronicles* have much to say about the king's profligacy, including 'abominable adultery', but nowhere does the play-text provide unambiguous evidence of this. The same sources also make clear that Richard has no desire to fight just as Queen Elizabeth had no wish to send troops to Ireland and could scarcely afford the expedition.

The play's exposition repeatedly opposes one judgement with another. While Bolingbroke's populist tactics are remarked on by Richard and his friends in Act I scene iv, in the next scene his two uncles have as much to say about Richard's 'unstaid youth' and 'rash fierce blaze of riot' (II.i.2, 33). An evocation of 'This blessèd plot, this earth, this realm, this England, / This nurse, this teeming womb of royal kings' is opposed to its present divided and ill-managed state and leads, just before Richard's entrance, to glowing praise of Richard's forebears:

> Fear'd by their breed, and famous by their birth,
> Renowned for their deeds as far from home,
> For Christian service and true chivalry,
> As is the sepulchre in stubborn Jewry
> Of the world's ransom, blessed Mary's son . . .   (ll. 50–6)

Such comparisons are dangerous to a new and untried authority, the more so when spoken by a person of great experience and attainments.

Having awakened an audience's questions at the start of this tragedy, Shakespeare then brought both Bolingbroke and Richard together for prolonged scrutiny: Bolingbroke taking more than he says he will: Richard finding that power is slipping away until he seems to have only his own self with which to counter the entire world that, he was told, he was born to rule. Issues are raised now that are more general and can be related to current issues of almost any age. What is the cost of success in pursuit of power and how can defeat and isolation be endured? To whom is loyalty due and how necessary is the 'cutting off' of ambitious heads or the 'rooting out' of incompetence?

Probing to the Centre

As at the centre of *Titus Andronicus* (III.ii), the hero suffers one setback after another and must find resources within himself with which to maintain his grip on sanity and follow his own will and purposes, so at the centre of *Richard II* is a similarly sustained scene. Here, however, the hero does not have to endure brutality and malicious cunning: more simply, but as devastating to his aspirations, he hears that his army has deserted and that Bolingbroke's power grows ever stronger. Like Titus, Richard makes 'senseless conjuration' to the stones beneath his feet, asking not for justice, but for the soldiers needed to maintain order in his kingdom (III.ii.23–6). The Bishop of Carlisle encourages him to accept what God offers and trust in that power, but only when his young cousin, the Duke of Aumerle, rebukes him for inaction is Richard shamed into asserting his rights and renewing his trust that

> Not all the water in the rough rude sea
> Can wash the balm off from an anointed king;
> The breath of worldly men cannot depose
> The deputy elected by the Lord.   (ll. 54–7)

When the Earl of Salisbury enters to report that twelve thousand fighting men have deserted, Richard's recovery does not last one moment more. Aumerle now comforts the king, telling him to 'remember who you are' (l. 82) and a second recovery follows, but that too fades to nothing when Sir Stephen Scroop enters with still more bad news. Now Richard seems to welcome – even to call for – defeat, on the grounds that man's relationship to God matters above everything else, but, told of his enemy's increasing strength in the 'fearful land', he wants to hear about his friends, fearing that they have 'made peace with Bolingbroke'. This confirmed, he curses them violently as 'villains, vipers, damn'ed without redemption!', worse than Judas tormented in hell. When he understands that, in fact, their peace had been made by death, Richard, like Titus, becomes totally silent. When he next speaks he, again like Titus, becomes a changed man, but to different effect: he does not seek ruthless revenge but envisages himself stripped of all power and conscious of his own needs as never before. Nothing is here of holy balm and authority, armed men, or 'great glory' (l. 87):

> I live with bread like you, feel want,
> Taste grief, need friends – subjected thus,
> How can you say to me, I am a king?   (ll. 175–7)

In performance, these simple words, referring to what everyone, everywhere, experiences, can draw members of an audience into the play so that, when Richard speaks of 'you' and of human necessities, they hear themselves addressed. The hero has become at one with his audience and the play's forward movement stalls.

Both Aumerle and the Bishop of Carlisle express alarm at Richard's 'weakness' and in response, for a moment, he seems to recover and think of winning back his power. This time it is only a pretence, for it lasts no time at all. When Scroop reports that his 'uncle York has join'd with Bolingbroke', Richard orders a retreat to Flint Castle; he will hear nothing more and cannot stay where he is:

> Discharge my followers; let them hence away,
> From Richard's night, to Bolingbroke's fair day.   (ll. 217–18)

Loss of power has not made Richard mad as Titus was mad, nor does he seek revenge: any violence is in his mind and it makes him renounce all authority and leave the stage without another word. The new element in this tragedy is Richard's recurring self-consciousness, his repeated revaluation of his own worth according to what he believes he truly feels: his 'want', 'grief', and 'need' for friends.

With his army, Bolingbroke now surrounds Flint Castle where Richard has taken refuge, and sends Northumberland as emissary. When the duke sees the king on the battlements, he compares him to an angry sun foretelling storms, but York, standing at his side, notices that:

> his eye,
> As bright as is the eagle's, lightens forth
> Controlling majesty; alack, alack for woe
> That any harm should stain so fair a show!   (III.iii.68–71)

During this parley, Richard recovers confidence, or seems to do so; he also foresees that his cousin's 'dangerous treason' will 'open / The purple testament of bleeding war' (ll. 91–100). The ideal of kingship and the reality of being overpowered, religious justification for authority and the use of force, political and truthful speaking are among the issues raised by this confrontation of the two young royal cousins. When Bolingbroke sends a message that he respects the king 'as he is a prince and just', Richard ignores the qualification and yields to his power, saying that he would give his 'gorgeous palace for a hermitage, . . . [his] large kingdom for a little grave'. But he knows he is talking 'idly' and, when he speaks of himself 'like glis'ring Phaeton / Wanting the manage of unruly jades', Northumberland senses that

> Sorrow and grief of heart
> Makes him speak fondly like a frantic man.   (ll. 185–6)

For an audience, the effect of all this is as baffling and unsettling as the start of the play had been, because it is not clear how submissive Bolingroke truly is or whether Richard's despair or courage is the stronger, or whether what is 'frantic' is about to become outright madness. When the cousins meet face to face, they play with words, not trusting one another:

> *Bolingbroke.*   My gracious lord, I come but for mine own.
> *Richard.*   Your own is yours, and I am yours, and all.
>
> (ll. 196–201)

Richard is the first to break away from this sparring, turning to his uncle, York, to ask him to dry his eyes: 'Tears show their love, but want their remedies' (l. 203).

Richard's divesting himself of power in Westminster Hall, Act IV, scene i, is more a confirmation of what has happened than a surprise. He calls for a glass to see himself and then smashes it because it does not show how he feels:

> . . . my grief lies all within,
> And these external manners of lament
> Are merely shadows to the unseen grief
> That swells with silence in the tortur'd soul.
> There lies the substance.   (IV.i.295–9)

This Deposition scene in which the political issues of this tragedy are presented with utmost clarity, in a style both highly formal and shockingly unconventional, is also the scene in which the personal distress of the tragic hero begins to take precedence over his public performance. This Richard does not 'gnaw his lip', hesitate, and become ruthless, like Richard III, or become crazed, blinded, and mysteriously wrapped up in his own 'contemplation', like Titus: he holds on to sanity by judging himself as he truly is and yet never loses entirely – or not for long – his earlier view of himself as a person of responsibility, dignity, and power, capable of admitting the truth and offering concern and love to others, as if all these were natural functions. The scene develops slowly and deliberately so that Richard holds the audience's attention and seems to share this exploration with them. An unseen, unspoken grief and a search for self-knowledge have become the substance of the tragedy.

In Richard's last scene, in prison and completely in Bolingbroke's power, the issue of kingship ceases to be a central concern. The stage is cleared for the king to speak in soliloquy and it is as a man alone that he speaks, setting one thought against another, and in 'none contented'. When music is played off stage, he struggles to make sense of it, and of time and thoughts of Bolingbroke, until his reason snaps:

> This music mads me. Let it sound no more;
> For though it have holp mad men to their wits,
> In me it seems it will make wise men mad.

Then, on the verge of madness, he has another thought:

> Yet blessing on his heart that gives it me,
> For 'tis a sign of love; and love to Richard
> Is a strange brooch in this all-hating world.   (V.v.6–65)

Shakespeare marked the importance of this thought, this movement out of the prison of self-regard, by inventing a Groom of the Stable to enter at exactly this point: he has come to look upon his 'some-times royal master's face' (l. 75). For Richard, this visitor is entirely unexpected and so, too, is the news he brings of the horse, Barbary, that he had fed with his own hand and has just carried Bolingbroke in triumph.

Again Richard 'needs friends' and again thinks of himself, asking forgiveness of the horse and remembering how he, himself, now bears a 'burden like an ass'. He seems unable to escape from self-wounding, but then enters '*one to Richard with meat* (S.D., Quarto) and orders the groom to 'give place'. The timing is again Shakespeare's – the whole of this last scene for Richard has, so far, been written with total freedom from any narrative necessity and without suggestion from any of the sources – and a very brief exchange follows that specifically reminds an audience of unspoken affections and Richard's concern for another person's love:

> *Richard.*   If thou love me, 'tis time thou wert away.
> *Groom.*   What my tongue dares not, that my heart shall say.
>   (ll. 96–7)

The words are not remarkable, but their effect is: a moment of still-ness, as events are about to draw the action to its end; a mutual silence between two persons who may never have spoken together before, certainly not with such laden words; an exchange of unspoken 'love' or, at least, of care for each other. The leading actor of the company and, probably, one of its youngest and least tried, will have to judge how to play this moment on each occasion the play is performed and to improvise whatever it is that the 'tongue dares not . . . say'. While *Richard the Second* is a tragical History with political issues clearly presented, it is also a personal and sensitive Tragedy which takes as its subject loneliness, loyalty, trust, uncertainty, near madness, need of friends – all matters of the 'heart'.

This is not the end of Richard and what happens next is almost totally unexpected. Faced with 'that sad dog', his keeper (l. 70), Richard experiences a surge of courage and impatience: he strikes out in protest and assassins '*rush in*'. They could overwhelm anyone weakened with imprisonment and sorrow, but not the man whom Richard has just this moment become. He kills one assailant and then is struck down by their leader, Exton. The text leaves no doubt about how Richard dies: the murderer not only realizes that his victim is 'As full of valour as of royal blood' (l. 113), but immediately repents what he has done. But how Richard is able to transform himself in this way, or to be transformed, the actor must discover from the meeting with the Groom that precedes the change and his solution must convince an audience of its truth and necessity. As with *Richard the Third*, the role of the tragic hero ends with positive action the force of which depends on the actor's performance.

Alternative Perspectives

Bolingbroke, the motor-force of the narrative, is presented in a very different way. Much of the action he decides upon is carried out by Northumberland and so, too, is the assertion of his rights. He says comparatively little, the majority of his speeches being of no more than three or four lines; of a total of twenty-four speeches in the entire last Act, nine are of one verse-line or less. He chooses words with care, frequently to conceal his thoughts rather than communicate them. Compared with what is known from Richard's fluent eloquence and careful debates with himself, Bolingbroke remains a cipher. This is not because he lacks evocative words: for example, he calmly takes 'advantage' of his power, knowing that this will:

> . . . lay the summer's dust with showers of blood
> Rain'd from the wounds of slaughtered Englishmen.　　(III.iii.43–4)

But his presence is powerful because he achieves so much with such little apparent effort. When banished from England in Act I, scene iii, he is back again before he seems to have had time to go into exile, and he comes with an army. Rumour serves him well, so that Richard's soldiers desert because they have been told their king is dead. His presence on the throne of England in the last scene of the play is achieved without struggle and no more than minimal ceremony; it seems inevitable. Yet he can still surprise his supporters and the theatre audience when, without debate, he pardons the Bishop of Carlisle who had taken part in rebellion against his seizure of power (V.vi.28–9).

Starting with his challenge to Mowbray with its implied challenge to the king, an audience has been led to listen carefully to Bolingbroke and to search his face for signs of what he is thinking under a mask-like face of authority and decisiveness. In contrast to Richard, he gains in power by his few words and an audience learns how to judge them. When his rival's corpse is brought before him in a coffin in the last scene, his expression of love for the murdered rival, his confession of 'woe' in his own soul, his dismissal of Exton without reward, and his intention to 'voyage to the Holy Land' as a crusader, may all be heard with the assumption that each speech is made for his own best advantage. Noticeably, none of his nobles responds verbally to Henry's final speech, although they may do so silently and formally, with tokens of allegiance or devotion to the God whom he invokes. In itself, the concluding political statement is bare and efficient in carrying an audience's expectation forward to subsequent history and yet, again, much is left to the actor: it is for him to decide how easily this political posture is assumed, how thorough the disguise of personal feelings.

As a further means of adjusting the balance of interests in the last

Act, Shakespeare developed the role of the Duchess of York, wife of the Duke and mother to Aumerle. There is no hint in the *Chronicles* that she took any part in the discovery or pardon of her son's treason against Bolingbroke, yet she dominates the presentation of this incident, York becoming a figure of comedy as he calls repeatedly for his boots in order to ride to London, and Aumerle content to be a submissive son who accepts mercy without speaking a word. Arriving at the court of Henry IV, the Duchess speaks from and for the 'heart', noisily demanding entry until she gains audience and then fearfully doubting what she hears when her request is granted. When Henry repeats his pardon for Aumerle, 'With all my heart', she has only one comment: 'A god on earth thou art' (l. 134) – which is, incidentally, an echo of Tamora's plea for her son's life in *Titus Andronicus*:

> Wilt thou draw near the nature of the gods?
> Draw near them then in being merciful.   (I.i.120–1)

King Henry says nothing in reply but he must know that he is no god; perhaps there is a brief silence here, before he pronounces that his other enemies 'shall not live within this world, I swear' (l. 140). The Duchess seems not to hear this but speaks to her son as she leaves with him: 'Come, my old son, I pray God make thee new' (l. 144) and so touches on the long-held Christian beliefs about sin and redemption with what may be genuine feeling or, possibly in this situation, consummate diplomacy and flattery.

   That the Duchess and the Groom have such important roles towards the end of this tragedy indicates Shakespeare's concern with balancing an audience's reactions, as he had used Aaron to challenge its judgement of Goths and Romans alike, or the wooing of Queen Elizabeth for the hand of her daughter to alert it to Richard's loss of effectiveness and clear judgement. All four of these late interventions were Shakespeare's invention and not suggested by any of his sources, and all help to identify some of the themes he wished to emphasize at the close of these tragedies. In *Titus* and *Richard II* these include love for child, master, or servant, and the courage that love can give, forgetting the entire world to satisfy its own impulses and facing out any opposition. In *Richard III*, reasons for adding the encounter with Queen Elizabeth are less obvious and its main purpose may have been to unsettle an audience's view of the play's hero, and this may also have been a factor in adding Richard's mock courtesy to the Groom, changing to concern for his safety, and Aaron's protection of his baby, contrasting with Titus's slaying of Lavinia. Contrasts are doubly effective in the Duchess of York's outright fight for the life of Aumerle, caring not at all what anyone might think of her, when viewed over against Bolingbroke's craft and Richard's almost continuous self-regard and attempted dignity. Each of these persons comes unexpectedly from unexpected places: a war camp, a defeated and bereaved family, a stable, and a home distant from court and battlefields. By these interventions, the field of vision is made wider at the end of these tragedies than at their beginnings as if neither death nor a hero was able to contain all that Shakespeare wished his tragedy to express.

5

Romeo and Juliet:
an Innovative Tragedy

While writing the earliest tragedies and a series of history plays about the long and jarring wars of the two noble houses of York and Lancaster, Shakespeare was imaginatively involved with two very different projects, each demanding special knowledge and techniques and as full of innovation as his other work. One resulted in the comedies that reached the public stages throughout the 1590s. Francis Meres' *Palladis Tamia, or Wit's Treasury* of 1598 noted that

> As Plautus and Seneca are accounted the best [writers] for Comedy and Tragedy among the Latins, so Shakespeare among the English is most excellent in both kinds for the stage; for Comedy, witness his *Gentlemen of Verona*, his *Errors*, his *Love's Labours Lost*, his *Love's Labours Won*, his *Midsummer's Night Dream*, and his *Merchant of Venice*. . . .

In contrast with the tragedies, the earliest comedies seem written as if in sport. For all their profusion of ingenious wit and complicated wordplay, mythological references and elaborate rhetorical speeches, they offer a world of fantasy that is almost innocent and childlike. Whatever happens in these plays does so lightly, with a freedom of invention which seems to spring effortlessly as if in release from the actualities of life and mortality. Anger, pain, and misunderstandings seldom last for long and almost all journeys end in lovers' meetings. The clashes between generations – or between

76

town and country, masters and servants, royalty and subjects, learning and ignorance, riches and poverty – provide occasions for both argument and laughter as the narratives of romantic and adventurous courtship twist and turn towards their neat conclusions. Increasingly, Shakespeare introduced elements that are destructive or irreconcilable and some individuals who stand apart from others to remind an audience that 'Youth's a stuff will not endure' or that all the men and women are 'merely players' (*Twelfth Night,* II.iii.51; *As You Like It,* II.vii.140), but nothing of this disturbs for long the surface of the earliest comedies written at the same time as the violent and harshly unsentimental tragedies. Only when we look closer can we see that, within the apparently fickle wordplay, a deeper current of thought is at work and, on second viewing, discern beneath the surface a carefully considered and developing view of love, involving service, idealism, unappeasable desire, and the unstable meeting of intelligence with sensual and sexual necessities. Death, too, is a lurking presence, in various and, often, insidious forms, familiar, unexpected, and irresistible, infecting even carefree thoughts and feelings. After more searching scrutiny, Shakespeare's comedies are seen to come from the same creative mind as the early tragedies and it was, perhaps, inevitable that these two lines of work should come together, sooner rather than later, as they did in *Romeo and Juliet,* first published in 1597 and probably first performed some two years earlier.

During the same early and productive years, Shakespeare was also engaged with non-dramatic poetry, writing numerous sonnets that circulated in manuscript 'among his private friends' (the phrase is from Francis Meres), a few of which were published in *The Passionate Pilgrim,* an anthology of poems by several hands of 1599. A collected edition appeared later, in 1609, but vocabulary tests and a few topical references indicate that many of these sonnets were written in 1593–5, the years of the early tragedies, others in 1598–9, and comparatively few in the early years of the seventeenth century. By 1598, on the strength of the poems that had come to his notice, Meres called Shakespeare one of the 'most passionate amongst us to bewail and bemoan the perplexities of Love', and his achievement in this manner obviously informed the writing of *Romeo and Juliet.* The lines:

> When, in disgrace with Fortune and men's eyes,
> I all alone beweep my outcast state,
> And trouble deaf heaven with my bootless cries,
> And look upon myself and curse my fate . . .   (Sonnet XXIX)

were not written about Romeo banished from his Juliet, but the 'passionate' impression they give, their images and ideas concerning 'disgrace', 'outcast state', 'sullen earth', and 'heaven's gate' are almost entirely relevant. In both the sonnets and this early tragedy, eyes are 'famished for a look', a 'heart in love with sighs himself doth smother', and a lover is 'happy to have thy love, happy to die' (Sonnets XLVII and XCII): a wide range of very personal and inward experiences are common to both.

Besides the sonnets and comedies, *Venus and Adonis* and *The Rape of Lucrece* (1593–4) helped to prepare Shakespeare for *Romeo and Juliet*. Written, it seems, while the theatres were closed on account of outbreaks of the plague, the stories told in these poems led Shakespeare to imagine an obsession with sexuality and resistance to its compulsions. Decorated and often decorous verses conduct a reader carefully into these narratives so that certain moments are held still, out of the pressure of action, illuminated by sensitive description (especially in the earlier poem) or explored almost methodically as rhetorical tropes are worked out to their last detail. Both poems give the impression that their author was in complete control of his subject and chosen mode of presentation as he extended his treatment of sexual experience beyond the pleasures and limitations of comedy.

All these imaginative streams flowed into the writing of *Romeo and Juliet* and seem to have encouraged a closer and more sustained commitment to its leading characters than in earlier tragedies. Here passionate complexity, expressed in sensuous and restless language, is linked in harness with direct and even simple engagement in the moment-by-moment life of the story. Images drawn from everyday experience carry speaker and listener into worlds of experience seldom realizable with words and still less often capable of being shared. The changing pulse of the dialogue suggests a wide range of feeling, from destructive compulsion to silent tenderness. In the sonnets, the poet claims frequently that his verses will give a death-less existence to his beloved and Shakespeare might have written the same of the heroine and hero of this first tragedy of love. In his own day, its success was immediate even though it was highly unusual for two young and inexperienced people to be the central figures of a tragedy, a form of drama thought to require noble persons of great consequence for its heroes. In its own day, *Romeo and Juliet* defied many generally accepted critical pronouncements and the flush of adventure can still be sensed in the energy and freshness of much of the writing; even today, it is still a tragedy that stands very much on its own.

Lifelike and Complex Dialogue

In *Romeo and Juliet,* speech is sometimes both highly contrived and extraordinarily ordinary – ordinary in the sense that it moves and breathes as if in life itself, as an audience will know it. Much of its dialogue can be spoken as an instinctive involvement with what is happening at the moment. As we read the text, these people come alive in our minds and, when presented on stage, they can convince us completely, carrying us away from our own thoughts so that we seem to share in theirs.

Not all the tragedy is written in this way, but that could hardly be: other tasks had to be done and an audience can respond to only so much immediacy. The play starts with a very formal sonnet as the Chorus addresses the audience, its tone and tempo respectful and its utterance obviously composed. Yet, even here, rhythms suggest that deeper feelings are involved and will be aroused later. The solemn forward flow of 'The fearful passage of their death-marked love . . . ' is off-set by the three close-linked stresses of 'death-marked love' that disturb the iambic measure and, two lines later, by the compact parenthesis within 'Which, but their children's end, naught could remove.' A lighter return to the present moment and practicalities – 'Is now the two hours' traffic of our stage' – prepares for a con-cluding couplet that politely requests an audience's attention. The fourteen rhymed iambic lines make a strong impression before the play itself begins, but that force is controlled delicately and, it seems, without effort.

Shakespeare also used a sonnet to bring Romeo and Juliet together for the first time, its lines and images shared between them, so that each speaker modifies the other's speech as if sharing a playful and sensitive consciousness. Formal verse-patterns establish a grave thoughtfulness while the words require the touching of hands and exchange of kisses. These specific actions ensure that the focus of an audience's attention is on the two bodies as much as – perhaps more than – what is said. Before the second kiss, the lovers' words have overflowed the measure of the sonnet, but their further speech has its own rhymes to show a new confidence in accepting both 'trespass' and necessity:

> *Romeo.*   If I profane with my unworthiest hand
>   This holy shrine, the gentle fine is this:
>   My lips, two blushing pilgrims, ready stand
>   To smooth that rough touch with a tender kiss.
> *Juliet.*   Good pilgrim, you do wrong your hand too much,
>   Which mannerly devotion shows in this;
>   For saints have hands that pilgrims' hands do touch,
>   And palm to palm is holy palmers' kiss.
> *Romeo.*   Have not saints lips, and holy palmers too?
> *Juliet.*   Ay, pilgrim, lips that they must use in prayer.
> *Romeo.*   O, then, dear saint, let lips do what hands do!
>   They pray; grant thou, lest faith turn to despair.
> *Juliet.*   Saints do not move, though grant for prayers' sake.
> *Romeo.*   Then move not while my prayer's effect I take.
>   [*He kisses her.*]
>   Thus from my lips, by thine my sin is purged.
> *Juliet.*   Then have my lips the sin that they have took.
> *Romeo.*   Sin from my lips? O trespass sweetly urged!
>   Give me my sin again.
> *Juliet.*   You kiss by th' book.   [*They kiss.*]

With a skill honed in a long series of sonnets, verse-making has been used to suggest the strength and wonder of shared sexual arousal. Developing imagery implies the solemn and carefully restrained impulses of a first, holy, and life-changing love: *good pilgrim*, *holy palmer*, *prayer*, and *devotion*. Management of the sonnet form captures the fresh sensations and creativity, mixed with pains-taking and irrepressibility, that can be experienced in the act of writing, and uses this to give credibility to the tragedy's two young heroes.

The word 'hero' sits uncomfortably on Romeo and Juliet in the first and longer part of the action when neither has any further intention than those arising from the moment and each other's presence. They do, however, even before their first meeting, show that other thoughts are deep within them, not moving easily with their immediate desires. This is most noticeable in Romeo's:

> my mind misgives
> Some consequence yet hanging in the stars
> Shall bitterly begin his fearful date
> With this night's revels . . .
>
> (I.iv.106–13)

But Juliet's reply to her mother's enquiry about her 'dispositions to be married' – 'It is an honour that I dream not of' (I.iii.66) – may also express, even if spoken lightly, an inner gravity of spirit and fear of 'consequence'.

Once they have met and kissed, their speech is bolder, quickly responsive to each moment and freely supplied with images that draw them far away from their former selves as they interact without impediment. By description, suggestive imagery, and varying syntax, physical presence is frequently implied in the words spoken, as if the flesh-and-blood actuality of the two speakers, their heart-beats, hands and bodies, and their eyes (especially) are all involved as they express wonder, fear, excitement, tenderness, solemnity, and an over-riding happiness that is instinct with both laughter and tears. The dialogue operates as music to which they move as in a dance, both together and apart, swiftly and slowly, forgetting every other need. The comparatively simple beginning can illustrate the new actuality and intimacy:

> *Juliet.* My ears have yet not drunk a hundred words
> Of thy tongue's uttering, yet I know the sound.
> Art thou not Romeo, and a Montague?
> *Romeo.* Neither, fair maid, if either thee dislike.
>
> (1)

Juliet.	How camest thou hither, tell me, and wherefore?
	The orchard walls are high and hard to climb,
	And the place death, considering who thou art,
	If any of my kinsmen find thee here.
Romeo.	With love's light wings did I o'erperch these walls; (2)
	For stony limits cannot hold love out,
	And what love can do, that dares love attempt.
	Therefore thy kinsmen are no stop to me.
Juliet.	If they do see thee, they will murder thee.
Romeo.	Alack, there lies more peril in thine eye (3)
	Than twenty of their swords! Look thou but sweet,
	And I am proof against their enmity.
Juliet.	I would not for the world they saw thee here.
Romeo.	I have night's cloak to hide me from their eyes, (4)
	And but thou love me, let them find me here.
	My life were better ended by their hate
	Than death proroguèd, wanting of thy love.
Juliet.	By whose direction found'st thou out this place?
Romeo.	By love, that first did prompt me to inquire. (5)
	He lent me counsel, and I lent him eyes.
	I am no pilot; yet, wert thou as far
	As that vast shore washed with the farthest sea,
	I should adventure for such mechandise. (II.ii.58–84)

Juliet speaks of hearing Romeo's voice as if this were drinking and had a physical effect, but she keeps some distance by speaking, not of his presence, but only of his 'tongue'. When questions follow, both speakers seek some reassurance and restrict themselves to practicalities. Romeo's first response is both respectful and assertive but his second has a far wider range of feeling with talk of levitation, stone walls or cliffs, risk, physical resistance. His third reply shows him to be gazing at her eyes in fear that he may not be loved, his imagination leading him to think of a brawl, lethally one-sided, and then of life-saving, protective armour. The fourth time he replies, confidence stems from Juliet's concern but is laced through with an assertion that again considers opposition and, at the same time, speaks of 'death'. In his fifth reply, Romeo again speaks of eyes, as if gazing at each other were still, for him, the one certain reality, but then he moves on to the more sustained image of merchants venturing across whole oceans. He speaks of the farthest limit of exploration, an idea that had captured many minds in London since Sir Francis Drake's circumnavigation of the globe in 1580 and treasure brought from across the seas had become a more common sight. The rhythms are longer in this fifth response as if in making the assertion Romeo's tensions were eased and his mind had accepted the possibility of infinite riches from a hitherto far-off and unknown world reached only by risking one's entire life on unknown seas. In these exchanges, speech seems to spring from two independent consciousnesses influenced by interplay between each other; it gives an impression of instinct and improvisation, not of deliberation.

The next sentence Juliet addresses to Romeo is carefully phrased and extended through three lines of verse, but then rhythms change as if speech had become more improvised. Faltering repetition and rapid contradiction reveal a renewed insecurity:

> Thou knowest the mask of night is on my face;
> Else would a maiden blush bepaint my cheek
> For that which thou hast heard me speak tonight.
> Fain would I dwell on form – fain, fain deny
> What I have spoke; but farewell compliment!
> Dost thou love me? I know thou wilt say 'Ay'
> And I will take thy word. Yet, if thou swear'st
> Thou mayst prove false.   (ll. 85–92)

Romeo says nothing while Juliet continues to take the lead in speech, her mind veering away from the present moment to imagine other times and idle talk about false love and the laughter of Jove, the greatest of gods in the strange, mind-haunting world of ancient myth: 'At lovers' perjuries, / They say Jove laughs.' Then, immediately, in yet another tone, she answers Romeo's continuing silence:

>   O gentle Romeo,
> If thou dost love, pronounce it faithfully,
> Or if thou thinkest I am too quickly won,
> I'll frown and be perverse and say thee nay,
> So thou wilt woo; but else not for the world.
> In truth, fair Montague, I am too fond, . . .

The speech is finely balanced and needs to be played delicately, in hesitation, emphasis, and repetition. Perhaps Juliet has instinctively laughed at her own contradictory feelings or at the excitement within her mind and body, and that has made her think of Jove. Perhaps she then continues in new confidence because Romeo has laughed too. Perhaps she remains solemn throughout all the variations in her speech.

Soon Romeo swears his constant love, or rather attempts to swear it and is stopped by Juliet who is afraid their contract is:

> . . . too rash, too unadvised, too sudden;
> Too like the lightning, which doth cease to be
> Ere one can say it lightens.   (ll. 118–20)

A moment later, they do exchange 'faithful' vows and then it is Juliet who finds an image with which she is so satisfied that it sustains speech over three verse-lines. Like Romeo's earlier extended image, it summons up a vision of the ocean, but now that lends its size to Juliet's capacity for giving and expresses no desire for possession:

> *Romeo.*   O, wilt thou leave me so unsatisfied?
> *Juliet.*   What satisfaction canst thou have tonight?
> *Romeo.*   Th'exchange of thy love's faithful vow for mine.
> *Juliet.*   I gave thee mine before thou didst request it;
>   And yet I would it were to give again.
> *Romeo.*   Wouldst thou withdraw it? For what purpose, love?
> *Juliet.*   But to be frank and give it thee again,
>   And yet I wish but for the thing I have.
>   My bounty is as boundless as the sea,
>   My love as deep; the more I give to thee,
>   The more I have for both are infinite.   (ll. 125–35)

Although separated on different levels of the stage, the two lovers will be still and rapt in thoughts of each other and in sensations that seem to have changed their very beings, but what happens next is not of their choosing:

> I hear some noise within. Dear love, adieu!

Anon, good nurse! Sweet Montague, be true.
Stay but a little, I will come again.   (ll. 136–8)

Another voice and, in effect, another world have made themselves
heard and Juliet takes command, quickened by fear that her 'Sweet
Montague' might not be true. In her haste, only simple words and
short phrases carry the play forward but tenderness and desire are
also able to speak even in the fears of such a moment.

Phrasing, rhythm, tension, relaxation, metrical variations, and the
breathing needed for utterance all require the actors' physical
engagement, and this conveys the characters' involvement in the situation as much as the words themselves, and sometimes more. In
performance, the activities in the actors' bodies, that are the necessary means of responding to the technical demands of the dialogue,
become a significant part of the play's effect. These are not fixed
signs, like words, and define no clear intentions, but they are an
instinctive and dynamic response to the play as it evolves moment
by moment. The physical presence of each actor changes before the
eyes of the audience and, with their bodies, their minds and feelings
will also change, half lost, perhaps, in sensation but quickened and
transformed by what is happening. Responding to this dialogue,
they speak physically as well as verbally, communicating to the
senses of an audience, perhaps more than to their minds.

On stage in Shakespeare's day, a young man would have played
the part of Juliet. He could not provide the sexual attractions of a
girl of fourteen (the age specified in the text), but an audience was
free to imagine those in whatever forms were attractive to their individual minds. What the male actor could provide was mental and
physical activity, the succession of changes in mind and body that
make it possible to speak the words. In giving form and pressure to
each moment, this was sufficient instigation for an audience to
follow the play and re-create it in their own minds. The use of a
young male actor meant that the task of completing the illusion of a
young woman in love had to be left to the audience, and this may be
one reason why in this tragedy actors and actresses are so often able
to give an impression of actual sexual arousal and ardent love: actors
speaking this dialogue can quicken an audience's instinctive desire to

complete – and so, momentarily, to re-create and possess – what it sees and hears enacted on the stage. In retrospect, we can see that this achievement was to be crucial in the writing of Shakespeare's later tragedies in which what happens on stage goes far beyond what any one actor has experienced or can adequately imagine.

Fate and Free Will

Freeing himself from the need to recount the 'true' history of monarchs and the state of England, Shakespeare shaped this more domestic tragedy with two other themes in mind and, against his usual practice, announced both in an opening Chorus: the operation of fate and the conflict between private 'strife' and social well-being. Both themes were present in Shakespeare's main source, Arthur Brooke's *The Tragical History of Romeus and Juliet* (1562), a narrative poem translated from a French version of still earlier Italian accounts, but the play's presentation of them is very different.

Fate often plays a part in the action as if by accident. Off-stage a messenger is prevented from delivering a letter because he has happened to stop in a plague-stricken house and this keeps Romeo in ignorance of what the Friar and Juliet have contrived and so provokes his suicide and, consequently, brings the tragedy to its close. Shakespeare has been criticized for using such a crude plot-mechanism, but it is at one with other accidental circumstances that seem to propel Romeo and Juliet forward in the 'fearful passage' of their love. Romeo had gone to Capulet's ball only to give himself more reason for loving Rosaline and so happened to see Juliet. For her part, she believes that some necessity has directed her choice:

> Prodigious birth of love it is to me
> That I must love a loathed enemy.   (I.v.139–40)

Prodigious meant ominous and fateful, as well as astonishing, monstrous, or oversized. A more general impression that events are being driven forward is given by Shakespeare's rearrangement of the narrative so that everything takes place in four or five days, and not over several months as in Brooke. Repeatedly, and without comment, the timing of entries seems fated, notably Tybalt's, Romeo's, and, in the last scene when exact timing is particularly crucial, the Friar's and the watchmen's.

Both Romeo and Juliet acknowledge fate's influence. Before he has even seen her, Romeo confesses:

> my mind misgives
> Some consequence yet hanging in the stars
> Shall bitterly begin his fearful date
> With this night's revels, and expire the term
> Of a despised life clos'd in my breast
> By some vile forfeit of untimely death. (I.i.106–11)

After killing Tybalt, Romeo is silent and then cries out, 'O, I am Fortune's fool' (III.i.138); for the moment, his own will seems paralysed and he has to be urged to leave the place where he is bound to be arrested. Juliet's premonitions of fate do not ring out so strongly, but she is repeatedly preoccupied by thoughts of death: in the midst of her 'joy', she senses that lightning will strike (see II.ii.116–20) and, while she waits for Romeo on their wedding night, she imagines him lying like 'snow upon a raven's back' and then metamorphosed into stars (III.ii.17–25).

This emphasis on fate is new in Shakespeare's tragedies and may have been suggested by the narrative presenter in Brooke's poem. From the start his Romeus is seen as a pawn:

> How happy had he been had he not been forsworn
> But twice as happy had he been had he been never born,
> For ere the moon could thrice her wasted horns renew,
> False Fortune cast for him poor wretch, a mischief new to brew.

Events follow each other inevitably:

> Whom glorious Fortune erst had heavéd to the skies
> By envious Fortune overthrown on earth now grovelling lies.

Brooke's Friar sums up the outcome as 'the wreck of frantic Fortune's rage' (l. 2840).

Shakespeare retained something of Brooke's sense that no one
could stop what was fated to happen, but he did not leave the matter
there. After Romeo's death, the Friar concludes that 'A greater power
than we can contradict / Hath thwarted our intents' (ll. 152–3), but
his view does not go unchallenged, not least because it is his conscious decision to leave Juliet alone in the tomb where she follows
Romeo in suicide. After Romeo and Juliet have spent their night
together, she sees death as imminent:

> Juliet.   [*looking down from her window*]
>   O God, I have an ill-divining soul!
>   Methinks I see thee, now thou art so low,
>   As one dead in the bottom of a tomb.
>   Either my eyesight fails, or thou look'st pale.
> Romeo.   And trust me, love, in my eye so do you.
>   Dry sorrow drinks our blood. Adieu, adieu.   (III.v.54–9)

Significantly, both lovers have a rational explanation for this premo-
nition of death and nowhere in the play does the operation of fate
release them, or anyone else, from making choices for which they
may be held responsible.

The new immediacy of the lovers' speeches is of crucial importance
in the presentation of fate because the spontaneous freedom, with
which their minds seem to function underneath the words spoken, is
the polar opposite of an inevitable and directed response to events. An
audience senses that these persons think and do as they wish, whatever happens to them. In their last moments they act decisively and in
unshakeable independence: Romeo insists on being alone in the tomb
where Juliet lies, drugged as if in death, and although he honours
Paris as 'One writ with me in sour misfortune's book' (l. 82), he has
already resolved to take his own life. Juliet disregards the Friar's advice
which until now has guided her: 'Go, get thee hence, for I will not
away' (l. 160). Fate or accident decrees that her suicide must be swift,
but it is, essentially, the result of a long process of self-determination.

When all is known at the end of the play, the Prince reconciles
free will and fate in a traditional way that accepts the outcome of
events as the response of divine justice to human actions:

Where be these enemies? Capulet, Montague,
See what a scourge is laid upon your hate,
That heaven finds means to kill your joys with love;
And I, for winking at your discords too,
Have lost a brace of kinsmen. All are punish'd.   (ll. 290–4)

This is not the only change from Shakespeare's source. To the very end, human decisions are seen to influence what happens. In the play, but not in the poem, the two families announce their reconciliation and clearly articulate their mutual remorse; Brooke's explanation of their reconciliation in a distant future is, simply, 'so mighty Jove it would'. After the two fathers have taken each other's hands and promised to erect golden statues to each other's children, the Prince takes up his duties as a mortal judge, calling on everyone to understand and to accept responsibility:

Go hence to have more talk of these sad things.
Some shall be pardon'd, and some punished.   (ll. 304–7)

The Social Context

While the Prologue speaks of the lovers as 'star-crossed', it also implicates 'fair Verona' in their fate, declaring that the wrongs of 'civil strife' between Capulets and Montagues preceded the beginning of the play and influenced Romeo and Juliet from their births; it warns that only 'their children's end' could change the families' deadlocked antagonism.

To widen the context of the love-story and so raise these issues, Shakespeare used devices that had been well tried in the comedies. He developed other characters – Benvolio, Tybalt, Paris, and Mercutio – well beyond their status in Brooke's poem so that they both spur Romeo to reveal more of himself and serve as reflectors in which the consequences of his thoughts and actions can be shown to the audience. Together they function in much the same way as Thurio, Launce, and Sir Eglamour in *The Two Gentlemen of Verona* or Costard, Jacquetta, Armado, and Moth in *Love's Labours Lost*.

Benvolio shows Romeo's capacity for friendship. Tybalt's passionate sense of family honour contrasts with Romeo's willingness to 'consort' with both Rosaline and Juliet. Paris, courteous and amenable, shows how powerful families expected to arrange their children's affairs. Together these three provide a context in which Romeo's single-minded love is more clearly viewed.

Mercutio, the fourth companion figure in *Romeo and Juliet*, is developed in an exceptional way. Like Tybalt, he dies because of the family feud but he fights out of personal choice, being kin to the Prince and neither a Capulet nor Montague. More significantly, he shares Romeo's immediacy and freedom of speech, in the more variable pace of prose as well as in verse, which means he can at times take command of everyone else on stage. He articulates an independent view of Romeo while Romeo responds to his company by becoming both 'sociable' and 'solely singular', his wit running a 'wild goose chase' (II.iv.72–4, 89, 65–6). Actors take great pleasure in creating their own interpretations of Mercutio. The role is so full of detail that they can surprise an audience by emphasizing what is reckless in the character, or what is disappointed, doomed, idealistic, immature, cynical, or frightened. He can be a prey to fantasies and sexually frustrated, or someone in love with Romeo or with himself. Every interpretation must, in some way, make credible Mercutio's combative energy of mind and persistent use of lewd sexual allusions. When explaining Mercutio's 'saucy' behaviour to the Nurse, Romeo provides a few clues to his personality which only deepen the mystery:

> One, . . . that God hath made, himself to mar. . . .
> A gentleman, . . . that loves to hear himself talk, and will speak more in a minute than he will stand to in a month.   (II.iv.114–15, 144–6)

This is no satisfactory explanation of Mercutio's buoyant comedic sense, his ability to turn any occasion into a carnival of laughter and bravado. Shakespeare has, through him, set Romeo over against an intellectually brilliant, physically alert, and highly sexed contemporary, with a generous capacity for friendship and, perhaps, an instinctive love of danger. Because Mercutio is in the tragedy, an audience cannot miss the 'mannerly devotion' (I.v.97) of Romeo's love or his attempts to make peace with Tybalt after he has been insulted by him.

Juliet does not have the support of companions as Romeo does. Except in soliloquies or scenes when the two are alone together, she becomes known to an audience through confrontations with her nurse, her mother and father, and Paris, her parents' choice of husband. However, the Nurse, like Mercutio, is presented in freely associative speech and intimate exchanges with Juliet. Her prose also has a kinship with Shakespeare's earlier writing for clowns such as Costard, Launce, or Bottom, and her role responds similarly to strongly independent and wittily timed performance. Hers is another role that has proved exceptionally attractive to actors: she takes time to speak self-indulgently from a long memory and quick affection; her frequent sexual innuendoes seem intuitive rather than calculated. She shares memories of a 'pretty fool' that is 'techy and fall[s] out with the dug' and of the time when 'She could have run and waddled all about' (I.iii.30–2, 37) and encourages an audience to imagine the 'prettiest babe that ere I nurs'd' and so appreciate the praise and affection that Juliet has always received, although not, it seems, from her mother.

As in the comedies, the relevance of these contrasts must speak for itself, but at a few crucial moments a clash of purpose has an effect that cannot be missed. When Mercutio associates Queen Mab with maids losing their virginity, Romeo interrupts him with:

> Peace, peace, Mercutio, peace.
> Thou talk'st of nothing.   (I.v.95–6)

In a flash, Mercutio accepts the charge, completing the half-line with 'True, I talk of dreams' and continuing to speak of 'an idle brain' and 'vain fantasy'. As if an entertainment had been completed, Benvolio urges them all to move off to the feast but Romeo, who had become silent, now holds them back to voice a very private misgiving of 'Some consequence yet hanging in the stars' which threatens 'untimely death'. Mercutio has shown Romeo to be alone in holding back and fearing such misfortune.

After Romeo's intervention has caused him to be fatally wounded by Tybalt, Mercutio's 'A plague o' both your houses' reaches beyond the accident of his death to mark the underlying antagonisms which are its less immediate causes. The next moment, his question, 'Why the devil came you between us?' marks personal responsibility just as clearly and provokes Romeo's helpless and ineffectual 'I thought all for the best'. Mercutio continues to insist on the wider view as he turns to Benvolio, leaving Romeo speechless:

> Help me into some house, Benvolio,
> Or I shall faint. A plague o' both your houses,
> They have made worms' meat of me.
> I have it, and soundly too. Your houses!
> *Exit Mercutio with Benvolio.*   (III.i.92–110)

When Mercutio's death off-stage has been announced and Tybalt returns, fighting starts again and Romeo kills his opponent rapidly but then, again, falls silent. Benvolio urges him to leave at once, saying that the Prince will have him killed for what he has done, but he has to repeat this message three times before Romeo responds with 'O, I am Fortune's fool' (l. 138). He still does not move, until Benvolio's further effort: 'Why dost thou stay?' In this scene, full of action and tension, first Mercutio and then Benvolio are the means whereby Shakespeare draws an audience to follow Romeo closely and fill out his speechlessness with its own imaginations.

By consciously taunting Juliet as she longs to be with Romeo and, later, unconsciously tormenting her with a muddled account of Tybalt's death and Romeo's banishment, the Nurse encourages Juliet to express her feelings more fully and strongly than she would to a more rational messenger. Later this intimate companion makes still greater impact when Juliet refuses to confide in her. The Nurse has argued that it would be better to marry Paris than stay faithful to her banished husband and have 'no use of him' (III.iv.212–25) and Juliet has listened in silence except for a brief hint of contrary feelings before pretending to acquiesce. Only when the Nurse has left does a passionate refusal break out with 'Ancient damnation' (l. 235). These two words have the greater strength by contrast with Juliet's earlier intimacy with the Nurse; they can suggest to an audience that her words that soon conclude the third Act – 'If all else fail, myself have power to die' – are likely to be no less than truth.

For the young male actors who were the first to play Juliet, the Nurse provided a contrast against which the complex and deep emotions of this scene could be expressed step by step and given credibility by a comparatively simple show of independence and strength of mind. Moreover, by encouraging an audience to pay attention to Juliet's silent presence while the Nurse has to wait for a response – an incomplete verse-line, 218, marks at least one pause – and when Juliet waits for the Nurse to leave, Shakespeare has ensured that an audience's imaginations will work to comprehend and fill out those silences. The scene may well find its fullest dramatic life, not on stage, but in the minds of spectators.

The Play's Structure

While its two lovers are an undisputed triumph, the rest of this tragedy is sometimes dismissed as crudely written, ineptly plotted, and far too long. Brutal sexual innuendo, clumsy literary artifice, rhymed moralizing, unnecessary amplification and repetition can all be held against Shakespeare's management of the drama. Directors, staging the play in present-day theatres, are apt to cut large sections of the text as well as making many smaller excisions. Yet in the face of these adverse judgements, the play has a long record of success in performance, regardless of changes in taste and methods of production. This implies that its basic structure is sound and outweighs any defects, both real and imagined.

The text has survived in two versions. By far the better is the second Quarto of 1599 (Q2), which was printed from an authorial manuscript. The Quarto of 1597 (Q1) is a shorter text, at some 2215 lines to Q2's 2986, and seems to represent a purposefully cut version, with longer speeches reduced in length, some phrasing simplified (and some muddled in consequence), some dialogue replaced with descriptive stage directions, and a number of smaller roles removed. What is notable about Q1 is that, in spite of some rewriting (or reliance on an earlier Shakespearean draft) and a smaller role for Juliet – its length and complexity in Q2 made greater demands on a young male actor than was usual – the structure of the play remains very much the same. The alternation of intimate love scenes with those involving the Capulet family, the Friar, and Romeo's companions, seems to have been accepted as necessary and effective at whatever length the text was played. The presentation of the story in this sequence of scenes – the 'argument' or 'plot' of the play, as Elizabethans would call it – was a great source of this tragedy's appeal, even in a greatly shortened version.

Its dramatic structure makes large demands on any company staging the play. In the first minutes a civic mutiny must build up rapidly with improvised fighting involving an unusual assortment of weapons. The arrival of the Prince with his peace-keeping force requires still more actors and changes the scene radically as they bring order and comparative silence for the pronouncement of judgement. On his order, large-scale exits follow, leaving the stage with signs of the recent 'fray' still visible (see I.i.115). Much the same happens all over again in Act III, scene i, except that its fighting is restricted to three young principals. In between these two violent crowd scenes is placed another which requires the entire company to change into other clothes that are suitable for dancing and lavish feasting. Again the spectacle has to be of two kinds, one more formal than the other: one with the excitement of 'lusty' masquers (I.iv.113), with their 'beetle-browed' vizors and torch bearers; the other more decorous for the entertainment provided by the Capulets. When the two parties eventually join in courtly dance, its concord is threatened by Tybalt's intervention and then reaffirmed and intensified by the formal sonnet shared between Romeo and Juliet.

At the end of the tragedy, for a fourth time, a crowd is required with two contrasting elements again opposing unruly improvisation and authoritative control. This time the build-up is very much slower over a series of short scenes and episodes that grow ever more fearfully alarmed before concluding with a stage crowded by awed and silent spectators. The process starts with busy entries and music that herald a formal wedding for Paris and Juliet. Before the expected order is fully achieved, it is fractured and replaced with violent expressions of grief and outrage. The scene then shifts to Mantua where Romeo has gone after being banished from Verona: here a frightened Balthasar arrives with news of Juliet's death and Romeo, 'pale and wild' (V.i.28–9), resolves to return and kill himself at his love's side. In another short scene, the Friar learns that his message to Romeo telling him to rescue the drugged Juliet from the grave had never reached him: it finishes with rushed preparations for breaking into the grave. The scene now shifts to the Capulet's monument and action is briefly both formal and tense as Paris sets a watch on the grave and mourns his intended bride. This carefully controlled business is disturbed very quickly, as Romeo and Balthasar arrive with '*a torch, a mattock and a crow[bar] of iron*'. Despatching his attendant to keep a look-out, Romeo forces open the tomb and is challenged by Paris; they fight; the Page hurries to summon the watch; and Paris is killed. This violence over, nothing further disturbs Romeo until, in his own time, he poisons himself and dies kissing his bride. Immediately after this, Friar Laurence enters, frightened and hurried; he finds, successively, the opened tomb, blood, and the dead bodies. Knowing that the watch is coming, and failing to get Juliet to leave, he hurries off. Juliet has only a short time alone, but kisses Romeo and then very swiftly kills herself with his dagger. After this, two different sets of watchmen enter and the alarm spreads; at first, even the Prince's entry does not stop the startling cries and shrieks of fear (V.iii.183, 189–93). After Montague's entry, the Prince takes complete charge and starts an investigation. Unlike the three earlier occasions when the stage has been crowded, everyone naturally becomes very still and quiet while the Friar tells the whole story as he knows it. For forty lines of verse, too involved in syntax to be spoken quickly, no one from either family interrupts, but as the Friar speaks of one person after another, he may well provoke audible cries and visible signs of grief and guilt: the text gives no guidance about this so the actors must improvise their characters' reactions as if drawn forth instinctively.

All four crowd scenes must be managed with both freedom and control as they alternately express unruly and dangerous reactions and peaceful acceptance of authoritative suppression. The same con-

trast is found elsewhere in the play, especially in reactions to the
deaths of Mercutio and Tybalt where the text is usually heavily cut
for performance. When the Nurse brings news of Tybalt's death and
Romeo's banishment, the verse, wordplay, and rhetorical forms are
stretched and broken repeatedly, as misunderstandings jostle with
forceful repetitions, exclamations, and antitheses. Only rarely does
strained and unruly speech yield here to simple statement or instruction. The next scene, in Friar Laurence's cell, sees Romeo 'on the
ground with his own tears made drunk' (III.iii.83–9) and on the
point of committing suicide. The Friar's arguments and hopes for a
peaceful solution at last calm the violent behaviour and lead the narrative forward. Capulet's plans for Juliet's marriage to Paris bring
further violence of language and action, and this time relief comes
only when Juliet, left alone, steadfastly resolves, 'if all else fail', to
commit suicide. In following scenes, Juliet accepts the Friar's plan to
take a potion which will render her as if dead and then, on her own
and on her marriage bed, she faces, in her vivid imagination, the
horrors of death itself before taking the drink as if in tribute to her
love: she has controlled the most unruly fears imaginable. The alternation of violence and calm formality in these scenes is seldom
managed with confidence in twentieth-century productions of the
play, and their text is often heavily cut. Nor will a reader find them
any more acceptable without a sense of the skill and energy needed
to bring the highly formal speeches alive in performance.

The new immediacy of thought and feeling returns to the text as
the tragedy moves to its deeply affecting climax. Briefly, Romeo
offers his own death as a 'favour' to Tybalt and asks for his forgiveness and then turns towards his wife and marvels at her beauty: 'Ah,
dear Juliet, / Why art thou yet so fair? . . .' A jealously possessive and
strangely fantastic question follows:

> Shall I believe
> That unsubstantial Death is amorous,
> And that the lean abhorred monster keeps
> Thee here in dark to be his paramour?

Before he kills himself, he must embrace Juliet and

> Seal with a righteous kiss
> A dateless bargain to engrossing Death.

This kiss, in which formality and passion mix, is bound to be different each time the actor takes hold of Juliet's inert body and that will ensure that his acting is, in part, improvised and draws instinctively on his deepest sense of what is happening. His mind reverts to the sea that had come, as if unsummoned, when he had first declared his love (see above, pp. 82–3); only this time the image draws together violent desperation and decisive control:

> Come, bitter conduct, come unsavoury guide,
> Thou desperate pilot now at once run on
> The dashing rocks thy seasick weary bark.

After this, Romeo is in command and can ceremoniously drink to his love and die with another kiss.

What an audience experiences here is both the brutal fact of Romeo's suicide and the utmost sensitivity of his feelings. It will know, as he does not, that he dies unnecessarily because Juliet is alive and not dead, and yet neither accident nor waste is likely to make the strongest impression: that stems rather from his physical and emotional courage when faced with appalling loss, and his calm resolve. In his eyes and, almost certainly, in an audience's, death is a shaking off 'the yoke of inauspicious stars' as he sets up his 'everlasting rest' (V.iii.110–12).

Juliet's suicide is no less remarkable, although hurried as she hears the watchmen's approach. Her dismissal of Friar Laurence, 'Go, get thee hence, for I will not away', marks decisively her inner assurance. In kissing Romeo's poisoned lips, she hopes to 'die with a restorative' and she does indeed respond to the warmth of their touch. She then becomes conscious of noise off-stage and, with two compact and charged lines, kills herself:

> Yea, noise? Then I'll be brief. O happy dagger.
> This is thy sheath. There rust, and let me die.

Although an audience hardly has time to follow each rapid step, the effect of all she has said and done is absolutely clear: however uncertainly the actor completes the hurried words and actions, Juliet so outpaces an audience's comprehension that her self-control is likely to be more amazing than her suffering. As in Romeo's death, a sense of achievement is present and here, possibly, a sense of a consummating sexual arousal, as strong or stronger than that experienced earlier in the play.

In *Romeo and Juliet*, Shakespeare brought an intense dramatic focus to bear on the last moments of its hero and heroine, and required of his actors the imaginative strength to sum up their involvement in the entire play, controlling wildest thoughts and feelings in consistent and compelling performance. Outwardly the result can be very simple and probably should be so that an audience's imagination will be aroused by what seems to be happening deep within the two young lovers. Wonder is likely to be its dominant response but it may also feel shocked, bruised, depleted, indignant, outraged, trapped, or bemused, implicated in some immediate and very personal way. The play proceeds to show the effect of the deaths on almost all the remaining characters and to invite an audience to search for degrees of responsibility and possible consequences of what has happened.

6

From *King John* to
Julius Caesar: Histories and
Heroes

As Shakespeare could not have written *Romeo and Juliet* without the experience of the sonnets and early comedies, so *The Tragedy of Julius Caesar* depends on the later history plays. The first Folio places it among the tragedies but the prefatory catalogue at the head of the book calls it *The Life and Death of Julius Caesar*, aligning it with *The Life and Death of King John* and other tragical histories. No definition of what a tragedy should be, as set out by the scholars of the time, will fit the structure and narrative of this play. Revenge and passion are not dominant motives. No single turning of Fortune's wheel accounts for the plot: its titular hero starts at the height of his power and is assassinated before the play is half done; the rise of Brutus or Cassius never appears secure and those of Antony and Octavius Caesar are achieved with scarcely any suggestion that a fall will follow.

Neither the sensationalism of *Titus Andronicus* nor the intensely experienced feelings of *Romeo and Juliet* are present here. Caesar's assassination is a bloody spectacle but the audience has been well prepared to witness it and interest is drawn to the perpetrators and their motives as much as to the man who suffers: the victim may sometimes be hidden to view as the conspirators gather around him. The deaths of Cassius and Brutus are neither spectacles in a public

place nor frightening acts in private: they are suicides, coolly executed on the field of battle as the means of avoiding greater shames.
Shortly after Cassius and before Brutus, Titinius takes his own life in
a very similar way, as if Shakespeare wished to make the deaths of
the play's leading persons less impressive than they would be in isolation. Nothing is here of the exceptional passion, moral outrage, or
sadistic cunning found in his earlier tragedies. The most gripping
horror is the ice-like opportunism with which victims are 'pricked
out' for death to counter the *coup d'état* that had eliminated Caesar
(IV.i.1–17). The most sensational episode is provided by a crowd of
anonymous Romans who tear Cinna the Poet in pieces on account
of his name and supposedly bad verses (III.i); and here, again, the
victim may be lost to sight behind the mob of his killers.

Death in the History Plays

The true predecessors of *Julius Caesar* are Shakespeare's late history
plays, none of them a tragedy by any recognized criteria. The death of
the king in *Henry the Fourth, Part II* is a central and crucial event, but
an audience's interest is held for much of the time by Falstaff, Hal,
and Hotspur, together with their various followers and supporters,
persons who initiate action more effectively than the king. None the
less, as he feels the approach of death, Henry surveys both life in
general and his own part in the history that has been shown on stage:

> O God! that one might read the book of fate,
> And see the revolution of the times
> Make mountains level, and the continent,
> Weary of solid firmness, melt itself
> Into the sea; and other times to see
> The beachy girdle of the ocean
> Too wide for Neptune's ships; how chances mock,
> And changes fill the cup of alteration
> With divers liquors! O, if this were seen,
> The happiest youth, viewing his progress through,
> What perils past, what crosses to ensue,
> Would shut the book and sit him down and die.   (III.i.45–57)

The speaker is neither passionate nor intent on some crucial action, nor is his suffering intensely realized. He observes 'rank diseases' and 'danger' near the heart of the state and recognizes his own responsibility for them but he acts now only out of 'necessity' (ll. 93–4) and does not have a tragic hero's mission.

Nevertheless, Henry's meditation is echoed in the questions and self-doubt of Hamlet's soliloquies, 'looking before and after' (IV.iv.36), Macbeth's sense that 'all our yesterdays have lighted fools / The way to dusty death' (V.v.22–3), and Lear's desire to view the world as if he were one of 'God's spies', interested in both who's in and who's out (V.iii.15–17), all arising out of the protagonist's accumulated experiences. His next tragedy, *Julius Caesar*, is like *Henry the Fourth, Part II* in still more ways than this: its titular hero is similarly withdrawn from the stage for much of the play while its audience is engaged by numerous other characters. His death is not the climax of the play, being followed by events that encourage a sceptical view of its consequences and the causes and motivation for all the play's varied action.

The hero of the earlier *King John* is more active than Henry the Fourth and, right up to his death at the end of the play, the fate of England lies ultimately in his hands. Numerous other persons, however, are also at work, among them his half-brother, the bastard Faulconbridge, Philip King of France, Pandolf a papal legate, all initiating independent action. For all John's efforts, he remains ineffectual: he is misinformed; his mother's death weakens him; Peter, the prophet of Pomfret, alarms the people with warnings that he will be forced to give up the crown. He is seriously impaired by his own lack of confidence and inconstancy. 'Do not seek', he tells the Bastard, 'to stuff / My head with more ill news, for it is full', and then apologizes:

> Bear with me, cousin, for I was amaz'd
> Under the tide; but now I breathe again
> Aloft the flood, and can give audience
> To any tongue, speak it of what it will.   (IV.ii.133–40)

John is dependent on others, needing their loyalty and learning the consequences of trusting it:

> It is the curse of kings to be attended
> By slaves that take their humours for a warrant . . .   (IV.ii.208–9)

As the play moves to its close with the country's enemies landed on its shores, he bends this way and that until forced to seek some relief from madness and the pain of poison. He sees himself now as

> . . . a scribbled form drawn with a pen
> Upon a parchment, and against this fire
> Do I shrink up.   (V.vii.32–4)

Rather than extolling the king's virtues, the Bastard's concluding speeches centre attention on the fate of an entire nation:

> Nought shall make us rue,
> If England to itself do rest but true.   (V.vii.117–18)

As an audience follows the twists and chances of John's life, it must also attend to many other voices, especially those of Elinore his mother, Constance his aunt, and Arthur his nephew, Humphrey his servant, and the supple-minded and pro-active Bastard. Opinions from all sides are questionable and the consequences of each action thrown in doubt: wars in France, dispute about succession to the throne of England, negotiations with Rome, loyalty of nobles. The play's mood is often uncertain, conviction and action provoking laughter as often as fear, and loss failing to awaken sympathy. The death of a king and his personal crisis are not given great emphasis at the play's conclusion. As the story of John unfolds, its general effect is to puzzle as well as to hold attention, to distance the drama and sharpen an audience's political consciousness. In these respects, this history also prepared for the writing of *Julius Caesar*.

Questioning Cause and Effect

Scholars differ widely about when *King John* was written, but all agree that it was some years before *The Life of King Henry the Fifth*.

Outwardly that later history play is a more assured play. Its titular hero does not die at the end, the action concluding with his success in battle and betrothal to a princess. Almost always, he speaks confidently and draws the audience's attention forward with a strong narrative interest. In the latter task he is assisted by a helpful Chorus, who speaks of Henry as the 'star of England' (Epilogue, 6) and claims that his army can pluck 'comfort from his looks':

> A largess universal, like the sun,
> His liberal eye doth give to every one,
> Thawing cold fear, . . .   (IV. Prol. 42–7)

Yet, even with this strong presentation, an audience is encouraged to see the contradictions that lie behind the front of decisive leadership and to question the king's achievements.

Many of the numerous persons placed around the central figure react in distinct and individual ways to the play's events and can directly affect an audience's reponse. At the very start, two prelates justify the king's right to wage war against France with such artful words and obvious self-interest that, even as his army is setting out for battle, the justification for the expedition can seem ill-founded or merely convenient. The argument, turning on rights of succession through a female line, is so finely and exhaustively presented that those in an audience who are able and willing to follow will do so only by excluding from their minds all thoughts of the military operations that the talk seeks to justify. A little later, Mrs Quickly complicates an audience's view of the king by remembering how he had broken Falstaff's heart by rejecting his claims for attention. She demonstates so vividly how the old knight still lives in her own mind that it seems as if she has brought him on stage in person, still wounded by his loss of Prince Hal's friendship (see II.i.14ff. and II.iii.9–44).

The way that the king wages war is not left unchallenged. Immediately after he has exhorted his men to attack Harfleur as the most valiant of soldiers, an anonymous boy is left alone to speak of the 'villainy' of the three 'swashers' he has followed to France (III.ii.27–50). Next on stage are four Captains in ill-tempered debate about whether they are being given proper orders and their skills appropriately used. Before the final battle of Agincourt, when the king walks in disguise among his troops, his easy assumption of their willingness to fight is undermined by the three common soldiers with whom he tries to talk. So charged with anticipation is the occasion that the single speech of Alexander Court – 'Brother John Bates, is not that the morning which breaks yonder?' (IV.i.85–6) – becomes eloquent in its simplicity, very effectively keeping his well-founded fears and his dependence on his 'brother' in the minds of an audience when the king and other soldiers seem to have forgotten them in abstruse and increasingly ill-tempered argument. In speech before battle, the king also addresses his soldiers as brothers:

> we band of brothers;
> For he today that sheds his blood with me
> Shall be my brother . . .   (IV.iii.60–2)

but here the idea of brotherhood is used as a means of persuading other men to risk their lives in battle: it is a powerful leader's bribe, an ideal vision and not the reality it was for Alexander Court.

Before the close of the play, with the long scene in which Henry woos Katherine, the French princess, comes the sharpest and most sustained spur for an audience to exercise independent judgement. The young French-speaking and chaperoned woman can be played many ways – bewildered, stubborn, subtle, flirtatious, or caught up in admiration and sexual desire – but even when poorly or uncertainly played, Katherine is sure to make an audience see Henry afresh, as he stands alone over her. He must now exert himself without help of physical strength or eloquent words. Many in an audience will judge him to be a bully in so pressing his suit upon a person who has little alternative but to listen. Others may take his own view of himself when he recommends his 'good heart'. Very few are likely to accept his claim to be 'the friend' of France, the country he has just defeated in battle – war-torn France in which Peace herself is 'naked, poor, and mangled' (V.ii.159 and 172–3, 34).

At first, as the Chorus's Prologue suggests, *Henry the Fifth* seems set to be a historical pageant-play about the amazing victories of

England's hero-king but, as its narrative unfolds in performance, an audience is shown reasons for making other judgements. Although Henry knows that his actions will cause thousands that are 'yet ungotten and unborn' to curse and weep, he threatens 'wasteful vengeance' without apology (I.i.259–96). When he convicts three friends of treachery, castigating them as devils and monsters who have caused 'another fall of man' (II.ii.142), he assumes that anyone who opposes his cause is opposing God himself. When he talks of his own dazzling glory and moral rectitude, this show of confidence before battle is offset by the loud-mouthed Pistol who knows that in war no one should trust anyone for anything:

> For oaths are straws, men's faiths are wafer-cakes,
> And Holdfast is the only dog, my duck.
> Therefore, *Caveto* be thy counsellor. . . .
> Let us to France, like horse-leeches, my boys,
> To suck, to suck, the very blood to suck.   (II.iii.49–55)

On the final battlefield, Henry acts as Pistol predicts. Thinking that the 'French have reinforc'd their scatter'd men', he does not hesitate to order that 'every soldier kill his prisoners' (IV.vi.35–7). He will praise God for eventual victory, but in winning it he has been responsible for an atrocity more fitting a 'tyrant' than a self-styled 'Christian king' (I.ii.241).

To these views of his hero, Shakespeare added yet another. Choosing to be alone before the last and crucial battle, Henry reveals thoughts and actions that have been hidden from an audience from the start of the play:

> Not to-day, O Lord,
> O, not to-day, think not upon the fault
> My father made in compassing the crown!
> I Richard's body have interred new,
> And on it have bestowed more contrite tears
> Than from it issued forcéd drops of blood;
> Five hundred poor I have in yearly pay,
> Who twice a day their wither'd hands hold up
> Toward heaven, to pardon blood; and I have built

> Two chantries, where the sad and solemn priests
> Sing still for Richard's soul. More will I do;
> Though all that I can do is nothing worth,
> Since that my penitence comes after all,
> Imploring pardon.   (IV.i.288–301)

An intense focus has been given to this confession by putting on
hold all other concerns of immediate and pressing importance.
Henry has just been speaking about ceremony and so has prompted
himself to fall on his knees and hold his hands in supplication to
heaven (see IV.i.252–3, 295–6). After all his public appearances, his
words are likely to sound closer to truth than ever before and, possibly, his posture may seem more appropriate: with so much at stake,
he dare not 'equivocate to heaven' (*Macbeth*, II.iii.13–14). Certainly,
both action and speech establish basic facts that must have underlain
every other moment, including those when Henry presents himself
as a righteous ruler, modest in the sight of his maker and confident
of being his instrument on earth.

Saying, plainly, that all that he has done is 'nothing worth', the
king's words reach to the very 'heart' of the play. An audience, if not
Henry himself, may remember them later when Williams, the trucu-
lent soldier, prays that his faults may be overlooked:

> All offences, my lord, come from the heart: never came any from mine
> that might offend your Majesty.   (IV.vii.45–7)

Further echoes come as Henry stumbles for words before the person
whom he must marry and asks her, as Williams had asked him, to
take his 'good heart' on trust; he knows all too well that a speaker
may be 'but a prater' (V.ii.158). Moments later, when he has formally kissed Katherine in front of a full assembly, Isabella, Queen of
France, takes centre stage and reminds everyone of the 'ill office or
fell jealousy, / Which troubles oft the bed of blessed marriage'; she
prays that God 'combine your hearts in one'. To this Henry can only
promise that their oaths 'may well kept and prosp'rous be!'
(V.ii.350–65) while many in a theatre audience will know that this
did not prove to be the case.

Repeated cues to view Henry sceptically and to question the worth of the war into which he draws his country are summed up in the play's Epilogue. While the Chorus speaks of him as the 'star of England', he also acknowledges that 'Fortune made his sword' and foretells his imminent death leaving an infant heir whose managers 'lost France and made his England bleed': nothing of permanent political value has been achieved and further bloodshed is about to follow. For his people, the consequences were to be loss and more suffering. Shakespeare has led an audience to question thought and action at the same time as it follows a hero's unique experience and shares in a celebration of his great achievement. This form of presentation is developed further in his next tragedy about the life and death of Julius Caesar: here both speech and conscious choice are often at variance with the course of events and, at the conclusion, little can be salvaged of individual worth or fulfilment. The crucial and unifying element of this tragedy is the progressive growth of an audience's perception, rather than the presentation of any one person's actions or consciousness. Such a play was suggested by no current theory of tragedy or any other dramatist's example, but it established what was to become a distinguishing mark of all Shakespeare's later tragedies and, perhaps, their most significant achievement.

7

Julius Caesar: Unsettling an Audience

When he turned from the English wars to the history of Rome at the end of Julius Caesar's life and the beginnings of its long-lasting empire, Shakespeare tackled another well-known story and another famous hero. As he had found some years before in *Titus Andronicus*, he also gained an opportunity to reflect the political realities of his own times in a guise that had less risk of being censored for dealing with matters of state and religion. The first few hundred lines of *The Tragedy of Julius Caesar* introduce enough that is specifically Roman for its author and actors to claim a measure of immunity from prosecution while they presented a situation that would be easily recognized by a local London audience as a reflection of their own world.

Most educated persons of the time would have known Caesar's story in outline and something of its background. His *Gallic Wars* was a standard textbook in grammar schools and it was reported that, when Britain was a Roman province, he had erected the Tower of London, then more dominant on the city's skyline than it is now. In Rome, the name of Caesar lived on after his death because all the emperors from Augustus to Hadrian took it as their title on succession to office. In the Gospels and Acts of the Apostles, he is repeatedly named as the ultimate political authority. Any person wielding great power might be called a Caesar; in more than a dozen of Shakespeare's plays, not counting those with a Roman setting, the name is used in this proverbial way. Taking this man as his hero,

Shakespeare chose someone known to everyone as a soldier and statesman who had risen to greatest power, ruled over huge territories, and started a line of emperors. His story raised issues of ambition, loyalty, trust, personal freedom, and sovereignty; fortunately, because he had not ruled, as the Queen of England did, by inherited right, it avoided matters of the succession, for dealing with which the author and actors might be punishable at law. In a play about Julius Caesar, Shakespeare could invite his audience to follow its action and draw on whatever connections their own experiences might suggest between distant Rome and the politics of their own times. Like the enchanted forests and exotic courts of the comedies, the classical world encouraged the quickening of consciousness that comes from a mixture of recognition and unfamiliarity.

Alerting the Audience

From the start of this tragedy, Shakespeare encouraged his audience to think for themselves. Instead of introducing his titular hero in the first scene, as in *Richard III* and *Richard II*, Shakespeare started off-centre, setting up a wide political context in a way that was sure to provoke uncertain and opposed reactions. A stage direction asks for a crowd of '*certain commoners*' to come on stage already engaged in a quarrel with two officious politicians. They might be Londoners for all that is said and done as they are reprimanded for failing to wear the marks of their crafts in accordance with regulations like those in force among Shakespeare's first audiences. A carpenter bears the first reproof in silence, but the second is directed to a cobbler who proves well able to cut officials down to size, playing with words so that that first one and then the other is riled by his taunting and ironically polite replies. He also plays to his on-stage audience of fellow commoners so that an appreciative circle will gather around to jeer at the regulators of behaviour and encourage their own spokesman, the game becoming more enjoyable with each old joke. Only after some thirty lines is the occasion for all this identified: the crowd is taking an unofficial holiday to 'see Caesar, and to rejoice in his triumph' (ll. 30–1).

Yet, even now, Shakespeare does not get to the heart of his matter. The two Tribunes of the People (this is their function, though it is not identified in the text) are supporters of Pompey, Caesar's rival in success and popularity, and one of them starts to belittle Caesar's triumph because he brings no captives home to Rome, tied to his chariot's wheels according to custom. This is a roundabout way of saying that the victory being celebrated was in a civil war against the sons of Pompey and not against foreign enemies. Leaving all this obscure, Marullus, the less forceful Tribune, reminds his hearers that previously they had greeted the triumph of Pompey with such

> . . . universal shout,
> That Tiber trembled underneath her banks
> To hear the replication of your sounds . . .   (ll. 44ff.)

This reference to the river that runs through Rome helps to locate the drama and is intended by the speaker to remind his hearers of the power they can wield by expressing strong opinions. From a London audience's point of view, Tiber could be a reminder of the Thames, making them feel more at home among the Romans. Flavius, the other Tribune, takes up the reference asking his hearers to weep into the river 'till the lowest stream / Do kiss the most exalted shores of all'. His meaning is not altogether clear: he is probably telling the commoners that they have the means to influence great estates, such as Pompey's or Caesar's. Unexpectedly, the elaborate rhetoric works and the commoners 'vanish tongue-tied in their guiltiness' (l. 62): clearly, they have been manipulated, but with such oblique references to off-stage events that a theatre audience may scarcely know why and be left to debate with themselves what it all means. When Tribunes go off to tear down any trophies that have been hung on statues of Caesar, the Roman context is clearly re-established and the stage prepared for the great man's entry, not with praise or precise information, but with a warning that personal freedom is threatened:

> These growing feathers plucked from Caesar's wing
> Will make him fly an ordinary pitch,

Who else would soar above the view of men,
And keep us all in servile fearfulness.   (ll.72–5)

At this very moment, Caesar appears in a procession, moving
through a 'throng' that is liable to hide him from the view of some
people in a theatre's audience.

At once some limitations on Caesar's power are made evident in a
stark and economical manner. When he calls 'Calpurnia!', and Casca
calls for silence, she does not come forward. He calls her name again
and this time she does answer with 'Here, my lord', an incomplete
verse-line that indicates a short silence before or after its few simple
words. Probably the hiatus should come first, because Caesar
answers with an unhesitating imperative and follows this with
another curt command:

Calpurnia.   Here, my lord.
Caesar.   Stand you directly in Antonius' way
                 When he doth run his course. Antonius!

                                            (I.ii.3–5)

Although this is yet another fact not mentioned in the text, an audience will understand that this woman is Caesar's wife, apparently
both necessary and submissive to her 'lord'. Antony's response is very
similar to hers:

Antony.   Caesar, my lord?
Caesar.   Forget not in your speed, Antonius,
                 To touch Calpurnia; for our elders say,
                 The barren, touchèd in this holy chase,
                 Shake off their sterile curse.
Antony.   I shall remember.
                 When Caesar says 'Do this', it is performed.
Caesar.   Set on, and leave no ceremony out.   (ll. 6–11)

Now an audience will also know that Caesar is without an heir and
would probably notice that Antony flatters him beyond all reason
since, whatever he has 'performed' with Calpurnia, she remains
barren and is treated abruptly, if not demeaningly. A stage-direction

stipulates that Antony is dressed '*for the course*' so that a much younger man stands before Caesar ready for strenuous and competitive exercise. (Shakespeare's source explained that young men of noble house would compete by running 'naked up and down the city anointed with the oil of olive'.)

The words spoken during Caesar's first short appearance leave much unsaid, but Shakespeare has contrived a meaningful tableau each time Caesar intervenes, that create images of power and dependence, and also of male and female, experience and youth, the established and the competitively aspiring, all set out within the crowded grandeur and slow-motion ceremonies of a Roman triumph. Many facets of these images may also have reflected the court of Elizabeth in her childless old age – not all, of course, for that would be unthinkable and undesirable, but sufficient to announce that this play is to be about the limitations of personal power and political initiative at a time of great and imminent change.

Before Caesar has left accompanied by music, a cry of 'Caesar!' is heard, which he answers at once, somewhat unexpectedly since an assassin could be hidden in the crowd. Casca twice orders silence before Caesar says he 'is turned to hear', so letting it be known that, even at a time of personal triumph, this great man is accessible. At length a Soothsayer stands before Caesar and repeats a mysterious message: 'Beware the Ides of March'. Those in the audience who do not recognize the date of Caesar's assassination should be able to catch the urgent tone of this message. Then, with one line, Caesar ignores the disturbance, as if unable or unwilling to pursue such prophecies: 'He is a dreamer. Let us leave him. Pass' (l. 24). These abrupt phrases leave an audience to draw its own conclusions about Caesar's pride, constancy, good sense, or refusal to listen to counsel. He is not seen again until well into the second Act: the first exposure of the title-hero has been brief and hard to assess.

Much more expansive means are used to present the persons who will plot the assassination of Caesar. Brutus and Cassius are the only persons left on stage when the procession has made its slow way off:

> *Cassius.*   Will you go see the order of the course?
> *Brutus.*   Not I.

Cassius.   I pray you do.
Brutus.   I am not gamesome. I do lack some part
             Of that quick spirit that is in Antony.
             Let me not hinder, Cassius, your desires.
             I'll leave you.
Cassius.   Brutus, I do observe you now of late;
             I have not from your eyes that gentleness
             And show of love as I was wont to have.
             You bear too stubborn and too strange a hand
             Over your friend that loves you.
Brutus.   Cassius,
             Be not deceived. If I have veiled my look,
             I turn the trouble of my countenance
             Merely upon my self. Vexèd I am
             Of late with passions of some difference. . . .   (ll.25–40)

The two politicians do not immediately resolve to take action, as do the disaffected nobles after the exit of the king in *I, Henry IV* (I.iii.125ff.): with half-lines indicating hesitations, they assess the situation carefully and are more deeply concerned than either wants to admit openly.

The narrative moves forward only through crafty and competitive talk. Off stage, however, a great deal of noise marks three separate occasions when Caesar refuses the victor's wreath as a crown. When Casca joins the other two, he gives an eyewitness report that shows what impression an off-stage crowd of minor actors have to create:

> the rabblement hooted, and clapped their chopped hands, and threw up their sweaty nightcaps, and uttered such a deal of stinking breath because Caesar refused the crown that it had almost choked Caesar, for he swooned and fell down at it.   (I.ii.242–6)

On stage, a continually shifting focus remains on the three men who now move with difficulty towards committing themselves to ending Caesar's ascendancy: how that should be done, however, still remains unspoken.

An audience's attention is drawn to many small details and differences. Caesar's physical frailty that made him liable to fits and his efforts to conceal this were well known to history, but Shakespeare added a deafness in one ear and had Cassius tell how he had saved Caesar from drowning when the great man had shaken with a fever and asked for help like 'a sick girl' (I.ii.100–31). Speaking of this accentuates both Cassius's envy and his cunning: 'what should be in that "Caesar"?', he asks Brutus, 'Why should that name be sounded more than yours?' (ll. 142–3). In turn, this suggests a clear contrast with Brutus for whom the spur to action is a sense of his own worth:

> Brutus had rather be a villager
> Than to repute himself a son of Rome
> Under these hard conditions as this time
> Is like to lay upon us.   (ll. 172–5)

An audience is invited to make its own comparative assessment of these politicians, as if there were differently skilled players in a single game. When Caesar is again seen briefly as he returns from the festivities with '*his train*', spectators are cued to observe the silent centre of the procession as Brutus speaks of the 'angry spot' glowing on Caesar's brow and the 'pale' cheek of Calpurnia; Cicero is said to have 'such ferret and such fiery eyes' that he seems to have been 'crossed in conference' (ll. 182–8). Caesar's one lengthy contribution to the dialogue is a character sketch of Cassius with his 'lean and hungry look' (ll. 208–10). An audience that has come to see a play about great Caesar has been led to look sceptically at several politicians, judging their potential for action, while the central character has little to say and major events happen off stage.

The mood of the play shifts when everyone disperses and thunder and lightning strike. Casca returns to be joined by Cicero and, when he has left, by Cassius. Besides the storm, that will be violent in off-stage effects and on-stage reactions, other portents are amazedly reported: a 'tempest dropping fire', fire burning on a man's hand like 'twenty torches', a lion stalking its prey near the Capitol, a 'hundred ghastly women, / Transformèd with their fear,' an owl haunting the market-place at noonday. Then all that is counterstated as, under a 'disturbèd sky', Cassius appears to be totally at ease: 'A very pleasing night to honest men,' he declares (I.iii.39–43). He then tests Casca's willingness to take action by talking of Caesar's tyranny. A new arrival is alarming at first, until he is identified as Cinna, a 'friend'. He brings news that other members of 'our party' (l. 141) have already met at Cassius' house and he is then sent away with papers to leave where Brutus will find them, all of which urge him to act against Caesar. In his absence, during these exchanges, Brutus is consistently portrayed as a potential leader for less 'noble' conspirators: 'Him and his worth and our great need of him / You have right well conceited,' Cassius tells Casca in the last moments of the scene (ll. 161–2). The general effect is that of a mechanism being slowly and secretly set up in order to accomplish some, as yet unspecified, act that will displace Caesar and in which Brutus must provide a missing and crucial element. As the stage empties, an audience will look for more information as the dramatic focus shifts to show Brutus alone *'in his orchard'* (II.1.0, S.D.).

The Close Focus on Brutus

The sequence of soliloquies given to Brutus has no parallel in Shakespeare's source and on many counts – in forms of speech, domestic details, repeated silences, self-awareness – form the most original episode in the play so far. In them, Brutus commits himself to action and expresses his own feelings, but he also thinks and speaks about own experience in all of this. Shakespeare's earlier heroes had soliloquized about their states of mind but only in adversity near the end of their stories: Richard III before the battle of Bosworth; Richard II imprisoned in Pomfret castle; King John knowing that he is powerless and about to die. Romeo and Juliet are exceptions here, but their self-awareness arises out of their interest in each other, not out of a political or moral crisis. In contrast to all these, Brutus is haunted by his own thoughts and feelings, before he has taken any significant action and before he has been curtailed in what he wishes to do: he seeks to understand the experience of making a decision, as well as defining it and preparing to carry it out.

Like earlier scenes, this one starts off-centre. Brutus calls Lucius and, as if needing to explain why, says he cannot tell the time by the movement of the stars. The boy does not come, so he calls again, this time wishing 'it were my fault to sleep so soundly'. Eventually, Lucius enters and Brutus asks him to set 'a taper in my study' and send word when it is lighted. Lucius leaves, with an incomplete verse-line – 'I will, my lord' – and then, after the implied pause, Brutus speaks of what has kept him awake and been the unspoken cause of his unease. That unease remains, for his words jump abruptly, several times, to new thoughts:

> It must be by his death; and, for my part,
> I know no personal cause to spurn at him,
> But for the general: he would be crowned.
> How that might change his nature, there's the question.
> It is the bright day that brings forth the adder,
> And that craves wary walking. Crown him that,
> And then, I grant, we put a sting in him
> That at his will he may do danger with.
> Th'abuse of greatness is when it disjoins
> Remorse from power, and, to speak truth of Caesar,
> I have not known when his affections swayed
> More than his reason.   (II.i.10–21)

Modern editors differ greatly in punctuating this speech, for much is still unspoken. When Lucius returns, Brutus asks if tomorrow is the Ides of March and, when the boy does not know, sends him off again to find out. His mind is busy: after another pause, he speaks of the portents and then turns to a paper that Lucius has brought, having found it in the window of his master's closet. Not knowing, as the audience does, that Cassius has written this, Brutus reads out the message and finds that he is called upon to strike and redress the wrongs Rome suffers. He 'pieces out' what he reads, repeating and rephrasing the words from this and other papers. Finally, he makes a formal promise to Rome that he will act as the papers instruct and at this point, as if fated to do so, Lucius returns to report that the Ides of March have indeed come. Then, at this very moment, again as if fated, a knocking is heard at the gate and the audience, rather better than Brutus, will know that the conspirators have come to draw him to their side.

With Lucius sent to answer, Brutus is alone once again and is, at first, almost matter-of-fact:

> Since Cassius first did whet me against Caesar
> I have not slept.

After that half-line pause, he tries to comprehend what has been happening within his own mind:

> Between the acting of a dreadful thing
> And the first motion, all the interim is
> Like a phantasma or a hideous dream.
> The genius and the mortal instruments
> Are then in council, and the state of man,
> Like to a little kingdom, suffers then
> The nature of an insurrection.   (I.ii.60–9)

In earlier plays Shakespeare had shown fateful decisions being made but here, with the action that will lead to tragedy only about to begin, thought and counter-thought are used to lead an audience into the mind of the speaker and hear what it feels like to live through such a crucial moment.

When Lucius returns to announce Cassius and other persons who keep their faces hidden, he is sent to let them in and Brutus again soliloquizes, now more aware of the immediate situation. He knows that 'conspiracy' is ashamed, even 'by night / When evils are most free', and that its true purpose must be hidden 'in smiles and affability'. From now on, Brutus must be prepared 'mask [a] monstrous visage' (ll. 77–85) and with this thought, after whispering with Cassius aside, he steps forward to take the hands of every person present. When a little later he talks of killing Caesar and calls these men his 'gentle friends' (l. 172), an audience will know what lies behind that courteous greeting.

After a long preparation, the focus has centred on the sleepless Brutus, tormented as if by an inner civil war. If the actor speaks as if in the physical grip of a terrible nightmare, as the text implies he should, his words and silences will be more intense than any others in the play so far: his thoughts and feelings will be the heart of the drama and, until the entrance of the conspirators fatefully on time, nothing deflects the attention from them. A similar immediacy will draw an audience into the mind of Hamlet and Brutus's moment of identification with 'There's the question', will help to breed a whole line of other tragedies, echoed in Hamlet's 'To be or not to be – that is the question' (III.i.56) and, more distantly, in Othello's

> It is the cause, it is the cause, my soul –
> Let me not name it to you, you chaste stars –
> It is the cause. Yet I'll not shed her blood . . .   (V.ii.1–3)

As Brutus knows he must assume a mask and hide his innermost thoughts, so Hamlet will be conscious of 'that within which passes show' (I.ii.85) and Macbeth will learn that 'False face must hide what the false heart doth know' and seek to mask his business 'from the common eye' (I.vii.82; III.i.124). The sleepless nights of Brutus will be echoed by Macbeth's: his awareness of 'a phantasma or a hideous dream', in which the state of man suffers 'an insurrection', will be further defined in Macbeth's:

>   Present fears
> Are less than horrible imaginings.
> My thought, whose murder yet is but fantastical,
> Shakes so my single state of man
> That function is smother'd in surmise,
> And nothing is but what is not.   (I.iv.137–41)

The double view that Shakespeare had created for the hero of *Henry the Fifth* is here more fully and explicitly employed and an audience may sense that the action of the play arises out of some inner unease or undefined compulsion, rather than from positive and willing choice.

The Operation of Fate

The main lines of the plot of this tragedy and many incidental details of its action stemmed from Shakespeare's use of Plutarch's

Lives of the Noble Grecians and Romans in Sir Thomas North's translation of 1579 or in a reprint of 1595; even the verse dialogue is often remarkably close to North's prose. Such fidelity was so unusual in Shakespeare's work that both departures from this source and adherence to it are important indications of how the play was meant to work in performance.

An emphasis on fate is Shakespeare's development of a recurrent motif in Plutarch. For example, he brought the Soothsayer very prominently on stage for Caesar's first appearance in Act I, scene ii, when in Plutarch his warning is given earlier and without a dramatic confrontation. Subsequent references to the Ides of March are Shakespeare's additions and only in the play do the conspirators knock at Brutus's gate at the very moment that he has been told that this day has come. Other small changes have much the same effect: for instance, in *The Lives*, Cinna the Poet has a 'marvellous strange and terrible' dream in which he chooses not to dine with Caesar, but in Shakespeare's play he has a different dream and says that some kind of compulsion has drawn him to leave home:

> I have no will to wander forth of doors,
> Yet something leads me forth.   (III.iii.1–4)

An audience has been alerted to watch his doomed progress towards death. Some changes are more general in effect, such as the dreadful portents added to those accompanying the storm of I.iii and Cassius's stronger forebodings before the final battle.

Clearly Shakespeare was much occupied with Plutarch's treatment of fate, accepting much of what he read and yet constantly modifying and supplementing it. The changes are not all one way: for their first meeting, he invented Cassius's argument to Brutus that

> Men at some time are masters of their fates.
> The fault, dear Brutus, is not in our stars,
> But in ourselves, that we are underlings.   (I.ii.139–41)

Underling was an ancient word deriving from feudal usages concerning a man's subjection to his 'master' or lord; it was no longer in common use and occurs only here in Shakespeare's plays where it marks the cunning with which Cassius slips from talking about fate to playing upon personal rivalry. Later, in contrast to what Cassius implies here, Brutus seeks to arm himself with patience 'To stay the providence of some high powers / That govern us below' (V.i.106–8); he is pursued by the Ghost of Caesar, seeing and identifying him twice and believing that this spirit will at last be satisfied only with his suicide (see V.v.51–2). In Plutarch, Brutus does not speak of 'high powers' and is visited by an unidentified evil spirit; he dies without speaking of Caesar or the anonymous spirit that had visited him.

In the last scenes of the tragedy fate seems to exercise its strongest force. The battle turns against Caesar's enemies by a series of chances and both Brutus and Cassius slay themselves, acknowledging that 'the time' has come and that Caesar will be revenged. For an audience, however, a tension continues between a fated inevitability and the apparent freedom with which these persons do what they decide to do. Sensing that his enemies 'have beat us to the pit', Brutus still wants to make a choice:

> It is more worthy to leap in ourselves
> Than tarry till they push us.   (V.v.23–5)

Even when events are beyond his control, he insists on control over himself. An audience is left to judge how far this freedom is an illusion and what difference belief in it might make. If Brutus is not free here, was he free to act otherwise than he did when 'Cassius first did whet him against Caesar' (II.i.61)? Shakespeare prompted such questions by changing Plutarch's account so that Strato makes a decisive choice to hold the sword on which Brutus dies: was it fated that one of those whom Brutus asked would do this service for him? Was Brutus's death dependent on the free choice of another person?

Fate had a significant role to play in the story of the 'star-crossed lovers' of *Romeo and Juliet*, but in that tragedy the quarrel between the parents' families offers a clear moral justification for its operation. In *Julius Caesar*, Shakespeare leads an audience to recognize an inevitability in what happens and some degree of moral justice in its operation and yet, at the same time, implies that how fate operates depends on the manner in which individuals live their lives and how they think and feel about crucial events.

After the deaths of Cassius and Brutus, and the defeat of their armies, the relative power of fate and the action of individuals remains an open issue. Over the dead body of Brutus, Antony speaks of his personal contribution to events, using words which, in substance, Plutarch had given him very much earlier:

> This was the noblest Roman of them all.
> All the conspirators save only he
> Did that they did in envy of great Caesar.
> He only, in a general honest thought
> And common good to all, made one of them.
> His life was gentle, and the elements
> So mixed in him that Nature might stand up
> And say to all the world 'This was a man!' (V.v.69–76)

For an audience that has witnessed this spokesman's political ruthlessness earlier in the play, especially when he agrees to murder his 'sister's son' without sign of reluctance (IV.i.6), these words may well sound more politically convenient than heartfelt or philosophically responsible; an audience is almost sure to question his personal commitment to them. When the young Octavius Caesar takes charge with great efficiency and looks ahead with optimism, his intentions may be questioned in much the same way:

> So call the field to rest, and let's away
> To part the glories of this happy day. (ll. 81–2)

In this context, *happy* could mean 'appropriate, fitting' or 'fortunate', but its other, more usual, contented and light-hearted meanings cannot remain entirely absent in the speaker's or his hearer's minds. The final line, alluding to the 'glories' of a civil war in which noble Romans have been killed, runs smoothly enough within the final couplet to support an entirely self-satisfied meaning for 'this happy day'.

Which of these two victorious leaders takes precedence as they leave the stage with their armies, and how they bear themselves, will provide a concluding show during which an audience is invited once more to make a judgement about individuals and their effect on events. At the end of *Romeo and Juliet*, the two rival families come together in reconciliation and remorse: at the end of this later 'fateful' tragedy, two persons whose armies have won a battle carry with them a burden of personal rivalry and individual political responsibility.

The Issue of Trust

In performance, a major effect of this play is that its audience becomes involved progressively with the inner life of its leading characters, with what they think and feel when they are speaking and acting. One way that Shakespeare achieved this was by emphasizing their rivalries in such a way that differences are continually being demonstrated without being defined in words. Cassius's talk with Brutus at the beginning of the play, in which they agree to move against Caesar, provides the story with much of its impetus but leaves a great deal unsaid. They appear to talk openly and yet, immediately afterwards, Cassius is planning to deceive Brutus. This is only the first of many contentions between these two political allies and mutually professed friends in which they differ instinctively, responding to events in distinctive ways which, with repetition, an audience will come to recognize and, even, to expect. They are frequently at odds about tactics, on whether to bind the conspirators with an oath (II.i.112–40), whether Antony should be eliminated along with Caesar (II.i.155–92), whether he should be allowed to speak at Caesar's funeral (III.i.231–43), and whether to engage in battle sooner or later (IV.ii.246–75 and V.i.74–6). Their differences come to a head in a prolonged encounter which has become famous as the 'Quarrel Scene'. For this, Shakespeare drew on scattered episodes in Plutarch's *Lives* and, with unusual care, prepared an audience to watch the encounter with a less limited and less partisan view than either of the participants.

Before Cassius enters at the head of his army, Brutus calls for a private report: 'A word, Lucilius, / How he received you: let me be resolved' (IV.ii.12–13). The soldier phrases his reply carefully and Brutus himself, although not present at the interview, sums up this halting description and proceeds, instinctively, to demonstrate his own superior understanding and ability to see beyond the present circumstances:

> *Brutus.*   Thou hast described
> A hot friend cooling. Ever note, Lucilius,
> When love begins to sicken and decay
> It useth an enforcèd ceremony.

For some unstated reason, he is compelled to blame Cassius for being devious and, by inference, to boast of his own straightforward virtue: 'There are no tricks in plain and simple faith.' After Cassius's army has joined that of Brutus on stage, the two leaders attempt to speak together in public and fail to do so. After an exchange of accusations, with varying forms of address and each speaker refusing to follow the rhythms of the other's speech, two lieutenants are told to send the armies away and the two leaders face each other waiting in the silence for privacy. In effect, the audience has been prepared to watch a show-down and the duologue that follows is more sustained than any in earlier plays. At times finely wrought, it is also outright and pas-sionate. It shudders to a halt in blatant contradictions and lurches forward when a particular word strikes deeply. Both speakers goad each other at times, but whether consciously or not is far from clear.

From the start, Brutus seems to be the more secure and deliberate. He makes a very particular argument (ll. 70–8) and, when Cassius does not answer, continues, as if compelled to speak of himself: 'I had rather be a dog and bay the moon / Than such a Roman'. Cassius may well consider the argument irrelevant, since it cites events before the assassination and makes only general reference to the case at issue. A theatre audience could be further puzzled because this motive for killing Caesar has not been mentioned in the play before. Cassius calls a halt:

> Brutus, bait not me,

> I'll not endure it. You forget yourself
> To hedge me in,   (ll. 80–2)

Now he baits Brutus in return, claiming greater authority as a
soldier: 'Older in practice, abler than yourself / To make conditions'
(ll. 82–4). He has hit home, for Brutus responds immediately, with
blatant tit for tat:

> *Brutus.*   Go to! You are not, Cassius.
> *Cassius.*   I am.
> *Brutus.*   I say you are not.   (ll. 85–6)

This last retort is left as an incomplete verse-line and the silence after
it will register fury, frustration, or rigid determination – whatever
pressures come authentically to both the actors as the play is in performance – but with sufficient power to hold the two men confronting each other with nothing more to say. After this hiatus, in
short phrases, Cassius speaks first, as if only he is aware of the
danger of being carried away:

> Urge me no more, I shall forget myself.
> Have mind upon your health. Tempt me no farther.   (ll. 87–8)

With an insult, Brutus attempts to end matters: 'Away, slight man!'
(l. 89). Another pause and then Brutus insists on prolonging the
quarrel, charging Cassius with belligerence and madness. He presses
on, the passion in his response marked by demeaning nouns and
phrases – *rash choler . . . testy humour . . . venom of your spleen . . .
mirth . . . laughter . . . vaunting*. Both call on the gods and both
protest disbelief.

At the end of this outburst, Brutus returns to what Cassius had
said earlier but, significantly, misquoting him: 'You say you are a
better soldier' (l. 103). He appears more sober now and continues
scathingly, filled with a sense of his own nobility:

> Let it appear so; make your vaunting true,
> And it shall please me well. For mine own part,
> I shall be glad to learn of noble men.   (ll. 104–6)

This time Cassius is the more reasonable, pointing out that he had said 'elder', not 'better' and, in doing so, substituting the less perjorative 'elder' for 'abler.' When asked the direct question, 'Did I say 'better'?', Brutus replies insultingly, as if what Cassius thinks is of no importance: 'If you did, I care not.' At this point, Cassius and then Brutus may put their hands on their swords as two very measured and fully laden verse-lines indicate a squaring up to each other. Cassius takes the initiative by calling up the memory of how they both had stabbed Caesar, he before Brutus:

> *Cassius.* When Caesar lived he durst not thus have moved me.
> *Brutus.* Peace, peace, you durst not so have tempted him.
>
> (ll. 110–11)

Their past actions and their entire lives are, now, on the line and keep them facing each other:

> *Cassius.* I durst not?
> *Brutus.* No.
> *Cassius.* What, durst not tempt him?
> *Brutus.*   For your life you durst not.
>
> (ll. 112–14)

A change has occurred: by repetition, words cease to be remarkable and feelings are no longer verbally explicit. The persons the two actors have become as they played their roles now provide almost the entire substance of the drama in this shared and nearly silent moment. An audience will not so much be puzzled by this as caught up with what is happening, transfixed by the very being of Brutus or Cassius, or of both of them.

Notably, this is a shared moment. Earlier, in *Richard III* and *Richard II*, and in *Romeo and Juliet* as the two lovers separately approach their deaths, Shakespeare had created just such an intense focus on the very presence and innermost feelings of isolated tragic heroes: now the truth and thrill of the moment depend on two actors meeting a similar challenge together while drawing instinctively on their entire performances until this very moment. The drama will be different each time it is played, but it can also seem inevitable as it springs from deep within each performer, beyond the reach of calculation or predetermination. The tragedy has moved beyond what can be fully expressed in words so that any meaning it possesses will depend in part on its audience's ability to grasp what the drama can only suggest.

Cassius is the first who attempts to say more, his words more measured now and provoking a measured response:

> *Cassius.*   Do not presume too much upon my love,
>   I may do that I shall be sorry for.
> *Brutus.*   You have done that you should be sorry for.   (ll. 115–17)

Brutus, acknowledging the 'terror' of what has occurred between them, moves on to praise his own 'honesty' and to make a second very particular argument, this time blaming Cassius for not sharing with him the money that he had procured by 'vile means' (l. 123) and which, by implication, is not in keeping with the 'honesty' he himself professes. Again, short-phrased contradictions follow, but this time Cassius does not hesitate to open up an entirely new range of feelings and sensations:

> *Cassius.*   I denied you not.
> *Brutus.*   You did.
> *Cassius.*   I did not. He was but a fool
>   That brought my answer back. Brutus hath rived my heart.
>   A friend should bear his friend's infirmitites,
>   But Brutus makes mine greater than they are.
> *Brutus.*   I do not, till you practise them on me.

Cassius continues to insist on the new level of engagement:

> *Cassius.*   You love me not.
> *Brutus.*   I do not like your faults.
> *Cassius.*   A friendly eye could never see such faults.   (ll. 136–41)

When Brutus does not respond with the same sober seriousness, Cassius pauses as if for deliberation and then starts a careful and consciously dramatic approach, a self-projection rather than a further appeal to Brutus. Weary and on the verge of tears, he strips his breast naked and offers his dagger to Brutus. The large and, perhaps, grotesque gesture gains silent attention; so, too, may an element of calculation in Cassius's reference to Pluto, god of gold and silver, which can remind Brutus that he had earlier accused Cassius of having an 'itchy palm' (l. 62). It is also a second allusion to Caesar's assassination, coupled this time with direct reference to the disloyalty Brutus had showed in killing a friend he had professed to love:

> Strike as thou didst at Caesar; for I know,
> When thou didst hate him worst, thou lov'dst him better
> Than ever thou lov'dst Cassius.   (ll. 156–8)

With no hesitation, when Cassius has done, Brutus capitulates:

>   Sheathe your dagger.
> Be angry when you will, it shall have scope.
> Do what you will, dishonour shall be humour.
> O Cassius, you are yokèd to a lamb
> That carries anger as flint bears fire,
> Who, much enforcèd, shows a hasty spark,
> And straight is cold again.   (ll. 158–64)

All is not well yet: Brutus still maintains that his friend has used him with 'dishonour.' They do not take each other's hand until he has confessed his own fault and, even then, some awkwardness remains:

> *Brutus.*   I was ill-tempered too.
> *Cassius.* Do you confess so much? Give me your hand.
> *Brutus.* And my heart too.
> *Cassius.*   O Brutus!
> *Brutus.*   What's the matter?
> *Cassius.* Have not you love enough to bear with me,
>   When that rash humour which my mother gave me
>   Makes me forgetful?
> *Brutus.*   Yes, Cassius, and from henceforth,
>   When you are over-earnest with your Brutus,
>   He'll think your mother chides, and leave you so.
>   (ll. 167–74)

With passions spent, speech is more relaxed but the almost humorous mood may still sound less than whole-hearted.

A two-part coda follows. First a Philosopher–Poet insists on entering to utter moralizing doggerel that counsels the generals to 'love and be friends' (l. 181). He is sent away with a scorn that may well seem over-sharp in that he has recommended the very relationship the two leaders have just vowed to maintain. Only when Brutus calls for a bowl of wine do both relax again and Cassius can look back on their quarrel: 'I did not think you could have been so angry' (l. 193). Even now, trust between the two is insecure: Cassius's scepticism and Brutus's half-concealed mockery are still present. As they wait for wine, however, Brutus speaks of feelings that he has not exposed before. To Cassius, as to the audience, his grief is totally unexpected: Cassius is lost for words and Brutus can only repeat the bare fact of Portia's death. Forward action seems to stall and then, when the wine comes, Cassius's heart is 'thirsty', he says, to pledge that he will 'bury all unkindness' as Brutus has done:

Brutus.	O Cassius, I am sick of many griefs.
Cassius.	Of your philosophy you make no use
	If you give place to accidental evils.
Brutus.	No man bears sorrow better. Portia is dead.
Cassius.	Ha! Portia?
Brutus.	She is dead.
Cassius.	How scaped I killing when I crossed you so?
	O insupportable and touching loss!
	Upon what sickness?
Brutus.	Impatient of my absence,
	And grief that young Octavius with Mark Antony
	Have made themselves so strong – for with her death
	That tidings came – with this she fell distract,
	And, her attendants absent, swallowed fire.
Cassius.	And died so?
Brutus.	Even so.
Cassius.	O ye immortal gods!
	Enter Boy [Lucius] with wine and tapers
Brutus.	Speak no more of her. Give me a bowl of wine.
	In this I bury all unkindness, Cassius.
	He drinks

Cassius. My heart is thirsty for that noble pledge.
Fill, Lucius, till the wine o'erswell the cup.
I cannot drink too much of Brutus' love.   (ll.193–212)

In performance, the exposure of feeling and then the rush of sympathy are unmistakable. The episode will dictate its own tempo and pitch for its very simple words; and physically it will usually look very simple too. Here rivalry is stopped short by a shared sense of loss and helplessness, and peace seems possible between these previously irreconcilable men.

Plutarch's *Lives* does not describe Portia's death until after the wars are done and Brutus has committed suicide. In Shakespeare's play, in the only version that has survived, it is reported on two occasions. On its later occurrence, at IV.iii.231–46, it is Messala who reports her suicide among other items of news and Brutus makes a very short formal farewell to her that demonstrates his patience more than his grief. This may have been intended for omission when Shakespeare moved the report of her death to the earlier and more prominent position and had Brutus announce the news. If both reports were intended to remain in the text, that would do nothing to diminish the quiet effectiveness of the first occurrence, in contrast to the violent and often loud quarrel that precedes it.

In the passage dealing with the Philosopher–Poet's entry, Plutarch tells how Brutus and Cassius could be heard 'loud within' as they 'grew hot and loud, earnestly accusing one another, and at length fell both a-weeping'; those outside are said to have been 'both amazed, and afraid'. From early performances onwards, the whole scene seems to have drawn attention for extremities of feeling much as Plutarch indicates. Leonard Digges in verses prefixed to the 1623 Folio edition of the plays vowed that he would not believe Shakespeare to be dead until some other writer out-did the passions of 'Juliet and her Romeo':

Or till I hear a scene more nobly take
Than when thy half-sword parleying Romans spake.

He added more when Shakespeare's *Poems* were published in 1640:

So have I seen, when Caesar would appear,
And on the stage at half-sword parley were
Brutus and Cassius: oh, how the audience
Were ravish'd, with what wonder they went thence . . .

Whether swords are drawn or not, the stage history of the play provides plenty of evidence of the intensity and 'wonder' of this quarrel.

The height of feeling in the tragedy of *The Life and Death of Julius Caesar* is not to be found in the deaths of its principal characters. The revaluations associated with the deaths of Richard III, Richard II, and Romeo and Juliet are entirely missing from the last scene, and so is the complex web of revenge and recognition that concludes *Titus Andronicus*. In this tragedy, the strongest feelings and most searching reappraisals are in the 'Quarrel Scene'; especially at its very end, when an audience is drawn to share closely in the experience of both Brutus and Cassius and the actors make present much that is unspoken. Shakespeare's later tragedies will not concentrate so much on how a tragic hero faces death: they will be more about what men and women do to each other and how that leads to disaster.

A Tragedy of State

Although the 'Quarrel Scene' is its emotional centre, this tragedy is not solely concerned with personal relationships. Intertwined with the exploration of trust and truthfulness are many other issues, such as leadership, responsibility, and the use of violence for political ends. The play starts with unruly citizens and political manipulation and the assassination of Caesar, staged with unmissable drama, is the central fact of the entire story. The conspirators then bathe their arms in the victim's blood to run through the streets brandishing their weapons and crying 'Peace, freedom, and liberty!'

The dramatic form developed for both history plays and comedies, where contrasts invite and stimulate comparative judgements, is here at the service of a tragedy. An audience that has been unsettled in its responses by the way in which the action has been presented, will be quick to notice further differences in reactions to the issues raised: Casca, Cinna, Cicero, Metellus Cimber, Trebonius, and Caius Ligarius provide a gallery of contrasted politicians, for each of whom the conspiracy to assassinate Caesar raises different issues. Portia, the noble and yet dependent wife of Brutus, is shown over against Calpurnia, who is silent and submissive except when seeking to restrain her husband from going to the Capitol in the face of the portents. In scenes with her, Caesar is shown as prey to flattery, even while disregarding her superstitious warnings and priding himself on constancy.

Most notably, Antony stands over against all the conspirators. At the start, he is flattering and obedient to Caesar and then becomes a subject of contention between Brutus and Cassius. That the latter was right to be wary of him is made apparent with a suddenness which is shocking in performance: having dealt circumspectly with Caesar's assassins, he is left alone on stage and reveals himself to be a political operator more skilful than the others and more obviously motivated by raw ambition. At first he sounds ashamed of the duplicity he has practised:

> O, pardon me, thou bleeding piece of earth,
> That I am meek and gentle with these butchers!   (III.3.254–5)

But later, he speaks of the war that will follow with an enthusiasm that accepts that 'all pity [will be] choked with custom of fell deeds', and calls for Ate, the goddess of cruelty and strife, to 'Cry "Havoc!" and let slip the dogs of war' (ll. 269 and 273). An audience may still be in two minds about him while it witnesses the unsuspecting Brutus propose that the two of them should both make funeral orations, but after Brutus has spoken carefully and with dignity, Antony's masterly address over Caesar's corpse will provoke divided judgements as it plays upon the crowd's own interests, makes a mockery of Brutus's claims of being an 'honourable man', and almost openly incites a riot. Those in the audience who are least suspicious of such rhetorical manipulation will be forced to reconsider when Caesar's body is taken off stage by the hooligan plebeians and Antony, surveying the scene, comments briefly in soliloquy:

> Now let it work! Mischief, thou art afoot,
> Take thou what course thou wilt.

Moments later, he tells Octavius's servant that his master's arrival in Rome

> . . . comes upon a wish. Fortune is merry,
> And in this mood will give us anything.   (III.ii.253–60)

Before long, Antony is seen with Octavius Caesar and Lepidus calmly planning retribution and, still more suprisingly, accepting Octavius's comments as if unconscious of the younger man's disdain. Later, he acquiesces when Caesar's heir-apparent countermands what he proposes: how powerful and how astutely political is Antony?

Provocative contrasts are also inherent in the handling of scenes, public ceremony alternating with private consultation, crowd scenes with soliloquies, personal anguish with careful concealment of fears and anxiety or with episodes of crude frenzy and violence. The most noticeable contrast is between the last Act and all the others. Here Shakespeare hugely reduced the complications of Plutarch's narrative, converting a succession of debates, hesitations, diplomacy, philosophizing, recruitment exercises, troop movements, and battle engagements into a swift-flowing sequence of short scenes in what seems to be a single and consecutive conflict. The progress towards the suicides of Brutus and Cassius seems almost inevitable, even though the fortunes of the battle change rapidly and are often difficult for the contenders to understand. An audience is liable to find itself straining to follow as the tide of events almost overwhelms Brutus and Cassius, the characters through whom it has previously made what sense it could of what was happening.

In arranging the last Act in this way, Shakespeare ensured another contrast. In great measure his source material had dictated that the citizens would disappear after they had taken a varied part in events at Rome, their intervention climaxing when they brutally and senselessly murdered Cinna the poet. But it was Shakespeare's choice that, when the same actors reappear in disciplined ranks of soldiers, their marches and counter-marches are managed with swift efficiency and often in quick succession: war has brought a new suppression of individuality. Yet many of the actors who reappear as soldiers, whether they had previously been senators or plebeians, are given a few highly significant acts and speeches that are well-controlled and forceful. As the main story draws to a close, an audience will find that it must attend to individuals whose names have not been heard before: Lucilius, Titinius, Messala, Young Cato, Voluminius, Strato, Pindarus, Dardanius, Labeo, Flavius, Varro, Claudius, Clitus. So an audience is encouraged to recognize the fall-out of the central tragic action in many other lives, and, by doing so, be once again unsettled in response and judgement. As the tragedy comes to its end, Shakespeare seems to be concerned with the intricacies of personal relationships, individual decisions, and the intransigence of politics and conflict. This aspect of *Julius Caesar* will be developed further in *The Tragedy of Hamlet* in which fully detailed and interlocking stories give rise to an awareness that no person suffers alone or is without some responsibility for what happens.

8

Hamlet I: Sources and Contexts

The Tragedy of Hamlet, Prince of Denmark, dating from some time in 1600, exploits the advances of *Julius Caesar*, written a year or so earlier. The philosophical and soliloquizing Brutus is replaced by a younger and more driven hero, who also questions what he should do but more insistently and feeling more frequently an insurrection within his being when caught between idea and action. The quarrel of Brutus and Cassius, in which they seem to forget themselves in anger, frustration, and grief, showed the way for Hamlet to forget himself (see V.ii.76) and engage fiercely with those nearest to him. Whereas Brutus shared only one scene with his wife, Hamlet has several with his mother and with Ophelia whom he loves and also repudiates. The brief but revealing moments of domestic life with Calpurnia, Portia, and Lucius are replaced by prolonged intimacies and frightening confrontations.

Whereas an audience's attention tends to be divided with the battles at the end of *Julius Caesar*, it is concentrated by sustained action in the last scene of *Hamlet*: on a crowded stage, cunning and accident give a concerted sense of danger and 'incensed' conflict (V.ii.307). Denmark's history was not as widely known as Rome's so that Shakespeare was much freer to choose what would happen and to imagine a group of persons closely involved with each other and with political crises at home and abroad. With this new tragedy, Shakespeare's imagination was more fully in control and at full stretch.

Earlier Hamlets

The story of Hamlet must have seemed a very strange choice to Shakespeare's fellow actors. At least one other writer had used it already in a manner far removed from his. No text has survived of the *Ur-Hamlet* (as scholars call this lost play or plays) but in 1589 Thomas Nashe alluded to a crude imitation of Seneca that was then current :

> English Seneca, read by candlelight, yields many good sentences, as 'Blood is a beggar', and so forth; and if you entreat him fair in a frosty morning, he will afford you whole Hamlets – I should say handfuls – of tragical speeches.
>
> (Preface to Robert Greene's *Menaphon*, 1589)

Thomas Lodge's *Wit's Misery and the World's Madness* of 1596 tells of a ghost with a pale vizard which had 'cried so miserably at the Theatre, like an oyster-wife, "Hamlet, revenge!"'. Shakespeare had never used that sort of effect. In *Julius Caesar*, the Ghost of Caesar appears only to Brutus and speaks only when it is addressed. Numerous apparitions enter and speak in the earlier *Richard III*, but they appear only in dreams before the final battle. Now, in this new tragedy, the Ghost of the hero's father was to be the main instigator of its action, appearing to numerous people on several occasions and twice giving very precise information and instruction to Hamlet.

Perhaps even more surprising would have been Shakespeare's choice of a story about brutal, drunken and, even, stupid people, refined in neither thought nor behaviour. The first fragmentary account of Hamlet dates from early in the twelfth century AD but a fuller account was given by Saxo Grammaticus in his *Historiae Danicae*, written at the end of that century and published in 1514. This was subsequently translated into French for the fifth volume of François de Belleforest's *Histoires Tragiques* of 1582. Now twice its original length with much moralizing added, the story was often reprinted but an English translation did not appear until 1608. This *History of Hamblet*, following Belleforest, warned its readers to make allowances for the story's antiquity:

> You must understand, that long time before the kingdom of Denmark received the faith of Jesus Christ and embraced the doctrine of the Christians, that the common people in those days were barbarous and uncivil, and their princes cruel, without faith or loyalty, seeking nothing but murder, and deposing or, at the least, offending each other, either in honours, goods, or lives; not caring to ransome such as they took prisoners, but rather sacrificing them to the cruel vengeance naturally imprinted in their hearts . . .

Shakespeare's playtext has many incidents and some phrases similar to those of both the Latin and French versions of Saxo but nothing to prove that he had made a close study of either of them. The *Ur-Hamlet* was probably another of his sources, but what we know of its ghost and rhetorical style argues against any close or sustained indebtedness. How far Shakespeare developed the story away from all these possible sources can be illustrated by the English account of the funeral banquet given on receiving news of Hamlet's death and during which he returns unexpectedly from England:

> When every man busied himself to make good cheer and Hamlet's arrival provoked them more to drink and carouse, the prince himself at that time played the butler . . . , whereby he gave the noblemen such store of liquor that all of them, being full laden with wine and gorged with meat, were constrained to lay themselves down in the same place where they had supped, so much their senses were dulled and overcome. . . . Seeing those drunken bodies, filled with wine, lying like hogs upon the ground, some sleeping, others vomiting the over-great abundance of wine . . . , [he] made the hangings about the hall to fall down and cover them all over, which he nailed to the ground . . . in such sort that what force soever they used to loose themselves, it was unpossible to get from under them; and presently he set fire to the four corners of the hall, in such sort that, [of] all that were as then therein, not one escaped away, . . . all of them dying in the inevitable and merciless flames of the hot and burning fire.

This Hamlet then pursued his uncle to his bedchamber and 'gave him such a blow upon the chine of the neck that he cut his head clean from his shoulders'.

Having chosen this story, Shakespeare started boldly by relocating its action in contemporary Europe. His Hamlet revenges his father's murder, by killing the uncle who is his mother's new husband, but he is not a pagan barbarian: he is a prince of Shakespeare's own times, university educated, skilled at rapier and dagger, brilliant in speech, knowledgeable in many subjects, an enthusiastic amateur of the arts, a sceptic in thought, a person capable of tenderness as well as fury, and quick to recognize faults in himself as well as in others. Ophelia speaks of him as the epitome of renaissance nobility:

> The courtier's, soldier's, scholar's, eye, tongue, sword,
> The expectancy and rose of the fair state,
> The glass of fashion and the mould of form . . .   (III.i.153–5)

But the pre-Christian and brutal revenger is still present within this paragon and at times takes command to unexpected and dangerous effect.

If we discount the familiarity of its words and respond to the confidence of its metre and phrasing, Hamlet's soliloquy on the way to visit his mother after his uncle's guilt has been confirmed, is both brutal and frightening, the pagan source coming to the surface intermingled with Christian superstition. Hamlet imagines a hellish corruption spreading over the earth:

> 'Tis now the very witching time of night,
> When churchyards yawn and hell itself breathes out
> Contagion to this world. Now could I drink hot blood,
> And do such bitter business that the day
> Would quake to look on.   (III.ii.379–83)

Disease, darkness, and graves all contribute to the horror of this crisis and yet the nightmare and infection are as real as it is to *breathe* or *yawn*. Hamlet speaks of *hot* blood, presumably fresh from an open wound, and imagines that he *drinks* it. He is then ready for action – *business* implying a clear and practical purpose – that would disturb the most basic of natural processes as if it were an earthquake.

Much simpler words follow – 'Soft, now to my mother / O heart, lose not thy nature' – expressing a gentleness that is a third element in Hamlet's make-up that neither comes from the pagan source nor is at all usual in depiction of renaissance heroes. He generously welcomes his fellow students and his 'good friends', the players, to the palace. In excusing her son's fury at Ophelia's grave, Gertrude associates him with the bird of peace caring for its offspring:

> Anon, as patient as the female dove
> When that her golden couplets are disclosed,
> His silence will sit drooping.   (V.i.279–83)

At Hamlet's death, Horatio bids 'Good night, sweet prince' (V.ii.364). Even his enemy, Claudius, acknowledges the 'great love' that ordinary Danes feel towards him, 'dipping all his faults in their affection' (IV.vii.18–19).

The mixture of compulsive brutality, courtly accomplishment, and gentle temperament is responsible for some of the tragedy's most characteristic and disturbing effects. Any actor of Hamlet must be able to manage great shifts of emotion. Having remembered his mother with natural affection, he must proceed immediately to think of the matricide of Nero, the Roman Emperor who was said to have cut open his mother's womb to see where she had given him birth (III.ii.384–6). Having greeted the actors cordially, he calls for a favourite speech that deals, as we have seen, 'with blood of fathers, mothers, daughters, sons' and, shortly after this, imagines himself 'fatten[ing] all the region kites' with his uncle's 'offal' (ll. 575–6). Having recognized the 'fair Ophelia', called her a 'nymph', and spoken 'humbly' to her, he must, immediately afterwards, renounce his love, question her honesty, and brutally deride her. As for himself:

> . . . it were better my mother had not borne me. I am very proud, revengeful, ambitious, with more offences at my beck than I have thoughts to put them in, imagination to give them shape, or time to act them in.   (III.i.123–7)

Elsinore, the setting of this tragedy, also has a double face. While the play reproduces many of the formalities and civilities of life at the court of Elizabeth and in the great houses of that time, this well-presented corporate world is hugely flawed, threatened by passions and impulses that have no part in the business of everyday life. A 'dram of evil', or a 'canker', grows under the surface that can overwhelm the 'noble substance' and acceptable 'nature' of society (I.iv.36–8 and V.ii.69–70). Corruption and political unrest are pervasive and affect the very fabric of this world. People are on edge, alert to differences of status and engaged in power-play. When the soldiers on the battlements see the Ghost, they know at once that 'There is something rotten in the state of Denmark' (I.v.90). In the first court scene, Claudius introduces Gertrude as his wife with bland words despite the fact that, without special dispensation, marriage with a brother's wife was considered incestuous throughout Christendom to whose God he will later pray. The new king pretends that all is well, speaking as if 'With mirth in funeral and with dirge in marriage' (l. 12), when shortly afterwards he acknowledges that war threatens his country and ambassadors must be hastily despatched. The court listens and watches this public presentation, alert to its importance (see pp. 43–6, above) but remaining silent, unless directly addressed. In the more domestic context of the following scene, Laertes is suspicious of his sister, Ophelia, while their father, Polonius, is suspicious of both daughter and son. At the end of the first Act, before a gap of some weeks in the play's narrative, Hamlet himself nails down the danger and recognizes that it is his task to deal with it:

> The time is out of joint. O cursed spite,
> That ever I was born to set it right.   (I.v.197–8)

Political unrest is felt throughout the court long before its causes are fully revealed or its effects become unavoidably apparent.

At a performance of *Julius Caesar*, an audience is unsettled as politicians state their differences and their rivalries are played out on stage but, in watching *Hamlet*, its members will have to watch closely to catch the dangers in what is unspoken or only hinted at in words and actions. Spectators are drawn into the action on stage as they probe for themselves, as Hamlet does, in order to get closer to the truth. As the tragedy draws near its conclusion in a graveyard, Hamlet describes the 'drossy age' in which a politician would 'circumvent God', a flattering courtier praise a lord's horse 'when he meant to beg it', and a lawyer use 'his tricks' to convey land to his own use:

> The age is grown so picked that the toe of the peasant comes so near
> the heel of the courtier he galls his kibe.   (V.i.76–137)

By the end of the tragedy, a whole way of life has been stripped bare and purposes are no longer mistaken. When Claudius calls on his 'friends' to defend him and claims that he is 'but hurt', Hamlet speaks with bitter passion and ruthless clarity, as he thrusts the poison intended for himself down the king's own throat:

> Here, thou incestuous, murd'rous, damned Dane,
> Drink off this potion. Is thy union here?
> Follow my mother.   (V.ii.329–32)

Innate barbarism co-exists here with civilized complexity and helps to destroy a corrupt power in a diseased society. Immediately after this, Hamlet changes back into the contemporary prince and politician; his next thoughts are about making his motives clear and ensuring the continued safety of Denmark. Shakespeare had found a way of representing a far subtler range of thoughts than he had before and feelings of dangerous force as well as great tenderness.

Intellectual Energies

Shakespeare made Hamlet a scholar, as well as courtier and soldier, and modern scholars have identified words or phrases that might have been taken, at first or second hand, from numerous learned writers, including Cicero, Apuleius, Plutarch, St Augustine, Erasmus, Stefano Guazzo, Geronimo Cardano, Michel Montaigne,

Timothy Bright, Thomas Nashe. Such a list can be neither complete nor unquestionable because the ideas expressed in *Hamlet* can be found at all hands among the most imaginative and thoughtful writers of the age. In England, Spenser, Donne, Raleigh, Marlowe, Jonson, Chapman all expressed similar ideas about matters of life and death, knowledge and uncertainty, society and the individual, fate and freewill, the earth and the sky above. They call on the same mythological persons and heroes: Jove, Mercury, Hyperion, Mars, Vulcan; Niobe, Damon, Priam, Hecuba, Aeneas, Dido, Caesar, Alexander, Roscius; Nemean lion and Hyrcanian tiger. Even more than most plays by Shakespeare, *The Tragedy of Hamlet, Prince of Denmark* belongs to a widespread interchange of ideas that might be called the great conversation of Renaissance culture, and has a hero who is exceptionally at ease in taking advantage of its eloquence.

In many texts by Shakespeare's contemporaries, quotations from earlier authorities stand out clearly, speaking in their own distinctive idioms; sometimes they are printed in italics or with other marks of quotation. In *Hamlet*, too, some sentences announce themselves as axioms or authoritative borrowings, although not often when Hamlet is speaking; Claudius and Polonius are more given to this kind of effect. But most quotations have been so re-thought that specific debts can seldom be identified; they seem to arise from the necessities of action and character, coloured and shaped as appropriate to the very moment. No 'handfuls' of wise sayings are to be found here; rather a quick interplay of individual thought and feeling.

The extensive reading in philosophy, morals, psychology, and politics that went into the writing of *Hamlet* was joined by quite different material from another and still more important source: a life-experience that was strongly sensuous and conscious of all manner of differences between people and within individuals. By drawing upon this, the play often gives an impression of life being lived, and this is one of the prime reasons why it was not only a highly sophisticated tragedy but also a most popular entertainment. In performance, speeches which require years of study to annotate – and then incompletely – are able to engage almost any hearer as an image or reflection of how men and women actually live and speak.

Of Hamlet's talk with Rosencrantz and Guildenstern in Act II, scene ii, much could be found in learned books: that Denmark is a prison might have come from Timothy Bright's *Treatise on Melancholy*, a book Shakespeare was almost certainly reading at the time:

> The house, except it be cheerful and lightsome, trim and neat, seemeth unto the melancholic a prison or dungeon.

In his *Essays* Montaigne had asserted that 'The taste of goods and evils doth greatly depend on the opinion we have of them.' In *Hamlet* these ideas become part of the prince's probing of his two supposed 'friends', each turn of the dialogue adjusted to an uncertain relationship and the desire that each has to hear more than is actually spoken:

Hamlet.	What have you, my good friends, deserved at the hands of fortune that she sends you to prison hither?
Guildenstern.	Prison, my lord?
Hamlet.	Denmark's a prison.
Rosencrantz.	Then is the world one.
Hamlet.	A goodly one, in which there are many confines, wards, and dungeons, Denmark being one o'th'worst.
Rosencrantz.	We think not so, my lord.
Hamlet.	Why, then 'tis none to you; for there is nothing either good or bad but thinking makes it so. To me it is a prison. . . . (II.ii.239–51)

When these persons manoeuvre around each other as the changing rhythms of their speeches suggest, repeating the same words and therefore watching each other closely, this talk is a game worth the watching, as well as hearing.

Similarly, Hamlet's soliloquies are packed with ideas and arguments, but these are not merely marshalled in words: the texts also imply that his mind hesitates, rushes forward, gathers strength, comes to a full stop, contradicts itself. By speaking the words, an actor becomes involved in the entire process of thought, feeling, and utterance, activity which inevitably engages his body as well as his mind. The process is so energetic and varied that an audience wants, instinctively, to know what is happening to this man. For example, much is verbally difficult and obscure in 'To be or not to be . . .' and occupies long notes in annotated editions and scholarly journals: is Hamlet concerned mostly about taking his own life, or the consequences of dying, or the courage necessary to take action against wrongdoing? Is the argument personal or general? Yet if we consider how this speech works, as opposed to what it unequivocally says, we find that its syntax insists that rhythms are constantly changing, as they build up, delay, and satisfy expectation, and the placing of words, with regard to both syntax and metre, insists that certain emphases are marked. If attention is paid to these practical elements of Shakespeare's writing, a reader will sense something of its varying dynamic, its points of strength or hesitation, its demands on the actor in terms of taking breath and extending or stopping a line of feeling. An actor will give a physical accompaniment to the movement of thought and feeling, occasionally being very still and using the simplest of means, and then moving away in doubt or confident elaboration.

Extensive quotation can illustrate this if, on first reading, time is taken to mark each new verb and to imagine, as fully and precisely as possible, the activity implied in nouns, adjectives, and adverbs. This will be a slow process:

> To be, or not to be, that is the question:
> Whether 'tis nobler in the mind to suffer
> The slings and arrows of outrageous fortune,
> Or to take arms against a sea of troubles
> And by opposing end them. To die – to sleep,
> No more; and by a sleep to say we end
> The heart-ache and the thousand natural shocks
> That flesh is heir to: 'tis a consummation
> Devoutly to be wish'd. To die, to sleep;
> To sleep, perchance to dream – ay, there's the rub:
> For in that sleep of death what dreams may come,
> When we have shuffled off this mortal coil,
> Must give us pause – there's the respect
> That makes calamity of so long life.
> For who would bear the whips and scorns of time,

Th'oppressor's wrong, the proud man's contumely,
The pangs of dispriz'd love, the law's delay,
The insolence of office, and the spurns
That patient merit of th'unworthy takes,
 When he himself might his quietus make
With a bare bodkin? Who would fardels bear,
To grunt and sweat under a weary life,
But that the dread of something after death,
The undiscover'd country, from whose bourn
No traveller returns, puzzles the will,
And makes us rather bear those ills we have
Than fly to others that we know not of? . . .   (III.i.56ff.)

Richard III's soliloquy on waking from his nightmare, Richard II's in Pomfret prison, and the deliberations of Brutus, all have some of the same qualities, but with Hamlet they are greatly developed and the basis for highly innovative elements in Shakespeare's writing for performance. Hamlet's mind travels widely across possibilities of both thought and action, draws in examples that go beyond his own first-hand experience, speaks with feelings that range between the bold and terrified, only momentarily standing still. He leaves an audience to make what it can of what he says and yet this does not leave his hearers behind: the soliloquy was written with such confidence that he seems fully committed to what is happening in his very being, even when in doubt and uncertainty, and so an audience travels with him willingly.

A confident dynamic is only part of the achievement. What Hamlet says relates the most complex ideas to practical images and so awakens everyday responses that appeal to a listener at a sensuous, as opposed to an intellectual, level. The verbs are either very simple or imply activity which any person can recognize. In the lines quoted, besides the verb *to be*, are found *suffer*, *take* (twice), *oppose*, *die* and *sleep* (several times), *say*, *end*, *wish*, *dream*, *come*, *shuffle*, *give*, *make* (several times), *bear* (twice), *grunt*, *sweat*, *return*, *puzzle*, *have*, *fly*, *know*. Some words relating to intellectual concepts are not at all easy to formulate – *question*, *noble*, *mind*, *fortune*, *consummation*, *devoutly*, *perchance*, *respect*, *contumely*, *unworthy* – but the majority of nouns relate to very tangible or everyday matters: *slings*, *arrows*, *arms, sea, sleep, heart-ache, shocks, flesh, heir, rub, death, dream, life, whips, scorns, time, wrong, pangs, law, delay, insolence, office, spurns, bodkin.* Much that is difficult or unexpected implies activity that is drawn from familiar and ordinary experiences: 'take arms against a sea of troubles', 'shuffled off this mortal coil', 'his quietus make / With a bare bodkin', 'grunt and sweat under a weary life'. A listener is conducted on firm stepping stones through the flooding words that seem to bring to the stage a person alive in his body and sensations, as well as in what he is saying and thinking.

The Ghost

A dramatist wishing to give credibility to a supernatural being would be well advised to decide on one particular kind of apparition and keep to that. Shakespeare, however, did not: the Ghost of Hamlet is of mixed pedigree and has a varying reality. It calls for revenge in the manner of the Senecan revenge plays of the time, but a 'martial stalk' and 'majestical' presence (I.i.66, 143) differentiate it from many others including the Ghost of the *Ur-Hamlet*. The Ghost of Julius Caesar in Shakespeare's previous tragedy is a likely source for Hamlet's continuing suspicion that his father's ghost might be an emanation of his own melancholy and not a supernatural being. Horatio, too, believes, at first, that the 'thing' seen on the battlements is 'but our fantasy' (I.i.24–6). In Plutarch's *Life of Caesar* Shakespeare would have read Cassius's long discourse to Brutus on this Epicurean view of ghostly appearances:

> Our senses being credulous, and therefore easily abused (when they are idle and unoccupied in their own objects), are induced to imagine they see and conjecture that which they in truth do not. . . . You being by nature given to melancholic discoursing and of late continually occupied, your wits and senses having been overlaboured, do easilier yield to such imaginations. For, to say that there are spirits or angels and, if there were, that they had the shape of men, or such voices, or any power at all to come unto us: it is a mockery.

In Shakespeare's play Caesar's Ghost announces itself as the 'evil spirit' of Brutus, another idea to which Hamlet alludes at the same time as he blames his melanchoy for the apparition:

> The spirit that I have seen
> May be a devil, and the devil hath power
> T'assume a pleasing shape, yea, and perhaps,
> Out of my weakness and my melancholy,
> As he is very potent with such spirits,
> Abuses me to damn me.   (II.ii.594–9)

Shakespeare is also indebted here to the protestant belief that no soul could ever return from the grave and that, therefore, all supposed ghosts were truly evil spirits or devils who are attempting to entrap mortals into their power. As Hamlet will later imagine graves opening and evil let loose on the world (see above, p. 137), on first seeing the Ghost, he cries out:

> Angels and ministers of grace defend us!
> Be thou a spirit of health or goblin damn'd,
> Bring with thee airs from heaven or blasts from hell,
> Be thy intents wicked or charitable,
> Thou com'st in such a questionable shape
> That I will speak to thee. I'll call thee Hamlet, . . .   (I.iv.39– 56)

Immediately after the Ghost has left the stage, Hamlet still does not know whether it has emanated from heaven or hell (see I.v.92–3) and, until he has other proof of Claudius's guilt, he remains ready to believe 'it is a damnéd ghost that we have seen' (III.ii.83).

The Ghost itself speaks of returning to purgatory (see I.v.10–13) and Hamlet at one time insists that it is 'an honest ghost' (I.v.144), but its exact nature is repeatedly called in question so that individual members of an audience are able to find their own opinion about the existence of ghosts reflected somewhere in the play and share Hamlet's perplexity. For him, what carries most conviction is the Ghost's likeness to his father and the closeness of what it says to his own thoughts. Immediately on seeing it, he promises, 'I'll call thee Hamlet / King, father, royal Dane' (I.v.92–3) and, on being told that his uncle had killed his father, he cries out 'O my prophetic soul! (I.v.41) as if he had known that already. Whenever the Ghost speaks, Hamlet is held gripped in silent attention and, once it has gone, he is transformed, weak in 'sinews' and emphatically accepting all that he has heard. His imagination has been so roused that the sheer energy of his speech, emotions, and action can communicate his conviction to an audience whatever its beliefs about ghosts. On this imaginative level, within Hamlet himself, the Ghost is most effective and its reality without question; and it is from here that the action of the tragedy springs.

In Act III the Ghost is presented differently. On this occasion, nothing that it says or does implies that it is other than a figment of Hamlet's imagination. Appearing now inside the palace of Elsinore, it is unseen by Gertrude, one of the two persons present. While Hamlet calls for 'heavenly guards', as if he needed protection from an evil presence, he speaks at once to its 'gracious figure' (III.iv.104–5) and thinks he knows what it will say. All Shakespeare's earlier ghosts are all present, either in dream or imagination, as the plays draw towards their close, but this one does not appear after Act III and no one makes further reference to it. Members of an audience no longer need to be reminded of the ghost and his message because they have been led to share in the working of Hamlet's consciousness which can now supply all that the Ghost had stood for. Once its narrative is fully under way, at the centre of the experience this tragedy offers is not an extra-terrestial intervention, but the thoughts and feelings of a troubled and mortal individual.

The Christian Context

With a play in which so much is open to speculation, it is not surprising to find that some elements require a more single-minded response. The force of one of these stabilizing factors has been greatly diminished by the end of the twentieth century when a large percentage of most audiences will be unfamiliar with church worship and the words of the Bible. For Shakespeare's contemporaries, however, a Christian context would have been unmistakably established at the very beginning of *Hamlet* when the Ghost fades 'on the crowing of the cock' and Marcellus remarks:

> Some say that ever 'gainst that season comes
> Wherein our Saviour's birth is celebrated,
> This bird of dawning singeth all night long;
> And then, they say, no spirit dare stir abroad,
> The nights are wholesome, then no planets strike,
> No fairy takes, nor witch hath power to charm,
> So hallow'd and so gracious is that time.   (I.i.163–9)

This speech signals belief in divine intervention in human affairs and the natural world and, more particularly, mankind's need for a Saviour, all of which is at odds with Hamlet's subsequent acceptance of the duty of revenging his father's death. The Christian God could do whatever he deemed necessary for his people, as St Paul's Epistle to the Romans stated unequivocally:

> Recompense to no man evil for evil. . . . Dearly beloved, avenge not yourselves, but rather give place unto wrath; for it is written, Vengeance is mine, I will repay saith the Lord.   (XII, 17, 29)

If Marcellus's disquisition on the crowing cock stays in the minds of some members of an audience, it will have a major effect on their response to the tragedy. Its allusions to Christ's incarnation, St Peter's denial of him before the crucifixion, and Christian doctrines of sin and responsibility are all at odds with Hamlet's quest for revenge. The effect might be to distance the play from their own lives, freeing them to follow its story as if it were entirely fictional and to experience thoughts and feelings from which they customarily turned away. For others in an early seventeenth-century audience, a memory of this speech might make them actively hostile to the play's hero so that they see his death as a judgement on what he has done. But this clearly placed Christian marker is never brought into plain and unavoidable relation to Hamlet's role as a revenger and so these orthodox Christian reactions are not actively encouraged. While Hamlet accepts that the Ghost might be from either heaven or hell, he never argues whether revenge, in itself, is either right or wrong.

Later references to Christian thought and feeling are either less specific or relate to offices of the church that customarily attended on birth, marriage, and death. Hamlet knows that 'the Everlasting' had 'fix'd / His canon 'gainst self-slaughter' and had given mankind the 'discourse of reason' (I.ii.131–2, 150); he speaks of 'angels' and 'heavenly guards' (I.iv.38; III.iv.104–5); he knows that his sins should be remembered in prayers (III.i.89–90). The Ghost speaks of 'sulph'rous and tormenting flames' that punish those who die 'Unhousel'd, disappointed, unanel'd', with no time to make a proper reckoning for their 'imperfections' (I.v.3, 76–9). Claudius asks angels for help as he acknowledges that, like Cain, he has slain his brother; and he knows that there is mercy 'in the sweet heavens', that can wash sins 'white as snow' (III.iii.36–7, 43–51). Encountering him at prayer, Hamlet is not reminded that revenge is wrong, but decides that to kill his uncle now would not be punishment enough since he would die forgiven by God and go to heaven (see III.iii.73–95). When he has killed Polonius, thrusting at him unseen behind an arras, he sees himself as 'Heaven's scourge and minister', as if his violent and instinctive reaction had been in accordance with God's will (III.iv.174–7). Such references, together with various calls upon 'God' or 'Heavenly powers', remind an audience of secure moral judgements that call for repentance and mercy or for punishment. They also awaken a sense that every event is part of some larger scheme in which all things work together for the best of purposes. They mark the play as contemporary, not belonging to a pre-Christian Denmark, and ensure that Hamlet's progress in revenge does not remove him entirely from customary judgements, even though he believes he could 'drink hot blood' and envisions evil spreading throughout the world. By avoiding the crucial argument that God is the only appropriate avenger, Shakespeare has presented a hero who is compelled instinctively to seek and exact revenge and yet lives in a world created by an all-seeing, all-powerful, and merciful God.

As the tragedy draws to its close the Christian references change in kind: less is heard of angels, hell, or purgatorial torments but more of pilgrimage, prayer, personal responsibility, and providence. The procession led by a priest that brings Ophelia's coffin, with 'bell and burial', to the graveside introduces familiar signs of Christian mourning and the 'service of the dead' that would be known to all

members of the play's first audiences, varied in form according to
their own place in society (V.i.229–31). At this point, however, all
expectation is disrupted when Laertes jumps into the open grave and
Hamlet follows him: while the two fight with each other, good order
is threatened and Christian procedures forgotten until Claudius
commands, 'Pluck them asunder'. A clearer influence of the barbaric
source of the story could hardly be imagined and yet, since no
Laertes-figure was in any of the three early versions, the fight is
entirely Shakespeare's own invention and a reminder that this
tragedy is concerned with instincts and passions that lie outside the
certainties and customs of Christian society.

The Christian context is again affirmed when Hamlet, near the
beginning of the last scene, quotes from St Matthew's Gospel (X, 29
and XXIX, 44) and alludes to St Luke's (XII, 40). By claiming a
'special [or particular] providence in the fall of sparrow' and
requiring a 'readiness' for death (V.ii.215–18), Hamlet does not
stress the necessity of repentance and purification at the moment of
death but, rather, that whatever happens in life should be accepted
as God's will and that, consequently, death should not be feared.
This was a familiar wisdom, deriving from many sources besides
holy writ, but the effect of quoting the Gospels so very closely and
immediately before the deaths at the end of the play will be similar
to the effect of the cock-crowing at the beginning: a means of suggesting another standard of judgement than those insisted upon in
the main action and its final outcome. They do not, however, deflect
Hamlet from revenge and he turns away from these thoughts with a
dismissive 'Let be' (l. 220).

The last Christian reference is still less specific:

> Good night, sweet prince,
> And flights of angels sing thee to thy rest.					(V.ii.364)

Such a prayer is unexpected coming from Horatio, who had only
half-believed Marcellus's account of the Christmas legend (see
I.i.170), and its mood is broken immediately with drums sounding
off-stage and Fortinbras's entry to take command supported by his
army. The momentary religious recognition is again overwhelmed by

the on-going action and by quite other political concerns. This tragedy does not insist on Christian judgements, but it does bring them into the reckoning and leaves an audience to make what it will of them. The most certain consequence of these comparatively fixed and clearly defined ideas is to emphasize, by contrast, the instinctive passions and fears and the political uncertainties that drive the story and grow to unmistakable and dangerous prominence.

Personal Contexts

For Ophelia's madness that follows Hamlet's rejection of their love and her father's death, the flowers, language, and customs of rural England make an unexpected entrance into both dialogue and action that creates a new context and draws upon other sources that are outside the parameters of the main story: On her first reappearance, she sings about simple and natural objects: 'grass-green turf', 'a stone', 'mountain snow', 'sweet flowers', and 'showers', together with a tale of a maid and her valentine (IV.v.23–73). The formality of music ensures that these new elements register clearly and evoke a rural and independent context of their own. On her second reappearance, Ophelia holds flowers in her hands and distributes them to the king and queen and her brother, choosing, naming, and presenting each one with deliberate care. This time she sings about a simple funeral and, in the words of a very popular ballad, declares that 'Bonny sweet Robin is all my joy.' She leaves with a prayer that is very specifically Christian and generally relevant: 'God a' mercy on his soul, / And of all Christian souls' (IV.v.164–97). These simple pieties and unaffected signs of tenderness, often thought to be appropriate to a simple rural life, have unmistakable influence on a scene in which major disasters threaten and no one can alleviate the suffering of this unwilling victim of Hamlet's actions. Later, when Gertrude enters to announce Ophelia's death by drowning, her careful, sensuous, wondering, and, to some extent, wandering description expresses her feelings of regret and tenderness in a form that encourages all hearers on stage and in the audience to attend to each detail and so share in the sights that she is reporting. Here

Christian references have all but disappeared and so has any offer of consolation.

In today's urban society it is hard to assess what effect these pastoral intrusions into the courtly and political world of Elsinore were intended to have. Modern nostalgia for a lost world can envelop them in pathos and generalities that displace any more thoughtful response. That is almost certainly inappropriate because their 'favour and prettiness' are the very qualities that Laertes takes as an expression of 'Thought and affliction, passion, hell itself' (IV.v.183–4). What seems undoubted is that, for Ophelia's suffering, Shakespeare filled an audience's ears with words that awaken visual images and, perhaps, personal memories that belong to the simplest of lives and the alternations of seasons, as if here could be found feelings appropriate for the loss of this young and bewildered life. The contrast with images and actions belonging to the passions, deceptions, and political purposes of the conclusion to the tragedy could scarcely be greater.

With the two clowns of the first scene of Act V and the earth that is being prepared for Ophelia's grave, rural England is again brought to the stage, but without either innocence or prettiness. Now, a blunt, tortuously slow, and tediously self-congratulatory humour takes over, and the songs are more egotistical and death-oriented. The effect on the play as a whole is rather more sure, however, because Hamlet enters, as if by accident, at this very place, and talks with a gravedigger who had started his labours, as if by accident, on the very day that Hamlet was born. As if by accident, too, the clown picks up what he says is Yorrick's skull and hands it to the prince who remembers how he used to ride upon the shoulders of this fool, the King's jester, and how he would kiss his lips, 'I know not how oft' (V.i.174–83). When Hamlet proceeds to comment to Horatio, 'To what base uses we may return' (l. 196), he cues members of an audience to see the tragic hero as one who will, in due time, lie in a grave, as they themselves are also bound to do. The effect of introducing these common and obvious considerations is heightened because the scene takes place outside the palace of Elsinore and Hamlet is not dressed as a prince: with his 'sea-gown scarfed' about him, he is incognito and no throne or courtly paraphernalia marks the centre of power and the advantages of wealth and influence.

The country gravedigger, Gertrude's strewing of flowers on Ophelia's grave, and Ophelia's flowers and country songs have moved the setting for this tragedy to a place that is widely known and does not recognize anyone's inherited power or lasting importance. If any memory of these scenes lingers in the minds of an audience, Hamlet's recognition of a silence in death – 'The rest is silence' (V.ii.363) – may provide, at the very last moment, some comparable simplicity to awaken such thoughts again and, in doing so, greatly complicate the audience's response to all that has happened. Overall, the effect on an audience is to bring the play and its hero closer to its own experience and to set its own memories to work as it follows the action.

The arrival at Elsinore of 'The Tragedians of the City' to perform at court is, like the introduction of Christian thought, very unambiguous in its basic effect on an audience although the consequences of introducing these actors into the play may be more difficult to assess. Their professionalism and performative skills accentuate excitement, intensity of feeling, and intentional deception and, as Shakespeare's addition to any story of Hamlet that he might have read, they bring with them observations drawn from his own experience as an actor and company member. Besides performing a play, the actors contact the hero very intimately, drawing from him feelings and thoughts that might otherwise have remained hidden and yet seem to be entirely his own. One effect is to impel Hamlet towards action at a time when he has failed to say or do anything that would bring him nearer to fulfilling the Ghost's demands. So close and crucial is the players' relationship to Hamlet, that a fuller account of their contribution must follow an attempt to understand the play's structure and story.

One other context for this tragedy must be mentioned even though almost nothing can be known about it and nothing certain can be deduced about its effect. Anne and William Shakespeare's only son, the twin of a second daughter, was baptised on 2 February 1585 and named Hamnet, a form of Hamlet then current in England. His name alone would bring this boy to his father's mind when writing about another Hamlet, but the fact that he had died at the age of eleven and a half, being buried at Stratford on 11 August

1596, must have brought the memory of his living presence and the shattered promise of his life into Shakespeare's conscious and unconscious mind as he wrote some four or five years later. Any treatment of a father's love and any suggestion of bereavement or loss of innocence is likely to have been keenly felt and, perhaps, not fully expressed.

9

Hamlet II: Stage Action and Audience Reaction

The signals that *Hamlet* gives to an audience are drawn from many sources and their messages are often very different in both kind and implication. While the political debates and personal motivations of *Julius Caesar* unsettle its audiences, uncertainties permeate every part of this tragedy. Its story is, however, more straightforward because its main development is centred firmly on a single character. In a series of varied incidents that repeatedly grip and hold attention, the narrative interest has proved so irresistible that over the centuries Hamlet's story has been told again many times over in many languages, in plays by other authors and in poetry, fiction, dance, opera, film, and television. Interpretations change with every retelling but not the story's ability to hold attention by means of its personal encounters and soliloquies, its formal set-pieces, unexpected developments, and unsolved mysteries. The tragedy's other enduring attraction has been its titular hero of such energy in thought and feeling that he seems to possess fresh life in every situation that the story yields and in contact with a wide variety of other persons. Continually, he shows new resources and yet remains the same questing, questioning, and responsive person. Both hero and story speak to an audience's instincts, quite as much as to its rational understanding, and draw upon the furthest reaches of an actor's imagination. To understand how this tragedy works in performance, we should hesitate to pin down particular meanings to words and actions before paying attention to the unfolding of the story and the changing involvement of an audience.

The Texts

The tragedy has survived in three different versions. Scholarly judgement is reasonably secure regarding the authority of the two earliest editions in Quarto format, dated 1603 and 1604–5, The first, Q1, was printed from a shortened and defective acting version that had probably been dictated to a scribe by an actor who had played Marcellus and Lucianus; it has much that makes little or no sense and some glaring omissions. The second Quarto, Q2, is obviously the better text and also the more complete, with nearly 3800 lines of type compared with some 2200 in Q1. Numerous features indicate that Q2 was set, although not very well, from a manuscript in Shakespeare's own handwriting. The presence of some first thoughts alongside their revisions, together with inconsistencies in speech prefixes and inadequate stage directions, indicate that this was a draft rather than a finished version. As a printer's copy, the manuscript was hard to read and the compositors sometimes turned for assistance to a copy of Q1, especially during the first Act.

The version published in the collected Folio edition of Shakespeare's plays of 1623 has many variants from Q2 and is some 230 lines shorter. Its compositors seem to have worked from another manuscript in Shakespeare's hand of a later date than the one used for Q2. The authority of the Folio text is compromised, however, because of the occasional reference that was made to Q2 and the probability that non-authorial changes had been introduced into the manuscript. Its printing took place seven years after the author's death and some twenty after he had written the manuscript used for Q2, time enough for any copy in possession of the players to be altered by other hands; authorship was not so respected in those days that changes could not be made solely for the benefit of the players, with or without the author's consent. These circumstances greatly complicate the authority of the Folio text which might otherwise have taken precedence over Q2 in all respects.

Some recent editors have taken a simple line and preferred the Folio wherever possible. They have banished Q's extra 230 lines from their editions and accepted many readings that almost all earlier editors had rejected. This policy has two great difficulties. Most important, from a structural and thematic view, is the deletion of the entry for Hamlet on his way to embark for England in Act IV, scene iv, which entails omitting a major soliloquy and having Fortinbras speak only seven and a half lines on his first appearance with little more than his name to individualize him. Such drastic economy for the only earlier entrance of a person who plays a signif-icant part in the conclusion of a play is found nowhere else in Shakespeare's plays. In Q2, Fortinbras leaves the stage at the same time as in the Folio, but a Captain remains to identify him and explain what has been happening. Moreover, Fortinbras continues to influence the scene until the end because it is his presence that gives rise to Hamlet's subsequent soliloquy in which, for the first time, he considers his own calling as a prince and the nature of greatness. It has been argued that Shakespeare was responsible for all the major cuts in the Folio because they were made paying respect to the meter and keeping the sense sufficiently clear, but little skill is required to place two half lines together or make a cut at the end of a line, and still less to stop a scene before very much has happened. Besides, the Folio's excisions often leave curious jumps in rhythm, imagery, or line of thought, that do not suggest an author's hand since he would have had no need to patch up the dialogue when he could have re-written to size, as many authors have done. The seventy lines that the Folio supplies that are not in Q2 are not affected by the authority of the cuts: many of these are obviously authoritative. One passage missing in Q2 appears to have been an accidental omission or due to an oddity in the copy (see, below, p. 181); two may have been deliberate omissions.

This is not the place for a detailed discussion of the authority of these two texts, but controversy about them is very active and has such an impact on any critical assessment of the play that the posi-tion from which this study has been made must be stated clearly at the start to avoid repetition or later confusion. I have accepted that Q2 was set from Shakespeare's autograph before it had been pre-

pared for performance and that the Folio was set from a later autograph that contained many corrections and changes and also various
notes and additions made by a book-keeper in the playhouse. I
doubt that Shakespeare was responsible for the Folio's major deletions; even if they were his, I assume that the text could have been
cut down to a more manageable length to please the acting company
rather than to satisfy his own ideas of what his play should be. I also
doubt whether Shakespeare was responsible for those additions in
the Folio which involve only a few words of little consequence: I
take these to represent the ad libbing of actors that a book-keeper
noted in the manuscript for his own purposes; as such they are inter-
esting indications of acting style rather than authoritative additions
to the text.

The Unfolding Narrative

Act I

Battlements, a bitterly cold night, a clock striking twelve, challenges,
recognitions, and worried consultations, voicing scepticism about a
ghost, all silenced by the entry of a commanding figure in complete
armour: these details from the first scene of *Hamlet* have become
clichés for dramatists, story-tellers, poets, and film-makers. When
first invented, their effect on an audience might well have been to
'harrow it with fear and wonder', as it does Horatio, Hamlet's sceptical fellow scholar from university, and even now, whenever clarity
is given to each moment in performance, this opening casts a spell
and starts the play's action in a context that extends beyond the
bounds of ordinary time and place. As the eye-witnesses go off to
seek 'young Hamlet' (I.i.178), the focus of interest narrows and
preparation for the hero's entrance is almost complete.

Throughout the first Act, Hamlet is a prince of a 'warlike state'
whose father, the king, has recently died and whose mother is now
married to the father's brother, Claudius, who has succeeded to the
throne. By the end of the Act, Hamlet has heard from his father's
ghost that he had been killed by this uncle who now 'wears the crown'.
The Act climaxes slowly towards this message – its appeal forceful and

composed; its pain precisely felt – and then the action moves rapidly forward with Hamlet's impassioned and convinced response. He acts now with an impulsive and almost crazed violence, deciding to obey the Ghost and revenge the 'foul and most unnatural murder' (I.v.25, etc.) and to hide his intention by a pretence of madness.

Within these over-arching concerns, further particular matters are also presented, in the more usual setting of a king's court. Hamlet is silent when he is first seen while his uncle's adroitly political address concerning his marriage holds attention (see Plate 4). Only after Ambassadors have been despatched to Norway, and Laertes, son of the counsellor, Polonius, has been given leave to go to France, is Hamlet drawn into public notice by first answering Claudius and then responding to his mother. When everyone else leaves the stage to celebrate the marriage, Hamlet alone remains and the first of a series of soliloquies follows. Its words are driven by strong emotion and vivid memories as he speaks of suicide, all that is 'gross' and rotting in the world, his mother's remarriage, and his own inability to speak from his heart. He stops abruptly as other people are approaching: the news they bring makes him decide to seek his father's 'spirit in arms' the next night (I.ii.255) (see Plate 5).

Before that happens, Laertes is seen saying farewell to his sister and urging her to write. After only four lines, he raises an entirely new issue:

> *Laertes.* For Hamlet, and the trifling of his favour,
> Hold it a fashion and a toy in blood,
> A violet in the youth of primy nature,
> Forward, not permanent, sweet, not lasting,
> The perfume and suppliance of a minute,
> No more.
> *Ophelia.* No more but so?
> *Laertes.* Think it no more. . . . (I.iii.5–10)

This presents the absent Hamlet in a surprisingly different light: a prince who secretly meets with Ophelia and has convinced her of his affection and love. The play is now in more private territory where secrets must be kept and 'blazes' must not be taken for 'fire' (ll. 117–20). When Polonius enters and takes proprietary charge of

Plate 4

4 and 5   Two contrasting views of *Hamlet*

In his early years as an actor, Gordon Craig had performed *Hamlet* in a number of productions, including one by his own company. After he had given up acting, for directing, design and teaching, the role continued to fascinate him and he made many drawings of it over the years. Plate 4 shows the prince at the beginning of Act I, scene ii, where he is alone among a crowd of courtiers, slouched in a chair and at a distance from the enthroned Claudius and Gertrude. Plate 5 shows him on the battlements in Act I, scene v, ready to meet his father's ghost, still alone but now a commanding and heroic figure. (*These plates are reproduced from a copy of Gordon Craig's* Towards a New Theatre *(1913), in the present author's possession.*)

son and daughter, his disdain for youth and respect for authority, together with his calculation and prurience, are as remarkable as the almost silent submission of Ophelia. Her presence and enigmatic behaviour displace, for a time, the concerns of earlier scenes, even though her belief in Hamlet's tenderness seems to belong to another story and another world.

No Act divisions are marked in the second Quarto, as usual in such texts, and in the Folio only the second Act is marked, which was more unusual, but editors down the centuries have questioned only one of the Act divisions that first appeared in a Quarto of 1679 and are repeated in almost all later editions. By no means equal, either in length or number of scenes, these divisions mark distinct stages in the development and handling of the action.

Act II

The switch in time and place at the beginning of Act II is unex-pected. Several weeks have passed and Polonius is instructing Reynaldo, a confidential servant, to follow Laertes to Paris and put him under private surveillance. Modern productions often cut this episode as unnecessary to the main narrative, but Reynaldo was not cut from either the Folio or the very abbreviated first Quarto (in which he is called Montano). For Shakespeare, and whoever pre-pared his texts for performance, these family concerns and a desire to probe beneath ordinary appearances were a necessary part of the exposition. Moreover, the episode strengthens its argument – what today is called its structural design – by keeping Laertes in mind so that, in the play's last scene, when Hamlet acknowledges in Laertes's 'cause' an 'image' of his own (V.ii.75–8), an audience may better remember him and, perhaps, the constraints the father had put upon this other son out of anxiety for his well-being.

A large part of Act II shows Hamlet with his student friends, Rosencrantz and Guildenstern. In the play as a whole, they stand alongside other young men: Laertes, Horatio and 'young Fortinbras', all helping to define Hamlet by contrast to him, in the same way as the conspirators serve to define each other in *Julius Caesar* (see above, pp. 130–1). In the very last scene this line-up of contempo-raries is joined by 'young Osric' (V.ii.193) who invites Hamlet to a

fencing match with Laertes: despite a 'waterfly' appearance and reputation (V.ii.355), he proves to be mysteriously efficient, superin-
tending the ensuing fight and ensuring that Laertes is in possession
of the poisoned rapier; he also announces Fortinbras's entrance
before anyone else knows about it. For this tragedy, an acting
company must be able to cast seven distinctive young male parts of
which only two can be doubled; all are crucial to the play's action
and together they mark inheritance and the responsibilities of a new
generation as significant concerns in this tragedy. They also serve to
underline Ophelia's isolation among other young persons of a different gender and greater personal freedom.

With Rosencrantz and Guildenstern, 'Being of so young days
brought up with him / And sith so neighbour'd to his youth and
haviour' (II.ii.11–12), Hamlet is instinctively at ease as Claudius had
intended when he hired them to act as informers or spies in the
court. They are told that Hamlet is strangely 'changed', his behaviour and 'understanding' both being transformed, and that their task
is to discover what is the cause of this affliction (II.ii.4–26, 34–7).
Although they fail to hide their mission from their former friend,
they draw Hamlet to speculate and speak his mind more freely than
he does with other persons. He may pretend to be mad, disguising
his true feelings with an 'antic disposition', as he had intended
(I.v.178–80) but, in their company, he often speaks with the accents
of sober and uncensored truth; for example:

> I could be bounded in a nutshell and count myself a king of infinite
> space – were it not that I have bad dreams.   (II.ii.254–6)

When he hears that actors are coming to Elsinore, he anticipates
their arrival eagerly and warmly: and yet here, as elsewhere in talking
to these friends, a bitter irony is also present, since the stage world is
unlike the real world in which intentions are not fulfilled and acceptance not given. Escaping from a duty to set right what is 'out of
joint' (I.v.196–7), Hamlet may be said to have come into his own in
this scene. Affection, frustration, anger, humour, and refinement are
all present as they talk; political cunning and a concern for noble
virtue and true beauty are also unmistakable. In performance, every

actor of the part is able to mark it with his own personal qualities as he gives life to the varied and spirited encounter.

When the Tragedians of the City come on stage, Hamlet welcomes them as his 'good friends' (ll. 417–20) and asks to be entertained with a taste of their quality. Mood, focus of attention, and manner of speech all change decisively when the First Player brings Act II to a climax by performing Aeneas's account of Pyrrhus, a speech that would be hard to equal as a representation of brutal violence and helpless suffering (see pp. 34–5, above). Hamlet's own soliloquy follows in which he elaborates his plan to confirm what the Ghost has told him by confronting Claudius with a play that shows 'something like' the crime that has been alleged; he also condemns his own idleness and ineffectual words. Besides its obvious emotion and eloquence, the player's speech has brought an increased awareness of performance so that, from now on, everything heard or seen is more open to question – including Hamlet's apparent madness and apparent sanity, and also his moments of silence and stillness.

The little said about Ophelia in this scene is largely innuendo at her expense, but earlier, at the opening of the act she had entered, immediately after Reynaldo had left, to tell how Hamlet had come to her closet looking as if he were mad, had stared at her for a long time, and, saying nothing, had left with a sigh that seemed about to 'shatter all his bulk / And end his being' (II.i.94–6). Being questioned, she says she has obeyed instructions and returned all Hamlet's letters and denied all access to him, which immediately leads Polonius to conclude that Hamlet is mad because of frustrated love for his daughter. He orders Ophelia to come with him to the king and, in the next scene, he reads one of the letters to Claudius and Gertrude, including verses that speak of the undying fire of Hamlet's love and claim an absolute truth. Hamlet may have written this letter as evidence of his pretended madness, but an audience can only speculate about its implications because he has still not said a word about his love; it is only after her death that he cries out:

> I lov'd Ophelia. Forty thousand brothers
> Could not with all their quantity of love
> Make up my sum . . .   (V.i.264–5)

Act III

As often in Shakespeare's plays, Act III brings an extended scene that draws all the main narrative lines together, its occasion being the performance of *The Murder of Gonzago* for which Hamlet has written an additional speech by which he hopes to 'unkennel' his uncle's guilt. The stage is once more filled for a royal occasion, probably using the same thrones and attendants that were on display in Act I, scene ii, but this assembly is at Hamlet's request so that he is in charge and his relations to the King, Queen, Polonius, and Ophelia are always part of the public spectacle. As only the second large-scale scene, it marks an important stage in the play's action, but it does not rise to new political business, as the first had done, until the play-within-the-play states personal and political issues with unusual boldness, as if the players were bound to 'tell all' (III.ii.138). The double stage picture of actors and audience is then shattered as the King rises and leaves the stage, calling for lights. The fall-out from this large-scale court scene eventually gives rise to two intimate scenes that complete the Act and take major narrative lines to crucial and intense confrontations.

The third Act has three intense and private scenes that present Hamlet in a series of new guises. The first starts the Act and, at last, brings Hamlet and Ophelia together. After Rosencrantz and Guildenstern have reported on their inconclusive mission, Polonius, with the agreement of Claudius, instructs his daughter to walk while reading a book in a place where Hamlet is bound to encounter her and, as they hear him coming, he and the King withdraw to overhear what happens. The text does not tell us whether Ophelia knows that she is being spied on, but Gertrude has told her, gently:

> I do wish
> That your good beauties be the happy cause
> Of Hamlet's wildness; so shall I hope your virtues
> Will bring him to his wonted way again,
> To both your honours.   (III.i.37–42)

She holds the book of devotions silently as Hamlet enters but the expected encounter does not happen at once. He seems totally rapt

in his own thoughts – 'To be or not to be. . . ' – as if he has forgotten everything else. He soliloquizes in general terms about action
and inaction, life and death, and, only when he has considered
'enterprizes of great pitch and moment' that 'lose the name of action'
(ll. 83–8), does he stop himself with:

> Soft you now,
> The fair Ophelia! Nymph, in thy orisons
> Be all my sins remember'd.   •   (ll. 88–90)

Again Ophelia is associated with beauty and with virtue, as if only
these general characteristics distinguish her from other people and
cause them to make demands upon her. The archaic and poetic associations of *orisons* and of *nymph* (perhaps a salacious tone here as
well) add to the uncertainties of this greeting and yet Ophelia's reply
is simple, respectful, and understanding: 'Good my lord, / How does
you honour for this many a day?' The effect of this on Hamlet may
also sound simple at first – 'I humbly thank you, well' – but these
are not the words of either lover or prince, or of a pretended
madman. The Folio text repeats the 'well' two more times, probably
recording an actor's way of expressing subtextual tension. When
Ophelia offers the gifts she has been told to return, Hamlet abruptly
refuses them, denying that he had ever given them to her, or anything else. Offered them again, he shudders with denial or, perhaps,
incongruously and helplessly laughs, and then challenges her
abruptly: 'Ha, ha! Are you honest?' (l. 103). Over-riding Ophelia's
bewilderment, he either tries to act more obviously mad or is,
indeed, deeply distraught and disturbed:

> Are you fair?
> *What means your lordship?*
> That if you be honest and fair, your honesty should admit no dis-
> course to your beauty.
> *Could beauty, my lord, have better commerce than with honesty?*
> Ay, truly, for the power of beauty will sooner transform honesty from
> what it is to a bawd than the force of honesty can translate beauty into
> his likeness. This was sometime a paradox, but now the time gives it
> proof.   (ll. 105–15)

Then suddenly, with no obvious connection, he adds: 'I did love you once'. To this Ophelia is able to respond more positively – 'Indeed, my lord, you made me believe so' – and, in many performances, both actors or just one of them will mark this recognition with a new tenderness or with passionate physical contact. For the moment all might be well between them.

Hamlet does not or cannot allow mutual understanding to last: he dares not trust her, or trust himself. Disbelief, fear, revulsion, or unappeasable desire – some inexpressible drive – makes him break away and attack the defenceless person who is so close and so open towards him. He denies loving her and dismisses her, villifying himself and the entire world of men (ll. 117–30). Just possibly, Hamlet is again acting madness but, in this long-delayed encounter, what he says has such headlong force and so often switches direction that any performance must, in some way, be deeply passionate and troubled. All his struggle either to hide or to express his feelings will be accentuated by the simplicity of Ophelia's replies and, later, by her steadfast prayers on his behalf when he seems yet more mad and turns to attack her more directly, and every other woman.

A crucial and problematic moment comes when Hamlet suddenly asks 'Where is your father?' Her reply could be either a conscious lie or what she imagines to be the truth: 'At home, my lord.' Why he should ask this question at this particular point is also unclear. Has he seen some sign in Ophelia's behaviour that suggests she is acting under orders in standing where he would meet her? Or has he actu-ally seen that he is being spied upon? Or has he assumed that nothing is likely to be private in Elsinore? If his words are to make consecutive sense in performance, some strong motivation must support the abrupt question and yet Shakespeare has denied any clear indication of what that may be. Perhaps the whole scene should skid around without any constant motor force, almost mindlessly lurid and pun-ishing, in which case Hamlet is a victim as well as Ophelia. By this time, the play is, indisputably, about inexpressible feelings and they are more, not less, powerful for not being defined by words. Hamlet's reply is a blatantly sexual and scornful dismissal of her father, an attack on marriage, and, in conclusion, renewed denunciation of all women and a threat, without naming him, to Claudius's life:

> You jig and amble, and you lisp, you nickname God's creatures, and
> make your wantonness your ignorance. Go to, I'll no more on't, it
> hath made me mad. I say we will have no mo marriage. Those that are
> married already – all but one – shall live; the rest shall keep as they
> are. To a nunnery go.   (III.i.146–52)

This is the fifth time he orders Ophelia to leave, but it is he who
goes, with frightening and, perhaps, frightened speed.

Ophelia stays for a soliloquy that expresses her feelings with
remarkable tenacity. After the praise of Hamlet that has been noted
already (see p. 137, above), she acknowledges her own wretchedness
for losing 'the honey of his music vows' (ll. 152–63) and so invokes
her memory of a Hamlet that an audience has not witnessed.
Speaking so comprehensively and clearly about a loved person
immediately after violent rejection is remarkable by any standards of
theatre or of life: Ophelia has little to say in the entire play, but the
self-control necessary for this sustained expression of her anguish
shows that her love for Hamlet is deeply anchored. Immediately
afterwards, Claudius enters convinced that Hamlet must be sent
'with speed to England': he has recognized that what he heard 'Was
not like madness' (l. 166) and that Hamlet is extremely dangerous.
An audience is more likely to believe that Hamlet is desperately torn
apart by loss of affection and trust, ashamed of his own faults, and
determined to achieve the task he has set himself. To use one of his
earlier phrases, physical contact with Ophelia has 'unkenneled' passionate feelings in Hamlet as nothing else has done, not even his
father's ghost.

Now begins Act III's long, varied, and crowded main scene. At
once Hamlet is very different, smoothly and confidently telling pro-
fessional actors what to do, insisting on the need for order and discretion, no matter how torrential passion may be, and ordering the
clowns not to obscure any 'necessary question of the play'. The First
Player politely insists that this is how they do act and so cues an
audience to realize that Hamlet's advice is applicable to himself: he
longs for perfection and for undivided attention to be paid to necessary judgements. In expressing this, he has caught his balance once
more: no sign of stress is here, but rather an earnest lucidity that sets

him apart from others. He seems to be everywhere: making enquiries and speeding up preparations, privately arranging for Horatio to watch the trap he is setting for Claudius so there will be a less passionately involved response to back his own. Horatio, who has not been seen since Act I, enters so quickly that he appears to have been ready and waiting, Hamlet having planned everything in advance. When the royal party enters, Hamlet assumes an 'idle' madness and in that disguise refuses the Queen's invitation to sit with her and goes to Ophelia whom he taunts with sexually provocative wordplay. His disruptive pretence of being mad stops when the Players enter and an audience, probably with some relief, will switch attention to the Players' Dumb Show. After more interruptions by Hamlet, the deliberate speeches and actions of the play itself take over until the Player-Queen's exit completes its first scene. Before the Player-Lucianus can enter, Hamlet intervenes again and then everything starts to go very wrong. Despite vocal criticism and prompting, Lucianus is soon poisoning the sleeping Player-King which, for Hamlet, is the moment when Claudius must be watched with particular care. When his victim remains silent and, probably, does nothing, Hamlet interrupts yet again, putting into words what the play has already shown and announcing what will happen next:

> A poisons him i'th'garden for his estate. His name's Gonzago. The story is extant, and written in very choice Italian. You shall see anon how the murderer gets the love of Gonzago's wife.   (ll. 255–8)

At this point, Ophelia cries out, 'The King rises', but still he has said nothing. After further silence, during which Hamlet, Gertrude, and Polonius all intervene, Claudius calls for lights and rapidly leaves the stage. In startled commotion (almost totally unrehearsed in an Elizabethan performance and, therefore, more uncertain and chaotic than in our theatres), everyone becomes active and soon all have gone, players as well as members of the court, so that only Horatio and Hamlet are left.

After being the busy manipulator and intrusive interpreter, Hamlet has received his cue for action: he elatedly declaims in verse and asks Horatio if this would not get him a 'fellowship in a cry of players' (ll. 265–72). With 'Half a share' and 'You might have rhymed', Horatio tries to restrain him but action soon presses forward when Hamlet is summoned to the Queen's closet: before he goes, he taunts Rosencrantz and Guildenstern, and then Polonius; and dismisses everyone. Once alone, he proclaims that he 'could drink hot blood' and the barbaric origin of the source-story surfaces, as we have seen in the previous chapter (p. 137).

The main lines of the narrative are now presented more intensely in two scenes that complete the Act and are as tightly focused as its first. Attention switches first to Claudius, still more convinced that Hamlet is dangerous and must be sent away to England. Although he does not say that he means to have him killed when he gets there, that plan is probably already in his mind when he engages Rosencrantz and Guildenstern in Hamlet's journey. Certainly, as he speaks with them and Polonius, other thoughts must be underneath what he says because as soon as he is alone he confesses to the murder of his brother, calling it an offence that 'smells to heaven' (III.iii.36). In a sustained soliloquy, stiff with physical as well as mental or spiritual pressures, he tries to pray and, eventually, falls to his knees. At this very moment Hamlet enters ready to kill him, and an audience unfamiliar with the play will catch its breath until, seeing Claudius in prayer, Hamlet unexpectedly stops and speaks, his sword ready in hand. It would be no revenge, he tells himself, to kill an enemy whose prayers might send him to heaven; he must thwart any possible divine mercy:

> Up, sword, and know thou a more horrid hent:
> When he is drunk asleep, or in his rage,
> Or in th' incestuous pleasure of his bed, . . .   (III.ii.89ff.)

After Hamlet has left to go to his mother, Claudius rises from his knees, admitting that he has been unable to pray.

At the beginning of the Act, Hamlet had been alone with Ophelia and now, at its close, he is alone for the first time with his mother. The meetings could scarcely be more different, for now he scarcely hesitates in what he says or does. When Gertrude thinks he has forgotten who she is and threatens to call for help, he insists:

> You go not till I set you up a glass
> Where you may see the inmost part of you. (III.iv.18–19)

He speaks with such obvious passion that she thinks he is about to murder her and so cries out for help. When Polonius, who is eaves-dropping, echoes her from behind an arras, Hamlet strikes out at once to kill, only afterwards wondering whether it was the King who had called out. Although blood has been violently spilt, Hamlet is not deflected from his purpose but presses forward and verbally attacks his mother for living:

> In the rank sweat of an enseamed bed,
> Stewed in corruption, honeying and making love
> Over the nasty sty. (ll. 92–4)

As he condemns her husband as 'A murderer and a villain. . . . A king of shreds and patches' (ll. 96–103), the Ghost briefly re-appears to 'whet [Hamlet's] almost blunted purpose'. The Queen, not seeing the apparition, thinks her son is mad so that he must again convince her of his sanity before she acknowledges that he has 'cleft [her] heart in twain' (l. 158). She now submits and asks, quite simply, 'What shall I do?' (l. 182). After an appalling battle of words, violent, intimate, sometimes strongly sexual, and accompanied with tears and near-madness, a new and steadily maintained concern for each other brings an acceptance of what has happened and a degree of peace between them. Hamlet is ready to leave:

> Once more, good night,
> And when you are desirous to be blest,
> I'll blessing beg of you.

He also submits to his own fate, accepting both Heaven's judgement and its control over mankind:

> For this same lord
> I do repent; but heaven hath pleas'd it so,
> To punish me with this and this with me,
> That I must be their scourge and minister. (ll. 172–7)

While the passions and violence of this scene are exceptionally unambiguous, an uncertainty remains with regard to any intimacy that is achieved between mother and son: how they touch each other, look at each other, or need each other is not specified and remains unclear. Certainly, both are left greatly affected, mentally and physically. As at the end of his encounter with Ophelia, Hamlet leaves the stage alone but this time 'lug[ging] the guts' of Polonius with him (l. 214); Gertrude says nothing as she struggles to draw breath and contain her emotion (see IV.i.1–2).

Affection, powerful and sometimes destructive emotion, and sexual awareness can by now be identified as driving forces in this tragedy, alongside political, moral, philosophical, and heroic concerns. While greatly developing one strain in *Titus Andronicus*, this marks a major change from *Julius Ceasar* and the historical tragedies, and from the more lyrical *Romeo and Juliet*.

Act IV

Some editors question the traditional marking of Act IV, scene i after Hamlet has left his mother, arguing that the previous scene must continue until the stage is empty once more. Yet the end of Hamlet's encounter with his mother completes the business of Act III and with Claudius's entry the narrative moves into a different gear: the focus settles on no one person for very long and sharply defined encounters follow each other in quick succession. In obedience to Hamlet, and to excuse his killing of Polonius, Gertrude has to lie, saying her son is 'Mad as the sea and wind when both contend . . .'. Her relationship with Claudius is now deeply troubled; having called her three times to leave with him, he has to call again, 'O come away', before leaving on the rhyme of a couplet, with: 'My soul is full of discord and dismay' (IV.i.44–5): this could be either a confession to his wife as she draws close to him or an isolated soliloquy as she makes her own exit.

The next scene is taken on the run, as Hamlet is pursued by Rosencrantz and Guildenstern and then, after he has insulted them both, agrees to go with them to the King. In the third scene, Claudius challenges Hamlet about Polonius's death and Hamlet uses his assumed madness to mock his adversary and express his own bitter sense of betrayal. He then leaves, as he is asked, to go to England, and Claudius reveals in soliloquy that Hamlet will be killed on reaching his destination. Claudius also confesses how 'like the hectic in my blood he rages' and that, until he knows he is dead, 'Howe'er my haps, my joys were ne'er begun' (IV.iii.68–71). The next scene is the first to be set outside Elsinore and, leading an army, Fortinbras enters at once. As he is leaving after only a few words, in the second Quarto, that represents Shakespeare's early complete draft, Hamlet enters on his way to England and in time to observe this ambitious young prince. Being told about this military expedition, he soliloquizes yet again and says, yet again, that he does not know why he delays his revenge; this time, however, he also considers what it is 'Rightly to be great' (IV.iv.53). A tight focus on Hamlet has been re-established to show that he now has a wider perspective on his predicament than before and a harsher objectivity about his own course of action:

> O, from this time forth
> My thoughts be bloody or be nothing worth.   (IV.iv.65–6)

The focus finally settles in this Act upon Ophelia in her madness provoking, as we have seen (pp. 151–2), a range of sensations entirely new to the play. The pathos of her two entries affects everyone on stage and shows them to be incapable of helping her. When momentarily alone with Gertrude, Claudius now directly claims sympathy from 'my dear Gertrude' only to be interrupted by a great noise from off-stage and news that Laertes has returned at the head of demonstrators demanding that he shall be king (IV.v.98–110). Doors are broken as they burst onto the stage and action takes a new turn. Laertes calms his supporters and then, with evident emotion, demands to know how his father died so that he may exact revenge. As Claudius reasons with him and promises help, Ophelia enters the second time and again the on-going action is deflected as Laertes fights back tears and stands helplessly speaking of her sweetness and kindness. Everything again seems at risk, especially if Laertes has been supported by a large and dangerous crowd.

Much happens very quickly now: news of Hamlet's return;

arrangements for his secret rendezvous with Horatio; a plan set by
Claudius and Laertes to kill Hamlet and make that certain by
employing three different ways of doing so; news of Ophelia's death.
For most of the time Claudius is firmly in control, but as he negoti-
ates with Laertes, other feelings surface:

> Laertes, was your father dear to you?
> Or are you like the painting of a sorrow,
> A face without a heart?
> *Why ask you this?*
> Not that I think you did not love your father,
> But that I know love is begun by time,
> And that I see, in passages of proof,
> Time qualifies the spark and fire of it.

The shortened Folio text then jumps abruptly to

> Hamlet comes back: what would you undertake
> To show yourself in deed your father's son
> More than in words?

Laertes's reply is chillingly ruthless: 'To cut his throat i' th' church'.
In the fuller version of the second Quarto, Claudius has a further
ten lines that show why he used this oddly personal and defeatist
argument to prepare Laertes for his question:

> There lives within the very flame of love
> A kind of wick or snuff that will abate it;
> And nothing is at a like goodness still,
> For goodness, growing to a pleurisy,
> Dies in his own too-much. That we would do,
> We should do when we would. . .

Claudius continues this argument drawn from painful experience
until, it seems, he has to remind himself of present necessities: 'But
to the quick of th'ulcer: / Hamlet comes back . . .' (IV.vii.106–25).

In this quick-moving Act IV, during which the story takes large
steps forward, progress is held up, not to elaborate on the emergency

caused by Laertes's rebellious army or clarify Hamlet's intentions, but to reveal how Ophelia, Laertes, and Claudius are all tormented by failure and loss, especially in kinship and marriage. Gertrude's suffering is more hidden: after a brief soliloquy about her 'sick soul' and continuing fears (IV.v.17–20) and an attempt to restrain Laertes, she becomes increasingly isolated and silent, until she bears the pathos of Ophelia's death by recounting it in precise detail.

Act V

Structurally, the play is simpler in the last Act, with two formal scenes, one a funeral and the other a fencing match, both taking time to prepare and inviting close-up views of the individuals involved. At the start of each, Hamlet clarifies his state of mind in talk with Horatio, on both occasions involving a third person, new to the play, the Gravedigger and 'young Osric', each establishing a wider perspective on Hamlet's intentions. So, as the story comes to its violent close, the presentation of the tragedy changes and offers a steadier view, restraining the forward pressures of the narrative so that an audience can follow terrifying events and complex struggles with more assurance and deeper involvement than has previously been possible.

Hamlet's Wordplay

Throughout the play, Hamlet is often difficult to understand. From the start, he uses words with an agility that requires an agile audience to keep up with him. He plays with words that sound alike, or nearly alike:

> *But now, my cousin Hamlet, and my son –*
>   A little more than kin, and less than kind.
> *How is it that the clouds still hang on you?*
>   Not so, my lord; I am too much in the sun.   (I.ii.64–7)

When the King withdraws from this exchange, his mother takes it up more sympathetically and on a different tack but Hamlet continues to take her words and return them changed or challenged:

Thou know'st 'tis common: all that lives must die,
Passing through nature to eternity.
    Ay, madam, it is 'common'.
                              If it be,
Why seems it so particular with thee?
    'Seems', madam! Nay, it is; I know not 'seems'.

Besides playing with words, Hamlet's first short speeches are also
puzzling in their intentions: do they consciously affront the public
celebration of his mother's remarriage or is Hamlet pretending to be
flippant, boorish, and ambiguous in order to keep his thoughts to
himself and so contain his frustration and pain? He uses rhetorical
devices that most critics considered improper for a prince. Cicero in
De Oratore (II.lxiii) insisted that obtrusive wordplay belongs to buf-
foons and pedantic scholars because it quickly becomes degrading or
insufferable. George Puttenham in *The Art of English Poesie* (1589)
warned that:

> sentences that hold too much of the merry & light, or infamous &
> unshamefast . . . become not Princes, nor great estates, nor them that
> write of their doings . . .

Ben Jonson, in his *Discoveries,* agreed that 'we must not play, or riot
too much with [words], as in *Paranomasies*', but he added that there
was no wordplay 'but shall find some Lovers, as the bitter'st confec-
tions are grateful to some palates'. Perhaps Hamlet's anger causes
him to speak aloud with such aggressive sarcasm.

Ambiguous and complicated speech is a distinctive element of the
'mind' with which Shakespeare has endowed Hamlet and challenged
an audience to follow. For him, words are restless, multiple in
meaning, shifting in form, quick to awake others close in sound but
different in meaning. They can be a disguise in which to taunt and
trick both adversaries and friends, so that he is not fully understood
while they are encouraged to disclose hidden thoughts:

Do you know me, my lord?
    Excellent well; you are a fishmonger.
Not I, my lord.

Then I would you were so honest a man.
Honest, my lord!
Ay, sir; to be honest, as this world goes, is to be one man pick'd out
of ten thousand. . . .   (II.ii.172–8)

Fishmongers smell, among other men; a *fishmonger* was a name for a
'fleshmonger' or bawd; a *fishmonger's* wife and daughter were said to
breed, fish-like, in great quantities. So Hamlet's mind runs on to 'so
honest a man', a word meaning 'honourable', or 'chaste', or 'truthful,
genuine', . . . and then to '*Modesties . . . craft . . . colour . . .* I know a
hawk from a *handsaw*' (II.ii.278–9, 375). Wordplay gallops easily
and can halt abruptly when it makes a bold and mocking challenge.

Words are so wanton in Hamlet's mind, feeding off his aggres-
sions and fears, that sometimes he seems to reveal more than he
knows, his unconscious, rather than conscious, mind directing
speech. Why should he treat Ophelia so harshly and openly before
the actors perform *The Murder of Gonzago*? Is he looking at his
mother and step-father all this time to see how they react? Does he
want everyone to hear so that they think he is mad and harmless? Or
is he forcing himself to talk in public to the young woman he now
distrusts and failing so thoroughly that he concludes with an epitaph
which is puzzling even to himself?

Lady, shall I lie in your lap?
  No, my lord.
I mean, my *head* upon your lap.
  Ay, my lord.
Do you think I meant *country* matters?
  I think nothing, my lord.
That's a fair thought – to lie between maid's legs.
  What is, my lord?
Nothing.
  You are merry, my lord.
Who, I?
  Ay, my lord.
O God, your only *jig*-maker! What should a man *do* but be merry?
For look you how cheerfully my mother *looks* and *my father died*
within's two hours.

> *Nay, 'tis twice two months, my lord.*
>
> So long? Nay then, let the devil wear black, for I'll have a suit of
> sables. O heavens, die two months ago and not forgotten yet? Then
> there's hope a great man's memory may outlive his life half a year. But
> by'r lady a must build churches then, or else shall a suffer not thinking
> on, with the *hobby-horse*, whose epitaph is 'For O, for O, the hobby-
> horse is forgot!'   (III.ii.110–33)

The wordplay upon *cunt, no-thing, jig, do, die, hobby-horse* converts
his private predicament into a public carnival. Perhaps Hamlet is
using it as a disguise, moving from polite behaviour to sexual
mockery so openly that his true feelings are never on the surface. Or
he may be carried away by his performance, saying more than he
actually feels or intends. An audience is likely to be more perplexed
than enlightened.

   In the soliloquies, an audience can perceive a mind working
simultaneously at different levels of consciousness. As soon as he is
alone in Act I, we hear: 'O, that this too too *sullied* [or sallied, or
solid] flesh would *melt* . . . '. After *melt*, particularly appropriate if
linked to *solid* (a reading adopted by some editors), Hamlet's mind
springs onwards to two other verbs: first *thaw*, bringing other physical associations of cold and change, and of dissolution; and then
resolve, adding to the range of meanings with dissolve, inform,
answer, dispel doubt. And so 'Thaw and resolve itself into a *dew*' –
that word introducing a phenomenon in nature that is mysterious
and almost imperceptible in operation; in association with some
senses of *resolve*, it also is a quibble on *due*, as a necessary 'payment'
or 'judgement'. So Hamlet's mind reaches:

> Or that the *Everlasting* had not fix'd
> His canon 'gainst self-slaughter.

With *Everlasting* comes a look backward, marking a contrast with
that which *melts, thaws,* and does *not* last. Wordplay becomes
complex in that this powerful and non-*flesh*ly presence *fixes* (no
melting or resolving now) his *canon* (both law and instrument of
destruction) against *self-slaughter* (not this weapon's usual target). At
times, members of an audience will strain to keep up as words con-

tinue to bend, buckle, extend, and change their meanings or sharpen their attack.

Hamlet is not always in control and sometimes makes a conscious withdrawal from speech, as if the management of words has bored him or perplexed him too painfully:

> Then are our beggars bodies, and our monarchs and outstretched heroes the beggars' shadows. Shall we to th' court? For by my fay, I cannot reason. (II.ii.263–5)

Or, again:

> Farewell, dear mother. . . . Father and mother is man and wife, man and wife is one flesh; so my mother. Come, for England. *Exit.*
> (IV.iii.52–56)

Although he renders the King speechless, Hamlet pursues him no further, preferring to go off-stage, silent and under guard, for the journey to England. He may be still less in control in the graveyard, after both he and Laertes have had to be restrained physically. He tries to use simple words, but then asserts 'it is no matter' and leaves abruptly with a taunting riddle:

> Hear you, sir,
> What is the reason that you use me thus?
> I lov'd you ever. But it is no matter.
> Let Hercules himself do what he may,
> The cat will mew, and dog will have his day. (V.i.282–6)

Much of the dramatic action of this tragedy is within the mind of Hamlet as it is torn by both positive love and the loss of it, as he seeks to be accepted or to punish, moves towards action or inaction, or wishes for an ideal fulfilment or for annihilation. Hamlet's multiple meanings and restless use of words adds to the narrative, strong and forward-drawing though that is, a kind of mystery that attracts an audience to probe underneath the ambiguities and disguises and so become keenly aware of an inner and irreducible dissatisfaction. There is within the very act of thinking a need that no single expres-

sion can satisfy: thought alters the person who has thought, and frequently this works against, and disables, the thought that has just
been realized in words. How then can we estimate Hamlet's progress
towards achieving what he sees as his duty or towards 'honest' relationships with others? These issues are brought to vivid life by the
play, but it offers no escape from the instabilities of Hamlet's use of
words, unless that is an acceptance of these conditions; otherwise,
the 'silence' of death can, indeed, seem like 'felicity' in comparison
with the restlessness of his mind (V.ii.352).

The Final Reckoning

Unsettled both by wordplay and by the changing focus of the dramatic structure, an audience will be ready for the slower if tantaliz-
ingly oblique progress of the talk between two clowns in a graveyard
at the beginning of Act V. When Hamlet arrives with Horatio, his
ruminations seem simple in comparison with the Gravedigger's
'equivocation' because an audience will know that he is thinking
about his own call to greatness and his own death when he meditates
on Alexander and Caesar returning to the earth from which they
were made. He has talked of death before, but now he seems ready
for some kind of ending and resolution, some unambiguous 'giving
out' which will report him and his cause aright to the unsatisfied.

After the fight with Laertes in Ophelia's grave, an even longer
preparatory duologue acts as prologue to the dangerous events that
must follow. At the very start of the last scene, Hamlet tells the story
of his sea voyage, his discovery of Claudius's plot to kill him, and his
own despatch of Rosencrantz and Guildenstern to their deaths. A
short exchange follows in which he is more explicit about the moral
rights of revenge than anywhere else in the play:

> Does it not, think thee, stand me now upon –
> He that hath kill'd my king and whor'd my mother,
> Popp'd in between th'election and my hopes,
> Thrown out his angle for my proper life
> And with such coz'nage – is't not perfect conscience

To quit him with this arm? And is't not to be damn'd
To let this canker of our nature come
In further evil?   (V.ii.63–70)

The two and a half lines after 'perfect conscience' are found only in
the Folio text, together with ten more lines in which Hamlet recognizes he has little time and that he has 'forgot' himself to Laertes at
Ophelia's graveside: 'the bravery of his grief did put me / Into a
tow'ring passion' (ll. 79–80). Either the compositor of the Quarto
missed these lines because they were part of an addition to the first
draft that had been written illegibly or in the margins where he
missed them, or else he accidentally skipped these lines (see p. 157,
above). Without the extra text supplied by the Folio, the talk breaks
off so abruptly on ' . . . perfect conscience' that some kind of unintentional omission must have occurred. But even with the extra
lines, an audience is not given a clear statement of all that is in
Hamlet's mind because he speaks with rhetorical questions as if
asking for reassurance; this is no 'plain and simple faith', such as
Brutus expected (*Julius Caesar*, IV.ii.22; see above, pp. 1–2). Besides,
after he has agreed to the fencing match with Laertes only minutes
later, 'perfect conscience' seems to have evaporated and now, uncertain of the outcome, he is reluctant to 'tell all', as a player might do:
'Thou wouldst not think how ill all's here about my heart; but it is
no matter' (ll. 203–4).

Horatio senses that Hamlet is still troubled – 'If your mind dislike
anything, obey it. I will forestall their repair hither and say you are
not fit' (ll. 213–14) – and, at this point, further intrusions of baffling wordplay cloud over the ultimate issues once more. At first,
Hamlet quotes and comments on St Matthew's Gospel, as if he
placed his trust in God's providence, not in his own acts:

> There is a special providence in the fall of a sparrow. If it be now, 'tis
> to come; if it be not to come, it will be now; if it be not now, yet it
> will come. The readiness is all.   (ll. 215–18)

But *can* Hamlet mean what seems so different from the argument
for action he has made with apparent earnestness a moment before?

A deliberate delivery of the repetitive phrases, stressing some of its words and not others, will give conflicting meanings and raise unanswerable questions, as in the most exotic wordplay. Actors can turn the speech into an assertion of cynical despair, every large issue being sparrowlike and footling, or into a committal to some holy duty with an all-powerful and all-knowing God ready to work on its behalf. Some Hamlets speak this passage lightly, making it a pretence of confidence to cover up a deeper scepticism or unspoken fears by giving only conventional answers about his problems. The word *readiness* establishes an unmistakable ambiguity: in this context, it can mean either preparedness for a particular action or submission to whatever brings the final end.

Hamlet's next words are so tricky that they baffled the original compositors and have set modern editors at variance. Neither the second Quarto nor the Folio makes sense and so various emendations have been proposed. *No/knows*; *ha's/leave/leaves*; *ought/all*; *of what/of ought*, all collide and change places with each other in the different versions found in modern editions: 'Since no man, of aught he leaves, knows aught, what is't to leave betimes?', or 'Since no man of ought he leaves, knows, what is't to leave . . .', or '. . . no man owes aught of what he leaves, what is't . . .', or '. . . no man knows of aught he leaves, what is't . . . .'. Is Hamlet thinking about a man's possessions, his self-knowledge, or the consequences of death? All he says more, as trumpet and drums announce the King's arrival, is the brief refusal to talk further: 'Let be.' An audience still has not been shown his 'perfect conscience'.

Encountering Laertes in front of the whole court, Hamlet offers a very different account of what he has done and is about to do. He starts very simply: 'Give me your pardon, sir. I have done you wrong', but then refers to his own supposed 'madness' as if that had been entirely real and absolved him of all responsibility:

> Who does it, then? His madness. If't be so,
> Hamlet is of the faction that is wrong'd;
> His madness is poor Hamlet's enemy.   (ll. 233–5)

But what *is* his 'madness'? Is it a 'sore distraction' by which he has been punished or his own invention for a somewhat theatrical disguise? Is Hamlet creating a cunning smoke-screen of words under which to hide his intent to kill the King? He does not speak of his 'madness' again.

An audience has been encouraged to expect that, at the end of this tragedy, the hero will unmask and everything will be clarified. In his first scene, he tells his mother: 'Seems, madam? Nay, it is. I known not "seems" / . . . / For I have that within which passes show' (I.ii.76–86). Later, he rounds on Guildenstern who tries to 'sound' him and 'pluck out the heart of [his] mystery' (III.ii.354–63). In most plays these would be pointers to a time when all will be revealed: what had 'jangled' a 'most sovereign reason' (III.i.159–60) and lain so 'ill . . . about [his] heart'. But, even at the moment of death, this does not happen. Hamlet's final speeches are so famous that for us they have an air of assurance and yet, if we try to imagine hearing them for the first time, we will find that much is still concealed in the ambiguities of wordplay. Hamlet could be experiencing thoughts too painful or too volatile to be expressed.

Knowing that Claudius has poisoned his drink with a 'union' or pearl (ll. 269–70, 284, 315–16), Hamlet puns as he kills his adversary: 'Drink off this potion. Is thy *union* here? / Follow my mother' (ll. 331–2). When he knows that he is himself dead, he is concerned about how much is 'unknown' and insists that Horatio should live to tell his story 'aright'. That is his friend's duty: he uses his last moments very differently, as if words remain as changeable and challenging as ever. He starts very simply:

> I am dead, Horatio. Wretched Queen, adieu!
> You that look pale and tremble at this chance,
> That are but mutes or audience to this act,
> Had I but time – as this fell sergeant, Death,
> Is strict in his arrest – O, I could tell you –
> But let it be. . . .
> (ll. 338–43)

Wordplay has come back, as if unbidden. *Strict* is 'cruel' as well as 'inescapably binding' and, perhaps, 'morally severe' (a sense common in Shakespeare's plays). *Arrest* can refer equally to stopping life and to stopping the 'act' which the audience is watching and Hamlet performing. When he tells Horatio, a third time, that he is as good as dead, the 'potion' mockingly becomes the 'potent poison' and, in a strange phrase (this is the only time that Shakespeare uses *o'ercrow*), the poison is said to cry in triumph over his spirit, rather than taking possession of his body:

> O, I die, Horatio.
> The potent poison quite o'ercrows my spirit.   (ll. 357–8)

An ironic allusion is here to the cock that heralds daylight after the night, not death after life. For Shakespeare, but not for his hero, the words may also be a reminiscence of the 'father's *spirit*' that had 'faded on the *crow*ing of the cock' (I.ii.255; I.i.162).

Hamlet has already heard the 'warlike noise' of Fortinbras's approach and now he gives his 'dying *voice*' – his 'vote' as well as his last utterance – to this young soldier for the next King of Denmark:

> He has my dying voice.
> So tell him, with th'occurrents more and less
> Which have solicited – the rest is silence.   (ll. 361–3)

Although its primary sense is dominant here, *dying* might also imply that the sounds Hamlet makes are now faint and so preparing for their 'silence'. With Hamlet's last line, meanings become as multiple and as baffling as anywhere in the play. *Solicited* could be a gentle solicitation or an urgent call; the word had been used in both senses by Shakespeare. The second is the more likely here, since 'solicited' and 'silence' are linked in sound and may therefore be held in opposition. But the main ambiguity is 'The rest is silence'. Most obviously, it means 'All that remains for me to say must be unspoken': so Hamlet implies that he withdraws intentionally from saying more, as he has done frequently in the course of the play, wordplay marking his escape without revealing what lies hidden 'about his heart'. Alternatively, Hamlet may be asserting that for the remainder, or 'the rest', of his life he has nothing to say or, perhaps, that he can make no noise, nothing like the 'warlike noise' of Fortinbras's approach

(l. 353) that is ringing in his ears. Either of these ways, he would be admitting his failure to tell all and acknowledge his ineffectuality as he dies. But *rest* could also allude to a time *after* life that would bring release from the noise and 'unrest' of this world. In this vein, Hamlet has told Horatio to:

> Absent thee from felicity awhile,
> And in this harsh world draw thy breath in pain
> To tell my story.   (ll. 351–2)

The actors of Shakespeare's company seem to have been dissatisfied with all these interpretations. Among the Folio's numerous small additions which probably record what actually happened on stage in performance (see p. 158, above), are the four letters, 'O, o, o, o' that it gives to Hamlet after 'The rest is silence' and before a stage-direction '*Dies*'. Perhaps Richard Burbage, the first Hamlet, believed that he needed extra time to express in inarticulate cries or groans whatever pain, disbelief, or courageous struggle seemed appropriate. We can have no idea what Shakespeare thought about the four O's, because the Folio was published after his death, but this addition became well enough established to get into print and serves to remind us that, however meaningful Hamlet's last words were intended to be, they had to be spoken while he faced the physical reality and pain of death from a poisoned rapier's point. The actor's way of accepting or resisting that 'strict arrest' will become part of what an audience sees and hears during the last moments of the play and will therefore affect how it hears what Hamlet is saying and, in consequence, its understanding of the whole tragedy. This will not be entirely a matter of the actor's conscious choice: Hamlet is a very demanding role so that the acting of it on any one occasion will be more than usually limited to what proves to be possible and what happens to occur in that performance. Whether or not four inarticulate cries or groans are heard, the 'harsh world' will influence how words are uttered and leave very physical marks on the play at the moment of death: a lot of blood or little, sweat, bleared eyes, contortion, weariness, and, finally, release from all tension may be among them.

When Fortinbras enters with Ambassadors from England asking 'Where is this sight?' Horatio directs attention to four dead bodies. After all has been said and done, Hamlet's corpse lies on the stage among the others. The dramatic focus has widened once more to take account of dynastic and political issues, as in the first court scene and the play scene. An audience will be unsettled yet again, as the army of another country stands beside the courtiers and while Horatio, who has wished to commit suicide, has not yet spoken on Hamlet's behalf. Young Osric, who has been in charge of the poisoned rapier, is also present and Fortinbras now in control, the inheritor of the Danish throne of whom very little is known except that Hamlet has said that he sought fame without regard for loss of life (see IV.iv.59–65).

Hamlet's Conscience

At a time when men and women laid down their lives or took the lives of others for clearly stated beliefs and when individual initiative in commerce and politics called for decisive action and, if possible, comprehensive strategies, *The Tragedy of Hamlet* pulled against the stream of most people's thoughts by dealing with personal uncertainties and actions that need very special reporting if they are to be understood 'aright' and not leave an audience 'unsatisfied'. Shakespeare created a final scene of great tension and, as in earlier tragedies, developed an increasingly intense focus on the play's hero but here, in its 'upshot', purposes are easily misunderstood. Individual members of an audience are left, it seems, to interpret as best they can and according to their own 'business and desire' (I.v.130–1).

An actor might seem well advised to make a very clear decision about Hamlet's final thoughts so that he can end strongly and have a sense of direction in making other innumerable choices during the course of the play. On the other hand, the many possible meanings of the last speeches would also allow him to choose which ones to emphasize in each individual performance according to the way in which he has been able to meet the varied challenges in that particular journey through the text, and according to performances by other actors and the response he has received from his audience. The choices are so numerous and so finely balanced that, whether made beforehand or at the moment of performance, some of them at the close of the play are bound to be intuitive, rather than intellectual, and suited as much to the performer and the occasion, as they are to the clues that the words of the text supply.

However we try explain his decision, Shakespeare chose, very positively, to provide a multiplicity of meanings at this crucial moment. Indeed, throughout the play, as well as in this final test, his hero seems to be drawn restlessly into engagement by his imagination, perhaps a little in the same way as his creator had been engaged as he wrote this play. Death, for such a person, could not be held in a single grip, in the fix of words used in a single sense, without 'tricks, in plain and simple faith'. To end this tragedy as Shakespeare has done, went against much of his previous practice for earlier heroes die with single-minded speeches, although in earlier scenes they have used wordplay to express unmanageable, complex, or cunning thoughts.

In going against expectation and unsettling an audience so continuously, we may see from hindsight that Shakespeare was leading his audiences towards a new sense of self and of the world in which they were beginning to live. Self-questioning and an attempt to be true to one's nature and the half-conscious promptings of instinct were part of a new consciousness that was to break up the last protections and restrictions of feudal society and threaten the formulations of authoritative religions. Shakespeare was not alone in exploring this new way of thought and, as we have already noticed, he was probably influenced by Michel de Montaigne's *Essays*, perhaps available to him in manuscript translation before writing *Hamlet*; their influence can also be traced in *Troilus and Cressida*, *Measure for Measure*, and *King Lear*, all close in date to *Hamlet*. When Montaigne wrote about his own consciousness, he might have been writing about Hamlet's:

> Shamefast, bashful, insolent, chaste, luxurious, peevish, prattling, silent, fond, doting, laborious, nice, delicate, ingenious, slow, dull, forward, humorous, debonaire, wise, ignorant, false in words, true-

speaking, both liberal, covetous and prodigal: all these I perceive in some measure or other to be in me, according as I stir or turn myself; . . . I have nothing to say entirely, simply, and with solidity of myself, without confusion, disorder, blending, mingling. . . .   (II.i)

Shakespeare's achievement was to give this new perception to a tragic hero, alive in mind and body, subtle and far-reaching in imagination, sensitive to a wide range of sensual experiences, always changing and often complex in thought. The handling of Hamlet's story is the other innovation of this tragedy, so that not only is the hero's conscience brought into prominence and the political and dynastic situation clearly presented, as in earlier history plays and tragedies, but emotions and sexual desire are also given full attention so that, occasionally, they take over from all other interests. Hamlet sees himself 'benetted round with villainies' (V.ii.29) as he seeks to put what is 'out-of-joint' to right (I.v.196–7), yet he is also aware of destructive and barbaric impulses within himself together with tender affection, sexual desire, and a longing for companionship and peace. Changeable, divided, and isolated in consciousness, Hamlet is drawn towards others who have some of the more durable qualities that he lacks: his father's Ghost, the actors, and Horatio, chief among them. He is also committed to his mother and Ophelia; with them, his emotions and sexuality are fully engaged, even though he finds little peace or assurance.

In all this, the role of Hamlet is so written that his thoughts and feelings are made apparent to an audience at the very moment that he is aware of them himself, or half-aware of them. In consequence, while following his course through the tragedy, an audience will seem to share in all that he endures and achieves. When Fortinbras announces a military lying-in-state and judges that Hamlet 'was likely, had he been put on, / To have prov'd most royal' (V.ii.400–8), members of an audience may believe that they know better than this, according to their own individual imaginations, and will value Hamlet for positive achievements, for having lived with great courage almost entirely alone in a 'harsh' and 'unknowing world' (ll. 352, 384). Hamlet's anticipation of the Players' arrival may speak better than Fortinbras for his own aspirations:

He that plays the king shall be welcome – his Majesty shall have tribute on me, the adventurous knight shall use his foil and target, the lover shall not sigh gratis, the humorous man shall end his part in peace, the clown shall make those laugh whose lungs are tickle a th' sear, and the lady shall say her mind freely . . .   (II.ii.317–24)

10

Othello: Sexuality and Difference

Whereas *Hamlet* is speculative and its imaginary horizons almost unlimited, *The Tragedy of Othello, the Moor of Venice*, is confined and direct. From the third Act onwards, an audience's attention is gripped by a fast-moving, single-line narrative that is increasingly dominated by the play's hero. In the last scene he is centre-stage almost continuously and speaks almost half of its three hundred and seventy lines. Another and obvious difference between these two tragedies, completed only a year or two apart, is that Hamlet was born a prince and is called to set the times to right; Othello is a famous soldier who has made a very personal choice in marriage and is employed by the state to fight against its Turkish enemies. He does not meet his death trying to fulfil a mission or serve the state: he kills his wife and then himself in a sequence of events which he imperfectly understands and over which he has little control. Watching *Hamlet*, an audience follows its hero sharing his thoughts, feelings, and uncertainties, and wishing him success; watching *Othello*, it is appalled by what its hero is driven to do, wishing that, somehow, the process could be stopped. *Hamlet* is a quest ending in death, *Othello* a catastrophe that seems increasingly unavoidable. *Hamlet* concludes with removal of dead bodies, the prince's held aloft by four captains as ordinance is fired in salute, *Othello* with hiding the 'tragic loading' of the marriage bed.

Increasingly during the last scene, Othello speaks of what is happening very simply, as if his ability to say more is entirely spent:

> My wife, my wife! what wife? I have no wife. . .
> O Desdemon! dead, Desdemon. Dead! O! O! . . .
> O fool, fool, fool!   (V.ii.96, 279, 321)

At one stage, all he can do is to fall down upon the bed and 'roar' out loud: 'O! O! O!' (ll. 196, 195). At other times his words have great resonance and acuity, as they had earlier in the play, but he suffers and grieves beyond the reach of that eloquence.

Instinctive Actions

Shakespeare had already forged the means to show a tragic hero impelled by unspoken thoughts and feelings. For all his sense of purpose, Hamlet retains his own secrets. While he talks of 'that within which passes show' (I.ii.85), he never shows what that is and an audience may doubt whether he ever knows so much. In preparation for the last confrontation, while telling Horatio 'thou wouldst not think how ill all's here about my heart', he avoids explanation, or it eludes him:

> It is but foolery; but it is such a kind of gain-giving as would perhaps trouble a woman.   (V.ii.204–9)

This could be a way of saying that tears are about to take over from words and 'woman's weapons, water-drops. / Stain [his] man's cheeeks' (*Lear*, II.i.276–7), or that his unease is unreasonable and inexplicable. Alternatively, he may have an intuition that what he has called 'the heart of my mystery' (III.ii.357–8) is chiefly experienced in the presence of women.

Hamlet seems least to understand what he is doing, least able to control words and actions, when he is alone with either Ophelia or Gertrude. The first of these encounters, reported and not shown, is when he comes into Ophelia's closet and says nothing at all. He may be acting madness but it goes beyond pretence when:

He rais'd a sigh so piteous and profound
As it did seem to shatter all his bulk,
And end his being.   (II.i.77–101)

Alone with his mother in her closet he is immediately so passionate
that she thinks he is about to murder her; later, as the scene reaches
an impassioned and, even, vicious climax, his father's Ghost enters
to 'whet [his] almost blunted purpose' (III.iv.90–111) but Hamlet
knows, without prompting, that in denouncing his mother, he has
'laps'd in time and passion' from his duty of revenge. While the narrative continues to be driven forward by a revenger's 'purpose', what
happens with these two women remains undeveloped and unresolved. Ophelia has to endure his lewd and self-assertive talk in
public before the 'Mousetrap' and she dies mad and alone. Gertrude
is able to speak on her son's behalf and to wipe his brow during the
final duel, but she dies before they can regain a mutual trust:
'Wretched queen, adieu!' are his last words to her. In choosing to
write of Othello, the Moor of Venice, Shakespeare took a great step
further into this region of instinct rather than rationality, hidden
feelings rather than careful words, towards a tragedy in which the
hero's relationship with a woman is of central importance. The tragic
action needs no ghost calling for revenge or any political or dynastic
duty to fulfil: the basic situation, neither understood nor secure,
provides the principal impetus. In words taken from *Hamlet*, some
'imposthume . . . inward breaks, and shows no cause without / Why
the man dies' (IV.iv.26–8). Why should Othello believe that his wife
is false to him? He, and others with him, die in response to what he
has instinctively felt.

In other ways, *Julius Caesar* also prepared the way towards this
new kind of tragedy. In its 'Quarrel Scene' (IV.iii), Brutus and
Cassius so goad each other that their differences are clearly exposed
and, eventually, a deeper trust is developed between them. This has
little direct effect on the tragedy's conclusion, which depends on
political decisions and the outcome of a battle, and yet, in consequence of it, an audience can sense that, in their separate suicides,
each of these men is affirming his own eradicable nature. The central
'Temptation Scene' of *Othello* (III.iii), in which Iago destroys

Othello's confidence in Desdemona, is sustained for almost four hundred lines and works in much the same way: his passions and uncertainties are so whetted that he is unable to hear or see anything that might deflect him from a course of action that destroys both himself and others. At first, Othello's vision of Desdemona's purity and personal beauty draws him away from Iago's suggestions:

> Look where she comes:
> If she be false, O then heaven mocks itself,
> I'll not believe't. (III.iii.281–3)

By the end of the scene, fear of losing this vision renders him powerless against the horror, shame, and helplessness that Iago has aroused; indeed, it reinforces them with the force of extreme physical torture:

> Her name, that was as fresh
> As Dian's visage, is now begrimed and black
> As mine own face. If there be cords or knives,
> Poison, or fire, or suffocating streams,
> I'll not endure it. Would I were satisfied! (ll. 389–93)

Both Iago's success in this central scene and the deaths in the final catastrophe are the results of Othello's obsession with a woman during the course of an enduring but fatally insecure relationship.

Sexuality

When plays were performed with women's roles performed by boys or young men, dramatists were sometimes content to portray sexual encounters within the restrictions of public behaviour. But intimate talk and physical contact had to be represented in some way if the stories and themes that were popular with the public and treated frequently in poetry and prose were also to find their place on the stage. In *Romeo and Juliet* and the later comedies Shakespeare had already shown skill in this, but *Othello* stands apart from these earlier plays by starting with marriage, not tentative wooing, and by bringing bodily presence and sexual activity to the very centre of attention.

The first scene sets up strong expectations. Instead of a regular exposition, it starts in a street at night in the middle of an argument about some secret matter which is then put aside so that Iago can show Roderigo that he hates his master, having been overlooked as lieutenant in favour of 'One Michael Cassio, a Florentine'. The explanation is circuitous and only at line 32 is the audience told that the speaker, Iago, is 'his Moorship's ancient', today the equivalent of sergeant major. For a further thirty lines, Iago continues to explain that he serves himself and not the Moor, and that he is not to be judged by any 'outward action: . . . I am not what I am' (ll. 60–4). An audience member, who has managed to disentangle all this talk, might well believe that a tragedy of ambition, resentment, dissimulation, and social disruption is about to follow. But at this point Roderigo obliquely broaches the reason why both have come here; his account is envious, salacious, derogatory, and racially insulting:

> What a full fortune does the thicklips owe
> If he can carry't thus! (I.i.65–6)

Iago answers that they should both rouse 'her father' which he proceeds to do:

> Zounds, sir, you're robbed, for shame put on your gown!
> Your heart is burst, you have lost half your soul,
> Even now, now, very now, an old black ram
> Is tupping your white ewe! (ll. 84–8)

While the father is identified early on as Brabantio, his daughter remains unnamed until later in the next scene, after Iago has told his master of Brabantio's 'scurvy and provoking' reactions and has asked if he is 'fast married'. Othello is both forthright and guarded in reply, naming Desdemona and hinting at careful deliberations that are completely at odds with Iago's earlier account:

> For know, Iago,
> But that I love the gentle Desdemona

I would not my unhoused free condition
Put into circumscription and confine
For the sea's worth.   (I.ii.24–8)

Desdemona's appearance on stage is further delayed until she is summoned to testify before the assembled senators of Venice. They are
meeting to commission Othello to defend Cyprus against the Turks,
and Brabantio has to interrupt this state business to complain of
his daughter's abduction, after being drugged, he says, by 'some
mixtures powerful o'er the blood' (I.iii.105). While waiting for
Desdemona to be brought as witness, the assembled men discuss her
as if some object to be prized, protected, and fought over, but
Othello gives a respectful account of how she had sympathized with
the stories he told of his life as a soldier and, then, how he had
wooed and married her. Expectation and curiosity have now been
whetted over the course of three hundred and seventy lines, some of
them overtly sexual or brutal in nature, others racially prejudiced,
others tender and respectful; and then, at last, she does enter.

Shakespeare could hardly have concentrated attention more on
the single, silent figure who stands waiting until called by her father
to approach and answer, 'Where most you owe obedience?'
(I.iii.180). She responds in the same terms and, claiming 'the Moor'
as her 'lord', denies all the lurid assumptions and prejudices that
have been voiced and all the panicked reactions that have led to her
entrance. Brabantio can do nothing but drop his charges and the
matter is concluded so quickly that an audience is left wanting to
know more. Othello, however, has nothing to say when Brabantio
gives him his daughter, and Desdemona remains silent until just
before the official meeting disperses. When Othello asks for provi-
sion to be made for his new wife when he takes up his new appoint-
ment in Cyprus, she interrupts discussion of this and, when given
leave, speaks her own mind. She will go with her husband and is
proud to do so:

That I did love the Moor to live with him
My downright violence and scorn of fortunes
May trumpet to the world. My heart's subdued

> Even to the very quality of my lord:
> I saw Othello's visage in his mind,
> And to his honours and his valiant parts
> Did I my soul and fortunes consecrate,
> So that, dear lords, if I be left behind,
> A moth of peace, and he go to the war,
> The rites for which I love him are bereft me,
> And I a heavy interim shall support
> By his dear absence. Let me go with him.   (ll.249–60)

Her words are public and not intimate so that this account leaves much that is still unsaid or obscure. Is she apologizing for his race when saying that she 'saw Othello's visage in his mind', or for his age or military appearance? Or does she ignore such matters to assert that her love engages at the deepest possible level? Which of the many meanings attaching to *rites/rights* are uppermost in her consciousness? How can she 'trumpet' feelings of downright violence and, in the same breath, 'consecrate' her soul? What can she mean by 'downright violence': her outspoken, unstoppable passion or, as the Arden editor glosses it, an 'absolute' and 'violent rupture with conventional behaviour'? Syntax, metre, and phrasing, together with frank and careful choice of words, combine to express strength of mind and tenderness of feeling, but an audience is left to sense Desdemona's most private thoughts and piece out with its own imaginations the dramatic reality of this young and confident bride. Whether played by an actress or young male, Desdemona may well be most compellingly alive in the consciousness of an audience, and not on the stage; in the fantasy of each spectator her presence can have the immediacy and particularity of sexual arousal.

After 'Let me go with him', Desdemona says little in this scene – just one interjection to question whether they must leave that very night – but the Duke, a senator, and her father all direct attention to the silent bride, Brabantio awakening earlier responses to her beauty and her marriage, most accutely with:

> Look to her, Moor, if thou hast eyes to see:
> She has deceived her father, and may thee.   (I.iii.293–4)

Othello's response, 'My life upon her faith', if spoken solemnly, may hint at a trial to come; even if spoken easily, an audience that has come to witness a tragedy may hear a dangerous boast. Othello then leaves Desdemona in the safe-keeping of 'Honest Iago', asking that his wife, Emilia, should attend on her: here, intimations of tragedy or, at least, conflict are certainly present, because an audience, having seen Iago at work, could never believe him to be 'honest'.

Desdemona is next seen at Cyprus in the company of Iago and Emilia. A great storm has separated the ships of the Venetian fleet and she must now wait for Othello, uncertain about what has happened and surrounded by soldiers and men of Cyprus. Cassio prepares for her arrival by announcing 'The divine Desdemona' as someone capable of taming 'high seas and howling winds . . .'. Questioned, he goes on less hyperbolically to identify her as 'our great captain's captain' and to talk of Othello making 'love's quick pants in Desdemona's arms' (II.i.68–81). When she enters and everyone kneels in welcome, an audience will recognize that the drama has been refocused and its action is ready to develop. Gone are allusions to racial difference, age, or violence but, in this new context, Desdemona is less assured and an audience may well feel closer to her in consequence. She plays along with Iago's cynical jokes about women, but protests against his conclusions. Her anxiety for Othello's safety is suggested as much by instinctive shifts of attention as by words and, possibly, by a forced familiarity with Cassio. As these two talk out of earshot, Iago interprets what is happening as a sexually potent encounter and plans his line of action against Othello.

With this preparation, the audience is ready for Othello's arrival in Cyprus and his greeting for his 'fair warrior' (II.i.180). He voices both contentment and fear that 'not another comfort like to this / Succeeds in unknown fate'. When Desdemona prays for an increase in 'our loves and comforts', Othello joins her prayer but then stops, momentarily incapable of speech, overcome either in sensation or in comprehension:

> Amen to that, sweet powers!
> I cannot speak enough of this content,
> It stops me here, it is too much of joy.

After this unexpected and unintentional break, Othello kisses his
wife. A single and formal kiss would suit this very public occasion
with all eyes fixed on them, but one kiss is followed by another:

> And this, and this the greatest discords be
> That e'er our hearts shall make.   (II.i.194–7)

A stage direction, '*They kiss*', found in the early Quarto edition, is
also unusual in suggesting that Desdemona is an active participant;
as the Arden editor comments, the conventional formula is '*Kisses
her*' or '*He kisses her*'. Both are silent, fully engaged in each other's
presence, while Iago comments:

> O, you are well tuned now: but I'll set down
> The pegs that make this music, as honest
> As I am.   (ll.198–200)

The play's action is now fully under way and the grounds for tragedy
clearly established in the privacies of a sexual relationship and at
least two threats to its continuance – Iago's antagonism and Othello's
instinct that 'stops' him before he kisses his wife and makes him
think of 'discords' as he does so.

At this distance in time, and in a very different cultural environment, we cannot know for sure what effect a young male performer
of Desdemona would have had in Shakespeare's day, but it is hard to
think of an introduction that would be more calculated to awaken
an audience's own imaginations, aroused at first by Desdemona's
silent presence and then by her words and the thoughts they only
partly express. The silent pleasure they take in each other's presence
on meeting again in Cyprus offers still freer scope to an audience's
imagination. Gertrude and Ophelia in *Hamlet*, and Juliet in the
earlier tragedy centred on love, are presented with less opportunity
and provocation for an audience's imagination to supply whatever
the actors do not.

Venice

While the love between Othello and Desdemona is the motor force of the tragedy, the settings of Venice and its military fortress of Cyprus influence almost every turn of their story. Othello is 'the Moor of Venice' and the course of his life is inextricably dependent on senators and soldiers. When he begins to think his wife is unfaithful, he imagines that 'the general camp, / Pioneers and all, had tasted her sweet body' (III.iii.348–9) and, as his jealousy grows, he takes her for a 'cunning whore of Venice' (IV.ii.91).

Although only the first Act is set in Venice, Shakespeare made its presence felt throughout the play according to the current reputation of *La Serenissima Republica* (see Plate 6). He may well have read in Lewis Lewkenor's *The Comonwealth and Government of Venice* (1599), a translation of several Italian sources, that while Venetians impressed many travellers with

> the greatness of their Empire, the gravity of their prince, the majesty of their Senate, the unviolableness of their laws, their zeal in religion, and lastly their moderation and equity,

more youthful visitors tended to

> extol to the skies their humanity towards strangers, the delicacy of their entertainments, the beauty, pomp, and daintiness of their women, and finally the infinite superfluities of all pleasure and delights.

The Duke, Brabantio, and numerous senators in the first Act, and Gratiano in the last, represent the men of power in Venice. They have wealth and status, and take care of their possessions; Brabantio speaks for their class to Roderigo:

> What tell'st thou me of robbing? This is Venice:
> My house is not a grange. (I.i.104–5)

Lodovico, a 'proper' man in diplomatic service, brings the proprieties of Venice to Cyprus for the last two Acts; his pronouncement

6   A Venetian festival in the early years of the seventeenth century

Reproduced from Giacomo Franco, *Habiti D'Huomeni et Donne Venetiana* (1609), this plate shows the Doge and his entourage entering the church of San'Giorgio Maggiore at Venice for Christmas Mass. It illustrates the wealth of the city and its pride as expressed in elaborate ceremonials. While the illustration is centred on the newly built church, ships and the open sea in the distance indicate the source of much of the power of the city-state and its openness to the rest of the known world. (*This plate is reproduced by permission of the British Library.*)

that 'This would not be believed in Venice' (IV.i.241) and his command to 'censure' Iago with torture and 'seize upon the fortunes of the Moor' (V.ii.63–9) re-establish official standards after disaster. The city's reputation for sexual licence is represented by Roderigo who squanders his wealth in pursuit of Desdemona and by Cassio who is gallant with Desdemona and treats his mistress, Bianca, as a 'customer' and 'monkey' (IV.i.120, 127). Cassio, a Florentine, not a Venetian, is a career soldier employed by the state. Fynes Moryson's *Itinerary Containing His Ten Years' Travel* (1617) gives a current explanation for the employment of strangers, such as Cassio and Othello: 'the gentlemen of Venice are trained up in plea- sure and wantonness, which must needs abase and effeminate their minds'; or, as Jean Bodin remarked in 1591, Venetians themselves were 'better citizens than warriors'. In consequence of its 'humanity towards strangers', Venice was also seen as a competitive world in which each person might seek his own advantage while daughters were jealously protected and wives watched with suspicion.

Private armed guards, foreign mercenaries, open hospitality, cele- brations with drinking and music, opportunities for personal advancement and sexual indulgence, all these elements in the play establish the Venetian setting in which Shakespeare chose to portray the love-match between an experienced and alien soldier and a young and beautiful heiress. Iago, who works to destroy that mar- riage, belongs to the same world but his restless mind does not settle into the luxuries and complacencies of Venice. He sees himself as a realist and sets out to be accepted as an honest man in an ambitious and deceitful world:

> Who has a breast so pure
> But some uncleanly apprehensions
> Keep leets and law-days and in session sit
> With meditations lawful? (III.iii.141–4)

So he asks Othello, at the very time that he refuses to utter his own thoughts: those are occupied in supplying 'poison' to Othello's thoughts of Desdemona and weaving a 'net / That shall enmesh them all' (III.iii.328 and II.iii.355–6).

In creating Iago who uses his knowledge of others for his 'own peculiar end' (I.i.59), Shakespeare reflected the ideas and reputation of Niccolò Machiavelli (1469–1527) of Florence that he had earlier drawn upon in *Parts I* and *II Henry VI*. In the words of Francis Bacon's *Advancement of Learning* (1605), Machiavelli had taught politicians to take into account 'what men do' and not only 'what they ought to do'. For this reason he is respected today as a social and political theorist, but among his contemporaries such an objective study of human nature gave him a reputation for cynicism and irreligion. Puns on the name were common, as in John Webster's *White Devil* (1612):

> Those are found weighty strokes which come from th' hand,
> But those are killing strokes which come from th' head.
> O the rare tricks of a Machivillian!   (V.iii.191–9)

As early as 1591 or 1592, the Prologue for Christopher Marlowe's highly successful *Jew of Malta* was 'Machevill' who told his audience that he should 'be envied and not pitied' because he was free to act as he wished:

> I count religion but a childish toy,
> And hold there is no sin but ignorance.

Addressing his audience, Iago has the same assurance:

> And what's he then that says I play the villain?
> When this advice is free I give and honest,
> Probal to thinking and indeed the course
> To win the Moor again?   (II.iii.331–4)

He takes pleasure in knowing that the 'heavenly shows' of his advice are, in practice, the 'Divinity of hell' (ll. 345–8). By using his 'Machivillian' knowledge of the motivation of other persons and by an appearance of honesty, Iago works secretly to his own advantage.

When he claims the right of silence that 'all slaves are free to' (III.iii.138), Iago brings still wider issues into play, speaking for everyone in his audience whose life is governed by men of greater power than themselves. In the same rebellious way, he had earlier explained to Roderigo that he follows Othello:

> to serve my turn upon him.
> We cannot all be masters, nor all masters
> Cannot be truly followed.

With sharply observed detail taken from everyday living that anyone in an audience at the Globe Theatre would have recognized, Iago speaks for a new consciousness to be found throughout Europe as individuals became increasingly dissatisfied with the position in society in which they found themselves and began to question established power and authority:

> You shall mark
> Many a duteous and knee-crooking knave
> That, doting on his own obsequious bondage,
> Wears out his time much like his master's ass
> For nought but provender, and, when he's old, cashiered.
> Whip me such honest knaves! Others there are
> Who trimmed in forms and visages of duty,
> Keep yet their hearts attending on themselves
> And, throwing but shows of service on their lords,
> Do well thrive by them, and, when they have lined their coats,
> Do themselves homage: these fellows have some soul
> And such a one do I profess myself. . . .
> Where I the Moor, I would not be Iago.
> In following him I follow but myself.   (I.i.41–57)

Iago has a double self: the honest Iago whom he plays successfully in other people's eyes, and the clear-eyed, calculating, ruthless, and self-promoting Iago. He takes pleasure in the difference, deriving 'sport and profit' from manipulating such a 'fool' as Roderigo with a profession of friendship (I.iii.382–5). Shakespeare had already created such a double consciousness by giving his characters a sense of performance and ability to control and comment on the impression they give. With Richard III, Richard II, Henry Bolingbroke,

Prince Hal and Henry V, and Brutus, this served political narratives; with Falstaff, Benedict, Rosalind, and Viola, it heightened and refined comedy. In *The Tragedy of Othello*, this cast of mind belongs to the hero's opponent who does not want to be 'known aright' as Othello, Hamlet, or Brutus do. At the start of the play, Iago takes the audience into his confidence, as Aaron or Richard III had done earlier, sharing his pleasure in dissimulation, but he does not remain so open: his last words, as he surveys the result of his 'work', are:

> Demand me nothing. What you know, you know.
> From this time forth I never will speak word.   (V.ii.300–1)

Iago's mind seeks satisfaction in its own independent self, not in relation to other people.

The Venetian setting was used by Shakespeare for a tragedy that is driven by two unstoppable forces within the principal persons involved; the thoughts and feelings aroused by sexuality in a society famed for 'the infinite superfluities of all pleasure and delight', and the pressures in active minds aroused by differences of status in a state where 'strangers' are tolerated and all men able to seek their own fortunes as servants of the state. Great 'content' in a love-match and independent ambition in service contain tensions that become increasingly intolerable during the course of the tragedy.

Narrative Drive

Once the play's action moves to Cyprus, events are driven forward both by Iago's manipulations and the private needs of its other principal persons. Desdemona's first appearances after Othello's arrival in Cyprus are brief, but revealing and crucial to Iago's plans. On her first entrance, she says only 'What is the matter, dear?' but, having come from the marriage bed that Othello had left when a riot caused the island's alarm bell to ring, her appearance is more vulnerable than before. Next she is seen with Emilia agreeing to speak for Cassio, Othello's friend and newly apppointed Lieutenant who is now disgraced for being the drunken cause of the disturbance.

When Othello and Iago enter and Cassio leaves, she takes Cassio's part as she has promised, showing greater verbal intimacy with her husband than before: she is playful, confident, affectionate, taunting, and she has her way. Othello, unable to resist, twice assures her: 'I will deny thee nothing' (III.iii.76, 83) and so she leaves, happily 'obedient'. In all this an audience knows better what is happening than either Desdemona or Othello: in a soliloquy at the end of the previous Act, Iago had planned to:

> . . . draw the Moor apart
> And bring him jump when he may Cassio find
> Soliciting his wife. . .   (II.iii.380–2)

After Desdemona has left, Iago goes to work with Othello, playing on the insecurity, the 'discords', that have already been suggested:

> She did deceive her father, marrying you,
> And when she seemed to shake, and fear your looks,
> She loved them most.
>   *And so she did.*
>   Why, go to then:
> She that so young could give out such a seeming
> To seel her father's eyes up, close as oak –
> He thought 'twas witchcraft.   (III.iii.209–14)

Iago stops there, for his task is almost done. When left alone, Othello doubts his ability to gain Desdemona's love because of his race, his military profession, and his age, and a nightmare takes possession of his mind:

> Haply for I am black
> And have not those soft parts of conversation
> That chamberers have, or for I am declined
> Into the vale of years – yet that's not much –
> She's gone, I am abused, and my relief
> Must be to loathe her. O curse of marriage
> That we can call these delicate creatures ours
> And not their appetites! I had rather be a toad
> And live upon the vapour of a dungeon

> Than keep a corner in the thing I love
> For others' uses.   (ll. 267–77)

Unable to bear the uncertainty, when he next sees Iago he threatens him: 'Villain, be sure thou prove my love a whore' (III.iii.362–6). From now on, Othello is increasingly driven by destructive passions, as if unable to resist them. His loss, he believes, is a 'destiny unshunnable, like death' (l. 279).

In their next brief encounter, Desdemona is solicitous about a new weakness in her husband. She ties a handkerchief around his head to ease a pain and, somehow, it drops to the floor. The dialogue in neither of the original texts specifies who is responsible for this, neither person being aware that it has happened; nor is there a stage direction to clarify matters, all directions in later texts being a modern addition. An audience may be unaware of what has occurred until Emilia picks up the handkerchief and explains, in soliloquy, that this was Othello's first gift and greatly treasured by Desdemona and that her husband has a hundred times 'wooed' her to steal it. She says later that Desdemona had dropped it, but she was not there to see. Iago takes the handkerchief, knowing instinctively that 'This may do something.' He can look further ahead now:

> The Moor already changes with my poison:
> Dangerous conceits are in their natures poisons
> Which at the first are scarce found to distaste
> But with a little art upon the blood
> Burn like the mines of sulphur.   (III.iii.327–31)

At the end of Act I, Iago was sure that Othello's 'free and open nature' meant that he 'will be as tenderly be led by th' nose / As asses are' (I.iii.398–401) and now he sets out to do just this by portraying Cassio and Desdemona as 'prime as goats, as hot as monkeys' (III.iii.406). When Othello again asks for proof, Iago invents a story about sharing a bed with Cassio who cries out in a dream:

> And then, sir, would he gripe and wring my hand,
> Cry 'O sweet creature!' and then kiss me hard

As if he plucked up kisses by the roots
That grew upon my lips, lay his leg o'er my thigh,
And sigh, and kiss, and then cry 'Cursed fate
That gave thee to the Moor!' (ll. 423–8)

For additional evidence, he tells how he saw Cassio wipe his beard with the treasured handkerchief. His torment growing, Othello at last cries out 'O monstrous! monstrous!' and vows to take physical revenge: 'I'll tear her all to pieces!' (ll. 428, 434). His participating imagination and passion climax in a single word, the cry of 'O blood, blood, blood!' (l. 454) that sums up many responses: dishonour, shame, doom, horror, revenge, sadistic pleasure, lust. He steadies himself by kneeling and making a 'sacred vow' to destroy both Desdemona and her supposed lover.

During Othello's silences while he listens, rapt and responsive, to Iago, an actor has to sustain a highly charged emotional performance so that his wounded cries will sound credible as expressions of great feeling until a strongly structured speech defines what Othello hopes will happen, rather than what has already occurred within him. Images and rhythms define the compulsion that physically and mentally has transformed him:

> Like to the Pontic sea
> Whose icy current and compulsive course
> Ne'er keeps retiring ebb but keeps due on
> To the Propontic and the Hellespont:
> Even so my bloody thoughts with violent pace
> Shall ne'er look back, ne'er ebb to humble love
> Till that a capable and wide revenge
> Swallow them up. (ll. 456–63)

With hindsight, looking back from the end of the tragedy, a reader may recognize 'humble love' as an amazing counter-thought, a sign of complexity and tension even among the pressures of such violence. Yet the powerful flow of utterance is not deflected: the metaphor of 'swallow' and the placing of this word, syntactically and metrically, show how completely and helplessly Othello longs for release from torture by embracing violence. Othello leaves the stage expressing torrid anger and precise purpose, as if both are needed to contain the wrenching pain that is fuelled by thoughts of Desdemona's dangerous sexuality:

> Damn her, lewd minx: O damn her, damn her!
> Come, go with me apart; I will withdraw
> To furnish me with some swift means of death
> For the fair devil. Now art thou my lieutenant.   (ll. 478–81)

The action now begins to take its course and Desdemona can do nothing to stop it. Not wanting to lose this treasured keepsake, she conceals the loss of the handkerchief only for Othello to speak of its magic power:

> To lose't or give't away were such perdition
> As nothing else could match.   (III.iv.69–70)

Trouble escalates. She wishes she had never seen it and he replies 'startingly and rash' (l. 81). She tries to minimize the problem by saying 'it is not lost' and, when he wants proof of that, she suspects 'a trick' is being played to put her from requesting Cassio's reinstatement. At this point, such strong feelings are aroused in him that he is at a loss for words, and he can only repeat three times, 'The handkerchief!', and leave the stage with an oath. Unwittingly, Desdemona has confirmed the 'dangerous conceits' with which Iago has poisoned Othello's mind and now burn in his veins like sulphur.

Before Desdemona returns to the stage, Iago brings Othello to overhear himself talking with Cassio about Bianca, his mistress, having told him they will be speaking of Desdemona. By a stroke of luck, Bianca enters to give back the handkerchief, the embroidery of which Cassio had asked her to copy. This still more convinces Othello that Iago has told the truth so that, when he is next with Desdemona in public, he strikes and abuses her to the astonishment of the Venetian delegation that has arrived to terminate his governorship of the island: when she weeps, he orders her away (IV.i.224–60). He leaves almost at once, his public demeanour destroyed again with a cry of 'Goats and monkeys!' (l. 263). Going to her room, he treats her like a whore and disbelieves all her protests. She is bewildered and helpless: 'I understand a fury in your words / But not the words' (IV.ii.32–3). When she approaches her husband, he orders her away and weeps; when she tries to sympathize, he calls her an 'impudent strumpet' although she swears on her salvation that she is not. At this point he calls Emilia and, throwing money at her as if she were keeper of a brothel, leaves the stage.

In a further public scene, when emissaries from Venice are about to leave, he scarcely speaks to her except to order 'Get you to bed' (IV.iii.5–7). In so far as an audience has been drawn to think and feel with Desdemona during the earlier Acts, it will have shared in the pain caused by Othello's violent onslaughts and his inability to hear what she says or see how she suffers. It will have been appalled, too, by Othello's failure to grasp what Iago has done and by his helplessness when he falls to the ground in a fit, after crying out as if he were witnessing Cassio sexually mastering his wife (see IV.i.35–43). An audience watches the approach of a disaster that seems unstoppable.

Reflection

Immediately after Othello and the Venetian visitors have left the stage, Desdemona is shown preparing for bed, helped by Emilia. This intimate and almost unhurried scene is a contrast to everything else, a release from the violence in which an audience's sympathies can strengthen and attention be paid once more to suggestion and half-expressed or unfamiliar feelings. Emilia sets a new tone with 'How goes it now? He looks gentler than he did' (IV.iii.9) and she becomes more outspoken when Desdemona does as Othello has 'commanded', dismissing her and asking for her 'nightly wearing'. Her quick 'Would you had never seen him!' prompts Desdemona to speak her mind too, in a re-affirmation of the love that had 'subdued' her heart (I.iii.249–60):

So would not I: my love doth so approve him

That even his stubbornness, his checks, his frowns
– Prithee unpin me – have grace and favour in them.
I have laid those sheets you bade me on the bed.
All's one. Good faith, how foolish are our minds.
If I do die before thee, prithee shroud me
In one of these same sheets.
                              Come, come, you talk.
My mother had a maid called <u>Barbary</u>,
She was in love, and he she loved proved mad
And did forsake her. She had a song of 'willow',
An old thing 'twas, but it expressed her fortune
And she died singing it.

Future and past are both present to Desdemona as she prepares for
bed and thinks about her childhood, dying, and the possibility of
going mad. Yet this complexity is unforced and unstudied; for an
audience, it will seem artless, as inevitable as changes in the sky as
night aproaches.

Emilia's unpinning of Desdemona's hair brings the two women
into very close physical contact and, because unforeseen pauses are
bound to occur as hair is shaken loose from its pins and carefully
handled, an element of shared improvisation draws their minds
together too. As Emilia, or perhaps Desdemona, brushes the long
tresses, a regular and soothing rhythm will be established. In this
calm, thoughts wander and settle where they will: Desdemona has
'much to do / But go hang [her] head all at one side / And sing [the
song] like poor Barbary'. Emilia tries to change the subject by
talking of the sexual attractions of Lodovico, their visitor from
Venice:

I know a lady in Venice would have walked barefoot to Palestine for a
touch of his nether lip.

This releases any reserve so that both speak familiarly in prose and
Desdemona sings a song she had remembered, one widely known in
Shakespeare's day as the complaint of a male lover who has been
rejected, not of a young woman:

> The poor soul sat sighing by a sycamore tree,
>> Sing all a green willow:
> Her hand on her bosom, her head on her knee,
>> Sing willow, willow, willow.
> The fresh streams ran by her and murmured her moans,
>> Sing willow, willow, willow: . . .

The song takes its own time and the repeated refrain and rhymes give a more regular pulse to the scene. The rural setting of the lyric, like those of Ophelia's mad songs and speeches, and of Gertrude's description of her death (see above, pp. 151–2), simplifies and softens the language while associating hopeless love with the endless stream of time and of death. Desdemona is so at ease now that she interrupts her singing to ask Emilia to 'lay by' some pins or ornaments. Soon she misquotes the song's words and so voices her own thoughts that still centre on Othello: 'Let nobody blame him, his scorn I approve' (l. 51). So an audience is shown that the constancy of Desdemona's love comes from her unconscious as well as her resolute mind.

Desdemona has become hyper-sensitive. She thinks someone knocks when it is only the wind and, bidding good night to Emilia, feels that her eyes itch. She is also aware of being alone and in need of companionship:

> O, these men, these men!
> Dost thou in conscience think – tell me, Emilia –
> That there be women do abuse their husbands
> In such gross kind? (ll. 59–63)

Emilia lightens the mood with humour:

> *Desdemona.* Wouldst thou do such a deed for all the world?
> *Emilia.* Why, would not you?
> *Desdemona.* No, by this heavenly light!
> *Emilia.* Nor I neither, by this heavenly light:
> I might do't as well i'th' dark.

Emilia's fantasy feeds on day-to-day circumstances of ordinary lives:

> Marry, I would not do such a thing for a joint-ring, nor for measures
> of lawn, nor for gowns, petticoats, nor caps, nor any petty exhibition.
> But for all the whole world? ud's pity, who would not make her
> husband a cuckold to make him a monarch? I should venture purga-
> tory for't.   (ll. 71–6)

As Desdemona holds her ground, Emilia rises to the challenge – 'I
do think it is their husband's faults / If wives do fall' – and follows
that with a manifesto for women's rights that scholars have found
nothing contemporary to match:

>   What is it that they do
> When they change us for others? Is it sport?
> I think it is. And doth affection breed it?
> I think it doth. Is't frailty that thus errs?
> It is so too. And have not we affections?
> Desires for sport? and frailty, as men have?
> Then let them use us well: else let them know,
> The ills we do, their ills instruct us so.   (ll. 95–102)

   In an open-air and popular theatre, such as the Globe, Emilia's
frank-speaking, sustained over eighteen lines, might well incite
members of an audience to cry out in support or, possibly,
in outrage. Desdemona's response is both affectionate and
apprehensive, while keeping more private and particular thoughts
to herself:

> Good night, good night. God me such usage send
> Not to pick bad from bad, but by bad mend!

They leave the stage at opposite sides, Emilia silent now. This scene
for two women counterbalances the long and contrasting scene in
Act III after which two men had left together in agreement after an
intense and impassioned meeting. In performance, its effect and
structural importance are far stronger and clearer than in a reading:
attention shifts away from action to intimacy and reflection; talk is
quiet and careful, pretension answered with humour, independence
of mind with suggestions of madness.

The Final Act

The next scene is the play's most fragmented and dangerous. As at the beginning of the play, action takes place in darkness but, instead of loud alarms and crowded entries, men enter stealthily, one or two at a time and speaking urgently; they hide and call out for help; they strike to kill and cry in pain. Othello appears and, believing Cassio to have been killed, leaves almost at once, hastened by 'fate' to go to Desdemona and kill her: 'Thy bed, lust-stained, shall with lust's blood be spotted' (V.i.36). Raised by the cries, Bianca runs onto the stage and is taken off under suspicion of having instigated the violence. All this is in stark contrast with Othello's entry to the sleeping Desdemona that follows immediately at the beginning of the last scene in the tragedy:

> It is the cause, it is the cause, my soul!
> Let me not name it to you, you chaste stars,
> It is the cause. Yet I'll not shed her blood
> Nor scar that whiter skin of hers than snow
> And smooth as monumental alabaster. . .   (V.ii.1ff.)

The 'cause' is not defined, but Othello's words and actions establish the depth of his response to the beauty of Desdemona's body. He had left the previous scene denouncing a 'strumpet' (V.i.33) and intent on violence, but now he is incapable of murder. He stands amazed at his wife's perfection – 'Thou cunning'st pattern of excelling nature' (l. 11) – and is drawn towards her tenderly:

> when I have plucked the rose
> I cannot give it vital growth again,
> It needs must wither. I'll smell thee on the tree;
> O balmy breath, that does almost persuade
> Justice to break her sword!   (ll. 13–17)

He kisses her, perhaps three times, and weeps (see ll. 17–21), justifying what he is about to do by quoting scripture: 'This sorrow's heavenly, / It strikes where it doth love.'

Torn betweeen responding to Desdemona's beauty and resolving to kill her, Othello's feelings change frequently and alarmingly as he delays her death. He asks, gently, whether she has prayed and 'walk[s] by' to give her time to do so; he prays for her; he is reduced to an inarticulate 'Hum!'; his eyes 'roll' and his whole body 'shakes'; he says his heart is turned to stone. In comparison, Desdemona is steadfast, struggling to understand and assuring him of her love, even as he means to kill her. After long and tense delay, thinking that she weeps for Cassio, he starts to force her down onto the bed to kill her and she begs for life or for a day's delay, a half-hour's, or time for one prayer. Then he '*smothers her*' (l. 83, S.D.). Only one of the two original texts gives her a verbal response: 'O Lord! Lord! Lord!' Probably, she attempts to pray or, perhaps, she cries out in alarm or pain. Rarely did Shakespeare call for a woman to be killed on stage and never was the act of murder protracted for so long, for the smothering is not immediately effective and, five lines after she is pronounced dead, Desdemona stirs only to be killed once more. Nor is there precedent for the murderer's swift realization of the effects of his crime or for his suffering:

> My wife, my wife! what wife? I have no wife.
> O insupportable, O heavy hour!
> Methinks it should be now a huge eclipse
> Of sun and moon, and that th'affrighted globe
> Should yawn at alteration.   (V.ii.96–100)

Even the second killing is not final. After Emilia has entered, Desdemona revives to life yet again and reasserts her innocence: 'O falsely, falsely murdered! . . . A guiltless death I die' (ll. 115, 121). When questioned, however, she changes her testimony to take the blame herself and so try to save his life:

> *Emilia.*   O, who hath done
>   This deed?
> *Desdemona.*   Nobody. I myself. Farewell.
>   Commend me to my kind lord – O, farewell!
>   (V.ii.121–3)

At first Othello seems willing to take the reprieve that Desdemona offers, but not for long: he needs to brand his wife as evil if he is to justify his own action: 'She's like a liar gone to burning hell,' he cries: ''Twas I that killed her' (ll. 127–8). Any doubt an audience might have about Desdemona's love of her husband, will be dispelled by her last words and further progress towards the tragedy's conclusion, although it involves highly dramatic events, will seem comparatively slow and inevitable. Shakespeare has ensured that Desdemona's contribution to the tragedy continues until its very last lines: repeatedly attention is drawn to her body, especially by Emilia who dies at her side and by Othello, although he recognizes that the sight is 'horrible and grim' (l. 201). His last act, after suicide, is to try to kiss his dead wife.

Desdemona

While Desdemona's part in the tragedy is not large in terms of the number of words she speaks, its effect is far greater because handled so differently from that of any other character. With so much for the audience to infer and for the performer to suggest by physical, non-verbal means, the part is capable of very different interpretations. In her *Lectures on Shakespeare* (1932), Ellen Terry said that Desdemona called for 'a great tragic actress, with a strong personality' because only a man of great nobility and valour would cause her to 'consecrate' her soul and fortunes. She also stressed Desdemona's unconventionality as a 'woman who being devoid of coquetry behaves as she feels'. For Irene Worth, who played the role at the Old Vic in London in 1951, an instinctive sensuality was a crucial element in the character. In a *Times* interview, she described Desdemona as

> a young Italian whose love is not a sentimental attitude of mind, but an awakened and canalized sensuality which yet sometimes breaks its bounds and unconsciously overflows.

She believed that this love is 'so jubilant' that it includes the friends of the beloved and thereby 'lends a dreadful hue of probability to Othello's suspicions.' More recently, Desdemona's courage has sometimes made the greatest impression. In *The Sunday Times,* John Peters commented on a production of 1997 at the National Theatre in London:

> Next time anybody tells you that Desdemona is not much of a part, send them to see Clare Skinner's delicate, poised, achingly generous performance. . . ; her voice and her slender body command the stage, and I shall not easily forget her little fists flailing in bewildered fury against Othello's chest: two doomed innocents in hellfire.

Such an impersonation may seem foreign to a text written to be performed by a young male actor, but one of the very rare accounts of any performance in Shakespeare's own day also comments on physical presence: when the tragedy was acted at Oxford in 1610, Desdemona's death 'moved us especially, when as she lay in her bed, her face only implored the pity of the audience.'

A further sign that the role of Desdemona has always been exceptional are some of the major differences between the two early texts of the play. The Folio of 1623 includes Desdemona's singing of the willow song and Emilia's singing of part of it just before she dies, while the Quarto of 1622 has neither. Ernst Honigmann, the Arden editor, believes that both passages were in Shakespeare's first draft and that he subsequently deleted them in another manuscript, probably because the King's Men lacked an actor who could sing well enough, and it was this second version that was responsible for the Quarto text. Both passages were retained in a third authorial copy that, through a scribe's copy, has given us the Folio text. Other explanations of the differences are also plausible, the matter being complicated because two other passages found only in the Folio, Roderigo's concluding account of Desdemona's elopement (I.i.119–35) and Emilia's speech about marriage (IV.iii.85–102), are most readily explained as additions made to clarify the action and its consequences; in Roderigo's case the speech is somewhat out of the speaker's character. Whether these four major changes are additions or deletions, they all affect how an audience will perceive

Desdemona, and the three occurring in the last two Acts lead us to think that Shakespeare was not easily pleased with what performance had achieved. In creating this heroine, he was pushing against limits in his own art and that of his actors.

Othello and Iago

The Tragedy of Othello, the Moor of Venice can be seen as a life-and-death struggle between Othello and Iago, the idealist and the pragmatist, the courageous and the ruthless soldier, a man at the height of his career and another dissastisfied with his, the Moor and the Venetian. While Iago has the more dynamic role in the first three Acts, Othello dominates the stage during the last long scene. In performance, the actors of these two parts will often vie with each other for the audience's sympathies and acclaim, Iago despite his obvious immorality and Othello despite his persistent gullibility and final cruelty. Yet this view of the tragedy is insufficient, most obviously because it tends to ignore the very different presence of Desdemona and, to a lesser extent, of Emilia.

Throughout, Othello stands alone in being 'the Moor,' arousing suspicion, misjudgement, fear, and hatred. As we have seen, racial slurs mark the opening scenes, imputing ugliness, bestiality, barbarity, and hellish 'practices' (I.iii.103). Even when praising Othello and urging Brabantio to accept him, the Duke alludes to an inherent racial disadvantage:

> If virtue no delighted beauty lack
> Your son-in-law is far more fair than black. (I.iii.290–1)

When Iago traps Othello into jealousy, he insinuates that Desdemona must have a will 'most rank' and thoughts 'unnatural' to have been attracted to someone who is not 'Of her own clime, complexion and degree' (III.iii.232–42). As soon as he is alone again, Othello concedes that 'Haply for I am black' he has lost Desdemona's love (III.iii.267–72).

Against the tide of suspicion and resentment, Othello seems at first to be secure. He is a soldier of impressive composure and command. Confronted by an incensed Brabantio and a mob of his armed servants, he speaks with authority and humour: 'Keep up your bright swords, for the dew will rust them' (I.ii.59). The account of his wooing that he gives to the Senate is reserved, observant, and modestly assertive; he speaks with gentle wonder of Desdemona's love for him. But, as we have seen, all this is precariously achieved and, when his confidence has gone and he believes his wife to be a whore, he becomes violent, roars out loud, falls down in a fit, and repeatedly calls himself fool. The man who had been 'all in all sufficient' (IV.i.265) becomes a murderer as if yielding to some inner compulsion. Racist prejudice surfaces yet again in Emilia's denunciation of Othello as the 'blacker devil . . . ignorant as dirt' and of the marriage as a 'most filthy bargain' (V.ii.129, 160, 153).

Neither text nor action implies that disaster occurs as a direct result of Othello being the victim of racial discrimination, rather that he is well able to withstand abuse and suspicion until he begins to fear rejection. If Othello is represented on stage as a dark-skinned, North African Moor, rather than a much blacker representative of central or southern African descent – and a portrait of the Moorish Ambassador to the court of Elizabeth painted around 1600 suggests that this was how Shakespeare could have imagined him (see Plate 7) – the allusions to his blackness would have been self-evidently prejudiced and false from the start and would belittle those who make them. Inevitably, an audience will be caught between several different views of Othello, as if Shakespeare had wished to test its responses: a leader of men, of great dignity and effectiveness; a gentle, even tender, man who is transformed by self-doubt and sexual passion; a 'black' Moor pursued by racial hatred and suspicion. Shakespeare seems to have encouraged doubt and argument as if to prevent an audience accepting any single explanation of Othello's insecurity and destructive impulses.

The much cruder story found in Giraldi Cinthio's *Hecatommithi* (1565), that was Shakespeare's source, either in the Italian or in some translation now lost, provided a number of judgements on its outcome. The original 'Disdemona' acknowledges that 'Italian ladies will learn by my example not to tie themselves to a man whom

7 The Moorish Ambassador to Queen Elizabeth, 1600–1

Although a contemporary drawing exists that differentiates Aaron the Moor from other characters in *Titus Andronicus* by showing his skin to be totally black, this portrait of Abdul Guahid, Ambassador from the King of Morocco, shows how Elizabethans would have seen a real-life and high-ranking Moor on an official visit to London. (*The painting hangs in the entrance hall of the Shakespeare Institute at Stratford-upon-Avon and is reproduced by kind permission of the University of Birmingham.*)

Nature, Heaven, and manner of life separate from us.' However, other people are said to have blamed the father for giving his daughter a name, which in the Greek means 'unfortunate'; others blamed the Moor for being too credulous. Shakespeare provided nothing so clear-cut: Lodovico's concluding speech which calls Iago a 'Spartan dog' and 'hellish villain', is much less judgemental about Othello, speaking in condemnation only of the 'tragic loading of this bed' that 'poisons sight' (V.ii.359–69).

An audience is given the clearest lead when Othello holds everyone back to make a last statement before he is led off as prisoner to wait until the nature of his 'fault be known' (V.ii.334). He begins simply: 'I have done the state some service, and they know't: . . .' and asks his captors to 'Speak of me as I am. Nothing extenuate, / Nor set down aught in malice.' Having gained attention, however, he sets out a number of different judgements on himself: he had loved 'not wisely, but too well', was 'not easily jealous, but, being wrought, / Perplexed in the extreme.' He then raises the racial issue by likening himself to 'the base Indian' who foolishly 'threw a pearl away / Richer than all his tribe.' This could be taken as a confession that he is 'base' because he is an alien but, in fact, he says only that he has been so foolish that he was 'like' such a person. (Some modern editors prefer the Folio's 'Judean' which introduces a possible, but otherwise unsupported, allusion to the betrayal of Christ.) Judgement is then further complicated by the tears that Othello sheds as he continues to give evidence:

> Set you down this,
> And say besides that in Aleppo once,
> Where a malignant and a turbanned Turk
> Beat a Venetian and traduced the state,
> I took by th'throat the circumcised dog
> And smote him – thus!   *He stabs himself.*   (ll. 149–54)

Here he presents himself as a proud and instinctive member of the Venetian state until, with another twist of his argument, he treats himself as a 'malignant and a turbanned Turk' to be dealt with as an alien 'dog'. His suicide is an unequivocal action but gives a double and contradictory evaluation, insisting that he has acted both as a Venetian and as an enemy alien.

As Desdemona's physical presence has exceptional effect in the conclusion of the tragedy, so Othello's physical act of suicide 'mars' or, at least, overtakes all that is spoken. After the suicide, he speaks a simply-worded couplet that is, once more, ambiguous, since it can be spoken with tenderness or bitterness, perhaps, even, with pride; its unmistakable purpose is to prepare for a last physical statement as he kisses his victim's corpse, or tries to do so:

> I kissed thee ere I killed thee: no way but this,
> Killing myself, to die upon a kiss.

Finally, an audience knows Othello not only in his words, but in how he speaks and what he does. The culminating effect of his part in the tragedy depends on a kiss, the regaining of physical contact in an act and avowal of love: an essentially private act in a very public context.

The sustained cruelty of Othello towards Desdemona has the effect of removing him from an audience's sympathies but, operating against this antagonizing effect, many of Othello's speeches have been written, as those of Hamlet had been, so that they reach deep into the consciousness of his audience by raising images and ideas of widest and instinctive appeal. Sometimes Othello seems so openly and instinctively inspired by some half-realized, entrancing vision that his audience follows regardless of his intention or accompanying actions. So, for example, at the beginning of the last scene, he brings to mind the stars, white skin, snow, and monumental alabaster at the very moment when he is about to murder his wife (see p. 213, above) and those that hear him will tend to think and feel with him, however much they reject his credulity and are repulsed by his ruthless and sustained cruelty.

Othello's words reverberate on many levels when least this might be expected. After the murder has been committed and he sees how he has been duped, he looks at his wife's body:

> Now: how dost thou look now? O ill-starred wench,

> Pale as thy smock. When we shall meet at compt
> This look of thine will hurl my soul from heaven
> And fiends will snatch at it. Cold, cold, my girl,
> Even like thy chastity. O cursed, cursed slave!
> Whip me, ye devils,
> From the possession of this heavenly sight!
> Blow me about in winds, roast me in sulphur,
> Wash me in steep-down gulfs of liquid fire!   (V.ii.270–8)

Much of this imagery may be expected from a Christian convert, although he has committed himself to 'black vengeance, from the hollow hell' (III.iii.450). Less expected will be the simple, everyday evocation of a pale smock and the sense of actual pain in the succession of active monosyllabic verbs: *meet, hurl, snatch, whip, blow, roast, wash*. After this build-up of sensation, crowned with the compact 'steep-down gulfs of liquid fire', an image of dizzying vastness, comes the simple calling of an intimate name, joined with inarticulate expressions of pain and sorrow that are affecting beyond any quality inherent in the words themselves: 'O Desdemon! dead, Desdemon. Dead! O, O!' (l. 279).

To follow all three major participants in the tragedy to its conclusion requires an understanding that outreaches anything they say. After Othello has died, Iago stands, a convicted 'viper' and 'devil', and says nothing when attention is again directed to him and he is told to 'look upon' his work (ll. 359–62). Othello, having kissed his wife, lies beside her with whatever expressiveness remains in his body that is dying so quickly that no one on stage thinks of trying to revive it. Desdemona has been long dead and all her considerable effect on the concluding events will draw upon an audience's memories, its complicity in her tender-hearted loyalty and its imaginative response to the 'heavenly' beauty and sexual attraction of her person. Shakespeare has written a tragedy that encourages an audience to see and judge its characters 'as they are' (see V.ii.340), without extenuation or malice, so that its members are individual arbitrators between personal worth and the fate that has seemed to hasten their destruction.

Inevitability

Towards the end of the earlier tragedy, Hamlet had said that

> There's a divinity that shapes our ends,
> Rough-hew them how we will. (V.ii.10–11)

Othello's pronouncement on fate occurs much earlier and concerns the handkerchief his mother had given him and he has already lost:

> That handkerchief
> Did an Egyptian to my mother give,
> She was a charmer and could almost read
> The thoughts of people. She told her, while she kept it
> 'Twould make her amiable and subdue my father
> Entirely to her love, but if she lost it
> Or made a gift of it, my father's eye
> Should hold her loathed and his spirits should hunt
> After new fancies. She, dying, gave it me
> And bid me, when my fate would have me wive,
> To give it her. I did so, and – take heed on't!
> Make it a darling, like your precious eye! –
> To lose't or give't away were such perdition
> As nothing else could match. (III.iv.57–70)

From the start, Hamlet had believed that his 'fate cries out' (I.v.81) and so follows the Ghost in danger of his life; he both embraces his own fate and struggles to shape his own ending. In contrast, Othello meets his fate, as if drawn unwittingly into its net: it seems that the tragedy had to happen once Othello doubted Desdemona's love. In part, that net is woven by Iago (see II.iii.356–7) but his plans develop fully and with astonishing speed because of circumstances beyond his contrivance.

Fateful events start before the handkerchief is lost: the unusually high and monstrous storm at sea plays into Iago's hands before Othello's arrival in Cyprus; so does Roderigo's infatuation with Desdemona and Othello's choice of his own wife as her attendant. Cassio enters and leaves at the beginning of the Temptation Scene exactly as Iago would have wished. The handkerchief is brought into play and dropped by accident when, immediately afterwards, Emilia enters at just the right time to find it and Iago at the right time to be given it in secret. Cassio's mistress is conveniently able to receive the handkerchief and enters to give it back in jealous anger just at the right time to be seen by Othello. Desdemona's earlier advocacy of Cassio gives quite contrary and unintended meanings to her words at the very last moments when Othello is about to murder her. If any one of these accidents were taken away, the house of cards which is the tragedy's plot could have tumbled down and disaster been avoided. Critics have frequently observed that a double time-scheme operates in the play whereby events on Cyprus seem to take a matter of weeks while, simultaneously, those involving the principals seem to occupy no more than a couple of days: this, too, gives an impression of a relentless and unwilled forward pressure towards the tragic conclusion.

An audience that believed in devils might see Iago as someone working in close allegiance to an evil power that is greater than any human agency. So Othello's suffering might appear to be caused by some superior power that wished to test him to the uttermost, rather as the Old Testament God allowed Job to be tempted. Othello gives a hint of this when he tells Desdemona:

> had it pleased heaven
> To try me with affliction, had they rained
> All kinds of sores and shames on my bare head,
> Steeped me in poverty to the very lips,
> Given to captivity me and my utmost hopes,
> I should have found in some place of my soul
> A drop of patience . . .   (IV.ii.48–54)

But, even in the absence of any ghost or supernatural intervention, the pressure of events and collusion of accidents are sufficient to suggest, and even encourage, an impression that this tragedy is the work of some unstoppable power. If not playthings of the gods, all three protagonists appear to be driven by their sexuality and instincts, as if these were 'a destiny unshunable' claiming them all as victims.

Using accident and coincidence in this way helped Shakespeare to lift this tragedy into a new arena. *Sexuality* was not a word current in his day, but its reality is always present and the fateful action of this play exposes its influence on individuals of different gender and origins, raising many other issues such as the nature of affection, confidence, fear and self-doubt, physical strength and intelligence. Besides being the thrilling and very moving play that everyone who has seen it in performance knows it to be, *The Tragedy of Othello, the Moor of Venice* may be judged the most innovative of Shakespeare's tragedies with regard to sexuality, gender, racial inheritance, and social relationships.

11

King Lear: Part One

Uncertainties are all around *The Tragedy of King Lear* and can be found at its very centre. From some perspectives the tragedy is about uncertainties. 'Who is it that can tell me who I am?', 'Do not abuse me', 'He knows not what he says' (I.iv.221; IV.vii.77; V.iii.291): such signals follow the hero throughout the action and echoes of them can be heard everywhere. When Lear is most sure of what he thinks, an audience may believe that he is most mistaken. When he speaks very simply, it may scarcely grasp what he thinks and feels.

Some speeches are clearly intended to deceive or puzzle so that, as Cordelia says, only time can 'unfold what plighted [or pleated, plaited] cunning hides' (I.i.282). Others are only a part of what is communicated, so that Goneril gives 'strange oeillades and most speaking looks' when she talks politely to Edmund (IV.v.27–8). Conscious absurdity or grotesque exaggeration sometimes distort what words normally convey and in ways that will keep an audience unsure in its response. Early in Act I, the Earl of Kent foresees that Lear may become 'mad' (I.i.146–7), in Act II Lear prays Goneril not to make him mad (II.ii.407) and, a little later, he foretells or, possibly, threatens, 'O fool, I shall go mad' (l. 475), and yet, in Act III, Kent says that his wits are only beginning 't'unsettle' (iv.158). Not surprisingly, actors have taken very different views on when Lear actually does go mad, with significant effect on their interpretations of large sections of the text. In reading the play, we will often be tempted to stop and ask whether words are spoken to deceive or to communicate openly, or whether the speaker is in his or her 'perfect mind' (IV.vii.63). Much of this confusion is also found in *The Tragedy of Hamlet* but here, in *King Lear*, speakers struggle to control what they say or become caught in what is inexplicable or unbearable; they are seldom exhilarated, as Hamlet is, by the pursuit of appropriate expression. In this tragedy, language becomes part of an oppression of mind and spirit that must be lived through and is not always conquered.

The Texts

Uncertainty will be in the minds of readers on quite another account which must be considered before any responsible reading of this tragedy. In recent years, scholars have shown that the surviving texts have no straightforward authority. The first Quarto (Q) of 1608 was inexpertly printed and, in places, is so corrupt that it makes little or no sense. The compositors may have worked from an early draft in Shakespeare's own hand but, whatever their copy, it proved very difficult, at times, to decipher. The first Folio (F) of 1623 was printed from a second Quarto of 1619 that has no independent authority, but F's compositors also referred to the first Quarto and, more significantly, to another manuscript that was probably a copy of an alternative version of the play possibly written in Shakespeare's own hand. Major differences are found between Q and F, as well as hundreds of minor ones, and frequently the readings of both texts seem sufficiently Shakespearian for later editors to make different choices between them. Some three hundred lines are found only in Q while more than one hundred are only in F. By printing a conflation of Q and F, choosing the 'better' reading according to informed guesswork and omitting passages from neither, a third composite text has been created that never existed in Shakespeare's day. Rather than do this, a few editors have provided two texts, one based on Q and the other on F; one is called *The True Chronicle History of the Life and Death of King Lear and His Three Daughters*, following Q's title-page, and the other *The Tragedy of King Lear*, following F. Other editors have based their text wherever possible on F, arguing that this represents a later revision by Shakespeare himself.

Reliance on the Folio offers a clear solution and would be the most acceptable option if we could be sure that it was the author who had wished to cut, alter, and add to his play as this text presents it. However, some differences may have been casually or accidentally made or be due to a scribe miscopying Shakespeare's manuscript in the copy used by F's compositors. Some of the smaller additions in F may have been corrections of accidental omissions in Q and not second thoughts about the play. In some of the larger changes, Shakespeare may have modified a first version to better suit the actors or to respond to his audiences' reception of the original text so that, in these respects, F represents a second-best version, rather than an improvement on the first; for example, in the last scene, a long speech for Edgar that prepares for Kent's re-entry (ll. 203–20) may have been cut reluctantly because audiences grew restless, not because Shakespeare thought it unnecessary. In general, the text may have proved too long in performance so that cuts were forced upon its author. Additions may have been made because Lear's intentions in the first scene had been found too mysterious for clarity and the consequences of some of his later actions too narrowly presented; such changes could well have been against Shakespeare's better instincts and the way in which he wanted his play to develop. Sometimes he may have found attention was being drawn to the wrong incidents: for example, when Gloucester has been blinded, the two servants in Q who comment on Goneril's and Cornwall's inhumanity and look to the old man's needs may have been cut from the Folio because they slowed the play down too much at this juncture or were beyond the abilities of the inexperienced actors who had to play them (III.vii.98–106). The same might be true of the Captain's heartless comments when Edmund sends him to follow Lear and Cordelia to prison (V.iii.39–40). In contrast, the actor of the Fool, whose part is comparatively small, may have asked for more opportunities in the middle section of the play and a stronger final line (see III.ii.80–96; III.vi.82); other additions may imply that Lear's affection for his fool had been missed by earlier audiences. In all such matters, the author may have modified the play in the interests of his audiences and cast, rather than to bring it closer to his own conception.

All the cuts and additions that distinquish F from Q cannot be simply or consistently explained. When Q and F differ, arguments can often be made in support of each as Shakespeare's preferred version; elsewhere, both readings seem to be of equal validity. If Shakespeare cut Lear's arraignment of Goneril, with Fool and a supposed madman sitting in judgement, he left his hero in the Folio with little to say or do in III.vi and turned what was an impressive and revealing scene into little more than a series of comings and goings. Perhaps the most crucial and debatable difference between Q and F is at the very end of the play, where neither version is entirely clear about what the king thinks and feels as he dies. Many of these textual issues must remain speculative, as must the further possibility that a still earlier version had shown the King of France returning to Britain at the head of his army rather than leaving the task to his wife, Lear's youngest daughter, Cordelia. The business of a war between the husbands of Lear's two older daughters has been left very understated in both surviving versions for such a significant development in the final Acts. One upshot of all these textual problems is to add more uncertainties to those that are essential to Shakespeare's handling of the action, themes, characters, and dialogue. We can never have a single definitive text of this tragedy and it may well be that one never existed.

The Main Narrative

Amid all these confusions, Lear's story is the one clear and indisputable element. Shakespeare did not find this story in any single source; he probably read several accounts of the early British King Lear and then modified them all to tell the story as he wished it to be, focusing attention more on the king and less on the fate of the country and the struggles between daughters and sons-in-law.

Complications have been kept to a minimum. While in width of view this tragedy is as demanding as any of the others – in some ways, it is the most epic of them all – this amplification is developed independently, very much for its own sake rather than directly involving King Lear. The story starts formally as a king, aged 'fourscore and upward' (IV.vii.61), gives his power away to two of his daughters and, going to live with them, refuses to submit to either of their demands.. He has banished Cordelia, his third and youngest daughter, from the land. The course of his story is that of a journey or pilgrimage in which he faces a series of challenges that go beyond all that he brings upon himself; it has an almost abstract quality like that of much earlier morality plays. Changes of place are significant: the king in his presence chamber is followed by the king asking for his supper after a hunt, going on a journey, demanding entrance to a castle, going off into the storm in open country attended only by his fool. Two other attendants soon join him and serve as markers for the king's progress: one is the Earl of Kent in disguise as an outspoken common servant, the other the Earl of Gloucester's son Edgar who pretends to be Poor Tom, a madman pursued by fiends. With the increasingly frightened Fool, they help Lear to survive and to reconsider the necessities of his life in a hostile environment.

After moving from the open heath to a hovel, the king is taken to the seashore where, now alone and crazed in mind, he meets the Earl of Gloucester, who has been blinded and is now suicidal. This unfortunate, but still sane, subject causes the destitute amd now crazed Lear to present himself once more as 'every inch a king' (IV.vi.106) and to address many persons from his former life as if they were all present around him: Goneril, his eldest daughter, nobles and attendants, thief, judge, beadle, whore, usurer, cozener, 'scurvy politician' (IV.vi.96–168). When Lear at last recognizes Gloucester, he can only counsel tears and patience:

> Thou must be patient. We came crying hither:
> Thou knowst the first time that we smell the air
> We wawl and cry. I will preach to thee: mark me.
>
> *Gloucester.*   Alack, alack the day!
> *Lear.*   When we are born we cry that we are come
> To this great stage of fools.   (IV.vi.172–9)

Lear can no longer distinguish 'which is the justice, which is the thief' and knows that 'the strong lance of justice hurtless breaks' when aimed against sin that is plated with gold (IV.vi.149–50, 161–2). Having lost authority and power, he no longer trusts those who are meant to protect individual rights and maintain good order in society.

At this point he is found by soldiers who have been sent by Cordelia and is reunited with her. In the Quarto version he is cared for by a grave and learned Doctor who calls for 'louder' music (IV.vii.25), a replacement for the sounds of storm and sea that had earlier accompanied Lear. This respite lasts only until king and daughter are defeated in battle, taken captive, and sent to prison. They are seen again after Cordelia has been killed and Lear is about to die, his heart broken of its own accord. Kent, having tried to make his true identity known, recognizes this:

> Vex not his ghost; O, let him pass. He hates him
> That would upon the rack of this tough world
> Stretch him out longer. (V.iii.312–14)

Lear has completed a journey that has been like a slow and progressive torture or a painful investigation conducted before spectators in the theatre. To understand this tragedy, which is confusing in many other ways, his story must be followed step by step.

Physical Suffering

Not only at the end, but throughout, Lear's story is presented in stark and unavoidably physical terms. In a way that was new to himself and almost unknown in the theatre of his time, Shakespeare constantly drew attention to what his hero undergoes in body as well as in mind, in his senses as well as his thoughts and feelings, achievements, and relations with other people. Despite large-scale scenes of ceremony, quarrel, interrogation, and debate, the king is reduced, in one encounter after another, to being silenced by misfortune and unable to articulate his thoughts. An audience often has no alternative but to follow his physical experiences as bewilderment and anger become pain and grief for what he has lost and what he, himself, has done. Shakespeare seems at times to have relied on an audience's sense-reactions rather than its understanding of verbal statements or argument.

At first, Lear stands alone and orders everything, and everyone responds to his slightest word or hesitation. Later, however, in scene after scene, he has to wait upon other people's initiatives: pauses occur and sudden shifts of mood or directions of address, until he impatiently leaves the stage. He weeps and struggles not to weep. He stammers and suffers repeatedly from a giddiness and choking in the throat, which he calls 'the mother' (II.ii.246–8, 310). He kneels to his daughter, against all convention, and behaves with 'unsightly tricks' (II.ii.342–6). When he goes out into the storm, Gloucester and an unnamed Knight prepare an audience for his re-entry by reporting that the heath offers no shelter from the high winds and cataracts of rain; his white hair is torn and he cries out loud to 'contend' with the storm (II.ii.485–92; III.i.1–17). Alternately, he says nothing and then, refusing comfort, relates his physical and very visible pain to a further inward, nameless suffering:

> Thou think'st 'tis much that this contentious storm
> Invades us to the skin: so 'tis to thee,
> But where the greater malady is fixed,
> The lesser is scarce felt.   (III.iv.6–9)

Again he kneels as physical helplessness inspires his first soliloquy:

> Take physic, pomp,
> Expose thyself to feel what wretches feel
> That thou mayst shake the superflux to them
> And show the heavens more just.   (III.iv.33–6)

Having been exposed to suffering himself, he knows that those who live without hope need a restitution that will 'shake' the *status quo*.

Lear's physical suffering continues after the storm is over. On her reappearance in IV.iv, Cordelia has heard that he is 'as mad as the vexed sea' and, when he does reappear at Dover beach, he is a 'side-piercing sight' before which Edgar can say nothing (IV.iv.1–6) and the blind Gloucester, recognizing his voice, 'quakes' in sympathy

(IV.vi.85, 107). When Cordelia meets her father two scenes later, movement, touch, and instinctive physical responses sometimes take precedence over speech. She holds back at first and then, having kissed him, withdraws once more to watch from a distance. When at last they speak, exceptional pauses and reiteration of the simplest words draw the audience's attention to deepset and physical suffering. Slowly, as if feeling his way step by step, Lear regains self-assurance:

> Where have I been? Where am I? Fair daylight?
> I am mightly abused. I should ev'n die with pity
> To see another thus. I know not what to say.
> I will not swear these are my hands: let's see –
> I feel this pinprick. Would I were assured
> Of my condition.   (IV.vii.52–7)

Father and daughter try to kneel to each other and both weep; he touches her tears to make sure they are real (see ll. 57–9, 47–8, 71). At the beginning of the scene, Lear had been brought sleeping on to the stage and, according to a Folio stage direction, carried in a chair, but now he leaves able to walk again. For an audience, their intimacy and mutual concern, and then Lear's recovery, have been made tangible and unmissable.

Lear's most amazing physical actions come later when he enters in the last scene carrying Cordelia's dead body in his arms and tries, against all hope, to find proof that she is still alive. As he strains to listen and speak, it is not always clear whether she is dead or alive and, as his life ebbs slowly away, it is not always clear what he is thinking. Physical actions often take over from words. He calls for a looking-glass and then peers in it to see if her breath will stain it. Meanwhile, those who watch can do nothing but comment, chorus-like:

> *Kent.*   Is this the promised end?
> *Edgar.*   Or image of that horror?
> *Albany.*   Fall, and cease.   (V.iii.261–2)

Lear looks to see if a feather stirs with her breath and, later, seems to hear her speak. He struggles with 'eyes not o'the best' (l. 277), as he tries to recognize the Earl of Kent in the man who has followed him as his servant, Caius. The audience has waited long for this recognition but, now that it comes, it is painfuly incomplete and Albany warns, 'He knows not what he says and vain it is it / That we present us to him' (ll. 291–2).

Lear has become entirely silent, but soon Albany redirects attention back to him with 'O, see, see!' (l. 303) and then, believing Cordelia to be dead, he does speak again until he is again caught up in physical activity and asks for a button to be undone (l. 307). While silent he has been struggling for breath, as any old person will do whose heart is failing and greatly strained. His release from this physical effort is marked when Lear thanks whoever deals with the button. Before now, he had thanked only Kent when, in disguise as a common servant, he had given an unexpected show of loyalty. Such courtesy as this, with no hint of irony, is not equalled by the king anywhere else in the play. Here, together with his need for air and earlier small physical actions, it emphasizes his new dependence on others and new sense of himself.

In the Quarto version, 'Thank you, sir' are Lear's very last words. Afterwards comes only 'O, o, o, o', which is exactly what the Folio text gives to Hamlet after his last words, but in that tragedy, the string of vowels are in conflict with 'The rest is silence', the hero's last words in both texts, making it likely that this late addition was not supplied by Shakespeare but was taken from a book-keeper's record of the usual stage practice. Typographical and bibliographical evidence supports this deduction, so that the *Hamlet* Folio is not a strong argument for keeping the inarticulate *o*'s of the *Lear* Quarto or for omitting the following two lines of text which only the Folio supplies. To do either would make Lear's last words 'Thank you, sir', following a bitter and extended expression of his own despair and sense of injustice:

> And my poor fool is hanged. No, no, no life!
> Why should a dog, a horse, a rat have life
> And thou no breath at all? O thou'lt come no more,
> Never, never, never, never, never.
> Pray you undo this button. Thank you, sir. O, o, o, o.   (ll. 303–8)

With the extra text supplied by the Folio, Lear's last physical actions are to turn back to Cordelia's corpse and towards those attending on him; his last words express an instinctive desire to share and to verify:

> Do you see this? Look on her; look, her lips,
> Look there, look there!   *He dies.*

But the Folio does not remove all confusion because its simple and repetitive final words could be spoken either to share his joy in the illusory belief that Cordelia is alive or, quite the opposite, to insist that attention is paid to Cordelia's death and that others share his distress.

In the course of this tragedy, an audience witnesses a succession of painful experiences that will be felt like one load after another that it must bear. However forcefully the dialogue questions 'the cause in nature' that makes both hard hearts and physical suffering (III.vi.74–5), an accumulative effect of the action is to place a burden on the senses of an audience so that inarticulate feeling may be its dominant response to the tragedy and one of its unique achievements. As Edgar [or Albany in Q] sums up at the end:

> The weight of this sad time we must obey,
> Speak what we feel, not what we ought to say.   (V.iii.322–3)

Emerging from a performance, members of an audience may well want to seek release from the experience in their own chosen company or walk off alone into the darkness of night. However familiar with the text one may be, and whatever the quality of the actors, attending a performance of *King Lear* provides an unavoidably physical and therefore individually experienced sense of its hero's extraordinary journey and death; it is, indeed, like bearing a 'weight'.

Questioning Authority

In scene after scene, along his journey, Lear calls on yet more of his resources and so progressively revalues himself, his family, and his subjects. At times he questions others, seeking some form of reassurance, and often he asks for patience or strength to endure. He struggles to avoid weeping or madness, or to gain attention, respect, revenge, or justice, or to express his anger and hatred in words spoken against the force of the storm. Slowly he comes to recognize what he owes to Cordelia and to the disguised Earl of Kent, and the comfort their presence brings. And he learns the need to be forgiven and for others to bear with him as someone who is 'old and foolish' (IV.vii.84). The distance is great from the authoritative exercise of power at the beginning of the play to such admission of weakness. But this is no simple resolution: even as he clasps Cordelia to him, he wants to 'starve' his enemies before he'll weep and, failing that, curses them as 'murderers, traitors all' (V.iii.24–6, 167). An audience that witnesses and, in some measure, shares in Lear's long journey may well find, when the play is done, that what stays in their minds most vividly is his will to live and to respond to every change of fortune. As Kent says, 'The wonder is he hath endured so long' (V.iii.315–16).

Shakespeare used a wide variety of means to ensure that an audience's understanding is alert to the changes in Lear at each stage of his journey. From one perspective, much goes as might be expected. A father with three children who cannot see that only the youngest is to be trusted is a common theme in fable and folklore, giving rise, for example, to many versions of the Cinderella story; and so is a verbal competition or riddle as a test of worth. An old man hanging on to social position and yet disclaiming responsibility was a well-known type in contemporary life: proverbs and common experience made Jacobeans very aware, as would a lawyer's advice today, of the dangers of parting with property in old age, particularly when proposing to live with one's children. Yet while much goes as might be predicted, this first scene is full of divergent messages, setting one statement against another and leaving contradictions unresolved.

For a man exercising great power, Lear is exceptionally isolated and unpredictable. Before he enters, Kent and Gloucester are puzzled about his decisions and, after giving curt orders, his very first words are about expressing some 'darker purposes'. In the fuller Folio text, the king announces to his sons-in-law, the Dukes of

Albany and Cornwall, how he will divide his kingdom and, in both texts, it is in them that he invests his 'power' (ll. 40–5, 128–32). This seems straightforward, but the arrangement is complicated by Lear's assurance that his 'largest bounty' will extend according to how each daughter publicly declares her love for him (I.i.48–53), which implies that his possessions should go to the most loving daughter, regardless of the worth or status of her husband. In effect, Lear is uncertain whether political reality or personal affection is the more important.

Unexplained reactions continue to invite an audience to question what is happening. When Cordelia, the youngest daughter to whom Lear had expected to give the most 'opulent' share, refuses to say how much she loves her father, why does she use only the one abrupt word 'Nothing', until forced to say more? She has the first long aside in the play to make clear that she distrusts her sisters' words as her father does not, but that does not explain why she is tactless to the point of rudeness when first replying to her father. An audience may also question why she says nothing to the King of France when he publicly betroths himself to her. And why is Kent allowed sufficient time to bid separate farewells to the king and his daughters after he has been banished the land for daring to dispute Lear's rejection of Cordelia? An audience is almost bound to question Lear's judgement when he leaves the stage saying 'Come, noble Burgundy' (l. 268), preferring him to the King of France whose love for Cordelia has proved to be unshakable.

Different ways of addressing the gods can also lead an audience to draw its own conclusions. The setting of the story allowed Shakespeare to escape the ban on treating matters of religion on stage, since Christian theology and rituals are not appropriate to early pagan Britain, and he used this freedom to show how an individual's respect for the gods declared that person's intentions in earthly matters. Lear calls on the gods to authorize his own objectives and, perhaps, to boost his personal confidence. On his rejection of Cordelia, Lear swears comprehensively:

> . . . by the sacred radiance of the sun,
> The mysteries of Hecate and the night,

By all the operation of the orbs
From whom we do exist and cease to be . . .   (ll.110–13)

Faced with Kent's opposition, however, he swears more personally by
Apollo and Jupiter, to which Kent answers with absolute contradiction: 'Now by Apollo, King, / Thou swear'st thy gods in vain' (ll.
162–3). The proprietary attitudes of Lear are contrasted with Kent's
respect; he prays for Lear (l. 143) and commends Cordelia to the
'dear shelter' of unnamed gods – this last, perhaps, the most gentle
expression of sentiment in the entire scene (ll. 183–4). France also
refers to the gods, but as if ignorant of their purposes:

> Gods, gods! 'Tis strange that from their cold'st neglect
> My love should kindle to inflamed respect.   (ll. 256–7)

Among these ways of calling on the gods, none appears more
authentic than another: the action of this tragedy begins to unfold in
an uncertain and contentious world.

   After Lear has left the stage, the consequences of his actions both
sustain the drama's forward impetus and revalue earlier statements.
Cordelia still does not speak to her newly betrothed lord, but her
hostility to her sisters and fear for her father's well-being are now
established beyond question. When she has left, Goneril and Regan
openly criticize their father:

Goneril.	He always loved our sister most, and with what poor judgement he hath now cast her off appears too grossly.
Regan.	'Tis the infirmity of his age, yet he hath ever but slenderly known himself.
Goneril.	The best and soundest of his time hath been but rash; then must we look from his age to receive not only the imper-fections of long-engrafted condition, but therewithal the unruly waywardness that infirm and choleric years bring with them.

This private talk between the sisters also suggests a rivalry that is not
dependent on their father's prompting, but instinctive and self-pro-
tective. They reveal unmistakably that personal and family concerns

are linked with the more political issues of inheritance, authority, and the exercise of political power that are the subject of the large-scale public ceremonies.

While setting this tragedy in the ancient times to which it belongs historically, Shakespeare's treatment of social, political, and intellectual issues is relevant to the uncertainties of the time at its first performances, years that saw an end of the Tudor dynasty and the accession of a Stuart king, the rise of capitalism, renewed religious controversy, and stirrings of social and political unrest. The action moves further into this wider perspective with Lear's next appearance.

Lear with Goneril and Regan

Although he had said that he would 'crawl toward death' (I.i.40), while resident with Goneril he has been out hunting, a pastime for men in their prime, recommended in 1575 by a poem by George Gascoigne because 'It exerciseth strength, it exerciseth wit, / And all the pores and spirits of man'. '*Horns*' are heard from offstage and Lear enters calling impatiently for his dinner and then, for some hundred and eighty lines that are mostly in prose, he is caught up in the domestic activity, complicated in days of formal ceremony, of returning from hunting and preparing for dinner. He also hires Caius, who is Kent in disguise, strikes Oswald, Goneril's personal servant, for lack of respect, and then commends Caius/Kent for tripping him up and mocking him. After Fool's entry, the king's attention is drawn to his fooling. In these various ways, the story of Lear is related to issues of household government, service, loyalty, and long-established customs; and, in doing so, gives rise to anarchic comedy.

Shakespeare has left a great deal to those who stage the play. Being 'bloody as a hunter' (*Twelfth Night*, III.iv.198) and therefore sweating and dirty, Lear will have to change clothes and, probably, wash on stage. The text specifies a hundred knights, but even a mere dozen on stage can create a great deal of business as they help Lear out of his hunting clothes and boots and get ready for his dinner. Meanwhile, having greeted him as 'my pretty knave', Lear allows

Fool to control what happens. His first song 'sounds proverbial', as the Arden editor notes, and is so repetitive in phrasing and general in reference that if he beats out a rhythm, the knights and, perhaps, Lear himself are likely to join in, adding to the noise and, possibly, starting a ring-dance. Feste in *Twelfth Night* demonstrates how, late at night, a fool can lead a company in 'coziers' catches' as if in an 'ale-house' (II.iii.83–8). By now the knights may be drinking in readiness for dinner and creating the sort of commotion in which Yorick poured a 'flagon of Rhenish' on young Hamlet's head (*Hamlet*, V.i.174–5). Yet soon the favoured ringleader has become a 'bitter fool', not least when he traps Lear into repeating the words that had marked Cordelia's rejection:

> *Fool.* Can you make no use of nothing, nuncle?
> *Lear.* Why no, boy; nothing can be made out of nothing.
>   (I.iv.129–30)

Immediately after this, he asks his master to stand by his side and demonstrates that he is another fool (ll. 137–43). Repeatedly, Fool forces Lear to think about his division of the kingdom, his daughters, and his own present situation, perhaps drawing laughter from the knights at their king's expense. Tales of Yorick setting 'the table on a roar' (*Hamlet*, V.i.88–9) suggest how the knights might respond and, as Lear faces the indignities of this crazy disorder, an audience might well join in the laughter.

Eventually Fool risks 'the whip' for his unsettling entertainment and, at this point, Goneril enters and reproves her father for his 'insolent retinue' and 'rank and not to be endured riots' (l. 194). In return, having been roused into reckless spirits, the knights may join together and flagrantly demonstrate their hostility towards her – in much the same manner as Feste and company when interrupted by Malvolio. How far their behaviour is riotous is not specified in the text, but the combination of Fool's jokes and Goneril's reproof is sufficient to bring Lear face to face with his present, unprecedented situation:

> Does any here know me? Why, this is not Lear.
> Does Lear walk thus, speak thus? Where are his eyes?

Either his notion weakens, or his discernings are lethargied – Ha! sleeping or waking? Sure 'tis not so. Who is it that can tell me who I am?

To this the Folio has Fool reply 'Lear's shadow'; in the Quarto it is Lear who says this. Either way, when Lear now asks his own daughter what is her name (l. 227), unreality as well as uncertainty seems to be taking over Lear's mind. Goneril, however, makes a factual reply:

> As you are old and reverend, should be wise.
> Here do you keep a hundred knights and squires,
> Men so disordered, so debauched and bold,
> That this our court, infected with their manners,
> Shows like a riotous inn.

Game-playing is finished. As if disorientated by criticism and lack of respect, Lear calls on 'Darkness and devils' and decides to seek refuge with Regan, his other daughter whose mind, the audience has heard, is at one with Goneril's, 'not to be over-ruled' (I.iii.15–17).

A great change has taken place in the audience's view of Lear and his view of himself. He now sees why he is suffering and alternately his words regain their power and stumble into simplicity, repetition, and inarticulate cries; he also responds physically:

> O most small fault,
> How ugly didst thou in Cordelia show,
> Which like an engine wrenched my frame of nature
> From the fixed place, drew from my heart all love
> And added to the gall. O Lear, Lear, Lear!
> [*Striking his head*] Beat at this gate that let thy folly in
> And thy dear judgement out. Go, go, my people. (ll. 258–64)

Cursing Goneril with sterility, he leaves to go to Regan and yet something unspoken holds him back because he returns to the stage weeping 'hot tears'. He curses his daughter again and, although half-doubting whether it can have 'come to this', vows that he will regain his former power and authority:

                    Thou shalt find
     That I'll resume the shape which thou dost think
     I have cast of for ever. Thou shalt, I warrant thee.   ll. 300–2)

Preparing to ride away, Lear is alone with his fool who once more
attempts to 'be merry' (I.v.11–12). The contrast with his previous
status could hardly be greater. Except for an early 'Ha, ha, ha' from
Lear, laughter is likely to be almost entirely absent, especially after
Lear suddenly talks of Cordelia, saying 'I did her wrong' (l. 24).
After more lame and, probably, forced fooling, Lear recognizes a new
danger and addresses the gods in a very different way than before:

     O let me not be mad, not mad, sweet heaven! I would not be mad.
     Keep me in temper, I would not be mad.   (ll. 43–5)

To this, Fool has no answer but, when called to follow his master off
stage, he stays behind to make a bawdy and generalized joke, probably addressing the audience and daring its members to laugh:

     She's that's a maid now, and laughs at my departure,
     Shall not be a maid long, unless things be cut shorter.   (ll. 49–50)

Out of the fooling, riot, and revaluations of these two scenes at
Goneril's palace, the next movement of Lear's journey brings him,
wearied by a night's travel, into confrontation with both his older
daughters. The setting is now Gloucester's castle to which Regan and
Cornwall, her husband, have gone so that Lear should not find them
at their own home. The mood and substance of the play also
changes yet again: Fool says very little to Lear while father and
daughters openly challenge and test each other, both sides claiming
moral authority. While Lear tries to reassert his authority with
prayers, more curses, and threats of revenge, in reply Regan and
Goneril refuse to allow him a retinue of a single knight. Proved
wrong in thinking that Regan will be kinder towards him, he is left
with nothing with which to bargain except to say, helplessly, 'I gave
you all' (II.ii.439). By the end of the scene, he is torn between two
reactions: he asks the heavens for patience, declaring that 'You see

me here, you gods, a poor old man / As full of grief as age, wretched in both' (ll. 460–2), and then, a moment later, he promises 'revenges' on both daughters – what they will be, he does not know, 'but they shall be / The terrors of the earth.'

Earlier Lear had called for revenge to strike at Goneril from the skies:

> All the stored vengeances of heaven fall
> On her ingrateful top! . . .
> You nimble lightnings, dart your blinding flames
> Into her scornful eyes!   (II.ii.351–5)

Now, as he is about to leave for the open country, a great storm threatens just such violence on himself. As it breaks, he gathers courage and, at the last moment, turns again to Fool who has been silent for almost two hundred lines:

> You think I'll weep,
> No, I'll not weep.   *Storm and tempest.*
> I have full cause of weeping, but this heart
> Shall break into a hundred thousand flaws
> Or e'er I'll weep. O fool, I shall go mad.
> *Exeunt Lear, Gloucester, Kent, Fool.*
>   (ll. 470–5)

Much of this long scene might be thought predictable: Lear's inability to change his daughter's minds and recognition of his own 'folly'; Kent and Gloucester's inability to help him. His last call to Fool is, however, very new: as Lear is on the verge of what can be endured and feels his reason to be failing, he turns to his fool, who is now the only person he can trust and whose fellowship he needs, the fool who has derided his wisdom.

Fool says nothing but must make the physical response of leaving with his master. Does he try to give him some silent comfort or support, or is he too frightened to touch or approach him? Does he go willingly or not? The king might ask where are his gibes, gambols, songs, and flashes of merriment now, as Hamlet had asked Yorick's skull, but the text gives no words to either actor to show

how they should make this *Exeunt* together. Lear could draw Fool to his side or wait for him to come, or he might speak only to himself, breaking away from Fool because he associates him with the madness he fears. Whatever is done must be the actors' choices and be influenced by the progress of their entire performances until this moment. Such delegation of responsibility has been the dramatist's chosen strategy at the close of earlier tragedies, but here the action is only beginning and Lear is about to enter wilder territory where still more will depend on the quality of performance and the impulses that arise within the actors on each occasion that it is played: words alone will be unable to contain and transmit the experience. If an audience wishes to understand the progress of this tragedy, it will have to watch Lear closely and attempt to probe beyond what is said, associating closely in imagination with characters and action.

Lear on the Heath

Act III begins with the storm still raging while Kent and a Knight conveniently provide information. Lear has been 'contending with the fretful elements', alone except for Fool, who 'labours to outjest / His heart-struck injuries' (III.i.16–17). Albany and Cornwall are in dispute and an army from France is on its way to England. Kent sends a message to Cordelia who will be at Dover. Then, with a new scene, Lear enters, 'bareheaded' and calling for the storm to destroy the world and 'all germans spill at once / That make ingrateful man' (III.ii.60, 1–9). His words are driven by violent and sexual visions that are teeming in his mind. Fool says nothing at first and, when he does, it is to beg his master to seek shelter and ask for his daughters' blessing. To this, Lear makes no response but continues to address the storm, now seeing himself as its slave against whom its might is pitted on behalf of 'two pernicious daughters' (l. 22). Then he seems to lose confidence, crying out helplessly, 'O, ho! 'Tis foul.' At this sign of weakness, Fool once again offers mockery and wisdom about unbridled passion and misplaced affection, finishing with an allusion to Goneril and Regan: 'For there was never yet fair woman but she made mouths in a glass.' If Lear notices him, it is only to assert his own separate way as he continues to struggle against wind and rain:

> No, I will be the pattern of all patience.
> I will say nothing.   (ll. 37–8)

Lear has decided to submit and suffer: this is another significant stage in his journey.

Kent, disguised as Caius, has now entered and, recognizing Lear, speaks directly and sympathetically to him. Lear makes no reply but addresses the gods as if the storm were their instrument for punishing deceitful criminals and himself among them, as 'a man / More sinned against than sinning' (l. 60). Kent can only counsel taking shelter in a nearby hovel while he tries to negotiate a return to Gloucester's castle. This time Lear does hear and although, at first, he says only, 'My wits begin to turn' (l. 67), his next speech is sensible and shows him to be concerned with his fool as he has not been before:

> Come on, my boy. How dost my boy? Art cold?
> I am cold myself. [*to Kent*] Where is this straw, my fellow?
> The art of our necessities is strange,
> And can make vile things precious. Come, your hovel.
> [*to the Fool*] Poor fool and knave, I have one part in my heart
> That's sorry yet for thee.   (ll. 68–73)

On the brink of madness, he has discovered a need to look after his fool who has, perhaps, been shivering or whimpering as he huddles close to his master, saying nothing. Alternatively, Lear may have gone to the fool for fellowship, as he has before, and then found that pity for him leads back to an acknowledgement of his own needs. Fool responds by singing about 'content' as the storm still rages:

> He that has and a little tiny wit,
> With heigh-ho, the wind and the rain,
> Must make content with his fortunes fit,
> Though the rain it raineth every day.   (ll. 72–5)

Lear listens and approves: 'True, boy'; he says and, making common cause with the fool, asks Caius/Kent to 'bring *us* to this hovel'.

Lear's new relationship with his fool creates a special and crucial moment. In the Folio text it is marked by Fool remaining behind to address the audience with a mocking acount of the 'confusions' brought about by priests, brewers, nobles, tailors, heretics, wenches' suitors, and others, at some impossible time:

> When every case in law is right
> No squire in debt, nor no poor knight;
> When slanders do not live in tongues . . .   (ll. 81–96)

It would seem that, at one time, Shakespeare saw that Fool could mark the chaos in Lear's mind in terms with which an audience could readily associate. Perhaps he had come to doubt the holding power of a narrative that has brought a very old and nearly insane king to wander on a barren heath during a terrible storm.

In both Quarto and Folio, Fool has nothing at all to say when Lear next appears at the entrance to the hovel to which Kent has led them. With the storm still raging, Lear now cries out against 'filial ingratitude' (III.iv.14), not against the gods or the cold, but he soon recognizes that he must 'shun' those thoughts because 'that way madness lies'. He returns to his concerns at the end of the previous scene, remembering his fool and telling him to go in first. Alone, except for the silent Caius/Kent, he probably kneels down, but he does not pray; instead, he thinks of nameless others less fortunate than himself:

> Poor naked wretches, wheresoe'er you are,
> That bide the pelting of this pitiless storm,
> How shall your houseless heads and unfed sides,
> Your looped and windowed raggedness, defend you
> From seasons such as these?

The next moment he revalues his own life in a much wider context than before by echoing the New Testament's injunction that Christian charity should take pity on all who are helpless: 'O, I have ta'en / Too little care of this.'

All forward energy in Lear's mind seems to have been dissipated or exhausted and Shakespeare marked the moment by springing a surprise on both characters and audience: Gloucester's son Edgar cries from offstage as if he were a madman and a terrified Fool rushes back on stage, believing he has seen a spirit who says his name is Poor Tom. An audience has heard Edgar say that he would take this name but it will not have seen him in the nearly naked and filthy disguise in which he now appears where he is not expected. While the others are probably repulsed, since they say nothing, Lear accepts the apparition at once and identifies its needs with his own, asking, 'Didst thou give all to thy two daughters?' (III.iv.48). Edgar, as Tom, improvises an answer, at first almost unintelligibly as he talks about being tormented by 'the foul fiend' and the cold wind that blows through the hawthorn, but then pretending that he was once a 'serving-man' who is now being punished for his pride and rapacious sexuality (ll. 75–107). Lear, faced by a man he believes to be mad and destitute, sees in him an image of every human being and asks, in words probably derived from both Montaigne and the Old Testament: 'Is man no more than this?' Declaring that 'Unaccommodated man is no more but such a poor, bare, forked animal as thou art', he tries, physically, to become more like Tom by stripping off his own clothes and, with them, all respectability and all signs of power and ordinary sanity.

As Fool argues with Lear, yet another surprise is sprung as Gloucester enters at a distance carrying a light and searching for Lear. For Edgar, the arrival of his father, who had threatened to kill him, will be so shocking that he tries to hide by reverting to incomprehensibly crazy speech and behaviour. When Gloucester offers a better refuge, Lear agrees to go, but only after he has spoken in private with Poor Tom and on condition that he comes along as well. The dramatic focus has only been fitfully on Lear since Gloucester's entrance and it is not clear whether he insists now on listening to Tom because he is more wretched than himself or because he truly wants to know 'the cause of thunder'? Does he ask for private talk because he wants to learn Tom's secret of how to 'prevent the fiend and to kill vermin' (ll. 151, 155–6) or because he alone seems as thoroughly mad as himself? Finally, he leaves with Edgar now, mysteriously, set on spilling blood:

Childe Rowland to the dark tower came,
His word was still 'Fie, foh and fum,
I smell the blood of a British man.'   *Exeunt.*   (ll. 178–80)

The Quarto and Folio have very different versions of the next scene for Lear. In the Folio, it is very short and Lear says little; in the much longer Quarto, he proceeds to set up and superintend an imaginary arraignment of Goneril and Regan, with Fool, Poor Tom, and Caius/Kent all acting as judges. What is common to both versions is yet one more crucial stage in Lear's journey. He is more mad than before, Kent pronouncing that 'All the power of his wits have given way to his impatience' (III.vi.4–5), and, in both versions, Lear starts by asserting that a madman is a king and fantasizing about revenge and having 'a thousand with red burning spits / Come hizzing in upon 'em' (ll. 11–16). He seems to believe that he, like Tom, is pursued by fiends (see ll. 60–1) and so, like Tom, he may 'smell blood' in seeking to punish his daughters. Nevertheless, when Kent suggests that he lies down and rests, Lear agrees, asking for no more noise and for curtains to be drawn. Renewed and, now, destructive energy has exhausted him and, on Gloucester's instructions, Kent is able to carry him off stage to escape a 'plot of death' and take him to Dover where Cordelia should be waiting (ll. 85–94). His growing madness and wholly imaginary attempts at justice and revenge have exhausted him and brought him to what appears to be the end of his story – a long story, in which a king has considered who he is and what his resources are when he has lost everything and when his only counsellors seem to be a fool, a servant, and a violent madman.

Lear at Dover

The journey of self-revaluation is not yet complete. After more than six scenes off-stage, the largest interruption in the play, Lear enters alone, talking to himself and more obviously mad than before. His thoughts have little logical progression, claiming 'I am the King himself' and, immediately afterwards, concerned about a scarecrow, clothier's yard,

mouse, giant, soldiers, arrow and target (IV.vi.83–92). According to
Cordelia in an earlier scene, he has been sighted wearing a crown of
wild flowers and he probably does so now, for he seems increasingly
aware of his lost kingdom. When he sees Edgar, who is already on
stage, he asks for the password as if he were in charge of the situation.
Edgar has discarded his disguise as Poor Tom and, dressed like a
peasant, is accompanying his father, Gloucester, who is now totally
blind. At first Lear does not recognize either of them but, when they
pay him respect, his past comes back with a new sense of what it was:

> They flattered me like a dog. . . . To say 'ay' and 'no' to everything
> that I said 'ay and 'no' to, was no good divinity. . . . They told me I
> was everything; 'tis a lie, I am not ague-proof.   (ll. 96–104)

When Gloucester recognizes the voice and asks 'Is't not the King?',
Lear assumes his earlier authority but now proclaiming pardon for
sexual transgression:

> Ay, every inch a king.
> When I do stare, see how the subject quakes.
> I pardon that man's life. What was thy cause?
> Adultery?
> Thou shalt not die – die for adultery? No!
> The wren goes to't and the small gilded fly
> Does lecher in my sight. Let copulation thrive,
> For Gloucester's bastard son was kinder to his father
> Than were my daughters got 'tween the lawful sheets.   (ll. 106–14)

Recognition of Gloucester is further delayed by an obsessive denunciation of women's sexual licence and deceit. Thoughts of hell-tor-
ments mix with strange jests as if he had taken over the role of Fool
who, mysteriously, no longer accompanies him. When Gloucester
speaks of his blindness, Lear is unresponsive but begins a sweeping
accusation of officers charged with the administration of justice:

> See how yon justice rails upon yon simple thief. Hark in thine ear:
> change places and handy-dandy, which is the justice, which is the
> thief? . . . a dog's obeyed in office.   (ll. 147–55)

When he does recognize the blind Gloucester, he counsels patience and claims that tears are mankind's inheritance. Then, in a moment, all these thoughts vanish and he veers away to consider revenge once more; he will steal 'upon these son-in-laws, / Then kill, kill, kill, kill, kill, kill!' (ll. 182–3).

The effect of this scene will depend very much on the acting. Everything can be played very quietly, as if Lear views injustice and pain from a distance and is motivated by a wistful serenity or, possibly, a quiet humour that no longer takes any strife seriously. Or 'None does offend, none, I say none. I'll able 'em, . . .' (l. 164) can arise out of a numbing sense of his own guilt and a desire to 'forget and forgive'. It can also be a defiant call for anarchy to obliterate all distinctions or a warning that this will happen. However spoken, the repetition of 'none' seems to call for strong emphasis; perhaps Lear is assertive now because he feels his physical strength failing – moments later he asks for his boots to be pulled off. When he recognizes Gloucester and, presumably, comes close to the blind and stricken man, perhaps taking his hands, a simple gentleness takes over his words: 'I know thee well enough, thy name is Gloucester. / Thou must be patient . . . ' (ll. 172–9; see also pp. 230–1, above). As mad Lear and blind Gloucester maintain close contact with each other, these gentler feelings can be sustained, even beneath renewed thoughts of revenge, so that recognition of one another's suffering will have established a stable and immediately recognizable element in the progress of Lear's journey.

But this stability does not last. At this point, a search party sent by Cordelia enters and yet more contradictions follow. When the unknown men approach, Lear sees himself as 'The natural fool of fortune', someone in need of surgeons for his brain whose eyes would be weeping copiously; but, a moment later, he is determined to 'die bravely'. He insists that he is a king and, the next instant, that he is a quarry being hunted down. When the soldiers try to pay him due reverence, he runs off and they have to chase after him to apprehend him.

Once Lear starts to sense that he is going mad and, more particularly in this scene at Dover when he enters quite crazed and alone, sudden and unexplained alterations of subject and reaction will defeat any actor's attempt to maintain a consistent motivation or a clear through-line of intention and feeling. In a carefully rehearsed and organized modern production, a director can ensure that certain speeches are emphasized so that the madness becomes more comprehensible, but this would not have been possible under the conditions of performance for which Shakespeare wrote. He must have known that the physical accidents of each performance would affect what this tragedy became: how far the actors are apart, the intensity of their silences, the changing energy with which they speak, and all their instinctive and passing reactions to details of the complex and demanding text. However this scene is produced and performed, an audience is liable to become increasingly unsure about what is happening within Lear's mind. Resolution or abeyance of these confusions has to wait until he is reunited with Cordelia, when very simple speech and a few specific actions will ensure that performance becomes far more comprehensible and consistently sustained.

Lear and Cordelia

The physical delicacy of the scene in which Cordelia and Lear are reunited has already been considered (p. 233, above). Viewed again after following Lear through the contradictions, tensions, and violence of his madness, its simplicity is more remarkable in contrast but so also are some contrary elements which mark this recognition as only one stage further in Lear's journey and not its conclusion. Cordelia is now leading an army and, while she prays to the 'kind gods' to cure her father (IV.vii.14–17), she still has no doubt that her sisters are to blame for his suffering and is about to fight a battle against them. At first, Lear seems to be still in the grip of fantasy, thinking that he is dead and Cordelia is a spirit; later he believes himself to be 'abused' by those who are ministering to him. He is able to rise and walk off stage, seemingly recovered, only when Cordelia has addressed him as a king rather than as 'father': 'Will't please your highness walk?' This acknowledgement and Cordelia's loving presence give him physical strength but they also suggest that his recovery depends on factors out of his control: 'You must bear with me', he insists as he leaves the stage. While everyone else is speechless, he continues: 'Pray you now, forget and forgive; I am old and foolish' (ll. 83–4). Shakespeare has brought this tragedy to the point where its hero is totally dependent on others and makes no customary heroic vaunt, call for revenge, denunciation of others, or plan for the future. An audience's awareness of father and daughter being reunited and strengthened by the experience is likely to be the dominant reaction at this juncture and is an exceptional achievement, but the precarious nature of this renewal is a sign that its action is by no means finished.

Other characters and narratives provide the main business of the fifth Act. Out of a total of just over four hundred lines, Cordelia speaks only four and a half while Lear, instead of dominating much of the last Act as Shakespeare's other tragic heroes have done, speaks only fifty or so. Father and daughter are seen, however, in three very different ways. At the beginning of V.ii, to the sound of an '*Alarum*', they have no words to speak but pass '*over the stage*' with their soldiers; according to the Folio, they bring '*drum and colours*' with them and, according to the Quarto, Cordelia holds '*her father in her hand*'. To what extent Lear is restored in physical strength and kingly bearing is left to the actor, but a clear statement is made that, with Cordelia, he has committed himself to military action. An '*Alarum and retreat*' are heard, representing a battle lost and won, but how savage and how prolonged the conflict is another element open to variation; only the announcement of its outcome is unequivocal: 'King Lear hath lost, he and his daughter ta'en' (V.ii.6). Only five lines later an army enters '*in conquest with drum and colours*' and with '*Lear and Cordelia as prisoners*'. After these sounds and shows, during which few words are spoken by anyone and none by Lear or Cordelia, the action takes another decisive step forward with the order:

> Some officers take them away – good guard,
> Until their greater pleasures first be known
> That are to censure them.　　　　　　　　　　　　(V.iii.1–3)

Cordelia is the first to speak, accepting the change of fortune but wanting a fuller confrontation: 'Shall we not see these daughters and these sisters?' (l. 7). These are her last words in the play: she says nothing when Lear contradicts her, ready for solitude in prison, so long as he shares it with her:

> No, no, no, no. Come, let's away to prison;
> We two alone will sing like birds i' the cage.
> When thou dost ask me blessing I'll kneel down
> And ask of thee forgiveness. So we'll live
> And pray, and sing, and tell old tales, and laugh
> At gilded butterflies, and hear poor rogues
> Talk of court news . . .   (ll. 8ff.)

Although pinioned by soldiers, he is allowed to speak elaborately and at length, which implies that, for all the fantasy of his thoughts, he has regained authority. Despite the old-style imperatives with which he starts, this is yet another new voice: after the disruptive violence of his storm-driven speeches and the uncertain progress of those on Dover Beach, after tender and tentative talk with Cordelia, after many confusing messages, now he almost sings and his thoughts develop confidently. It is as if a cello had unexpectedly taken over from other instruments, sustaining a new theme with a single-minded clarity and soft resonance that have previously been almost entirely absent.

Lear is ready to submit to the will of God: he and Cordelia will 'take upon's the mystery of things / As if we were God's spies' (ll. 16–17): good fortune and power are no longer important to him:

> And we'll wear out
> In a walled prison packs and sects of great ones
> That ebb and flow by the moon.

Ignoring the renewed order, 'Take them away', Lear continues, held in this thought and justifying himself by reference to the gods: 'Upon such sacrifices, my Cordelia, / The gods themselves throw incense' (ll. 19–21). To this calm acceptance, Cordelia must reply in some silent, physical way, because now Lear does break the line of his thought and feeling to ask what has happened: 'Have I caught thee?' Probably he holds her in his arms, so becoming aware that she is weeping, and certainly he becomes defiant now, as if strengthened once more by closeness to her. Echoes from the Old Testament, boasts, threats, and prophecy, together with destructive physical images, all return and emphasize his confidence in the gods' approval:

> Have I caught thee?
> He that parts us shall bring a brand from heaven,
> And fire us hence like foxes. Wipe thine eys;
> The good years shall devour them, flesh and fell,
> Ere they shall make us weep!
> We'll see 'em starved first: come.
>
> *Exeunt [Lear and Cordelia, guarded].*

Lear's last entry with Cordelia dead in his arms and his attempts to see signs that she is alive have already been discussed (see pp. 233–5, above). Viewed now in a fuller context, his very entry from prison to speak to others becomes more remarkable by contrast to all his other entries when he had spoken almost wholly for himself. His first call is for companionship in sorrow and outcry against the injustice of the gods in heaven:

> Howl, howl, howl, howl! O, you are men of stones!
> Had I your tongues and eyes, I'd use them so
> That heaven's vault should crack: she's gone for ever. . . . (V.iii.255ff.)

He knows he must rely on his own efforts: he will look for signs of life; others are 'murderers, traitors all' (l. 267); although he has killed her assassin, he 'might have saved her' (l. 268). By following his own instincts, he asks 'are you not Kent?' and already senses that Goneril and Regan are dead (ll. 280, 290). After some silence, Lear speaks again to cry out against the injustice of fate and the finality of death: 'And my poor fool is hanged. No, no, no life!' Lear is not concerned now with his own life or activity: he neither prays to the gods for help nor curses them. Instead, his last efforts are to get others to share what he sees to be true and to plead for understanding as earnestly as he had insisted on his commands.

The end of Lear's long story can be viewed as a pittiable and inevitable disaster that overtakes an aged ruler who, despite momentary insights of blazing accuracy, had 'but slenderly known himself' (I.i.294–5). It can also be viewed as a significant step, in the instinctive recesses of his mind and being, towards a more open and humble fellowship with other persons. Possibly, both views can be taken together and seem to be unimportant in comparison with his suffering and endurance. Undoubtedly, for an actor, the conclusion places extreme demands on stamina and calls for a strong imagination to give substance to very simple words and actions. He also needs to act with an absolute openness or transparency so that nothing interposes between his audience and the man he plays, and free access is given for sharing the experience of these last and necessarily quiet moments. So little is expressed in words that each spectator is called upon to complete what is seen and heard with an act of his or her own imagination.

12

King Lear: Part Two

Around the story of King Lear, and intertwined with it, Shakespeare has placed sharply defined characters and strong action so that they amplify and reflect upon its central concerns. The most notable addition is the story of the Earl of Gloucester and his two sons, the illegitimate Edmund and the legitimate Edgar, which comes, in part, from an entirely different source, Sir Philip Sidney's pastoral narrative, *Arcadia*, of 1590. For much of the tragedy, the Gloucesters are presented in self-contained scenes like a subplot of one of the comedies. They could well have been added after the core of the play was complete or drafted in considerable detail; they are, in effect, a Part Two, a supplement to the tragedy that is focused on Lear himself.

In a Part One, without this additional material, the king would meet a real and not a counterfeit madman on the heath and, instead of encountering Gloucester on Dover Beach, he would talk with an old blind man and through this derelict learn that suffering craves a master to reverence and needs patience to endure. The absence of Edmund's interaction with Lear's daughters in the final Acts would have left scope for a fuller treatment of the differences between Albany and Cornwall which are very sketchily presented in both original texts. It helps, therefore, to understand the tragedy, as it has survived in print, to ask why these additions were made and what changes they effect to the reception of the core action. Adding all the additional material would not have been undertaken lightly because the augmented text is lengthy and places unusually large demands upon an acting company. Ten experienced actors have to be available who are able to command the stage alone and sustain individual characters throughout much of an action that changes frequently in setting and mood; all three daughters are further roles that require very strong performances. Other actors must be numerous enough to supply Lear with sufficient knights to represent a hundred and to bring three armies together on stage in the last Act.

The Second Narrative

A major difference between what may be called the two parts of *King Lear* is that much of the supplementary material is presented in a more outright way, using forms of drama reminiscent of Shakespeare's earlier plays and more readily understandable than his more mature styles. Each thread of the added story proceeds from explicitly stated decisions and ends by inviting clear moral judgements. The same is true of the contribution made by the Earl of Kent, who is so inextricably linked with Lear's fortunes that he must have featured to some extent in any early version: Part Two develops his independent stance and displays it to greater advantage.

The story of the Gloucesters is introduced after brief speculation concerning Lear's decision to divide his kingdom and, at once, two lines of narrative emerge very clearly. The first is a variation of Lear's relationship to his daughters: Gloucester does not accept Edmund, his bastard son, into his household, not for any supposed fault, but because he had come 'something saucily into the world' (I.i.20). The second story-line starts when Edmund, who has stood silently watching and listening, offers his 'services' (l. 28) to the Earl of Kent to whom he has just been introduced. The later demands of his role will call for an actor of quick mind and virile presence so that as he steps forward now personal promise and ambition may well be obvious.

The three members of the Gloucester family account for the whole of Act I, scene ii. It starts with a soliloquy for Edmund which is entirely at odds with the authoritative ceremonies of the first scene. He derides all notions of inherited duty and privilege:

> Thou, Nature, art my goddess, to thy law
> My services are bound. Wherefore should I
> Stand in the plague of custom, and permit
> The curiosity of nations to deprive me?
> For that I am some twelve or fourteen moonshines
> Lag of a brother . . . ?

By placing his own instincts and gifts against rules that have bound society together in established relationships, he may be echoing the scepticism of Montaigne's essay 'Of Custom', but he is also speaking, in practical rather than speculative terms, for anyone in his audience who has been thwarted by established hierarchies. He proceeds to deride prejudice against the base-born, takes pride in his own 'composition and fierce quality', and vows to take over the inheritance of his elder brother Edgar; in Goneril's words to Regan, he will 'do something, and i'the heat' to better his expectations (I.i.309). He is a dangerous person.

The confident metre and rhythm of Edmund's speech, its mental energy, humour, and direct address to the audience all ensure that an audience is drawn into his thoughts regardless of their wider implications. His flippant 'Now gods, stand up for bastards!' might raise memories of the irreverent Vice-characters in earlier plays and its contrast with the hypocritical and self-serving piety in the play's first scene can scarcely be missed or not welcomed. When Gloucester enters immediately afterwards, the contrast of his plodding speech will also encourage many to side instinctively with his son. The father has nothing but questions or exclamations to offer, while his troubled thoughts break the flow of each verse-line:

> Kent banished thus? and France in choler parted?
> And the King gone tonight? Prescribed his power,
> Confined to exhibition? All this done
> Upon the gad? – Edmund, how now, what news?   (ll. 23–6)

At this point the dialogue shifts into prose, which allows the actors considerable freedom in timing and choice of emphasis. The scene becomes a game that Edmund plays, sharing its deceits with the audience. He tricks his father into wanting to see a letter which he says is from his brother but was, in fact, written by himself. So he makes out that Edgar believes old parents should relinquish power to their children and is actively plotting to kill his father because he does not. By the way, Edmund pretends to be loath to distrust his brother and to be unshakeably loyal to his father. He gets Gloucester to leave on the promise of further proof and then, in another soliloquy, mocks the old man's credulity and the common prejudice against bastards: he concludes by taking pleasure in being 'that I am' (ll. 131–3). At this moment, just as he would wish, Edgar enters – 'Pat, he comes, like the catastrophe of the old comedy' (l. 134) – and Edmund shifts gears to put on a show of being simple-minded and concerned about the ills of the world. By this means he persuades his brother to trust him when he reports that, for some unspecified reason, his father is so enraged against him that he is in physical danger. He pretends an honest concern and, offering his own lodging as a refuge, sends Edgar off to arm himself. In fact, he plans to fight with him where his father will be a witness, as some in an audience may have guessed already.

Edmund now has a third and shorter soliloquy in which prose is exchanged for verse and crafty dissimulation for elation; it springs from another promise of 'service':

> *Edgar.* Shall I hear from you anon?
> *Edmund.* I do serve you in this business.   *Exit Edgar.*
> A credulous father and a brother noble,
> Whose nature is so far from doing harms
> That he suspects none – on whose foolish honesty
> My practices ride easy. I see the business.
> Let me, if not by birth, have lands by wit;
> All with me's meet that I can fashion fit.   *Exit.*
> (ll. 175–82)

The pursuit of 'lands' is an echo of the division of Lear's territories in the preceding scene, only here 'wit', not a profession of love, will obtain them. An audience has been shown all these encounters from Edmund's point of view so that it has seen how he handles his father and brother as puppets in a comic melodrama. As they enjoy his expertise, some will want to accept his argument that any action is permissible if it can be made to work. Others, however, may have heard the threat of anarchy and yet others a rousing call for independent action, free of inherited obligations and revolutionary in implication. Today Edmund can be understood as making a plea for free enterprise, a classless society, or social mobility. If the actor emphasizes the reference to his birth in the last couplet, many will judge Edmund to be motivated by the stigma of bastardy which he has already mocked in two earlier soliloquies. For most people in any audience, the comedy of Edmund's successful manipulations raises major social and moral issues and invites them to take sides in the dramatic action.

How far the scene is greeted with laughter depends on the actor's discretion and how often Edmund shares his thoughts with an audience: he can show his private satisfaction as his father reads the letter and takes it to be genuine; when Edgar declares 'Some villain hath done me wrong' and he replies 'That's my fear' (ll. 163–4), he can share with his audience the irony that he is just such a villain and standing on stage beside his brother. But other features of the text work against too broad a performance. For example, Gloucester can be truly worried when he relates his personal predicament to the state of the world in general:

> Love cools, friendship falls off, brothers divide: in cities, mutinies; in countries, discord; in palaces, treason; and the bond cracked 'twixt son and father.   (ll. 106–9)

The later Folio text adds more here, concluding with sentiments commonly voiced by the elderly immediately after Elizabeth's reign, at the time when *King Lear* was first performed:

> We have seen the best of our time. Machinations, hollowness, treachery and all ruinous disorders follow us disquietly to our graves.

The ease with which Gloucester has been duped may cause some hearers to ask whether too much prudence and a preference for earlier times might not weaken awareness of what is happening in the present.

Another unsettling element in this scene is Edgar's notably under-written part. Edmund calls his brother 'noble' but here he seems hampered from expressing his thoughts as if he were restrained by some unspoken unease. All his speeches are either questions pro-voked by Edmund's strange behaviour or brief responses to his ques-tions and information. This will change later when Edgar's motivation is made abundantly clear and his actions require consid-erable presence of mind and physical strength: he will invent suit-ably wild behaviour and fantastic speeches for a madman and then, changing his disguise, take responsibility boldly for his father and for political causes. Twice he will kill an opponent in single combat, the second being Edmund who seems here to have far superior resources. While none of this ability is on display as he falls into his brother's trap, an audience may, nevertheless, sense something within Edgar that suggests he is more than a docile and laughable victim. This hidden resource is not unlike that to be sensed in Cordelia in the previous scene when she says nothing to her father's demand and when she is betrothed to the King of France. While both are tongue-tied, they may 'have that in [their] countenance' (I.iv.27) and in their very presence, that promises far more. Enough is out of balance and unexplained to alert an audience to follow both of them closely: like Lear himself, they will be tested as the action progresses and will reveal more of their potential.

Service and Self-promotion

Three times and to three different masters Edmund has offered his 'service' and this continues to be a key word in the action that follows, drawing other persons into its orbit and referring to both feudal allegiance and domestic ties. *Serve* and *service* are words not often used today, because subservience to another human being, especially one more powerful by accident of birth or fortune, is likely to be considered demeaning, but in Shakespeare's day these words were used frequently and referred to such practices as we might call vested interest, career-building, company loyalty, mutual support, and security of tenure. Many of these aspects of *service* are written into the text of *King Lear* and can be made obvious in performance by the manner in which persons relate to each other on stage.

At the beginning of the seventeenth century, as a consequence of changes in the structure of society and greater opportunities for self-advancement, the proper function of both the *served* and the *servants* were live issues. They are raised repeatedly in Shakespeare's plays. In *As You Like It*, written some six years before *Lear*, after Adam has offered unpaid service and his life's savings so that his 'young master' may escape his overbearing older brother, Orlando tells him:

> how well in thee appears
> The constant service of the antique world,
> When service sweat for duty, not for meed!
> Thou art not for the fashion of these times,
> Where none will sweat but for promotion,
> And having that do choke their service up
> Even with the having.   (II.iii.56–62)

In *King Lear*, when Edmund offers his 'service' for *meed* (or reward) and *promotion*, he clearly sets the play's action in a world that is unsettled by acquisitive ambition and insecurity of service. This is the context in which Lear realizes that saying 'ay and no' to everything as a master wishes may not be 'good divinity' and learns, by the time he is dying, to say 'Thank you, sir' for a simple service (IV.vi.98–100; V.iii.308).

After the theme of service has been established in the secondary action of *King Lear*, it is taken up in the next short scene of the main action in which Goneril instructs Oswald, her '*Steward*', to see that other servants slack their 'former services' to her father and his hundred knights (I.iv.10). Who started this quarrel is not clear – the reason she gives is that Lear has struck one of her gentlemen in defence of his fool – but Oswald's subservience, as he says 'Ay' to whatever his mistress asks, demonstrates the tight control that Goneril exercises over those who serve her. The theme is repeated at the start of the next scene when Kent is shown assuming the humble disguise of Caius so that he can 'serve' Lear, his 'master', at risk of his own life (I.iv.5–7). A king would not be expected to accept a new servant without some personal recommendation, but Kent gains Lear's confidence by flattery and by claiming to be fearless and self-reliant; he further ingratiates himself when he humiliates Oswald by tripping him up. As Lear moves towards trusting this unknown man who wishes to serve him, he asks 'Dost thou know me, fellow?', recognizing that good service requires mutual understanding.

As we have seen, the reproaches, jests, and songs of Fool release such a 'riot' among Lear's followers that Goneril says her house has become like an inn, tavern, or brothel (see above, pp. 239–41). These are not careless strictures: family ties had always been forgotten in brothels and, by the end of the sixeenth century, the reputation of taverns was little better as they became increasingly popular with 'masterless men' and the poorer sorts of labourers and servants. After the Reformation, when churches and churchyards were no longer allowed to be used for public gatherings and folk celebrations, taverns began to take their place and, almost at once, regulations had to be devised to control how they were run and keep close check on tavern-keepers. Those in authority began to view them as centres of lawlessness so that, by 1611, alehouses were said to 'breed conspiracies, combinations, common conjurations, detractions, defamations'; they were 'nurseries of all riot, excess and idleness'. After heavy drinking, servants were known to 'have returned home to assault their masters' (*Puritans and Revolutionaries*, pp. 47, 58; and Clark, pp. 123–65). From Goneril's point of view, Lear's retinue threatens to overturn the very bonds of service by means of which her household functions. From Lear's point of view, the fault is Goneril's as an anonymous knight, very respectfully, points out:

> My lord, I know not what the matter is, but to my judgement your highness is not entertained with that ceremonious affection as you were wont. There's a great abatement of kindness appears as well in the general dependants as in the Duke himself also, and your daughter.   (I.iv.65–70)

When the action moves to Gloucester's castle, the demands of rival services continue to be dominant as Oswald and Kent exchange

insults and brawl with partly comic results. When Cornwall intervenes, Kent almost loses his disguise to castigate such 'smiling' servants as 'rats' and 'dogs' (II.ii.64–72). Cornwall responds by warning
Caius that blunt and saucy 'knaves' like him can:

> Harbour more craft and more corrupter ends
> Than twenty silly-ducking observants
> That stretch their duties nicely.   (ll. 100–2)

After Lear's arrival, the issue of a servant's loyalty is presented more
harshly as he repeatedly asks the single question: 'Who put my man
i'the stocks?' (II.ii.371, etc.).

The prominence given to Oswald and Kent, over the course of
more than three hundred lines, shows that conflicting demands of
service are a major concern in this tragedy. Although modern productions often cut all but the funnier exchanges between Oswald
and Kent, the whole of the episode is in both Quarto and Folio,
their texts varying slightly. That Gloucester trusts his deceitful son
provides an obvious parallel to Lear's misjudgement of his daughters,
but the supplementary story of the Gloucesters interacts more continuously with the core action in its treatment of service: Edmund
pretends to give 'loyal service' to both Cornwall and Lear's two
daughters; Gloucester is torn between loyalty to Cornwall and
Regan and his earlier loyalty to Lear, finally choosing the latter at the
risk of his own life and without hope of reward; eventually,
Gloucester's service saves the king's life and Kent's continues to
support him.

Conflicts of Service

At first, Gloucester relies on Cornwall, 'my master, / My worthy
arch and patron', to authorize his pursuit of Edgar and bring him 'to
the stake' (II.i.58–63). When the duke comes with Regan to lodge at
his castle unexpectedly, he immediately shows himself a true
servant:: 'I serve you, madam. / Your graces are most welcome'
(II.i.130–1). When Cornwall offers to employ Edmund and his son

replies, 'I shall serve you, sir, truly, however else', Gloucester is quick
to add, 'For him I thank your grace' (II.i.118–19). When they all
enter the castle together, the protocol of the time ensured they do so
in due order and with appropriate signs of dependence. But all these
signs of good service serve to emphasize its breakdown when Lear
arrives the next morning and finds that his servant Caius has been
placed in the stocks and that he, himself, receives no welcome and
must enter the castle alone to set matters right. Immediately,
Gloucester is in a predicament. He had protested reasonably against
the treatment of Lear's messenger (see ll. 137–44) and been over-
ruled, but now he has to face his other master's fury. Fool's mockery
underlines the crisis:

> That sir which serves and seeks for gain,
>   And follows but for form,
> Will pack when it begins to rain,
>   And leave thee in the storm;
> But I will tarry, the fool will stay,
>   And let the wise man fly,
> The knave turns fool that runs away,
>   The fool no knave perdy.   (ll. 267–74)

His point is sharpened with a pun: in the penultimate line, *knave*
means 'young male servant' and, in the last line, 'dishonourable
rogue': he asks whether Gloucester will prove foolishly disloyal or
wisely a knave.

Trying to reconcile the demands of his two masters, Gloucester is
soon reduced to silence by Lear's fury and stumbling incredulity at
being treated as a servant:

> The King would speak with Cornwall, the dear father
> Would with his daughter speak, commands – tends – service.
> Are they informed of this?   (ll. 290–2)

During Lear's ensuing confrontation with both his daughters, alternately pleading and cursing, Gloucester has nothing to say. When
his old master goes out into the storm, predicting 'O fool, I shall go
mad' (l. 475), Gloucester does follow him but still saying nothing.

When he returns and reports on the king's rage, the pitiless weather, and the exposed country into which he has gone, he is too late to alter anything. Cornwall and Goneril assure him that Lear 'leads himself' and Regan argues that, having chosen the wrong servants, he has been misled by them and deserves any 'injuries' he may suffer. With 'Shut up your doors. / He is attended with a desperate train', Cornwall seconds her advice, implying that Gloucester should now look after himself:

> Shut up your doors, my lord, 'tis a wild night.
> My Regan counsels well; come out o'the storm.   (ll. 494–9)

All three direct attention to the tongue-tied and bewildered Gloucester who, finally, obeys the master who is now the more powerful and follows him off stage – how willingly is the actor's choice – still saying nothing as the gates of his own castle close behind him and the storm rages outside.

Gloucester is next seen with Edmund and in distress. They have come apart to talk secretly and, according to the Quarto, at night, for they both carry lights. Having asked Cornwall for permission to take pity on the king, Gloucester has now lost 'the use of [his] own house' and been charged 'on pain of perpetual displeasure' not to speak of the king or do anything to 'sustain' him (III.iii.1–6). He tells his son that he is about to disobey Cornwall and seek out the king, his 'old master', so that he may 'privily relieve him'. He is motivated by prudence as well as compassion and duty, having received a letter telling of an army on its way to support the king. Warning of 'strange things toward' (III.iii.8–19), he asks Edmund to cover for him by maintaining talk with the duke and leaves without further explanation. Once alone, Edmund must decide between his father's safety and his own advancement under his new master, and he does not hesitate. In a short soliloquy, alive with sarcastic wit, he resolves to tell the duke what his father intends and to use the letter to his own advantage: by this kind of service, he will be sole inheritor when his father is dead. A last rhyming line – 'The younger rises when the old doth fall' – expresses a confidence and self-satisfaction completely at odds with his father's hesitant but final resolution to risk everything in service of the king.

During the next few scenes, Gloucester speaks and behaves very differently. He is resourceful and determined to do his 'duty' by finding shelter and food for the king, even though 'grief' at what he believes is Edgar's treachery has almost 'crazed' his wits (III.iv.144–9, 166–7). When he next appears, he has arranged a litter to take the enfeebled Lear to greater safety at Dover. While achieving so much, however, he has not protected himself and in the following scene he is brought a prisoner before Cornwall and Regan. The audience is prepared for witnessing cruelty when Regan suggests they should 'hang him instantly' and Goneril that they should 'pluck out his eyes'. Edmund is told to leave with Goneril because the revenges intended on his father 'are not fit for your beholding' (III.vii.7–9). Then Gloucester is brought in and, after being tied to a chair, Regan plucks him by the beard. Under interrogatation, he tries prevarication at first, but his persecuters know too much for that to work and so he gathers strength to denounce their cruelty. Having heard him out, Cornwall retaliates with a physical threat: 'Upon these eyes of thine I'll set my foot' (l. 67). 'These' rather than *those,* indicates that he is close to his helpless victim, perhaps looking into his eyes in a physically tense and closely focused confrontation. Gloucester cries out for help as Cornwall tears out one of his eyes:

> He that will think to live till he be old,
> Give me some help! – O cruel! O you gods!   (ll. 68–9)

Enacting such calculated violence on a helpless old man has no parallel in Shakespeare's plays and rarely in those by anyone else. Its horror is accentuated, at least for its first audiences, because the punishment is for service to his king.

As if in recognition of the exceptional and sensational pressure this action places on an audience, Shakespeare relieved it by having one of Cornwall's servants interpose. He is first heard in silence:

> Hold your hand, my lord.
> I have served you ever since I was a child,
> But better service have I never done you
> Than now to bid you hold.   (ll. 71–4)

They fight and the 'villein' wounds his master and is then killed himself by Regan from behind. Cornwall has enough strength left to pluck out the 'vile jelly' of Gloucester's other eye and then Regan takes over the torture by telling Gloucester of Edmund's treachery. For the moment, physical pain is forgotten and the father cries out against his own 'follies', as Lear had done already by this stage of his journey (see I.iv.263–4, and p. 241 above):

> O my follies! Then Edgar was abused?
> Kind gods, forgive me that and prosper him.   (ll. 90–1)

Before her wounded husband leaves the stage, calling for the support of her arm, Regan orders, 'Go, thrust him out at gates and let him smell / His way to Dover': Gloucester is silent as he is dragged off so that, once more, the audience is left to supply his thoughts and feelings.

At this point, Shakespeare or his theatre colleagues were in two minds about leaving the audience with no more guidance. In the Quarto version, two other servants speak out against their master and decide to follow 'the old Earl' to make sure he finds someone to lead him; one of them goes to 'fetch some flax and whites of eggs / To apply to his bleeding face', praying heaven to help him (ll. 105–6). This coda to the terrible scene is cut in the later Folio version, which could imply that the actors had not been able to carry it off or that Shakespeare had decided that the sight of Gloucester, broken in spirit and stumbling in unaccustomed blindness, would hold attention without this support. The 'gentle Shakespeare', as his contemporaries called him, may well have been uneasy about bringing so much physical cruelty and pain onto the stage. Horrors in the early *Titus Andronicus* are more numerous, but not so vividly staged or so sustained: the lopping of Alarbus's limbs, the rape and mutilation of Virginia, and the beheading of Titus's two sons all happen offstage; the chopping-off of Titus's hand and the slitting of the throats of Chiron and Demetrius are staged before the audience, but in sudden and unreflecting action. Here, in *King Lear*, the violence is foreseen and then shown precisely, step by step, in spite of the victim's cries and a servant's protest. At the centre of this

tragedy, a helpless, enfeebled man is tortured, physically and psycho-
logically, in a manner that draws individual members of an audience
to share his torment or else to turn away their eyes.

Why would Shakespeare have taken the risk of involving
Gloucester in such agony? Perhaps to show the consequences of the
credulity that has led him to misjudge the son who loves him.
Possibly to show how he turns instinctively to the gods, whom he
now calls 'kind', and how readily Regan and Cornwall turn to
cruelty. Yet the cause of the suffering and the progress of the scene
depend on none of these factors, but on Gloucester's resolve to serve
Lear loyally, even though he does so after long delay and for mixed
motives. He has gained strength of will from his decision and now
does not consider his own well-being. By this violent means, the secondary narrative ensures that the tragedy is about service as well as
the arbitrary exercise of power and maintenance of family bonds.
And, since Gloucester is blinded well before the final suffering of
Lear, when that catastrophe does come, an audience's sympathies
have already been active and therefore will be more able to look
beyond Lear's pain and suffering to register other aspects of his
death: love and tenderness towards Cordelia and concern for those
around him. This might explain why Richard Burbage, principal
actor of the King's Men who died in 1619, was remembered for his
'*kind* Lear', not for an angry, grieved, mistaken, misused, or suffering one.

Consequences: Edgar and Gloucester

Whereas Lear becomes destitute by slow degrees, Edgar takes to isolation, poverty, pretended madness, and self-mutilation in one decisive step. Believing that his father seeks his life, his first soliloquy
explains:

> I will preserve myself, and am bethought
> To take the basest and most poorest shape
> That ever penury in contempt of man
> Brought near to beast. My face I'll grime with filth,

Blanket my loins, elf all my hair in knots
And with presented nakedness outface
The winds and persecutions of the sky.   (II.ii.177–83)

He will act like 'Poor Tom', a mad beggar, crying out and striking
gashes in his 'numbed and mortified bare arms', and, with this 'horrible object', he will from poorest people 'enforce their charity'. This
new self is so rapidly invented and his former self so quickly
becomes 'nothing' (ll. 184–92), that he seems to be drawn to this
disguise.

When the king, unexpectedly encountered on the heath, accepts
his pretence, Edgar's performance grows in confidence and range.
From his conscious or subconscious mind, Edgar calls up nightmare
images of depravity, deceit, pride, beast-like behaviour, and, not
least, suffering: 'Tom's a'cold' and 'Through the hawthorn blows the
cold wind' recur like refrains, fixed points in the headlong and
crazed performance. When Gloucester arrives to 'relieve' the king,
Edgar elaborates his performance further to escape recognition,
speaking now of 'the fury of his heart' (ll. 126–7). Yet he is not
entirely in control for, as the king grows weaker and more crazed, he
almost drops out of his disguise to 'bless [Lear's] five wits' and
his own tears begin to 'mar [his] counterfeiting' (III.vi.56–60).
Although fantasy and anger have supported a pretence of madness,
Edgar cannot face the reality of suffering until he makes common
cause with Lear by energetically attacking the imaginary fiends that
threaten them both in the form of vicious dogs. This leaves Edgar so
exhausted that he cries out 'Poor Tom, thy horn is dry' (l. 72) and
then is silent. Lear and he have come very close together, like two
dazed and driven beasts of burden.

While the king is carried to Dover, Edgar again encounters his
father who now is 'poorly led', defeated, and helpless. Even though
his life can no longer be at risk, he must still believe he has lost his
father's love and so he keeps his distance. Almost certainly he does
not hear Gloucester speak of his 'dear son Edgar' who has falsely
been 'food' for his wrath (IV.i.23–6); if Edgar *had* heard, he would
surely have reacted in some way or other, but he only speaks aside
about his own ill-fortune. When he does address his father it is to

bless him, disguise again forgotten in sympathy for suffering. At this, Gloucester asks an Old Man who has been guiding him to leave and calls out to the 'naked fellow'. For Edgar, 'Poor Tom's a-cold' is no defence now and he does make contact to find himself looking into his father's bleeding eyes and blessing them. He does not hesitate to say he knows the way to Dover but, as Gloucester's despair becomes increasingly evident, he is at a loss for sympathetic words, accepting the role of a servant with the deceptively simple, 'Ay, master'. When his father makes quite clear that he intends to commit suicide, Edgar resumes his role-playing with his service: 'Give me thy arm, / Poor Tom shall lead thee' (ll. 81–2).

While Lear is absent for a total of six scenes, Edgar becomes the most active person on stage, the gullible son of Act I, scene ii now providing forward impetus for the action as his brother Edmund had done earlier. At the start of IV.vi, Edgar has already decided to trick his father out of suicide by saying that they are approaching the top of Dover Cliff when they are still on level ground but he has still not revealed his identity. In carrying off the deception, his fantasy is again successful: the dizzy height, from which his father intends to plunge to his death, he describes so vividly that it can seem as if he is encountering the terrifying prospect on his father's behalf. When Gloucester 'falls' on the level stage (as the Quarto directs), he is simultaneously both pathetic and absurd so that this action is famously difficult to stage convincingly: it can seem to be merely unbelievable and will nearly always emphasize the strangeness of the manipulating device that Edgar has chosen. Such effects are likely to be momentary, however, because the focus shifts back to Edgar who fears that his deception has gone so terribly wrong that he has killed his father. When Gloucester revives and tells him 'Away, and let me die', Edgar reacts at once and his purpose will become far clearer to an audience. He takes on another persona and, speaking less out-landishly, he declares 'Thy life's a miracle' and tells Gloucester to look up, as if he does not know that he is blind. With a new leap of weird fantasy, he invents a 'fiend', with horns and 'a thousand noses', and says that this creature had brought him to the cliff-top (ll. 41–72). This further deception succeeds in persuading his father that he has been saved by divine intervention:

Edgar.	Think that the clearest gods, who make them honours
	Of men's impossibilities, have preserved thee.
Gloucester.	I do remember now. Henceforth I'll bear
	Affliction till it do cry out itself
	'Enough, enough' and die. (ll. 73–7)

Edgar may well believe that his task is finished, but Gloucester's resolve is not firmly expressed, there being little distinction between a personified 'Affliction' and his own reaction to it.

At this point Lear enters, more obviously mad than before. Gloucester recognizes him almost at once by 'the trick' of his voice, but Lear either does not recognize Gloucester or chooses not to acknowledge that he does. Nevertheless, as 'the subject quakes' before his monarch, Lear pardons him for adultery as if knowing that he had fathered the bastard Edmund. Gloucester is again silent until he asks to kiss the hand of the master in whose service he has lost his sight. This moment provokes both men to a keener sense of their own predicaments, Lear remembering his failings and Gloucester imagining the loss of an entire world that once had seemed strong and now is powerless:

Gloucester.	O, let me kiss that hand!
Lear.	Let me wipe it first, it smells of mortality.
Gloucester.	O, ruined piece of nature, this great world
	Shall so wear out to naught. Dost thou know me?
	(ll. 128–31)

Eventually Lear acknowledges 'Thy name is Gloucester' and insists, as Edgar had done, 'Thou must be patient.' The reason he gives for this, however, is very different: instead of being cared for by the 'clearest gods', man is born to weep and play a part on a 'great stage of fools' (ll. 172–9); pain and folly are the common portions of all humanity and no 'special providence' cares for them (*Hamlet*, V.ii.212). When Gloucester responds with 'Alack, alack the day!', he may be grieving for Lear as much as for himself, or for the loss of a 'great world' in which he had once served. The two narratives of the tragedy come together here as two men try to wrench significance from their different 'afflictions'.

These issues are not developed because Lear runs away, determined to resist capture, and Edgar moves away to ask about preparations for battle; Gloucester is left alone and silent once more. When Edgar returns, he finds his father praying aloud to 'gentle gods' and asking them to end his life; he no longer remembers 'the clearest gods' that could preserve him (ll. 73–7):

> You ever gentle gods, take my breath from me,
> Let not my worser spirit tempt me again
> To die before you please.   (ll. 212–15)

Blind Gloucester still despairs and when, immediately after this, Oswald enters drawing his sword to kill him, the assassin's hand is 'friendly' (l. 220) and seems an answer to his prayer. For Edgar, however, Oswald is another challenge and, using a mere 'baton' against the sword, he confronts and kills him. Their fighting can be an absurd interlude or long and bloody but, either way, when Edgar discovers a letter on Oswald's body, the two stories of the tragedy again combine and take a huge step forward. The letter reveals Goneril's plan for Edmund to kill Albany, her husband, and so to 'supply [his] place' in her bed. Perhaps Edgar now believes the gods have indeed made 'honours / Of men's impossibilities' (ll. 73–4) and, certainly, the chance encounter suggests his next course of action which is to report this treachery to Albany. Gloucester, in contrast, is left wishing he were mad like the king so that he could lose all knowledge of his griefs (see ll. 266–79). Drums are now heard '*afar off*' and Edgar hurries off stage taking with him his father who, yet once more, is silent.

As the play's action moves ahead with the reconciliation of Lear and Cordelia, a worrying uncertainty hangs over its complicated secondary narrative. Nothing in the text shows that Edgar knows that his father no longer seeks his life. Before throwing himself off Dover Cliff (as he thinks), Gloucester had prayed that Edgar 'should be blessed' (l. 40) but, as in their previous scene together (see p. 270, above), Shakespeare has so presented events that Edgar is unlikely to hear these words. Immediately before this prayer, Gloucester had told him 'Go thou, further off' and Edgar, saying farewell, had moved away far enough to make his blind father believe he was now quite alone, probably too far away to overhear his prayer. When his father calls out, just before his fall, Edgar does hear but his reply implies that he has to call back from a distance: 'Gone sir, farewell.' If, in spite of these signs to the contrary, Shakespeare intended Edgar to hear Gloucester pray or by some other means know that his innocence had been established, the son would be very perverse and cruel in not revealing his identity to his father; such a recognition would have lifted Gloucester's despair and longing for death. Edgar does recognize, in an aside, a need for self-justification – 'Why I do trifle thus with his despair / Is done to cure it' (ll. 33–4) – but this does not explain why he would presume to stifle an expression of his love if he knew his father was very ready to receive it.

Much later, Edgar reports that, after the battle had been lost by Cordelia and Lear, at this very late and despairing moment, he had revealed his true identity to his father and 'from first to last / Told him our pilgrimage.' The result of these revelations at this time was that Gloucester had died, proving too weak to support 'the extremes of passion, joy and grief,' and Edgar acknowledges that his earlier failure to reveal his identity had been a 'fault' (V.iii.180–98). Like Lear's rejection of Cordelia and Gloucester's belief in Edmund, both at the begining of the tragedy and both springboards for its action, Edgar's decision not to reveal himself to his father is presented as an impetuous and irrational action, the result of a self-confidence that made him blind to the needs of a person whom he greatly loves. Possibly all three had feared that their love was too great to be reciprocated or that they were unworthy and therefore fated to be estranged. These and other possible causes of misjudgement are not considered in the dialogue but they remain as underlying possibilities that may cause some in an audience to suspect that the disasters of this tragedy arise from dark secrets within the minds of the persons involved, feelings unrecognized and thoughts unnamed, not from any chance event or supernatural intervention of external compulsion.

In *Hamlet*, Shakespeare had created a hero who debates the problems of self-will, political and moral responsibility, and a 'destiny that shapes our ends'. In *Lear*, these issues are also very much alive but no one person carries their burden and no solution appears to be final. The various opinions expressed in different circumstances by different persons arise as products of the play's action, rather than out of self-conscious enquiry and single-minded argument. In his last advice to his father, after Cordelia and Lear have lost the battle, Edgar neither puts his hopes in the power of 'clearest gods' to preserve him, as he had formerly urged his father, nor accepts the stern judgement of 'just' gods, as he will later, when speaking of his father's blindness to Edmund:

> The dark and vicious place where thee he got
> Cost him his eyes   (V.iii.168–71)

At this time, he recommends a fatalistic and stoical acceptance of whatever happens:

> Men must endure
> Their going hence even as their coming hither.
> Ripeness is all.   (V.ii.9–11)

Gloucester's reply constitutes his last lines in the play: 'And that's true too', words that suggest he might be recalling other opinions, including his earlier 'As flies to wanton boys are we to the gods, / They kill us for their sport' (IV.i.38–9). Although Edgar has suffered and changed a great deal, his 'pilgrimage' has not conferred on him a lasting belief that all is for the best, or that he or anyone else will receive justice in their lives or after their deaths. He and others with him are caught in a net of ideas that offers a range of different solutions to such issues, expressed more or less confidently as experience dictates at the time.

These varied judgements bring uncertainties to the conclusion of the story of Gloucester and his sons which in other ways is very clear: on the one hand, a withdrawal from final judgement and, on the other, a continued effort to understand what has happened and find what course to follow. In this way, the secondary narrative greatly influences an audience's reception of Lear's story. He. too, has changed his view of the gods and the heavens over his head, of human responsibility, the pain of existence, and the need for patience; he has questioned what he himself and 'unaccommodated man' might be and how to distinguish a justice from a thief; he has enquired about 'the cause of thunder' and who makes 'hard hearts'. His mind has been engaged with all these issues, as the varying experiences of his journey have suggested, right up to the beginning of the battle in the last Act: after that, he pays no more attention to them except to see himself, indifferently, in two opposing roles, as one of 'God's spies' and as someone capable of exacting terrible revenge on the lives of others (see V.iii.15, 22–6). After his last entry he is almost wholly concerned with Cordelia and the other persons who gather around him. About providence or justice, he speaks only to regret his own failure to act – 'I might have saved her' – and to ask the anguished question: 'Why should a dog, a horse, a rat have life / And thou no breath at all?' (V.iii.268, 305–6). Further response is left to witnesses on stage and individual members of an audience who, immediately before Lear's last entrance, have been alerted by the complicated and strange story of Gloucester and his sons to consider questions of chance, fate, justice, the 'judgement of the heavens that makes us tremble' (V.iii.231), and hidden causes of human weakness and strength.

Consequences: Edmund

Edmund, who can be reckoned the tragedy's most modern person by reason of his critical and self-serving independence of mind, meets death at his brother's hand in accordance with a long-established notion of tragedy. Agreeing with Edgar's account of the 'just' gods who punish human vices, he adds, 'The wheel has come full circle, I am here' (V.iii.172). His fortune, that had risen in service of Cornwall, now must fall, and this view appears to be endorsed when other persons fall with him: Cornwall killed by his servant's sword, Regan poisoned by her sister, and Goneril committing suicide. As in many tragedies of the time, concealed evil is publicly exposed and punished by death. On hearing of Cornwall's death, Kent knows what to say:

> This shows you are above,
> You justicers, that these our nether crimes
> So speedily can venge. (IV.ii.79–81)

On the deaths of Edmund, Regan, and Goneril, Albany echoes him, but with less satisfaction:

> This judgement of the heavens that makes us tremble
> Touches us not with pity. (V.iii.230–1)

Although this sounds like an ultimate comment, safe in assurance of divine providence, the speed with which these 'tragic' events happen, experienced over against the slower movement towards death for both Lear and Gloucester, allows little time for an audience to feel horror and fear as Albany does. Moreover, Edmund's acknowledgement that Fortune's wheel has turned is not the end of his part in the play: he has more to do.

Towards the end of the play, Edmund may be uncertain as he stands aside and watches while others deal with his future but, once he has acknowledged defeat, he is again witty, frank, and, even, boastful: all that 'is past', he says of his crimes, 'and so am I' (V.iii.160). When told that Goneril and Regan are dead, a laugh may accompany his sharp reply: 'I was contracted to them both; all three / Now marry in an instant' (V.iii.227–8). A little later, he may enjoy a fleeting pleasure or, perhaps, regret in recalling what is past:

> Yet Edmund was beloved:
> The one the other poisoned for my sake,
> And after slew herself. (ll. 238–40)

Shortly after this, he makes a decision that he knows is unexpected:

> I pant for life. Some good I mean to do,
> Despite of mine own nature. Quickly send –
> Be brief in it – to the castle, for my writ
> Is on the life of Lear and on Cordelia. (ll. 241–4)

This speech has been judged a dramatist's convenience, a ready but not very plausible way of bringing the play's multiple narratives to a conclusion, and the actor does have a choice between treating the moment lightly, drawing as little attention as possible, or giving it full weight and bringing Edmund into close focus. The text supports a positive treatment because an incomplete verse-line suggests a pause of astonishment or disbelief at what has been said; he has to insist, 'Nay, send in time.' In such a pause, a theatre audience may also doubt whether it fully understands what he is about. Has he acted in this way because of a need, even now, to keep the initiative and so establish his self-esteem and an illegitmate son's right to be heard? Or does he take ironic pleasure in the incongruity of choosing to finish his life with a good deed against his undeniable 'nature'? One thing is certain: as he struggles for breath, Edmund insists on controlling events and is assured of his 'own nature', even as he does 'some good' against that nature. Edmund does not submit to a change of fortune; he is what he is, still, and so an audience's attention is drawn to 'long-engrafted conditions' that are as powerful in directing life and death as those very different ones that had been identified in the king at the start of the play (I.i.298).

Edmund's personal qualities have taken an increasingly important role in the play, overriding other concerns. Goneril is obsessed with sexual desire for him, even as she prepares for war against Cordelia and Lear. When she has to send him away on military business, she arranges for messages to pass between them and promises:

> Ere long you are like to hear –
> If you dare venture in your own behalf –
> A mistress's command.

Her meaning is ambiguous for it could imply either a social or a military relationship. He does not answer and so Goneril must do more: she offers Edmund a chain, probably taken from her own neck since she was not expecting to part from him. If this chain carries a single prominent jewel, as well it might, the sexual implications of her gift would be still more clear. When he obeys and bows his head, she kisses him, the verse-lines flowing unbrokenly:

                                    Wear this.
          [*She places a chain around his neck.*]
                                            Spare speech,
               Decline your head. This kiss, if it durst speak,
               Would stretch thy spirits up into the air.
               Conceive, and fare thee well.
Edmund.   Yours in the ranks of death.   *Exit.*
Goneril.   My most dear Gloucester.
               O, the difference of man and man!
               To thee a woman's services are due;
               A fool usurps my bed.   (IV.ii.19–29)

How the kiss is given and received can vary greatly in performance
and so send many different messages. The text, however, insists on
subtle meanings for ordinary words and on prolonged, intimate, and
physical contact between woman and man, as she dares to woo him,
against the social conventions implied elsewhere in the play and
regardless of the military urgency of the situation. Progressively,
speech becomes more highly charged so that, after a pause,
Edmund's brief response may well taunt Goneril by referring either
to death in battle or to intense sexual engagement. In both senses,
however, he accepts complicity and, according to the Folio's placing
of the exit, he takes her cue by leaving at once. When he has gone,
Goneril can speak more openly and, while her comparison of 'man
and man' will sometimes raise a laugh in performance, her anticipation of sexual 'services' has a detonating effect, as previously hidden
feelings are released. When Albany, her husband, enters at just this
moment, her greeting, before he can speak – 'I have been worth the
whistling' (l. 30) – shows, unmistakably, how *her* spirits have been
'stretched' out of sympathy with his. The sexual and subtle
encounter between Goneril and Edmund cannot have been easy to
play in the improvised conditions of a Jacobean theatre; perhaps it
was meant to be awkward in performance, the only strong motor-
force being her insistence on facing and offering her 'services' to the
almost silent Edmund.

    Until this point in the tragedy, the interest in Edmund that both
Goneril and Regan have shown appears to be of minor importance
in its secondary narrative. Now, however, its force becomes unmis-

takable until it draws all three to their deaths and written evidence
of it becomes Edgar's means of challenging his brother and reversing
the consequences of defeat in battle. Regan is not given a scene alone
with Edmund but at the start of Act V he is at her side when, in the
presence of their army, she discloses the strength of her jealousy of
Goneril:

> I am doubtful that you have been conjunct
> And bosomed with her, as far as we call hers.
> > *No, by mine honor, madam.*
> I never shall endure her. Dear my lord,
> Be not familiar with her.   (V.i.15–16).

Before this, in a private meeting with Oswald, who is carrying
Goneril's letter to Edmund, she has allowed her compulsive desire to
break down usual propriety. She inquires after Edmund's business,
asks what is written in the letter, proposes that Oswald should betray
his mistress's trust, asks again about the letter, and then, after a hesitation that may be calculated in effect, with 'I'll love thee much', she
asks to see and open the letter. Denied all this, she alludes to
Oswald's intimacy with his lady and then is more open:

> My lord is dead; Edmund and I have talked,
> And more convenient is he for my hand
> Than for your lady's. You may gather more.   (IV.v.1–34)

Words are still guarded and subtle, but Regan's purpose cannot
remain so. Like her sister, she has revealed that she is in thrall to
desire for Edmund. In view of what is expected between a lady and
another lady's servant, she may retain some measure of reserve and
even gain in authority as she begins to act as her instincts and crav-
ings dictate. Alternatively, however, she can be forcefully flirtatious
with Oswald or very obviously nervous and desperate, possibly on
the verge of madness. However played, the improprieties of this
short scene concentrate an audience's attention so that it establishes
that *King Lear* is, amongst other things, a play about sexual longing
and thwarted affection.

     In the last scene of all, when Goneril and Regan are together once more, they express their interests in Edmund without reserve, and interplay between them becomes both melodramatic and harshly comic. When Albany reproves Regan for treating Edmund as a husband, she mocks him confidently and Goneril intervenes:

Regan.	Jester do oft prove prophets.
Goneril.	Holla, holla!
	That eye that told you so looked but a-squint (V.iii.71–3)

Regan then proceeds, in public, to offer herself into Edmund's power completely: 'the walls is thine', she says, as if she has been defeated in battle. Goneril has already poisoned her sister and, when Albany speaks of her intentions with regard to Edmund, she is confident enough to brush it aside as an 'interlude' (l. 90). Almost immediately Regan leaves the stage, in what will prove to be her death pangs, and Goneril, the extent of her involvement disclosed, soon follows her, desperate and intent on suicide. These women die as if they had no alternative to obeying their sexual appetites.

Lear's love for Cordelia absorbs most of his attention when he is dying and here again the secondary story provides a context for understanding and prompts an audience's own instinctive responses. First, the bloody knife with which Goneril has killed herself is carried on stage, still hot and smoking. Then Regan's death from poison is reported and her sister's responsibility for it. Shortly afterwards, the bodies of both are carried on and will remain on display until the tragedy is over. By these means, a father's love for one daughter is shown over against the shocking power of his other daughters to destroy themselves, driven by passion for a man whose death is reported only minutes after theirs. At the beginning of the tragedy, the other occasion when all three daughters are present, the powerful and irrational passion of that scene stemmed only from the father when he believed himself to be rejected by his youngest daughter; Kent's passion was in reaction to the consequences of his king's. These contrasts and similarities between the beginning and end of the tragedy may prompt an audience or reader of the text to remember the obsessive sexuality of Lear's mad fantasies (see above, pp. 244, 249, etc.) and come to believe that, throughout the action in his impulsive and violent anger and, latterly, in his shame (see IV.iii.43), the father of three young women has been tortured by his own irrepressible and impermissible longings. As in *Othello*, a very human form of fate may be operating as Lear clutches the body of Cordelia, tenderly gazes at her, remembers her excellencies, wills her to live, and finally yields his own life: it seems that he could not do otherwise.

Military Conflict

The other factor that greatly affects the action towards the end of *King Lear* is warfare, a conflict of seemingly unpredictable outcome that briefly but completely takes over the narrative, in its sudden eruption not unlike the storm that had disrupted events earlier. We cannot know whether Shakespeare expected any evidence of the stage-direction's '*Alarm within*' to be enacted on stage – the Folio's '*within*' is missing in the Quarto – but, whatever is seen or heard, the only fixed point of reference while the fate of everyone is in the balance will be the sightless and hopeless Gloucester, whom Edgar has left on stage in the shadow of a tree, unable to make any response. For everyone else, the battle brings considerable changes and reversals. Almost the entire company will return to the stage bearing signs of the conflict in their appearance and clothes as speech becomes more practical and downright.

Together the battle and the subsequent duel between Edmund and Edgar serve to place the protracted concerns of the main narrative into a new perspective in which individual prowess in fight appears to have greater influence on the outcome than either conscious intention or those qualities of endurance and understanding that have drawn the main narrative towards its hard-won conclusion. Even Lear is influenced by the spirit of battle, being roused now to kill Cordelia's assassin while still in prison and off stage. Albany, who has several times seemed weak and hesitant, takes full command after the battle even though, that crisis past, he resigns all power in the 'gored state', in favour of the friends of his soul, Edgar and Kent. Kent has taken no part in the battle, but arrives on stage

when it is over, having been left 'tranced' by Edgar after he had 'bel-
lowed out / As he'd burst heaven' in grief for Lear. He enters
searching for the king and eventually leaves the play refusing any
more responsibility than a continuation of his former service:

> I have a journey, sir, shortly to go.
> My master calls me; I must not say no.   (V.iii.198–9)

When all is over, Edgar suddenly has to take the responsibility of
kingship without any formal handover of power. These three, with
many unnamed, weary soldiers, stand around the dead bodies of
Lear and Cordelia: two master-less men with their service finished
and one newly empowered as master of those who remain; all now
being almost silent. With this framing for the last view of the tragic
hero, the future beyond this moment is scarcely suggested, as if no
one, not even the author, knew what would follow. Edgar (or Albany
in the Quarto) speaks for everyone:

> The oldest have borne most: we that are young
> Shall never see so much, nor live so long.

13

Macbeth: Power and the Imagination

I have't, it is engendered! Hell and night
Must bring this monstrous birth to the world's light.

So Iago ends the first Act of *Othello* and he continues to speak his
mind to the theatre's audience until the end of Act V, scene i, when
he knows that 'this is the night / That makes me or foredoes me
quite' (V.i.128–9). From then on, he speaks only when impelled to
do so and an audience must guess at his thoughts while his plans
come to nothing: Shakespeare was not able, or not willing, to show
what disaster meant for its chief instigator. With *The Tragedy of
Macbeth,* which followed *Lear*, probably at the end of 1606, this was
not so: the mind of its secretive hero, who kills his king and slaughters innocents, is open to an audience until the very end. In this
respect, *Macbeth* was a return to unfinished business.

Witchcraft

Three Witches, accompanied with '*Thunder and lightning*', start the
play to brief and startling effect. They are also puzzling, having time
to speak little more than a riddle and a promise to 'meet with
Macbeth'. Summoned by familiar spirits, they depart immediately
with another riddle and the suggestion that they or someone else, or

some thing, will 'Hover through the fog and filthy air' – that is, fly with the beating of wings, for so *hover* implied at that time. A mere dozen lines, written in simple-sounding, rhymed octosyllabics, predict the 'hurly-burly' of a battle and a return by 'the set of sun'. This tragedy may take an audience beyond 'mortal knowledge' (I.v.3) and 'mortal consequences' (V.iii.5) and certainly outside the palaces of kings and established courts of justice. The concluding choral speech shows that individual characteristics and purposes will not always have prime importance; an effect that will be increased if chanting, ritual, and dance are introduced here, as they are specifically required in the Witches' later scenes. The whole episode is an unmistakable announcement that this tragedy will take place against a huge perspective, a setting that includes a storm in the sky and all the elements of air, fire, water, and earth.

How much is achieved in this opening episode, how puzzling it is, and how far distant stylistically from anything in earlier tragedies can best be indicated by full quotation. This also shows its varying, drum-like rhythm and the near-comic effect of the Witches' self-absorption: if the scene were less driven or less elementally suggestive, it would be merely odd and ridiculous.

> *Thunder and lightning.*
> *Enter three Witches*
> *First Witch.*   When shall we three meet again?
>   In thunder, lightning, or in rain?
> *Second Witch.* When the hurly-burly's done,
>   When the battle's lost and won.
> *Third Witch.*   That will be ere the set of sun.
> *First Witch.*   Where the place?
> *Second Witch.*   Upon the heath.
> *Third Witch.*   There to meet with Macbeth.
> *First Witch.*   I come, Graymalkin.
> *Second Witch.* Paddock calls.
> *Third Witch.*   Anon.
> *All.*   Fair is foul, and foul is fair,
>   Hover through the fog and filthy air.   *Exeunt*

Today, very few people believe that witches have supernatural

8   The punishment and practice of witchcraft, 1589

This title-page from *The Apprehension and Confession of three notorious Witches, Arraigned and by Justice Condemned and Executed at Chelmsford in the County of Essex, the 5 day of July, last past, 1589* illustrates both the public punishment given to three convicted witches and also a fourth who is occupied with her familiars; these may be compared with Paddock and Graymalkin to whom the Witches call out in the first scene of *Macbeth*. The author reports that this fourth witch 'had nine spirits; 2 of them were like unto a black dog, having the faces of a toad'. (*The only known copy of this pamphlet is in Lambeth Palace Library, London, by whose permission it is reproduced.*)

powers, enabling them to prophesy with certainty and cause diseases and death, and so productions of *Macbeth* tend to rely on scenic spectacle, lights, and music to support the Witches with large-scale and nightmarish fantasy. In the nineteenth century, whole orchestras were used with large choruses of Witches, some of whom flew through the air. Shakespeare and the King's Men took much the same view on how to gain credibility, for they too could not take belief for granted. While King James's *Demonology* (Edinburgh, 1597; London, 1603) had argued that Witches threatened the lives and souls of their victims and while men and women were still being tried and burned as Witches (see Plate 8), not everyone took claims of possession and divination seriously. Reginald Scott's *Discovery of Witchcraft* (1584) had been totally sceptical and the king, like many others, became less convinced as later investigations continued to expose fraud and dementia. When *Macbeth* was first performed, some people in the audience would have been genuinely scared by its witches, but others would have been in two minds or frankly incredulous: in this situation, both author and players, like many modern directors, introduced as much elaborate stagecraft as possible.

After the succession of James I in 1603, the King's Men had become involved with the hugely expensive masques that were an established feature of court life. Here they would have experienced the attractions of spectacular sets and stage machinery, exotic costumes, music, dance, ceremony, and visual symbolism and, in *The Tragedy of Macbeth,* Shakespeare gave them opportunity to put this into practice in their own theatre. The Witches' second scene features a charm that is 'wound up' (I.iii.37) with chanting and a dance involving nine circles in alternate directions. Then, after ritually hailing Macbeth and Banquo and delivering their prophecies, some eye-catching device makes them seem to 'vanish' or melt 'as breath into the wind' (I.iii.79–82). In Act IV, scene i, the Witches' last scene, a succession of apparitions ascend and descend through a trapdoor, eight kings parade in line with the last holding a mysterious '*glass*', and a cauldron sinks into the ground, and all this is accompanied with ceremonial reverences, music, and dancing. The drama is a supernatural fantasy in which a succession of strange 'shows' – a severed human head, '*bloody child*', uprooted tree, and many crowns – display symbols of power and violence, success and defeat. The effect can be awesome but riddling prophecies and peremptory commands will also provide undercurrents of taunting comedy and inanity. The whole may seem like a nightmare activated by ambition and fear.

After early performances, the King's Men probably augmented the stage-effects by adding a new scene, Act III, scene v, in which the goddess Hecate summons her 'beldams', the Witches, to meet her 'at the pit of Acheron' where Macbeth will arrive the next morning. Hecate's arrival and her long speech might have been in Shakespeare's original version of the play, but not the song called for by a stage-direction in the one version of *Macbeth* that has survived in the first Folio of 1623: '*Sing within. Come away, come away &c.*' The full song, for Hecate, a cat, and three spirits, is given in Thomas Middleton's *The Witch*, a play that was suppressed by the censor around 1613 and survives only in manuscript. The song's words and the stage-business they imply fit the later play far better than they do Shakespeare's, where they must have been a late addition, dating from after the composition of *The Witch*. Hecate's re-appearance in the Cauldron Scene (IV.i) of the Folio text of *Macbeth*, together with the first two words of another song from *The Witch*, three extra witches, and a few lines of rather brash dialogue, can all be cut without harm to the scene and must also be a late and imperfectly recorded addition. This makes it more probable that the entire first Hecate scene as printed in the Folio was also an addition to the play as first written; it, too, can be cut without loss to continuity or clarity, and it usually is in modern productions. Most scholars believe that Middleton, who was working for the King's Men around 1615, was involved in making all these additions, either with or without Shakespeare's help.

The tragedy has thrived when spectacle, music, ceremony, and witchcraft have helped to establish the presence of evil and supernatural powers. Yet ambiguities remain about who or what the witches might be. The playtext gives two contrary explanations that probably derive from Shakespeare's main source for this play, Raphael Holinshed's *Chronicles of England and Scotland* in its second edition of 1587. There the witches are first introduced as 'three women in

strange and wild apparel, resembling creatures of elder world' but
then, a little further on, they are 'the weird sisters, that is (as ye
would say) the goddesses of destiny'. In the same vein, Holinshed
also conjectures that they might have been 'nymphs or fairies,
indued with knowledge of prophecy by their necromantical science'.
What seems to have lodged in Shakespeare's mind is that the
Witches could be identified either as strange and wildly dressed old
women or as the three Fates of classical mythology. The Folio's stage-
directions and speech-prefixes always refer to 'Witches' but the word
is used only once in the dialogue, where they are always identified as
'weird sisters' (five times) or 'weird women' (once). *Weird* was not
used commonly or casually, as in some modern usage, but seems
always to have meant 'fateful' or 'able to control the fates'. An association with the three classical Parcae or Fates is not insisted upon in
Shakespeare's text but remains a suggestion through the persistent
use of *weird*.

In contrast, Banquo's greeting establishes the Witches, more mun-
danely, as Holinshed's 'three women in strange and wild attire':

> What are these,
> So withered, and so wild in their attire,
> That look not like th' inhabitants o' th' earth
> And yet are on 't. . . .
>   You should be women,
> And yet your beards forbid me to interpret
> That you are so   (I.iii.39–47)

When Macbeth seeks them out later in the play, he twice calls them
hags, a word that could be applied to dispossessed, crazy, or rebellious women, as well as to those who were old or disfigured (IV.i.62,
130). Many of the items that they throw into the cauldron suggest a
life of scavenging poverty spent in the wilds; the implausible ingredients, such as the 'pilot's thumb', 'nose of Turk', or 'baboon's blood'
(I.iii.28; IV.iii.29–37), could be products of fantasy or madness.

Among all this confusion of names and nature, the play makes
clear beyond all doubt that these women can prophesy correctly.
Macbeth is created Thane of Cawdor immediately after they have

hailed him by that title, and this power of divination continues to be endorsed throughout the play and is so presented in the unfolding narrative that it draws an audience's attention. When Macbeth says that one of their apparitions 'hast harped my fear aright' (IV.i.88), it is possible to understand the prophecies and, perhaps, the Witches themselves as emanations of his own thoughts, subconscious and prophetic, as well as deliberate and guilt-ridden. As we have seen, the ghost of Caesar is this kind of hallucination and, on its last appearance, the ghost of Hamlet's father (see pp. 120, 145 and 147, above). But the Witches in *Macbeth* cannot be entirely explained as reflections of Macbeth's own imaginings because, right at the start, Banquo sees and hears them as well as Macbeth. Shakespeare has closed this option and placed the Witches and their prophecies in a sequence of events that must be received as mysteriously para-normal, if not supernatural.

As Macbeth proceeds to satisfy his ambition by killing Duncan, King of Scotland, and becoming king himself, and then tries to become more secure by having Banquo assassinated, revisiting the Witches, killing Macduff's wife and children, and committing other unspecified crimes that cause Scotland to weep and bleed as 'each new day a gash / Is added to her wounds' (IV.iii.39–40), the Witches' prophecies are progressively fulfilled and their riddles explained. Macbeth does become Thane of Cawdor and King of Scotland; an army, by carrying green branches to hide its move-ments, does appear to make Birnam Wood approach Macbeth's castle of Dunsinan; Macduff who, in one sense, was 'not of woman born', does decapitate him. The Witches' greeting to Banquo, 'Thou shalt get kings, though thou be none' (I.iii.67), is partly fulfilled when Fleance unexpectedly escapes assassination and is corroborated in the Witches' last apparition, the eight kings that Banquo 'points at' for his heirs (IV.iii.127–39).

Terror

The Witches' influence is mysteriously widespread, not least because the words, phrasing, and rhythms of their speeches are echoed, as if instinctively, after they have disappeared from the stage. The effect can be eerie, as when the Witches' talk of a battle 'lost, and won' is heard again in Duncan's pronouncement at the end of the following short scene: 'What he hath lost [referring to Cawdor], noble Macbeth hath won.' Their concluding couplet in the first scene, 'Fair is foul, and foul is fair . . .', is echoed in Macbeth's very first words, 'So fair and foul a day I have not seen' (I.iii.38), and his first extended soliloquy is driven by similar oppositions: 'This supernatural soliciting / Cannot be ill, cannot be good . . . Nothing is / but what is not' (I.iii.131–2, 141–2). Later, the antitheses, repetitions, alliteration, and insistent beat of the Witches continue to be heard, as in Lady Macbeth's short soliloquy during preparation for the banquet:

> Nought's had, all's spent,
> Where our desire is got without content:
> 'Tis safer to be that which we destroy,
> Than by destruction dwell in doubtful joy. (III.ii.4–7)

Repetition comes in other forms as well. Once he has returned to his own castle, Macbeth encounters a series of strange happenings, all associated with the spilling of blood. As he goes to kill Duncan, he sees an air-borne dagger pointing the way: he tries to clutch it and cannot; when he draws his own dagger, the apparition is still there but now covered with blood. When Banquo's murderer enters to give his report, Macbeth can see blood on his face and, moments later at the banquet, Banquo's Ghost shakes his 'gory locks' as he appears twice to Macbeth. A 'blood-baltered Banquo' (IV.i.138) is raised as an apparition by the Witches. Repeatedly, blood is shed on stage or off: the 'bleeding Captain' who arrives unheralded as soon as the Witches have first left; blood on both pairs of hands after the murder of Duncan and the bloodying of his drugged attendants; blood of the final battle, including that on the head of Macbeth as it is raised for all to see in sign of victory. The sleep-walking Lady Macbeth is obsessed with the non-existent blood she sees and tries to wash from her hands. Blood permeates the play, as if it had a supernatural power to make its presence felt. Macbeth comes to believe this: 'It will have blood, they say: blood will have blood' (III.iv.123).

Other prodigies, seen or reported, suggest that the entire world suffers from Macbeth's crimes. It is an 'unruly' night when Duncan is murdered, with 'lamentings heard i'th'air, strange screams of death' (II.iii.54–62). The next day scarcely dawns; as Ross reports:

> The heavens, as troubled with man's act,
> Threatens his bloody stage. By th' clock 'tis day,
> And yet dark night strangles the travelling lamp . . .   (II.iv.5–10)

Duncan's horses are said to have broken out from their stalls so wildly that they 'ate each other' (ll. 14–20). Most uncanny, perhaps, because they are comic and occur immediately after the king's murder, are the visions seen by the drunken Porter: he imagines he is guarding Hell Gate where he encounters a neo-capitalist farmer, an equivocating traitor, and a Frenchified English tailor who are all applying for entrance. He talks to them as if they were actually present and it can seem as if a phantom world, a contemporary Jacobean one, has momentarily taken over from an actual and ancient Scotland.

The apparitions whose reality may be most convincing and threatening are those that take possession of Macbeth's mind but are given no visible or no fixed form. After Duncan's murder, he begins to hear an insistent voice crying:

> 'Sleep no more' to all the house:
> 'Glamis hath murdered sleep, and therefore Cawdor
> Shall sleep no more.'   (II.ii.40–2)

Planning Banquo's murder, he speaks of 'terrible dreams / That shake us nightly' and confesses to 'restless ecstasy' or near madness (III.ii.20–3). Increasingly, words and actions reveal a mind full of monstrous fantasies, more brooding and solitary than anything associated with the Witches:

> . . . ere the bat hath flown
> His cloistered flight, ere to black Hecate's summons

> The shard-born beetle with his drowsy hums
> Hath rung night's yawning peal, there shall be done
> A deed of dreadful note.   (III.ii.43–7)

He wants to be in darkness, although it will bring more blood and wrenching pain:

> Come, seeling night,
> Scarf up the tender eye of pitiful day,
> And with thy bloody and invisible hand
> Cancel and tear to pieces that great bond
> Which keeps me pale.   (ll. 49–53)

He feels at one with unseen and mysterious powers:

> Light thickens,
> And the crow makes wing to th' rooky wood;
> Good things of day begin to droop and drowse,
> Whiles night's black agents to their preys do rouse.   (ll. 53–6)

Speaking with the accent of the Witches, he senses that the world he inhabits is beyond his wife's knowledge:

> Thou marvell'st at my words; but hold thee still,
> Things bad begun make strong themselves by ill.   (ll. 57–8)

Before leaving the stage, he calls for his wife in an almost gentle half-line, 'So prithee go with me' (l. 59): experiencing all these terrors, he is still in the real world.

Oppositions

Macbeth's mind is 'full of scorpions' (III.ii.36), but not always entirely so. He retains an instinct for 'the good things of day', even as he loses them. When he considers murdering the king, he knows that his guest is there 'in double trust' and

> . . . hath been
> So clear in his great office, that his virtues
> Will plead like angels, trumpet-tongued against
> The deep damnation of his taking-off . . .

He becomes aware of pity and then a cherubim, angel of truth, takes over his mind, with piercing and irresistible force:

> And pity, like a naked new-born babe,
> Striding the blast, or Heaven's cherubim, horsed
> Upon the sightless couriers of the air,
> Shall blow the horrid deed in every eye
> That tears shall drown the wind.   (I.vii.12–25)

These contrary ideas, expressed in palpable images, have immediate effect on Macbeth and, for the time being, his resolve to murder evaporates. Having 'Put rancours in the vessel of [his] peace' (III.i.66), his mind has become a battleground for opposed forces.

When Macbeth chooses to return to the Witches, he knows that they stand over against everything that promotes virtue, health, wealth, and wisdom in the world:

> I conjure you, by that which you profess,
> Howe'er you come to know it, answer me:
> Though you untie the winds, and let them fight
> Against the churches; though the yeasty waves
> Confound and swallow navigation up;
> Though bladed corn be lodged, and trees blown down,
> Though castles topple on their warders' heads;
> Though palaces and pyramids do slope
> Their heads to their foundations; though the treasure
> Of nature's germen tumble all together,
> Even till destruction sicken: answer me
> To what I ask you.   (IV.i.64–75)

This single long sentence is so written that continuous control of breath and phrasing, together with concentration and sustained energy of thought, are all needed to make sense of it. The witches are rendered silent while he speaks and, if well spoken, an audience can be spellbound as well. More than a command, it is a deliberate act that accepts all that the Witches might do while demonstrating that Macbeth retains a knowledge of all that is good, even as he repudiates it. Despite the spectacular and prophetic impression made by the Witches, the core and main conflict of the tragedy is within the mind of its hero.

Much later, committed to battle and surrounded with enemies, his wife withdrawn and overcharged with 'thick-coming fancies' (V.iii.37), Macbeth still knows what life might have been and is accutely aware of its loss:

> that which should accompany old age,
> As honour, love, obedience, troops of friends,
> I must not look to have – but in their stead
> Curses, not loud but deep, mouth-honour, breath
> Which the poor heart would fain deny, and dare not.   (V.iii.24–8)

As darkness and blood are pitted against the good in Macbeth's mind, so the Witches' prophecies and rituals are offset in the play's action by their opposites. Having attended on both Duncan and Macbeth, Ross enters with a nameless man who is more than seventy years old and they talk about ominous portents in the sky. When Macduff joins them, the old man falls silent and, being neither introduced nor greeted, probably withdraws to stand apart. He speaks again only after Macduff has gone and Ross has bid farewell, and then his words are a prayer that directly echoes and contradicts the Witches' incantations:

> God's benison go with you, and with those
> That would make good of bad, and friends of foes.   (II.iv.40–1)

Ross has twice called this man 'father' and so Shakespeare may have intended him to be played as a priest or hermit but omitted, in pru- dence, to say so in the text. To speak of God so openly with a formal bestowal of blessing is rare in Shakespeare's Jacobean tragedies because it could be censored.

A more explicit presentation of peace and holiness comes much later, in Act IV, scene iii. When, after intense testing of his loyalties, Malcolm, Duncan's exiled elder son, welcomes Macduff to England and speaks with him of Scotland's suffering under Macbeth's tyranny, another anonymous person enters unannounced. What Malcolm is saying must be kept secret and so he breaks off to identify the stranger as a Doctor attending the King of England who is that day to 'touch' many wretched and sick persons: 'Such sanctity hath Heaven given his hand, / They presently amend' (IV.iii.144–5). After the Doctor's exit, Malcolm reports further about this king's 'most miraculous work', his 'heavenly gift of prophecy', and the 'sundry blessings that hang about his throne' and 'speak him full of grace'. As Hecate is imagined by Macbeth as a power behind the creatures of night (see III.ii.44) and, in the extended version of the play, appears twice on stage in charge of the Witches, so King Edward the Confessor is introduced as a contrasting off-stage presence demonstrating the supernatural powers of the Christian God.

The two opposing forces controlling human events are only occasionally unmistakable or unavoidable, but repeated visions of horror and trust, bloodshed and peace, darkness and light, heaven and hell are often compelling presences in Macbeth's mind and establish the widest perspective against which the tragedy's human action unfolds. Drawn both ways, its hero is tormented, grieved at heart, afraid, and self-abused; as he loses his grip on the power he had won, he acts as if he is mad:

> He cannot buckle his distempered cause
> Within the belt of rule.   (V.ii.13–16)

Struggling to keep his sanity and authority, life becomes for him:

> . . . but a walking shadow, a poor player
> That struts and frets his hour upon the stage,
> And then is heard no more. It is a tale
> Told by an idiot, full of sound and fury
> Signifying nothing.   (V.v.24–8)

The tragic hero seems about to end his part in meaningless defeat, but that is not so; he will confront death fighting.

Sensing that he is 'tied to a stake' so that 'bear-like' he must fight the course (V.vii.1–2), Macbeth rejects playing 'the Roman fool' and committing suicide (V.vii.31–2). Then, learning that Macduff was from 'his mother's womb / Untimely ripped' and so, in one sense, 'not of woman born' (V.vii.38–45), he believes that he is about to be killed in accordance with the Witches' prophecy that he should fear such a man. This moment is critical because his first instinct is not to fight; then a contrary thought takes over his mind and, accepting that he is doomed, he decides to 'try the last':

> Before my body
> I throw my warlike shield: lay on Macduff,
> And damned be him that first cries 'Hold, enough!'   (V.vii.63–4)

After these abrupt and practical words, only Macbeth's actions in single combat speak for him. The messages given will vary on each occasion that the play is performed according to how the two men fight wordlessly. In the Folio there are three consecutive stage-directions – '*Exeunt fighting*', '*Alarms*', and '*Enter fighting, and Macbeth slain*' – but no words at the moment of death. Later Macduff re-enters '*with Macbeth's head*' and proclaims, 'Behold where stands / Th'usurper's cursèd head' (V.vii.64–5), but these words of the victor add nothing to what is known about the tragic hero and how he met his death.

In *King Lear* Shakespeare had also left great deal for the performer and audience to supply when he gradually withdrew the hero's ability to think, speak, and act. In *Macbeth* the actor has a different and, in some ways, more difficult task because, after a long and demanding performance, he must have the imaginative and emotional strength to show Macbeth's onset of courage and the sheer physical energy needed to engage with a resolute Macduff played by a much fresher actor. 'Giving a good fight' at this late stage – and the last Act needs nothing less if it is to hold interest and excitement to its end – is also a test of nerves because the most carefully arranged stage fight is especially dangerous for a tired actor; in fact, this fight is renowned for the accidents it has caused. Even though this tragedy has very clear indications of what is good and what is bad, Shakespeare has insisted that the actor, in his performance, and members of an audience, in their imaginations, experience death itself without help from the text. Final judgements on the hero are supplied in Macduff's 'hell-hound' and Malcolm's 'dead butcher' (V.vii.33, 99), but the actor of Macbeth and an audience can supply alternative ideas about the will, courage, madness, isolation, and suffering of the man, and about the loss of 'honour, love, obedience, troops of friends.'

Macbeth and his Wife

For much of the play, any uncertainty about supernatural intervention or the reality of the apparitions is offset by the strong forward impulse of the narrative. Events follow each other with a minimum of delay or explanation: among Shakespeare's plays, only the early *Comedy of Errors* and *The Tempest* are shorter. The entire play is a sequence of short scenes, only two being of more than a hundred and fifty lines. At times the Folio text deals with important actions in such a summary fashion that some scholars have argued that Shakespeare's original text has been more severely cut than it was subsequently lengthened. When Malcolm is named Prince of Cumberland and Duncan's heir and, in the last scene, when Malcolm announces that the thanes are to be created earls, so little preparation or reaction is provided that an audience can easily miss the political significance of these events. From first to last, the play has the grip of a thriller, not only until the murder but afterwards as well: the situation continues to be highly unstable as the consequences of ambition and treachery become increasingly evident.

This exceptional narrative drive enables other, very different aspects of the play to be developed. Sometimes it seems as if time stands still so that mental and emotional experiences can become the centre of attention. Macbeth's crimes take place offstage or are undertaken by other people, unlike Shakespeare's treatment of violence in *Hamlet*, *Othello*, or *King Lear*, but reactions to them are vividly present on stage in his soliloquies and in interaction with his wife. Lady Macbeth is crucial in this because, as the stories of Gloucester and his sons or of Polonius and Laertes help to define and sharpen the audience's understanding of the main action of *Lear* and *Hamlet*, so Lady Macbeth's actions, thoughts, and feelings throughout the entire play reflect on those of Macbeth. A continuing duologue between man and wife reveals the steps by which the decision to commit the crimes is reached, denied, and then ratified; it also shows the effects of having undertaken them.

Throughout much of the first Acts, Lady Macbeth seems the stronger partner. Whereas the Witches had chosen to 'meet with Macbeth' (I.i.8), she had, in her first appearance, invoked supernatural powers and willingly submitted to them:

> Come, you spirits
> That tend on mortal thoughts, unsex me here,
> And fill me from the crown to the toe, top-full
> Of direst cruelty. . .
> Come to my woman's breasts
> And take my milk for gall, you murd'ring ministers,
> Wherever, in your sightless substances,
> You wait on nature's mischief. . . (I.v.39–53)

Lady Macbeth makes the practical plans for murdering Duncan and, when Macbeth decides 'We will proceed no further in this business' (I.vii.31), she strengthens his will to continue. When he returns from murdering Duncan holding daggers dripping with blood and 'afraid to think' what he has done (II.ii.50), she completes the task by returning the daggers and smearing the faces of sleeping grooms with blood. When Macbeth's horror at seeing Banquo's ghost breaks up the banquet, she takes command, at first trying to cover up and coax her husband back to the table, and then ensuring that their guests leave as soon as possible (see III.iv.84–5, 118–22).

By challenging Macbeth's motives for what he is doing and intervening to strengthen his resolve, Lady Macbeth unsettles other judgements an audience might otherwise make. Whereas everyone in the play blames Macbeth for the disasters brought upon Scotland, it has seen that he 'proceeds' in the matter only after his wife insists

that he does. While Macbeth soon becomes 'Steeped' in blood
(III.iv.137–9), he is known at the start of the play as Duncan's
'valiant cousin, worthy gentleman' (I.ii.23) and, even after many
atrocities, Malcolm speaks of his 'good and virtuous nature' that has
given way to 'an imperial charge' (IV.iii.19–20). While 'Fate and
metaphysical aid' (I.v.28) seem to insist that he commits great sins, a
person watching the play may come to believe that this was not his
necessary destiny – as might be said, for instance, of Iago or
Edmund in earlier tragedies. The question of whether he would have
murdered Duncan had he not been persuaded by his wife is never
posed, yet that possibility can arise very readily when man and wife
talk in private.

When they are together, words are more than usually charged
with precise meanings and, sometimes, no words are needed for
mutual understanding; for example:

> *Macbeth.*   My dearest love,
>   Duncan comes here tonight.
> *Lady Macbeth.*   And when goes hence?
> *Macbeth.*   Tomorrow, as he purposes.
> *Lady Macbeth.*   O never
>   Shall sun that morrow see.
>   Your face, my thane, is as a book where men
>   May read strange matters; . . .   (I.v.57–62)

'As he purposes' says all that is needed for Lady Macbeth to know
that he thinks of murdering his king and her indirect answer communicates both her understanding and complicity in this. She then
warns him that he must hide the thoughts that she has 'read' exactly
although he has not spoken them. At the end of this introductory
scene, husband and wife have not yet used the word murder: 'this
night's great business' is how she refers to it and his 'We will speak
further' is a further avoidance of the word (ll. 66, 69). However, by
the time they leave the stage together, an audience knows what they
think and that they both know each other's unspoken thoughts as
well as hearing the words they speak.

In scene after scene, husband and wife are so aware of each other's
presence that words signal only a part of the messages that are given

and received. An audience has been made aware of an intimate, unspoken and, even, unconscious intercourse. When she persuades him a second time to proceed with the murder, by accusing him of cowardice and of not being the man she believes he could be, he says nothing in reply but responds by being there and staying there, hearing all she says and being aware of her presence, as she must be of his. They watch each other closely, as two persons in single combat must do, and they respond instinctively:

> . . . What beast was't then
> That made you break this enterprise to me?
> When you durst do it, then you were a man:
> And to be more than what you were, you would
> Be so much more the man. Nor time nor place
> Did then adhere, and yet you would make both –
> They have made themselves, and that their fitness now
> Does unmake you.

Perhaps he moves or his body stiffens at this point because she now, in an instant, shifts the grounds of argument and, speaking of herself, dares him to equal her resolve and courage:

> I have given suck, and know
> How tender 'tis to love the babe that milks me:
> I could, while it was smiling in my face,
> Have plucked my nipple from his boneless gums
> And dashed the brains out, had I so sworn
> As you have done to this.   (I.vii.47–59)

Now he does speak: 'If we should fail?' Silently, he has followed all she had said and is ready to move a step further, not as 'I' but, with her, as 'we'. Her reply is yet more simple verbally: 'We fail?' These two words are a line to themselves, the rest of the expected pentameter left empty to indicate that they are both silent now, before or after she speaks.

Editors and actors have tried many different ways of punctuating and phrasing this exchange after 'If we should fail.' Does her 'We fail?' prevent him saying more by abrupt and scornful rebuttal or, even, ridicule? Does she answer after some time, with an echoing question that accepts his doubts as reasonable, or pretends to do so? Or does she make an exclamation, rather than ask a question? (Scribes and compositors often used a question-mark in this way.) Does she stress the 'we' and at the same time move closer towards him, perhaps taking him in her arms? How assured or insistent are her next words as he, again, remains silent: 'But screw your courage to the sticking place, / And we'll not fail'? Every pair of actors will weigh their words differently and be in a different physical relationship to each other, but all of them need to show a mutual involvement so deep that speech is not always necessary. Her next words show that she has planned the murder with some exactness but also emphasize that they will act together now and, speaking in questions, invite him to respond to the prospect of a shared dominance:

> What cannot you and I perform upon
> Th'unguarded Duncan? What not put upon
> His spongy officers who shall bear the guilt
> Of our great quell?   (ll. 70–3)

His answer is indirect, but immediate and sustained in phrase as it refers back to her invocation of motherhood; acceptance of her leadership is implied in what follows:

> Bring forth men-children only:
> For thy undaunted mettle should compose
> Nothing but males. Will it not be received
> When we have marked with blood those sleepy two . . .   (ll. 73ff.)

Moments later, with 'I am settled' (l. 80), he calls her to follow him off stage and she is the one who is silent.

By the close of its first Act, the tragedy has announced that its main action springs out of a childless marital relationship that depends on listening as much as speaking and responds to reactions that are not spoken at all. Although the man speaks of his own intentions as they leave the stage, the woman has controlled his thoughts and actions. Over the course of a number of performances, two actors will develop ever more subtle and deeply realized understanding of each other's impersonations and changes are bound to creep into their finely balanced relationship. It becomes an adventure for both actors and audience as the play is realized in subtly new ways with each repetition.

Lady Macbeth

From start to finish, this tragedy is clearly about regicide and usurpation, treason and violence, but as soon as Macbeth and Lady Macbeth hold the stage together the focus intensifies to include the story of their relationship. While the Witches foretell the course of the political narrative, what happens between these two is impelled by what they are in themselves, scarcely influenced by any other person.

Although Lady Macbeth seems formidably in charge of what happens at first, signs of insecurity are soon evident and disturb the progress of the drama. The very first time she is alone on stage and a Messenger enters, she asks for his 'tidings' before he has chance to speak. When he replies, 'The King comes here tonight' (I.v.30), the speed with which she answers, 'Thou'rt mad to say it', betrays a mind that has raced ahead dangerously and so thinks of her husband as king, not of Duncan, as if the prophecies she has just read in his letter were already fulfilled. As she will tell her husband:

> Thy letters have transported me beyond
> The ignorant present, and I feel now
> The future in the instant. (I.v.55–7)

When he has gone to murder Duncan, she does not keep to her room but enters and seems almost to apologize and to excuse herself by reference to the grooms she has drugged:

> That which hath made them drunk, hath made me bold;
> What hath quenched them, hath given me fire.

She stops, as if apprehensive, to listen for sounds in the near silence:

> Hark, peace;
> It was the owl that shrieked, the fatal bellman
> Which gives the stern'st good night. He is about it, . . .   (II.ii.1ff.)

After the murder has been discovered and the entire court has been aroused, her husband covers his guilt in a masterful speech that gives credibility to his excuses for killing the grooms by drawing on the compassion he had earlier expressed for the slain king (see II.iii.113–20). In contrast, Lady Macbeth faints, almost without a word (l. 120). This incident cannot be missed, because everything else has to stop while she is helped to her room and because there is no means of knowing whether this is a genuine and surprising weakness or an astute trick to draw attention away from her husband.

When they both enter crowned for the first time in a public celebration that is heralded by a trumpet call and surrounded with 'Lords, and attendants' (III.i.10, S.D.), Lady Macbeth holds centre-stage with her husband and she speaks formally and graciously when he prompts her but, as soon as the court is dismissed, she leaves in silence while the whole assembly must wait for her to take precedence and bow as she passes. A few minutes later she re-enters with a servant asking for confirmation of Banquo's absence and sending for her husband to come and speak with her. Once alone, she speaks a soliloquy in which, as we have already noted (p. 291), her words echo the manner of the Witches; they also echo her husband's soliloquy of a few moments before. He had started with: 'To be thus is nothing, /But to be safely thus . . . ' (III.i.47–8); she starts as if more defeated: 'Nought's had, all's spent, / Where our desire is got without content . . .' (III.ii.5–6). When Macbeth joins her, she argues that 'what's done, is done' and tells him, as she had previously, to conceal his thoughts:

> Come on –
> Gentle my lord, sleek o'er your rugged looks,
> Be bright and jovial among your guests tonight.   (ll. 29–31)

But the tone is different now: 'Gentle my lord' is a new form of address and he answers very promptly: 'So shall I, love, and so I pray be you'. He has 'read' in her face and bearing (I.v.61–2) that she is the one who needs this advice now. He had called her 'My dearest love' on first returning to their castle (I.v.57), but no further endearments have been spoken until now. Now, the simple 'love' is followed by 'dear wife' and 'dearest chuck' (ll. 39, 48): perhaps she is so disturbed that he feels a need to reclaim her attention and confidence. While she insinuates that Banquo and Fleance may not live – 'in them nature's copy's not eterne' – he replies more positively, 'There's comfort yet, they are assailable'; when she is prompted to ask 'What's to be done?', he warns her to be 'innocent of the knowledge . . . / Till thou applaud the deed' (ll. 41ff.). The balance between them has radically altered and he is now in charge.

Although this tragedy presents supernatural, violent, and politically significant events in bold forms, highly refined and verbally understated ways are used to draw attention to the inward suffering of those most engaged in the sensational narrative. After the banquet has broken up in disorder and Lady Macbeth has pronounced 'A kind good night to all' (III.iv.122), Macbeth does most of the talking. She answers his questions, tells him that the night has almost passed, and follows his question about Macduff's absence with one of her own: 'Did you send to him, sir?' When he says that he is about to revisit the Witches and is already engaged in 'Strange things', she asks nothing more, responding only by saying 'You lack the season of all natures, sleep' (l. 142) and then, probably, following him off stage. The text gives no indication how she should leave, except the very general direction '*Exeunt*': sometimes, in performance, Macbeth and Lady Macbeth leave in two different directions or with very different bearing and tempo; sometimes he has to take hold of her and physically draw her off the stage.

Man and wife do not appear together again. The next that is heard of Lady Macbeth is that since 'his majesty went into the field' she has walked and talked in her sleep. A Waiting Gentlewoman and Doctor of Physic are waiting for her entry and then watch in silence while she rubs her hands together, as if washing them, and then, at last, speaks: 'Yet here's a spot' (V.i.30). Another silence follows until, with a sudden rush of varying sensations, she appears to relive much of the action of the play:

> Out damned spot – out I say, One – two – why then 'tis time to do't
> – Hell is murky. Fie, my lord, fie, a soldier, and afeard? What need we
> fear who knows it, when none can call our power to account? Yet who
> would have thought the old man to have had so much blood in him.
>
>   (V.i.13–38)

At the time of the murder, she said that had Duncan 'not resembled
my father as he slept', she would have killed him (II.ii.13–14) but
she had not been appalled as her husband had been when he saw the
blood on his hands. She was concerned then only with practicalities
and her husband's inaction: now she is haunted by blood stemming
from the old man's wound.

   After another silence, she speaks of Lady Macduff, her husband's
more recent victim – 'The Thane of Fife, had a wife – where is she
now?' – and, again, of the need to clean her hands and take charge
of her husband. Yet another silence and then she starts to wash her
hands once more:

> Here's the smell of the blood still – all the perfumes of Arabia will not
> sweeten this little hand. O, O, O.   (ll. 48–50)

Now she is conscious of a permeating smell, implying that the blood
is still hot in her imagination and she is reliving the murder, but
contrary thoughts are now present as well: the sweetness of exotic
perfumes in impossible abundance and the smallness of her own
hand. After this heightened and acutely present awareness, all words
are stopped by three inarticulate cries, the sound of a heart strained
to breaking point, as the Doctor interprets them. She speaks in two
other disjointed bursts, both concerned with her husband's inactivity:

> Wash your hands, put on your nightgown, look not so pale: I tell you
> yet again Banquo's buried; he cannot come out on's grave.
> *Doctor.   Even so?*
> To bed, to bed – there's knocking at the gate – come, come, come,
> come, give me your hand – what's done, cannot be undone. To bed,
> to bed, to bed.   *Exit.*   (ll. 59–66)

Performance in response to these fragments of speech and compulsive actions will show Lady Macbeth reaching towards a more sensitive awareness, as if towards shafts of light, or, perhaps, becoming increasingly appalled, as if fleeing from the prospect of a 'murky' hell. Her last words and actions are to draw her husband towards the comparative security of their shared bed.

To read the text of this scene, looking for hints of meaning and points of certainty, is unlike the experience of watching it in the theatre where we are held by this woman standing alone and, now, so open to our scrutiny. When a clear performance has been achieved, our understanding can seem crystallized and fixed for ever in her presence. Paintings and photographs show that Shakespeare has provided opportunity for very personal and distinctive impersonations (see Plates 9, 10 and 11). Even with an unskilled or uncer-

9   Henri Fuseli's sketch of Lady Macbeth sleepwalking

One of three sketches of this incident by Fuseli. Probably based on Mrs Pritchard's performance which he had seen in 1764, it suggests the great violence and sense of danger that she may have used. (*Reproduced by permission;* © *The British Museum.*)

10   George Henry Harlow's painting of Sarah Siddons as Lady Macbeth sleepwalking

Mrs Siddons first played the role in London in 1785. This portrait suggests the inward and transfixed nature of her performance in this scene; Leigh Hunt wrote of 'the death-like stare of her countenance' (*Dramatic Criticism*, ed. 1949, p. 72). (*The painting hangs in the Garrick Club, London, and is reproduced by the club's permission.*)

11   Ellen Terry as Lady Macbeth sleepwalking

This Lady Macbeth has recovered self-command; holding her light high, she is probably calling her husband to follow her 'to bed' (V.i.63–6). (*Reproduced from a photograph in possession of the present author.*)

tain performance, the Doctor and Gentlewoman are present to guide us in attentive whispers so that our imaginations can fill out the cues of the text according to our immediate experience of the earlier Acts. In performance, Lady Macbeth's prolonged silences in her final scenes, like Desdemona's silences (see pp. 198, 213, etc. above), give scope for an audience's responses to grow and take possession of their minds.

After 'The cry of women' (V.v.8) is heard from off stage, Macbeth is told 'The Queen, my lord, is dead' (l. 16). For the moment, as he defends his castle with depleted forces against well-provided enemies, Macbeth forgets himself and, after a silence indicated by the incomplete verse-line, speaks first of the inadequacy of his response:

> She should have died hereafter;
> There would have been a time for such a word –

That acknowledged, his words, like King Lear's 'Never, never, never, never, never' (see above, p. 234), show that he is overwhelmed by how little is left for him to live or fight for:

> Tomorrow, and tomorrow, and tomorrow,
> Creeps in this petty pace from day to day,
> To the last syllable of recorded time;
> And all our yesterdays have lighted fools
> The way to dusty death.   (V.v.17–28)

Unlike Lear, his thoughts centre on life and death as if they were his own and he only a player 'signifying nothing'. Lear had reached a similar sense of the folly of life during the strange dream-like encounters on Dover Beach (see above, p. 230) but, nearer to death, anger possessed him and a determination to share his experience with others. Close to death, Macbeth is more alone and more in charge of his thoughts and actions. He is able to choose to live on and, for all his recognition of the folly of living, this is exactly what he does when a messenger enters: 'Thou com'st to use thy tongue – thy story quickly' (l. 29), he says, before the frightened man has time to speak.

When Macbeth hears that Birnam Wood has been seen coming to
Dunsinan, Malcolm's army having been hidden by leafy boughs torn
from the trees, he threatens the messenger with torture if he has
spoken falsely and then begins to 'pull in resolution' and call his
remaining followers to arm themselves. While this reaction is clear
and can be played boldly, the contradictions in the scene, alternating
between hope and despair, reflection and action, will test actor and
audience with demands similar to those of Lady Macbeth's sleep-
walking. The only constant elements are his tired body and the will
which enables him to grasp each new thought and to fight on, rather
than accept a meaningless sequence of days and nights:

> Arm, arm, and out –
> If this which he avouches does appear,
> There is nor flying hence, nor tarrying here.
> I 'gin to be aweary of the sun
> And wish th' estate o' th' world were now undone.
> Ring the alarum bell, blow wind, come wrack,
> At least we'll die with harness on our back.　　　　(ll. 46–52)

After this speech, its thoughts separately defined and yet held
together in three contrasting couplets, the stage is emptied of people
while drums sound and Malcolm's army marches on.

The men opposed to Macbeth are single-minded and confident,
as Malcolm reminds them: 'Now near enough; your leafy screens
throw down, / And show like those you are' (V.vi.1–2). This operation, involving the handling of bulky camouflage and then a display
of '*colours*' by a largish body of armed men, is not easy to achieve in
a theatre. Considerable time must be taken in its accomplishment,
during which an audience is required to re-adjust its attention from
an inward struggle to the speech and action of men ready to engage
in battle with total belief in the righteousness of their cause.
Macduff speaks for them all as they leave to fight and '*Alarums*' continue to be heard:

> Make all our trumpets speak, give them all breath,
> Those clamorous harbingers of blood, and death.　　　(V.vi.9–10)

From now on, the focus of attention alternates between these resolute soldiers and the tragic hero, increasingly alone and wearied in
mind and body, as he determines to 'try the last'. Lady Macbeth has
continued to influence the tragedy after she left the stage for the last
time because the sound of her off-stage death has helped to sensitize
an audience to the pain that underlies Macbeth's words and only
further action can mitigate.

The Kingdom of Scotland

The tragedy is not complete until Macbeth's severed head is shown
to the victorious army and Malcolm denounces 'this dead butcher,
and his fiend-like Queen' (V.vii.98). None of this takes a 'large
expense of time' (l. 90) but all is carefully managed, as the affairs of
Scotland and the workings of 'watchful tyranny' have been
throughout the play.

An economy of means is used for almost all the political scenes
but they are marked by contrasts that make contradictions evident
and provoke questions about many of the judgements that are made
in them. Duncan is said to be a good king but, having declared that
there is 'no art / To find the mind's construction in the face'
(I.iv.11–12), he proceeds to welcome Macbeth with unguarded generosity. Banquo can sound like a man of religious faith – 'In the
great hand of God I stand' (II.iii.132) – but he is politically adroit,
carefully probing Macbeth's intentions after meeting the Witches
and guarding his own words; he tries to play safe by absenting
himself and his son from the coronation feast. Macduff suffers
deeply and nearly silently – 'Give sorrow words', advises the young
Malcolm (IV.iii.209) – and yet he is the most outspoken in pursuing
revenge. Malcolm goes to ingenious lengths before trusting Macduff
as an exile in England, although he and his brother had earlier taken
refuge in separate countries as soon as danger threatened.

Similar disparities in less central elements create an impression of
an uneasy world beyond the protection of the royal presence. Lennox
remains close to Macbeth throughout the first four Acts and accompanies him when he revisits the Witches but, meeting with an un-

named Lord, he takes great pains to test his loyalties before disclosing his own (III.vi). Ross and an unknown messenger both advise Lady Macduff to take refuge, but without committing themselves to any action that might help her. Whether Lady Macduff trusts her absent husband is far from clear, since the words she uses about him have double meanings that are obvious even to her very young son. When Old Siward learns that his son is one of the very few casualties of the final battle, his grief in public is so brief that Malcolm urges 'He's worth more sorrow, / And that I'll spend for him' (V.vii.80–1). In the concluding speech of the play, Malcolm spends little time on any topic and draws the story briskly towards the future:

> what needful else
> That calls upon us, by the grace of Grace,
> We will perform in measure, time, and place:
> So thanks to all at once, and to each one,
> Whom we invite to see us crowned at Scone.   (V.vii.101–5)

Treatment of the political dimensions of this tragedy is masterly, but held in by very tight reins. Nevertheless, a number of scenes make large-scale ceremonial or military demands upon the acting company and provide occasions for corporate and political concerns to dominate. Duncan is provided with '*Attendants*' on every entry and is often announced with trumpets: although he does not himself fight, soldiers show his military might, and processions of servants demonstrate the respectful hospitality accorded him at Macbeth's castle. Similar ceremonies are repeated when Macbeth and his Lady enter crowned for the first time and when the lords take their seats for the banquet respecting their 'own degrees' (III.iv.1) and drink healths that are formally proposed. This ceremony is broken up 'in most admired disorder' (III.iv.111) because Macbeth is met, not like Duncan by a 'Bleeding Capatain' who has saved his son's life, but by Banquo's bloodied ghost. The next ceremonies are the highly elaborate ones at the pit of Acheron, where another centre of power is presented and Macbeth does obeisance to the Witches. A climax is provided by the apparitions that fill the stage with a royal procession of eight kings and cause Macbeth to fall silent and 'stand . . . amazedly' (IV.i.141).

When viewed in this sequence of ceremonies and rituals, Macbeth's isolation on stage after the Witches' apparitions, stripped of any representation of power and authority, is a crisis with political implications. This is the point at which he is ready to act decisively without respect for others, no longer remembering his place in the kingdom:

> From this moment
> The very firstlings of my heart shall be
> The firstlings of my hand.   (ll. 161–3)

After the Witches' ceremonies have proved to be impermanent and taunting, Macbeth who had sought them out is revealed as foolishly unreflective and desperately ruthless:

> The castle of Macduff I will surprise,
> Seize upon Fife; give to th'edge o'th'sword
> His wife, his babes, and all unfortunate souls
> That trace him in his line. No boasting like a fool,
> This deed I'll do, before this purpose cool;
> But no more sights.   (ll. 165–70)

No more ceremonial 'sights' of witches or peacetime royalty will follow. When the stage fills again it is with an army in battle order. Shortly afterwards Malcolm enters the castle which has been 'gently rendered' (V.vii.25) and Macbeth is hunted down and killed among the '*Alarums*' of battle. Only when his lifeless head is put on display does a final ceremony take place that is both military and royal, soldiers hailing Malcolm as King of Scotland and he announcing that the thanes shall become earls in a new political order. This is effected very quickly and, after the switch of allegiance, everyone leaves the stage with no words to express their thoughts or feelings. The tragedy does not end with the convincing demonstration of inherited authority or of holy blessings that would provide a full conclusion for the series of ceremonial scenes.

The concerns of society as a whole have their most detailed presentation in a scene that is almost unnecessary to the story. Macbeth talks at length to two nameless men, trying to persuade them to kill

Banquo, even though he has spoken to them already. He needs to be confident of their willingness to act – to 'make assurance double sure', as he will say later (IV.i.97) – and so, in troubled prose, he reminds them:

> how you were borne in hand, how crossed; the instruments; who wrought with them – and all things else that might to half a soul, and to a notion crazed, say 'This did Banquo.'

He insists that they should have neither patience nor pity:

> Are you so gospelled to pray for this good man, and for his issue, whose heavy hand hath bowed you to the grave and beggared yours for ever? (ll. 76–90)

He assures them that, as dogs are different from each other, so are men, and that he is looking for those with 'a station in the file / Not i' th' worst rank of manhood'. On the first occasion offered, these two assure him that they are 'reckless' and ready to set life 'on any chance / To mend it, or be rid on't'; they are 'weary with disasters, tugged with fortune', 'incensed' by the 'vile blows and buffets of the world' (III.i.108–14). These murderers need no persuasion, but Macbeth has not finished until he has also revealed himself more fully: Banquo, he says is his enemy as he is theirs:

> and though I could
> With bare-faced power sweep him from my sight
> And bid my will avouch it, yet I must not,
> For certain friends that are both his and mine,
> Whose loves I may not drop, but wail his fall
> Who I myself struck down . . . (ll. 115–26)

So, when there is no need to speak, Macbeth talks about 'love' and explains that he lives in a world of distrust and secret crime. Later, he will send a third murderer after these two to ensure that they do as they promise and, probably, to kill them afterwards. Malcolm shows much the same view of the Scotland he intends to rule when he describes himself as evil in order to discover Macduff's intentions when he left wife and children without apparent thought for their safety: 'modest wisdom,' he says, 'plucks me / From over-credulous haste' (IV.i.119–20). It is the same Scotland, too, which the Porter imagines, when he rises from drunken sleep to answer knocking at the gate, and which audiences at the Globe would have recognized as the dark side of politics in the world in which they lived, the conspiratorial and dangerous world of the Gunpowder Plot that intended to blow up the king and parliament as recently as November 1605.

Although this political breeding ground for Macbeth's history is only sketched in at the side of the main action, rather than having a full presence on the stage, it contributes importantly to an audience's view of the tragaedy. As the main narrative unfolds with its various conflicts and uncertainties, in the distance a heavy cloud of despair is gathering, a sense that everything is part of a wider anxiety. This is why the Old Man who talks to Ross after Duncan's murder prays for 'those / That would make good of bad, and friends of foes' (II.iv.40) and why the Doctor attending on Lady Macbeth can 'think, but dare not speak' (V.i.77). When Macbeth, after the death of his wife, sees that 'all our yesterdays have lighted fools / The way to dusty death' (V.v.22–3), his words are not a vague generalization by which he tries to escape from an acute sense of personal loss, but a condemnation of a way of life in which men and women strive for individual advantage, maintaining their own purposes no matter how they had been 'gospelled' to behave. The conflicts of this tragedy have their roots among the great variety of men:

> . . . the swift, the slow, the subtle,
> The house-keeper, the hunter, every one
> According to the gift which bounteous nature
> Hath in him closed.   (III.i.96–9)

This wider perspective is only lightly sketched in, as if Shakespeare could not find full scope for his interest in these matters in this tragedy and needed to move on to other plays that would deal more thoroughly with political and social issues.

14

Antony and Cleopatra: a View of Greatness

Before late 1606, the probable date of *Antony and Cleopatra*, Shakespeare had relied increasingly on the hero to draw a tragedy to its conclusion: in facing adversity, these individuals reach the end of their resources so that needs and aspirations, their inner or essential selves, are more clearly revealed than before. Tragedy became an endurance test that draws upon new kinds of speech and action as other options are closed, a progressive isolation and exposure in which pretence has to be dropped. From the first, however, in *Titus Andronicus* and *Romeo and Juliet* as well as, more obviously, in the historical tragedies, Shakespeare also maintained a wider view of the narrative: the end of *Hamlet* brings a new beginning for Denmark as Fortinbras views the 'quarry' of the dead (V.ii.256–9); emissaries from Venice witness Othello's suicide; the story of *Lear* and his daughters is linked with that of Gloucester and his sons; besides close attention to Macbeth and Lady Macbeth, the kingdom of Scotland comes, occasionally, into sharp focus. In the two tragedies which followed *Macbeth*, the balance between these two interests is tipped increasingly towards the wider view. Neither *Antony and Cleopatra* nor *Coriolanus* uses extended soliloquies or duologues to draw an audience to think and feel with the central characters. Death is encountered by choice or a sudden intervention: it no longer brings a discovery of new personal resources; rather it confirms what has been apparent almost from the beginning. Speech, dialogue, stage action and interaction, and the deployment of the acting company are all significantly different from those of earlier tragedies. In exchange, a more extensive perspective, a more judicial presentation, and, almost certainly, a greater sense of waste and inevitability are achieved.

This departure from Shakespeare's previous form did not bring these two tragedies the same success as their predecessors: neither was published in quarto, neither folio text shows signs of preparation for use in performance, and no record of a performance has survived from before the Restoration. In some ways, both of them represent a return to the successful manner of *Titus Andronicus*, the first of the tragedies: again Shakespeare has chosen the freedom of a Roman setting for showing the interplay of political and personal motives, public and private lives, but the violence, sensational plotting, and preponderance of youthful characters are all gone, together with the surprising variety of rhetorical and poetic effect. The new Roman tragedies are consistently composed and masterful in management of a complex narrative; they also make new and exceptional demands on actors and audiences.

Towards a New Theatrical Idiom

Antony and Cleopatra made new casting demands. Besides the protagonists, only two major roles play a continuous part in the action and both of these are limited in function: Octavius Caesar consistently represents the political opposition that destroys Antony's army and leaves Cleopatra defenceless; Enobarbus, although he deserts Antony after his military defeat, has an otherwise consistent presence as commentator, go-between, and facilitator. In its dependence on two protagonists, the new tragedy is most like *Macbeth* but differs from all predecessors in calling for twenty-seven named characters, most of whom have no more than a few dozen lines to speak. They make individual contributions to the action on one or two occasions and then leave the play or are lost to view as the story moves forward, bringing new associations and new challenges. Lepidus, who as one of three triumvirs shares power with Caesar and Antony in the early Acts, and Charmian and Iras who attend on Cleopatra throughout, have more to contribute but achieve little on their own account. Nevertheless, many in this large supporting cast are individually characterized and reflect significantly on the protagonists. An audience can understand Antony more fully when Pompey threatens war; Menas suggests treachery; Agrippa proposes Antony should marry Caesar's sister, Octavia; Ventidius rates politics above personal advancement; Octavia is deserted; Candidus and Scarus give independent military assessments; Eros shows unquestioning devotion and courage. Cleopatra's personal qualities are revealed in dealings with Mardian, Thidias, Proculeius, Dollabella, and Seleucus. Other nameless roles are also strongly featured in brief encounters: the soothsayer, schoolmaster, clown, captain, boy, messengers, soldiers, and servants. Each of these contributes to the story, as many tributaries to its main flow in the persons of the protagonists.

Often the stage must be crowded with anonymous eunuchs, servants, soldiers, guards, and less specific 'trains' taking part in a formal meeting, celebration, elaborate banquet, or a battle that ranges over numerous scenes. A small band of soldiers carry the dying Antony and help to haul him aloft into Cleopatra's monument; others arrive in the last moments of the tragedy to represent Caesar's unassailable victory. In Shakespeare's theatre, which did not use elaborate scenic devices, these nameless attendants helped to identify the location of the action as it moves frequently from Egypt to various parts of the Roman empire and back again. They also emphasize political and social conflicts because each new group appearing on stage will wear costumes by which their allegiance to one party or the other is instantly recognizable.

The demands made on the book-keeper and tiremaster, together with their assistants and every available member and part-time employee of Shakespeare's company, were in all these respects exceptional and have a pervasive effect on an audience's view of the play in any style of production. The two protagonists are famous and exceptional persons who lead protected lives and make their own decisions, but Shakespeare has ensured that, unlike his previous tragic heroes, they are very seldom seen alone or in private. All their actions have implications for others and these colleagues, attendants, and servants are also tested by the play's action. As they show fear, ambition, courage, cunning, affection, endurance, allegiance to truth and to friends and masters, these smaller, individual personal crises will affect an audience's awareness of the protagonists by providing contrasts, a sense of scale, a measure of individuality and personal freedom of choice. They may be those parts of the tragedy with which an audience member most closely identifies, leaving Antony and Cleopatra as figures to reckon with rather than persons whose experience is shared. Together, the subsidiary characters in *Antony and Cleopatra* – that is the majority of persons on stage for much of the play – serve as a kind of chorus whose changing roles, costumes, and behaviour provide a context and a sounding board for the main drama as the heroes live and die.

The actors in early performances were also faced with what amounted to a new kind of dialogue. Most noticeable are the large number of very short phrases, sometimes providing highly compact and forceful speech, at other times seemingly unstudied or almost thoughtless. In Shakespeare's texts, incomplete verse-lines within a single continuous speech are comparatively rare and indicate exceptional pauses; here they are frequent. When one verse-line is shared between two or more speakers, the correct alignment is usually obvious; here it is often debatable and difficult to respect in performance. For example, after Antony has fallen on his own sword:

Antony.	. . . How, not dead? Not dead?
	The guard, ho! O, dispatch me!
	Enter a [Company of the] Guard.
1 Guard.	What's the noise?
Antony.	I have done my work ill, friends.
	O, make an end of what I have begun!
2 Guard.	The star is fall'n.
1 Guard.	The time is at his period.
All.	Alas, and woe!
Antony.	Let him that loves me strike me dead.
1 Guard.	Not I.
2 Guard.	Nor I.
2 Guard.	Nor anyone. *Exeunt [all the Guard but Dercetus].*

(IV.xiv.103–14)

The Guard's image of a fallen star is not sustained and only simple, short-phrased speeches accompany departures from the stage. Antony's speeches are addressed very variously, some to himself, in both comment and resolution, and some to instruct and appeal to the Guard. Only one iambic pentameter is regular and, although some of the shorter speeches could be printed to form fairly regular verse-lines, none would be entirely convincing iambic pentameters. To hold attention, the actors have to realize the situation fully in action without the usual support of sustained phrasing, a strong metrical basis, or a sequence of images that arise out of each other. So an audience will follow the dramatic action, words only briefly commanding attention and significantly taking the action forward.

Reasoned debate can be no less fragmented and verbally simple. So, after a '*Flourish*', Octavius Caesar greets Antony for a council-meeting in Rome:

> *Caesar.* Welcome to Rome.
> *Antony.* Thank you.
> *Caesar.* Sit.
> *Antony.* Sit, sir.
> *Caesar.* Nay, then.
> *Antony.* I learn you take things ill which are not so,
> Or, being, concern you not.
> *Caesar.*   I must be laughed at
> If or for nothing or a little, I
> Should say myself offended, and with you
> Chiefly i' th' world; more laughed at that I should
> Once name you derogately, when to sound your name
> It not concerned me.
> *Antony.* My being in Egypt, Caesar, what was't to you?   (II.ii.30–42)

In performance, the bare civilities at the start can be tensely or good-humouredly spoken; either way, they will be followed by other persons on stage taking their appropriate places, all silent and awaiting the start of business. Briefly, Antony supplies this, his first line being both monosyllabic and without further courtesy; the half-line that completes his statement is phrased brokenly and negatively. Caesar's reply should probably be spoken to complete the verse-line, but it will do so irregularly and is followed by a full line which is sharply phrased and has a syntactical break before its very last syllable. Broken phrases and unexpected stresses continue until he concludes with a negative statement that is a half verse-line only. Antony's reply, presumably after a half-line pause, is again irregular metrically and ordered so that it, like Caesar's, concludes with a personal pronoun. Speech throughout this meeting is sharply focused, strangely stressed and phrased, and barely polite. The actors are left to ensure that each irregularity appears necessary for the speakers and that the simple words, 'thing' and 'nothing,' and the strongly placed personal pronouns all make meaningful challenges or replies. These tasks involve technical problems of verse-speaking and phrasing, but also depend on physical, mental, and emotional underpinning if they are to seem credible in performance. Above all, the actors need to maintain a keen sense of each other's presence and opposition. No striking images are here to provoke an audience's imaginative response, no confident flow of verse or syntax to draw its attention forward. An audience observes, rather than shares, a personal engagement that is tense with unspoken thoughts and feelings but has little development of either thought or feeling.

Many of the same features are found in passages of intense engagement between the two protagonists: the same broken verse-lines, metrical irregularities, short phrases, and unusual word-order. Although images and vocabulary are often astonishing and deeply evocative, such expressions are fleetingly present and associated with other simple and mundane words or phrases. When Antony is about to return to Rome to deal with military necessities and the death of Fulvia, his wife, Cleopatra, taunts him for deceit:

Antony.	I'll leave you, lady.
Cleopatra.	Courteous lord, one word.
	Sir, you and I must part, but that's not it;
	Sir, you and I have loved, but there's not it,
	That you know well. Something it is I would –
	O, my oblivion is a very Antony,
	And I am all forgotten.
Antony.	But that your royalty

	Holds idlesness your subject, I should take you
	For idleness itself.
Cleopatra.	'Tis sweating labour

Holds idlesness your subject, I should take you
For idleness itself.
Cleopatra.   'Tis sweating labour
To bear such idleness so near the heart
As Cleopatra this. But sir, forgive me,
Since my becomings kill me when they do not
Eye well to you. Your honour calls you hence;
Therefore be deaf to my unpittied folly,
And all the gods go with you! Upon your sword
Sit laurel victory, and smooth success
Be strewed before your feet!
Antony.   Let us go. Come;
Our separation so abides and flies
That thou, residing here, goes yet with me,
And I, hence fleeting, here remain with thee.
Away!   *Exeunt.*
                    (I.iii.86–105)

Cleopatra's two amazing images, one mysterious and apocalyptic, the other intensely physical, are able to burn themselves in a hearer's consciousness and yet both are briefly expressed and arise out of the simplest phrases and in relation to a 'Something', that is neither defined nor alluded to again. Antony's concluding paradox transcends time and place, playing with action and inactivity, the transient and established, and suggesting an inevitability in what is happening that outstrips ordinary concepts of 'I' and 'Thou'. Yet this speech, like others, holds each thought and feeling for no more than a brief moment. Having called for exceptional qualities in performance the effect of which on an audience will not quickly dissipate, the words of both speakers revert to more immediate concerns which include flattery and evasive wordplay, a plea for forgiveness, a formal blessing for military success, and response to each other's presence. Antony's simple injunctions for leaving the stage suggest an instinctive haste, as if he fears that their shared experience would be threatened by hesitation or continuation. In viewing this scene, members of an audience may find themselves out of step with what is happening.

Presenting the Protagonists

Lacking the kind of thought-sharing soliloquies and sustained
encounters that produced notable changes of intention, emotion,
and action in Macbeth and Lady Macbeth, the protagonists of this
tragedy change in an instant, about-facing without arguing the cause
or considering consequences. Each of them has several conflicting
roles to play: Antony a powerful statesman, brave soldier, and lover
enthralled by Cleopatra; she a wealthy queen, independent woman,
and lover enthralled by Antony and sometimes taking possession of
him. Both slip easily from one role to another, often without preparation or warning.

Statements of purpose often sound absolute and unshakeable but,
in the event, prove incomplete and impermanent; some are intentionally misleading. Antony tells Octavia whom he has just married
in Rome that, in future, all shall 'be done by th' rule' and bids good
night to this 'dear lady', but he then meets the Soothsayer who
warns that he cannot thrive near Caesar. Antony changes at once
and speaks a short, and rare, soliloquy about political business that
ends in a bare statement that denies the pledge he has just given to
Octavia:

> I will to Egypt;
> And though I make this marriage for my peace,
> I' th' East my pleasure lies. (II.iii.4–40)

After Antony has furiously accused Cleopatra of being 'Cold-hearted
toward me', he accepts her denial in a single, everyday phrase: 'I
am satisfied' and immediately passes on to military matters
(III.xiii.162–71). Cleopatra pretends to faint because Antony is
leaving her, calling, 'Cut my lace, Charmian, come!' and, in the next
line, she countermands the order: 'But let it be; I am quickly ill, and
well, / So Antony loves' (I.iii.67). She asks for mandragora so that she
may sleep and the next moment is eagerly asking questions about
Antony, recalling their intimacies and feeding herself 'with most deli-
cious poison' (I.v.3–228). Twice she '*strikes*' the messenger who brings
news of Antony's marriage and '*hales him up and down*', threatening

to whip him with wire and stew him in brine; she draws a knife, so that he runs out in terror, and then, the very next moment, she calls him back and blames herself for what has happened:

> These hands do lack nobility, that they strike
> A meaner than myself, since I myself
> Have given myself the cause. (II.v.62–85)

When they are together, Antony and Cleopatra differ from each other instinctively, not by degrees or with reluctance. To his solemn avowal of their peerless love she replies with irony, deprecation, and play-acting:

> Excellent falsehood!
> Why did he marry Fulvia, and not love her?
> I'll seem the fool I am not. Antony
> Will be himself.

With so much that is both changeable and extraordinary, spokesmen are provided to establish long-term qualities and achievements. The play starts with two Romans commenting on Antony's military prowess and sexual dependence on Cleopatra and, when the lovers make their entrance, his political status is also remembered: 'The triple pillar of the world transformed / Into a strumpet's fool' (I.i.12–13). Later, Caesar faults Antony for being 'not more manlike' than Cleopatra and for rating 'voluptuousness' before affairs of 'state', but then, at length and in the same scene, he praises his military victories and soldierly hardiness (I.iv.1–33, 57–72). Pompey, as he prepares to wage war, rates Antony's 'soldiership' as twice that of his other oponents (II.i.35–6). The most favourable assessment follows a report of his death: 'A rarer spirit never / Did steer humanity' (V.i.31–2). Cleopatra is also thoroughly and variously appraised throughout the play: in its opening lines, she is a 'strumpet', but when soldiers talk of her in Rome she is 'a most triumphant lady' and 'royal wench'. Enobarbus, Antony's closest associate, describes in great detail her ostentatious display of wealth and beauty when the two had first met and then concludes with testimony to her superhuman qualities:

> Age cannot wither her, nor custom stale
> Her infinite variety. Other women cloy
> The appetites they feed, but she makes hungry
> Where most she satisfies. For vilest things
> Become themselves in her, that the holy priests
> Bless her when she is riggish.   (II.ii.196–250)

Superlatives are frequent. Antony is 'most worthy sir' and 'noble emperor'; Cleopatra is 'a wonderful piece of work' who can work 'magic'. Venus, Mars, Isis, and Hercules provide comparisons, as if these two lovers occupy a mythical world of absolutes. They call themselves *great*, *greatest*, and *peerless* and use many other outsized epithets. Antony's very first words claim that their love can only be 'reckoned' in a 'new heaven, new earth' (I.i.14–17). In his view:

> The nobleness of life
> Is to do thus, when such a mutual pair
> And such a twain can do't .   (I.i.38–40)

Cleopatra speaks of the time when:

> Eternity was in our lips and eyes,
> Bliss in our brows' bent; none our parts so poor
> But was a race of heaven. They are so still
> Or thou, the greatest soldier of the world,
> Art turned the greatest liar.   (I.iii.35–9)

Such encomiums create huge problems for the actors who have to substantiate them in performance, both in words and in physical presence and action. But here the 'infinite variety' of their appearances is a positive advantage: actors are able to mark contrasts boldly so that, for much of the play, they dazzle and amaze, rather than draw attention to half-hidden thoughts and feelings or slowly accumulate subtlety and power in the manner of Shakespeare's earlier tragic heroes. An audience is likely to observe, shocked or delighted by what happens, trying to keep abreast of the changes.

Only the onset of disaster and, eventually, of death, brings any notable modification to this form of presentation. When Antony

and Cleopatra are defeated in battle at sea because he has followed
her flagship when she had fled from danger, he sends all his soldiers
away and, according to Shakespeare's stage-direction in the Folio
text, '*sits down*', saying nothing. Shakespeare may have intended him
to be alone on stage for some time because in Plutarch's *Lives of the
Greeks and Romans*, the source for this play, he had read how
Antony:

> went and sat down alone in the prow of his ship, and said never a
> word, clapping his head between both his hands, . . . and so lived
> three days alone, without speaking to any man.

In the play, Cleopatra enters at some distance, accompanied by
Charmian, Iras, and Eros, and she, too, is silent at first. When
Antony does speak, he has heard nothing and makes no attempt to
communicate or acknowledge her presence.

Eros.	Nay, gentle madam, to him, comfort him.
Iras.	Do, most dear queen.
Charmian.	Do. Why, what else?
Cleopatra.	Let me sit down. O Juno!
Antony.	No, no, no, no, no.
Eros.	See you here, sir?
Antony.	O fie, fie fie!
Charmian.	Madam!
Iras.	Madam, O good empress!
Eros.	Sir, sir!
Antony.	Yes, my lord, yes. He at Philippi kept
	His sword e'en like a dancer, while I struck
	The lean and wrinkled Cassius, . . . (III.xi.25–37)

To follow Antony and Cleopatra here, an audience has little guidance but its own sympathies and imaginations. Cleopatra has to ask
attendants to 'sustain' her before she can approach Antony with her
head down, looking as if 'death will seize her' but still saying
nothing. At last he makes contact, first with a wordless cry and then
an accusing question: 'O, whither hast thou led me, Egypt?' and, in
return, she begs 'Forgive my fearful sails! I little thought / You would

have followed.' To Antony's 'Egypt, thou know'st too well / My heart
was to thy rudder tied by th' strings . . .', she cries, as if wounded,
'O, my pardon!' When Antony speaks of the consquences of defeat,
her cry is still more simple: 'Pardon, pardon!' By now, she is weeping
and Antony changes, completely:

> Fall not a tear, I say; one of them rates
> All that is won and lost. Give me a kiss.
>   [*They kiss*]
> Even this repays me. – We sent our schoolmaster,
> Is a come back? – Love, I am full of lead. –
> Some wine within there, and our viands! Fortune knows
> We scorn her most when most she offers blows.   *Exeunt.*
>
>   (ll. 68–73)

The kiss will bring a further silence that can establish a more mutual
awareness than before. The actors will have to judge how long to
hold this silence, adjusting to each other's performance and so establishing, however lightly and temporarily, a hard-won trust and
dependence on each other or an acknowledgement of some ultimate
necessity or 'Fortune'.

Cleopatra is yet again silent as they leave together so that whoever
acts this role will be able to control the effect of this exit and the reconciliation it represents. Does she stay close to Antony or move at a
distance from him, in sympathy with his rhythm or in her own very
distinct tempo and manner? Does she still feel a need for 'pardon' or
is she intent on lightening Antony's leaden burden? Are tears still in
her eyes or is she, once more, reassured in his presence? Is she
subdued by his suffering, dominant over him, or deeply uneasy
about him or herself? Her wordless physical performance as she
leaves the stage may now hold more attention than his words. In the
manner of earlier tragedies, Shakespeare has left actors and audience
to supply what words do not, but here, by means of a sequence of
silences and a very few, simple words, he has drawn attention to the
presence of feelings that have been so private and unexpressed that a
sense of mystery is maintained.

Deaths and Affirmations

The reconciliation of the protagonists after defeat at Actium establishes a new depth and subtlety of presentation that prepares actors
and audiences for the conclusion of the tragedy. The deaths to come
will not be brought about by violence or physical suffering but are
self-willed, the means of assuaging personal loss and satisfying individual feeling and imagination.

In the midst of short scenes full of orders and action, an audience
is further prepared for the first deaths by a short scene in which one
guard, relieving another at night, hears '*Music of the hautboys under
the stage*' (Folio stage-direction; IV.iii.12). In Plutarch's *Lives of the
Greeks and Romans*, music is heard as if in the streets and through
the gates of the city as a great crowd dances in honour of the god
Bacchus; this is said to imply that Antony's favourite god was for-
saking him. In the play, the music is played on woodwinds and
heard more mysteriously as if from beneath ground; it is taken as a
sign that 'the god Hercules, whom Antony loved, / Now leaves him'
(ll. 21–2). The ebbing of his military power is further suggested
when Enobarbus, a 'soldier only' who has deserted Antony
(II.ii.114), is the first to die on stage.

Enobarbus receives only passing reference in Plutarch's *Lives* but
Shakespeare greatly expanded his role so that he is present in both
Roman and Egyptian scenes and voices truths that the protagonists
are unable or unwilling to recognize. Speaking aside, and often provoking laughter, the actor will have developed a rapport with an
audience that is unique in this play and now he is given a series of
short soliloquies in which he at first decides to stay with Antony and
then to leave him. Recognizing that events draw a person's 'inward
quality after them', he concludes that he 'will joy no more'
(III.xiii.32–4; IV.vi.17–19) and, when Antony sends all his possessions after him to Caesar's camp, he goes to find a foul ditch in
which to die. By moonlight, another group of sentries find him
alone and overhear him repent, pray for death, and ask for Antony's
forgiveness. This last soliloquy for Enobarbus is formal and not an
intimate and deeply felt preparation for death, such as Gloucester's
soliloquy before attempting suicide in *King Lear*. An audience is

likely to feel closest to him when, having branded himself 'a master-leaver and a fugitive', he loses control of sustained speech and utters the simple cry, 'O Antony! Antony!' (IV.ix.7–23). This moment of regret, pain, or affection – whatever feeling the actor has given to the cry – is so quiet and unstressed that the sentries think that he has fallen asleep or fainted; even as they carry his body off-stage, one of them believes 'He may yet recover.' An audience has been attuned to witness, if not to share, a private and mysterious suffering.

Antony's death is quite different, being approached through a series of encounters which he confidently dominates: both he and Cleopatra have attempted to negotiate with Caesar; battle is renewed; and, once again, contrasting views of the action are given, none of them long-lasting. In what is, perhaps, their most relaxed and intimate scene, Cleopatra helps Eros to arm Antony. When they are joined by captains and soldiers, Antony declares that the morning is like the 'spirit of a youth / That means to be of note' and he leaves after giving 'a soldier's kiss' to his 'dame' (IV.iv.26–34). Cleopatra has fallen silent but, now that he has gone, she asks to be led away and, in lines of varied and broken rhythm, recognizes that the man who 'goes forth gallantly' cannot 'determine this great war in single fight' (ll. 35–8). After brief scenes, cross-cut with trumpets and sounds of battle, Antony returns surrounded by his soldiers and proclaiming victory. He greets Cleopatra with words in which soldier and lover seem, at last, to be entirely at one:

> O thou day o' th' world,
> Chain mine armed neck; leap thou, attire and all,
> Through proof of harness to my heart, and there
> Ride on the pants triumphing!   (IV.viii.13–16)

The imagery, that is sustained now, carries physical and sexual implications that are both triumphant and absurd. She hails him as an absolute of manhood and virtue (here likely to mean valour rather than moral goodness) but she is also alert to the danger of another and wider reality:

> Lord of lords,
> O infinite virtue, com'st thou smiling from
> The world's great snare uncaught?   (ll. 16–18)

The actors probably interact more closely here than ever before. Antony takes this cue to call her 'My nightingale' and boast that he has beaten his enemies to their beds. Then, calling her 'girl', he acknowledges, as he rarely has, his greater age and confidently commands 'brazen' trumpets and 'rattling' tambourines to sound together in celebration. Cleopatra's renewed silence here is not likely to make a great impression over against his sustained vaunting and the music that has been set to 'blast . . . the city's ear', but this is one element of the drama that has now been repeated from scene to scene and, like her contrasting comments, will tend to distance an audience from Antony's out-going euphoria.

The quiet death of Enobarbus follows and then sounds of another battle, '*as at a seafight*' (IV.xii.3, Folio S.D.). After several short scenes, a transformed Antony returns to the stage:

> All's lost!
> This foul Egyptian hath betrayed me. . . .   (IV.xii.10–11)

After ordering his soldiers to fly, Antony's only sustained soliloquy follows in which he gives himself over to denouncing the 'triple-turned whore . . . grave charm . . . right gipsy', the queen who has betrayed and beguiled him 'to the very heart of loss'. He no longer changes between one reaction and another and his words are powerful and vehement. When Cleopatra enters, he dismisses her with 'Ah, thou spell! Avaunt!' (l. 30) and does not listen to her greeting and enquiry. She speaks only a single line before he tells her to follow Caesar's chariot and be hoisted up to the shouting plebeians. She leaves at once, silent again, and Antony continues in soliloquy, asking Hercules, his ancestor, to teach him 'rage' as he plans suicide and vows that 'The witch shall die' (l. 47). When he leaves the stage to find Eros, Cleopatra enters with her women saying that he is mad and agreeing with Charmian to lock herself in the royal monument. She sends Mardian, her eunuch, to Antony with news that she has slain herself and yet implies that she will do no such thing by telling him to 'word' his message piteously and return to tell 'how he takes my death' (IV.xiv). Once more, she is dissembling to Antony and an audience will wait for his return knowing more of the true state of affairs than he.

Antony returns with Eros and speaks of strange sights in the air and of himself as equally insubstantial. Saying that Cleopatra has 'packed cards with Caesar and false-played my glory / Unto an enemy's triumph', he is ready to end his life. Eros is now weeping openly so that it is Antony who sees Mardian enter and immediately vows that Cleopatra 'shall die the death' (IV.xiv.16). On being told that Cleopatra is dead, Antony is at first stunned and then changes instantly, submitting to his fate:

> *Antony.*   Dead, then?
> *Mardian.*   Dead.
> *Antony.*   Unarm, Eros. The long day's task is done,
>   And we must sleep.   (ll. 14–16)

These few words express the consequence of hearing news of Cleopatra's death but none expresses how it is received until Eros unarms him and Antony starts a slow-paced threnody for life, valour, and love that maintains a single course although varied with acknowledgement of heart-felt pain, torture, and darkness. Sending Eros away, he resolves to take his own life and so overtake Cleopatra and 'weep for my pardon'. Words and images are now charged by physical and emotional suffering but the rhythms of speech and flow of consciousness are repeatedly disturbed as Antony issues orders and calls out to Cleopatra. Only when he imagines a reunion after death is any one thought sustained for as much as a line and a half:

> Where souls do couch on flowers, we'll hand in hand,
> And with our sprightly port make the ghosts gaze:
> Dido and her Aeneas shall want troops,
> And all the haunt be ours.   (ll. 51–4)

After the short phrases of this soliloquy, Antony anchors his thoughts in a vision of celebratory pride and intimacy with Cleopatra. This is the moment, near death, when an audience may feel closest to Antony and, at last, share the pride and sensual fantasy that have inwardly sustained him thoughout much of the play's action.

Eros is recalled and asked to kill his master who had freed him and so keep the promise to do so if 'disgrace and horror' threatened. When he refuses, Antony tells him that all his previous services would be worthless if he does not do as he is commanded and save his master from the shame of being tied to the wheels of Caesar's chariot. After exchanging farewells, Eros kills himself behind his master's back and so Antony must fall on his own sword. When he does not die at once, much happens very quickly: he calls the guard so that they can dispatch him; they also refuse and leave while one of them takes his sword to Caesar. Then a messenger brings news that Cleopatra is alive and, still more abruptly than when he had heard of her death, Antony accepts almost in silence. He calls his guard and asks to be carried to her monument; as he tells the bearers not to weep it is clear that he now hides his true feelings with a Roman soldier's discipline:

> Bid that welcome
> Which comes to punish us, and we punish it,
> Seeming to bear it lightly. Take me up.   (ll. 141–3)

Arriving at Cleopatra's mausoleum and treasure-house, Antony asks to kiss her lips and, since she will not leave her place of refuge, he is drawn up to its only access above the level of the main stage. As this is done, a repetitive rhythm begins to exert an influence on the scene: it had started earlier, with 'O, Antony, / Antony, Antony! Help, Charmian, help, Iras, help! / Help friends below' and 'I am dying, Egypt, dying', but now it is accentuated by the physical efforts of the women as they haul him up – 'O, come, come, come! / And welcome, welcome!' – and by Antony's repetition of 'I am dying, Egypt, dying' (IV.xv.12–43). She kisses him repeatedly and, interrupting him, rails against the 'false huswife Fortune' and will not accept his advice on how to seek honour and safety at Caesar's hands. He insists that she should not to lament the 'miserable change' of his end but, rather, please her thoughts:

> In feeding them with those my former fortunes,
> Wherein I lived the greatest prince o' th' world,
> The noblest.   (IV.xv.54–7)

So, as he begins to lose consciousness, he reasserts his former self. He is caught within his own idea of himself as the 'greatest' and the 'noblest' so that, except for pride at committing suicide, he has nothing new to say about himself or his feelings for the woman who has caused him to risk everything. Such a death for a defeated and helpless hero would be brief and unremarkable if Cleopatra were not, in consequence, transformed in speech and bearing. As soon as he was brought dying to the monument, she had called out:

> O sun,
> Burn the great sphere thou mov'st in; darkling stand
> The varying shore o' th' world –

Now she praises his life in words that outreach his own in superlatives while responding to the 'miserable change' and her own loss:

> The crown o' th' earth doth melt. My lord!
> O, withered is the garland of the war;
> The soldier's pole is fall'n! Young boys and girls
> Are level now with men; the odds is gone,
> And there is nothing left remarkable
> Beneath the visiting moon.   (ll. 65–70)

Through her praise of Antony, the focus of attention shifts to Cleopatra. She is physically so altered by emotion that her women think she must be dead too. When they rouse her, she dramatizes her new role:

> No more but e'en a woman, and commanded
> By such poor passion as the maid that milks
> And does the meanest chares.   (ll. 78–80)

She tells her women to 'take heart' and imitate Antony by dying in the 'high Roman fashion' and 'make death proud to take us'. They must act alone:

Ah, women, women! Come, we have no friend
But resolution and the briefest end.   (ll. 95–6)

Cleopatra's response to emissaries from Caesar and to the emperor himself is managed with alert and varying cunning. Sending submissive messages to Caesar, bowing low as Caesar approaches, making false account of her possessions: these tactics are intended to give the impression that she means to live and so lessen the vigilance of the guards Caesar has placed on her. But the ruse does not work and when the guards seize her, she draws a knife to kill herself; disarmed, she then threatens to kill herself by refusing food, drink, and sleep. The constant element in this last scene is Cleopatra's unfaltering authority that stems from a conviction of greatness that is most fully realized in her image of an all-powerful Antony. When Dolabella, one of Caesar's messengers, greets her royally – 'Most noble empress' – she describes to him the hero of her 'dream'. Now unquenchable words stream forth as if unstudied, and yet they are so confidently ordered that a hearer might equally well assume she has been in continual practice:

I dreamt there was an emperor Antony.
O, such another sleep, that I might see
But such another man!
                    If it might please ye –
His face was as the heav'ns, and therein stuck
A sun and moon, which kept their course and lighted
The little O, the earth.
                    Most sovereign creature –
His legs bestrid the ocean; his reared arm
Crested the world; his voice was propertied
As all the tunèd spheres, and that to friends;
But when he meant to quail and shake the orb,
He was as rattling thunder. For his bounty,
There was no winter in't; an autumn 'twas
That grew the more by reaping. His delights
Were dolphin-like; they showed his back above
The element they lived in. In his livery
Walked crowns and crownets; realms and islands were
As plates dropped from his pocket.

> *Cleopatra* –
> Think you there was or might be such a man
> As this I dreamt of?   (V.ii.75–93)

The speech has to be read in full to appreciate how it stands out among the shifting, brilliant, taunting staple of the play's dialogue, and also from its other powerful passages. Acted with the necessary technical control and a responsive imagination, it stands as an unshakeable monument to her thoughts and feelings, for all its fanciful impracticality and hyperbole, it is lucid and confident, commanding attention in every detail. Yet this 'dream' is no surprise: it draws together earlier superlatives and glowing images, that have been fleeting and fragmentary, and brings them to a timeless summation. Drawing on her imagination and feelings for Antony, Cleopatra's words create an impresssion of the 'new heaven, new world' that he had, far more simply, claimed as theirs in the very first scene (I.i.14–17).

Counting on Dollabella's evident admiration, Cleopatra asks 'what Caesar means to do with me' and learns that he will lead her in public triumph. Later, after Caesar has visited the monument and talked of friendship and dealing with her according to her own counsel, Dollabella returns alone with a second message: his 'love', he says, 'makes religion to obey' as he gives the secret information that Caesar will within three days send her with her children before him while he journeys back towards Rome. The prospect of public humiliation prompts Cleopatra to activate her plans for suicide immediately. She calls for her best attires, her 'crown and all' (ll. 126–31), and when 'a rural fellow' calls with poison-biting asps concealed in a gift of figs, she is ready to greet him:

> He brings me liberty.
> My resolution's placed, and I have nothing
> Of woman in me. Now from head to foot
> I am marble-constant; now the fleeting moon
> No planet is of mine.   (ll. 236–40)

Before this promised transformation, Cleopatra talks with her visitor whose talk of the 'worm' he has brought is part of a sequence of sexual innuendos about 'a very honest woman, but something given to lie', in which 'dying' alludes to sexual orgasm and the feeling of 'pain' to its extreme pleasure. Further wordplay raises issues of belief, salvation, 'kind' (that is one's nature), goodness, worth, joy, wisdom, the devil, gods, and human fallibility. When he has gone, having offered this vista of every person's life, Cleopatra is ready to create a 'marble-constant' monument to her own life and Antony's:

> Give me my robe. Put on my crown. I have
> Immortal longings in me. . . .   (ll. 274ff.)

And yet, in killing herself, uncertainty and variety of impulse will still remain. Her phrasing is short as imperatives are followed by questions, more imperatives, and more exclamations. In turn, she addresses her women, herself, Antony – now, for the first time, her 'husband' – and the asps. Enthroned at centre-stage, she will also seem to speak to a far wider audience: the spectators in the theatre, for sure, and also the rest of the world that, perhaps a long time later, will hear of Caesar's deeds as well as her own.

Having claimed 'I am fire and air; my other elements / I give to baser life' (ll. 283–4), she makes sure that she is fully attired – 'So, have you done?' – and calls her women to kiss her lips. When Iras falls and dies, a pang of self-taunting jealousy makes her think of Antony's kiss that after death would be her 'heaven to have' and so she bares her breast for the 'poor venomous fool' to be 'angry and dispatch'. She imagines the serpent calling 'great Caesar ass / Unpolicied' but a moment later, as it continues to poison her, she sees it as 'my baby at my breast, / That sucks the nurse asleep.' Plutarch's account tells how Cleopatra was bitten on the arm by the asp but Shakespeare has Dollabella find the 'vent of blood' on her breast. She has said there would be 'nothing of woman' in her death but, as she prepares to die, she imagines a hungry infant feeding on her milk. She speaks now of what is 'sweet', ' soft', and 'gentle', until that line of thought breaks down and, as if from deeper within her being, she calls out 'O Antony!' She then takes another asp, impatient to finish life, and dies as she is starting another sentence. At some time a sudden movement has caused her crown to fall 'awry', so that Charmian will 'mend it' before she also takes an asp to kill herself. Queen, 'fire and air', and a woman commanded by her 'passion': Cleopatra in her death affirms these 'inward qualities' that events seem now to draw from her and have, occasionally and fit-fully, been present throughout the action (III.xiii.32–4). Seeing her, sitting dead in her robes and crown, Caesar imagines that she is still alive:

> she looks like sleep,
> As she would catch another Antony
> In her strong toil of grace.   (V.ii.340–2)

Caesar and Rome

None of Shakespeare's other tragedies finishes with the focus so con-tinuously and firmly fixed on the death of a single person and none other has an opposing figure of such proved authority enter the last scene to conclude its action. Caesar has opposed Antony's obsession with Cleopatra throughout the action and now, having beaten him in battle, he confronts her as well. By this time, he is ready to lament Antony's death 'With tears as sovereign as the blood of hearts' and offers friendship to Cleopatra, but he still believes that, 'perforce', he had to oppose them and so lance a 'disease' within the body of the state (V.i.36–41). He now does everything possible to trap Cleopatra into ignominious capitivity, calculating that 'her life in Rome / Would be eternal in our triumph' (ll. 65–6). When Cleopatra has out-tricked him and committed suicide, he orders his army to make the funeral of the two lovers a 'solemn show' that will mark both pity for them and his own 'glory which / Brought them to be lamented' (V.ii.354–60). In *Romeo and Juliet*, the suicide of the two lovers had brought a 'glooming peace' to Verona; here the funeral will be manipulated to honour the power of Caesar.

Caesar's presence throughout the action speaks for the world that Antony and Cleopatra reject in favour of their love. This opposition of two 'worlds' has repercussions that extend outside the action of the play since, ironically, Caesar's Roman world carries within itself the origins of another 'new world', more widespread and powerful than any the lovers could imagine, let alone achieve. His world will become the great empire founded when he takes the name of Augustus as its first sole emperor. As his army closes in on Antony, he looks ahead to what will be called the *Pax Romanum*:

> The time of universal peace is near.
> Prove this a prosp'rous day, the three-nooked world
> Shall bear the olive freely.   (IV.vi.5–7)

This prophecy is soon forgotten in the alarms, drums, and trumpets of battle and its changing fortunes, but it may have alerted some in early audiences to Rome's great future and, possibly, to the time, some thirty years later, when a new Christian world would also begin with the birth of Christ.

In the tragedy, the territories Rome has conquered are still divided but Caesar's decisiveness and control are everywhere apparent. Welcoming his sister, Octavia, back to Rome he assumes a god-given right to intervene:

>   the high gods,
> To do you justice, makes his ministers
> Of us and those that love you.   (III.vi.90–2)

This small sample is representative of his use of words: large issues efficiently stated, subsidiary phrases neatly and firmly marshalled, meaning defined by personal pronouns. He is unprincipled and ruthless in pursuing his own ends. He gives his sister in marriage to Antony for his own political advantage and deposes Lepidus as a triumvir, arbitrarily taking his revenues for himself: as Pompey says, Caesar 'gets money where / He loses hearts' (II.i.13–14). He does not hesitate to oppose Antony with the largest force he can muster, and places in the foremost ranks those soldiers who have deserted Antony to join him.

The alternative world that Antony and Cleopatra wish to inaugurate in their relationship is presented neither ideally nor peacefully. Caesar faults Antony for stooping 'to tumble on the bed of Ptolemy

[and] give a kingdom for a mirth' (I.iv.16–33). Other Romans say much the same: after his defeat at Actium, Scarus. a Roman fighting on Antony's behalf, rates him as a 'noble ruin', a 'doting mallard' who violates 'experience, manhood, honour' (III.x.18–23). Mostly it is the lovers themselves who praise their new world in glowing, lyrical, and, sometimes, plain and physical terms. Yet, in another sense they do not speak alone, for their words echo those that Shakespeare's lovers have used before, in the comedies, sonnets and poems, and *Romeo and Juliet*; for example, behind Antony's belief that there's 'beggary in the love that can be reckoned' and Cleopatra's claim that his autumn 'grew the more by reaping' lies Juliet's earlier:

> My bounty is as boundless as the sea,
> My love as deep: the more I give to thee,
> The more I have, for both are infinite.   (II.ii.133–5)

Love in this tragedy has been given yet further dimensions by Antony's reference to Dido and Aeneas brought together again in an after-life, Cleopatra's association with the Goddess Isis marked by wearing her habiliments (III.vi.16–19), and allusions to Venus that conclude with Charmian's choric 'O eastern star!' as the asp sucks at her mistress's breast. More vaguely and mysteriously, some ideas and phrases echo *The Book of Revelations*, the last book of the New Testament, in which St John declares, quoting the prophet Isaiah, 'I saw a new heaven and a new earth: for the first heaven, and the first earth were passed away . . . '. He also saw a 'mighty angel' bestriding the sea, lifting his hand to heaven, and speaking in a voice of thunder; his face, like Antony's, 'was as the sun'.

The large cast demanded by this tragedy and the sweep of its narrative present these oppositions in a wide context within which no one person is able to deflect the course of events. Charmian and Iras wish to do so but can only die with their mistress. Enobarbus tries to change allegiance but that leads towards a lonely and despairing death. The conflict between Rome and the world that the lovers inhabit in their imaginations and imperfectly realize in their lives seems unresolvable, the faults and virtues on both sides being presented as permanent and indelible. After Cleopatra has chosen and achieved her own death, an audience may well find that its sense of loss is not adequately represented on stage but only within themselves who have witnessed the story of two sets of people each confident in their own concept of greatness. Other persons who have been caught up in the action and have survived are either unable to respond to such an experience or can only, momentarily, catch a sight of it. This tragedy is remarkable for the number of persons who, at best, can do little more than stand by and watch.

15

Coriolanus: Power and Uncertainty

'The nobleness of life is to do thus', says Antony of the 'peerless' love
he shares with Cleopatra (I.i.36–40), and their tragedy concludes
with Caesar declaring that 'No grave upon the earth shall clip in it /
A pair so famous' (V.ii.356–7). As if in counterbalance, *Coriolanus*,
Shakespeare's next tragedy, written some two or three years later in
1608 or early 1609, is about a peerless soldier, a hero who repeatedly
stands alone, even as he fights in battle or asks for the people's votes.
He leaves Rome alone, banished by the state and, in reply, banishes
it from himself. In enemy territory, he vows to

>   . . . stand
> As if a man were author of himself
> And knew no other kin.   (V.iii.35–7)

At the end of the tragedy, praise for Coriolanus matches that for the
pair of lovers at the end of its predecessor:

> The man is noble, and his fame folds in
> The orb o' th' earth.   (V.vi.126–7)

In means of presentation, the two tragedies also have much in
common. Both use soliloquies very sparingly, relying on sharply
defined, nervously alive dialogue to show the effect of personal reactions rather than the processes whereby conviction has come about;

both make occasional use of a plain, short-phrased, almost ordinary way of speaking. *Coriolanus* does not have so many named and individualized characters as *Antony and Cleopatra* but, in their place, eight are in contact with the hero throughout the action, helping to define his intentions and the effect of his actions, and anonymous persons, in considerable numbers and variety – citizens, soldiers, patricians, conspirators, lords, and officers – speak for themselves and still further highlight the unique qualities of Coriolanus. These two tragedies, when viewed side-by-side, may be seen as twins, each presenting a grand example of a widely admired concept of human excellence.

Peerless Valour

As with Antony and Cleopatra, the virtues and faults of Coriolanus are described repeatedly during the course of the play. Citizens say that he has 'done famously' but is 'proud . . . to the altitude of his virtue' (I.i.36–7); officers laying cushions in the capitol agree that he is 'a brave fellow, but he's vengeance proud and loves not the common people' (II.ii.5–6). Menenius, his old and intimate friend, implies that these two attributes necessarily go together;

> His nature is too noble for the world.
> He would not flatter Neptune for his trident
> Or Jove for 's his power to thunder. (III.i.257–9)

Sicinius and Brutus, Tribunes of the People and professed enemies of Coriolanus, elaborate on his faults:

> A worthy officer i' th' war, but insolent,
> O'ercome with pride, ambitious past all thinking,
> Self-loving –
> > And affecting one sole throne
> Without assistance. (IV.vi.32–5)

These moral judgements echo so consistently throughout the play that an audience might well lose interest or wait for an eventual

denial that never comes. What holds attention is the daring and
success of Coriolanus in battle and a sequence of interactions with
others, including members of his own family, that raise a number of
issues about good government and personal aspiration that were
urgent in Shakespeare's day and are finding new forms today.

Coriolanus' aptitude for fighting is demonstrated spectacularly in
a sequence of eight scenes that conclude the first Act of the tragedy.
After talk about his valour and pride earlier in the play, an audience
now witnesses the intrepid deeds that earn him the surname
Coriolanus. When Roman soldiers will not follow him into the
Volscian town of Corioles and he is trapped alone within its gates,
he re-emerges, a little later, wounded but still fighting. Back in
Rome, Cominius will report how:

> From face to foot
> He was a thing of blood, whose every motion
> Was timed with dying cries.   (II.ii.106–8)

The soldiers who, in his view, had shown the 'souls of geese',
respond now to his example, join the fighting, and start to sack the
city. Refusing to rest, Coriolanus leaves immediately to find
Aufidius, his opponent in earlier battles, who has repulsed other
Roman soldiers under the command of Cominius. He arrives so
covered with blood that he looks as if he has been 'flayed' alive; at
first, he is unrecognizable. Declaring himself to be 'in heart / As
merry as when our nuptial day was done, / And tapers burnt to
bedward', he embraces Cominius and is greeted as the 'Flower of
warriors'; he is riding on a high of achievement and expectation. He
calls for volunteers to join him in attacking Aufidius but takes only
those who can thoroughly identify with him:

> If any such be here –
> As it were sin to doubt – that love this painting
> Wherein you see me smeared; if any fear
> Lesser his person than an ill report;
> If any think brave death outweighs bad life,
> And that his country's dearer than himself,
> Let him alone – or so many so minded –

Wave thus to express his disposition,
And follow Martius. (I.vii.68–75)

As he waves his own sword, the previously defeated soldiers acclaim
him with instinctive enthusiasm:

They all shout and wave their swords, take him up in their arms and cast
up their caps. (Folio S. D.)

He responds with pride and valour but his cry is ambiguous: 'O, me
alone! Make you a sword of me?' So the Oxford editor punctuates
the line; the Folio text, probably printed from a manuscript close to
one of Shakespeare's own, has simpler punctuation that does not
mark a question: 'Oh me alone, make you a sword of me: . . . '. As
he is carried aloft, his words could signal either agreement and affir-
mation, or a command, or a rebuke: what he is thinking, as often in
this tragedy, is not revealed. Single combat with Aufidius finishes
inconclusively when other Volces come to his aid, but the battle is
soon over: all the Volscians are '*driven in breathless*' and a '*retreat is*
sounded' (I.ix.13 and I.x.0, S.Ds.).

No matter how carefully rehearsed, the danger of a prolonged and
impassioned sword fight will encourage an audience to pay close
attention as the actors improvise in response to many small accidents. In Shakespeare's tragedies, combat is usually reserved for the
final Act, by which time an audience will know what is at stake and
be able, in imagination, to enter into the thoughts and feelings of
the protagonist; so, for Hamlet and Macbeth, a fight reveals their
ultimate resources and tests their 'resolution'. In contrast, the
thrilling encounters come so early for Coriolanus that an audience is
likely to feel remote from him, unable to enter into a mind so ruth-
lessly engaged in slaughter. Why does he have such appetite for risk
and valour? Talk of his pride, ambition, and insolence cannot
explain everything, not least because he is now called 'modest' when
he tries to stop the 'acclamations hyperbolical' lavished upon him
and refuses a special allotment of booty (I.x.11–58). In Plutarch's
Lives of the Noble Grecians and Romans, Shakespeare's chief source for
this as for other earlier plays, Coriolanus ensures that a former friend

and host in Corioles is saved from being sold into slavery: in the tragedy, this incident becomes a last-minute request that proves to be ineffectual because he has forgotten the man's name (I.x.79–92). What redounds to Coriolanus' credit in Plutarch has been used so that it further unsettles an audience's reactions to a man who gives himself totally to fighting and danger.

Politics, Popularity, and Power

Back in Rome, Coriolanus is welcomed as a hero:

> Stalls, bulks, windows
> Are smothered up, leads filled and ridges horsed
> With variable complexions, all agreeing
> In earnestness to see him. . . .
> Such a pother
> As if that whatsoever god who leads him
> Were slily crept into his human powers
> And gave him graceful posture.
>
> (II.i.201–17)

Proposed for consul by fellow patricians, Coriolanus now becomes involved in political processes that Jacobean audiences could recognize as close to those of their own times and many other viewers will have encountered in analogous forms.

When the Tribunes of the People, Brutus and Sicinius, manipulate the opinion of citizen voters against Coriolanus, he denounces these elected officers as demagogues, who 'prank' themselves 'in authority / Against all noble sufferance' (III.i.24–5). For him, the plebeians are a 'mutuable, rank-scented' crowd that threatens 'rebellion, insolence, sedition' (III.i.69–77). He blames the 'good but most unwise patricians' for granting this mob the right to 'choose their magistrate':

> My soul aches
> To know, when two authorities are up,
> Neither supreme, how soon confusion
> May enter 'twixt the gap of both, and take
> The one by th' other
>
> (III.i.93–114)

He questions why corn had been given in a time of scarcity to citizens who were not ready to fight in defence of Rome:

> Being pressed to th' war,
> Even when the navel of the state was touched,
> They would not thread the gates. This kind of service
> Did not deserve corn gratis. (III.i.124–7)

For voicing these autocratic sentiments and questioning established political rights, the Tribunes denounce Coriolanus as 'a traitorous innovator' (l. 176) – in usage of the time, an instigator of rebellion. At this point '*a rabble of Plebeians*' join the senators on stage to shout or chant one-word slogans and '*bustle about Coriolanus*' (l. 185, S.D.). As 'confusion' grows, the Tribunes intervene and pronounce Coriolanus worthy of death by being thrown from the Tarpeian rock outside the city and, in reply, he '*draws his sword*' and defies them all:

> No I'll die here.
> There's some among you have beheld me fighting.
> Come, try upon yourselves what you have seen me. (III.i.223–5)

For the time being, the plebeians yield ground and Coriolanus escapes. Menenius remains to face the '*rabble*' and warn that civil war is imminent; he persuades the Tribunes to 'proceed by process' and promises that Coriolanus will answer their charges 'by a lawful form' of trial.

Canvassing, casting votes, political argument, public address, private consultation, denunciation, a yelling crowd, and, finally, civil violence have become the substance of the action and threaten the 'hurlyburly innovation' that was more often the concern of Shakespeare's history plays. Political conflict plays its part in *Julius Caesar* and *Hamlet*, but in neither does public responsibility or poverty become an issue; in *King Lear*, both authority and justice are repeatedly in question, but only the king remembers 'poor naked wretches' who are represented on stage only in Edgar's pretended madness. In contrast, Coriolanus is himself confronted by 'fickle

changelings . . . starving for a time / Of pellmell havoc and confusion' (*I, Henry IV*, V.i.72–82) and personally advocates political
change. Moreover, the plebeians in this tragedy can be seen as representing the turbulent dissidents of Jacobean England. Present-day
scholars have identified echoes of the riots of 1607–8 that troubled
the peace of rural areas of England, including some villages around
Stratford-upon-Avon, by means of which the poor protested against
enclosure of common land and scarcity of corn. The Tribunes,
basing their authority on precedent, echo the disputes about traditional rights which occupied James I and Parliament in the early
years of the century. Throughout England, voting rights and election
procedures for membership of official bodies were being challenged.
A dispute about the 1601 election of a Warwickshire member of
parliament and another, in 1607, about voting rights in the election
of churchwardens for St Saviours, the parish church for London's
Bankside, could have brought both issues to Shakespeare's particular
attention. A new society and a new culture were emerging and the
dependent relationships of nobles, landowners, financiers, merchants, members of professions, skilled and unskilled workers,
family members, and the needy poor were changing year by year.
Ancient authority was being challenged and new wealth increasing
in power. All these social and political uncertainties so influenced
the writing of *Coriolanus* that over subsequent centuries this tragedy
has been staged on many different occasions in support of current
issues on both the right and left of politics.

The popular appeal of a military hero and his opposition to political careerists provided other reflections of English politics at the
time. Some among Shakespeare's London audiences would have
remembered the attempted military coup led by the Earl of Essex at
the end of Elizabeth's reign for which he stood trial and was subsequently executed. Failing to rouse the citizens to his cause, this military hero had taken refuge in Essex House together with a few
remaining supporters. Shakespeare's young patron, the Earl of
Southampton, was among these and it was he who climbed onto the
roof to announce that no harm was intended to the Queen and that
he and his fellows would all rather die like men, with swords in their
hands, than end their lives on the scaffold. Essex then joined him to

say he intended good service to God and his country by seeking to root out the 'aetheists and caterpillars' who had procured undue influence in government (Akrigg, pp. 116–19). Coriolanus drawing his sword can be seen as representative of political activitists of Shakespeare's time and all those of other times who have promoted their cause by a show of force, confronted hostile crowds, or seen only their own side in a confrontation.

While political issues are clearly and repeatedly established, their personal implications for Coriolanus are presented in a more uncertain and, indeed, puzzling way. Either pride or modesty, or political principle, could make him unwilling to wear the 'gown of humility' (III.iii.38) and show his wounds to citizens when he asks for their vote as consul. When, on Menenius' persuasion, he does agree to conform to these precedents, knowing that he will 'blush in acting' what is required (II.ii.144), his motives for doing so are not revealed. An audience is not drawn to share in his thinking as he changes his mind because he shows none of the hesitation, fear, foreboding, step-by-step argument, or gathering conviction that are characteristic of Brutus, Hamlet, Macbeth, or Lear. Even Titus Andronicus and Richard the Third in much earlier tragedies are occasionally presented more openly and with show of more raw and accessible feeling. The probable effect of this less inward focus is to free an audience to identify with either side in the political conflict or with both, or, possibly, with neither; perhaps to become aware that still greater discord and suffering is to come.

Personal motives are more clearly presented when Volumnia persuades her son to return to the Tribunes and stand trial for treason. After public places and battlefields, she establishes a domestic context for the play's action, albeit one that is dominated by her pride in the military honours Coriolanus has won. On her first entry in Act I, she boasts of his prowess and enumerates his battle-scars as welcomed signs of valour. When she hears that Martius, her grandson, has destroyed a butterfly, she promptly recognizes 'one on 's father's moods', as if savouring the resemblance (I.iii.60–9). In Act II she hails the trumpets announcing her son's return from war with:

These are the ushers of Martius. Before him

> He carries noise, and behind him he leaves tears.
> Death, that dark spirit, in 's nervy arm doth lie,
> Which being advanced, declines; and then men die.   (II.i.154–7)

But their relationship is more complex than this. When they meet, her persuasive energy and his long silences are equally remarkable. His few abrupt rejoinders hide any deeper or hidden feelings that he may have and leave his friends to respond more fully. When she promises greater praise if he will 'perform a part' he has not undertaken before, his resistance seems to disappear but his words are ambiguous because, as he imagines what will be involved, exaggeration hints at irony or sarcasm :

> Well, I must do't.
> Away my disposition; and possess me
> Some harlot's spirit!   (III.ii.112–14)

Soon he denies what he had first agreed:

> I will not do't,
> Lest I surcease to honour mine own truth,
> And by my body's action teach my mind
> A most inherent baseness.   (III.ii.122–5)

Only when Volumnia tells him, 'Thy valiantness was mine, thou suck'st it from me, / But owe thy pride thyself' (III.ii.131–2), does he do as she wishes and return to the Tribunes to 'mountebank their loves' (ll. 130–9). For the moment, it seems as if a threatened estrangement from his mother has finally changed his mind but, when he leaves the stage promising to speak 'mildly', he may well be mocking his submission by the repetition of that single uncharacteristic word. In the event, when he is again condemned in public as a traitor, his new decision no longer holds. Forgetting his mother's advice, he cries out instinctively, 'The fires i' th' lowest hell fold in the people!' and tells the Tribunes that he 'would not buy / Their mercy at the price of one fair word' (III.iii.68–9).

When the Tribunes decree that Coriolanus' punishment shall be banishment rather than death and when their sentence is confirmed

by the cries of citizens, he immediately answers by banishing the
'common cry of curs' who have condemned him. As he grows
stronger in defiance, his imagination feeds on thoughts of how his
enemies will suffer:

> Let every feeble rumour shake your hearts;
> Your enemies, with nodding of their plumes,
> Fan you into despair! Have the power still
> To banish your defenders, till at length
> Your ignorance – which finds not till it feels –
> Making but reservation of yourselves –
> Still your own foes – deliver you
> As most abated captives to some nation
> That won you without blows! Despising
> For you the city, thus I turn my back.
> There is a world elsewhere. (III.iii.126–36)

The energy of this speech implies a strong tide of feeling while its
parentheses and changing rhythms mark the varying pressures in his
mind. He then rejects the whole proceedings by leaving the stage.

But, even now, uncertainty remains. By dwelling on an unspecified disaster for Rome, his thoughts may seem, to some degree,
inchoate and unfocused. In contrast to all his talk of nobility and
service to the state, he is now roused to violence against his fellow
countrymen as if this thought had lain hidden within his own mind,
ready to be awakened. As he prepares to leave Rome, Coriolanus
may well seem only partly to know himself since he fails to recognize
that in the new 'world' elsewhere that he is about to enter he will
become a traitor and seek to destroy all that he holds most dear. He
does not stop to think of any 'ill' that 'breeds about [his] heart' or to
realize any 'insurrection' in his mind (*Hamlet*, V.ii.203 and *Lear*,
III.vi.76; *Julius Caesar*, II.i.67–9). Lacking a settled focus on his
inner experiences, members of an audience are left free to make their
own judgements about the rights and wrongs of his words and
actions. Only later do they hear that he is leading the Volscian army
and looking 'like a thing / Made by some other deity than nature'
(IV.vi.94–5), his eye 'red as 'twould burn Rome' (V.ii.63–4).

The Women's Strength

Whenever Volumnia and Coriolanus meet, their confrontations are very different in kind from those between Gertrude and Hamlet or Lady Macbeth and Macbeth, an impression of immediate feeling and multiple levels of consciousness being almost entirely absent. In performance, by responding imaginatively to suggestions in the text, actors can develop an inner consciousness for both characters but the course of the action does not depend on this: the narrative is carried foward by political and personal decisions that appear single-minded and fully articulate.

Volumnia, who believes that her son commands death's 'dark' power (II.i.154–7), is the one person able to turn him back from destroying Rome. During a long interview, neither 'colder reasons' about nobleness and honour, nor signs of submission and grief in child, wife, or mother can change how Coriolanus intends to appease his 'rages and revenges' (V.iii.86–7): he will not be moved by any 'woman's tenderness' (ll. 130–1). Yet this resistance is not easily achieved: when he starts to go away, he finds he is unable to do so; he does not reply to direct appeals and, when Volumnia con-demns his failure in duty to a mother, he 'turns away' (ll. 149, 154, 169). He remains silent when she disowns him and asks to be given her 'dispatch'. But when Volumnia herself decides to leave and begins to do so, his resolve breaks and he *holds her by the hand, silent* (l. 183, Folio S.D.). By making physical contact with his mother, against the full strength of his conscious will, he silently acknowledges the bonds of kinship that will cause him to withdraw the army with which he was about to destroy Rome. In his own words at the beginning of their meeting, he has become 'a gosling' and obeyed instinct (V.iii.35). After a mutual silence – which actors are able to sustain far longer than any ordinary hesitation or delib-erate withdrawal – he confesses that he is helpless; as if on the world's stage, he has taken part in some unreal and laughable perfor-mance, and is appalled at the consequences:

> O mother, mother!
> What have you done? Behold, the heavens do ope,

> The gods look down, and this unnatural scene
> They laugh at. O my mother, mother, O!
> You have won a happy victory to Rome;
> But for your son, believe it, O believe it,
> Most dangerously you have with him prevailed,
> If not most mortal to him. But let it come. . . .   (V.iv.183–90)

He had intended to 'stand / As if a man were author of himself / And knew no other kin' (V.iii.35–7), but he cannot do that: his eyes 'sweat with compassion' (l. 197).

Volumnia's ultimate hold over her son does not lie in anything she says but in the fact that she is his mother. Her greatest power proves to be her silent presence. She may have had intimations of this when she accompanied her son to the gates of Rome. At that time she was withdrawn, her usual confidence gone, and she no longer loaded him 'with precepts that would make invincible / The heart than conned them' (IV.i.9–11). She spoke only when, as his mother, she cursed his enemies and offered him protective advice:

> Determine on some course
> More than a wild exposure to each chance
> That starts i' th' way before thee.   (ll. 14–15, 36–7)

After he had left Rome, she was so distraught that she was considered 'mad' (IV.ii.11) and had to overcome tears before she could denounce the Tribunes who were retreating before her. When Menenius tentatively suggested, 'You'll sup with me?', she spoke of herself as a life-giving mother forced feed herself and not her child, and so destroying herself:

> Anger's my meat: I sup upon myself
> And so shall starve with feeding.   (IV.ii.53–4)

After mother and son have met in the crucial interview outside Rome, she maintains the silence in which she had prevailed against his will, giving no word of acknowledgement or welcome to his capitulation. When she returns to the city and is hailed as the 'patroness, the life of Rome!', she again says nothing, although her intention had been to save the city. While her fellow Romans prepare to praise the gods and light bonfires, her last contribution to the tragedy is the silent act of '*passing over the stage*' (V.v.1–6, and Folio S.D.). Now her presence, informed by words and actions earlier in the play, provides the only clue to help an audience imagine what her thoughts may be and what will happen to her. And that is surely enough, for the tragedy is concerned here with feelings that can be appreciated by all people and are not particular to the consciousness of a hugely gifted individual: she is a mother who has lost her only son and has nothing more to say.

Virgilia, Coriolanus' wife, walks silently by the side of Volumnia when the women return to Rome, bringing with them young Martius, the son whose last words were to pledge himself to become a fighter like his father (V.iii.128–9). Her progress through the play is very different from Volumnia's. At first, she sits sewing and saying little as she waits for her husband to return from the war; he seems to accept and value this reticence, greeting her as 'My gracious silence' to which she replies with tears of relief and joy (II.i.171–5). Once he has been banished, however, Virgilia makes her hostility to the Tribunes explicit, telling Sicinius that her husband would 'make an end of thy posterity' (IV.ii.28). Reluctant to accept that Virgilia could change so suddenly, some editors have re-allocated this speech and part of another, giving them to Volumnia and leaving the wife almost silent throughout the parting with her husband. Yet, even as her anger surfaces in words, tender feelings are still evident, causing Volumnia to reprove her 'faint puling'. Taking part in the intercession with Coriolanus when he is on the point of razing Rome, she goes 'foremost' to greet him and her 'doves' eyes' make him realize he is not made of 'stronger earth than others' (V.iii.27–9). She is the first to intercede, by looking into his eyes, and the only one who kisses him – 'a kiss', he says, 'Long as my exile, sweet as my revenge!' (ll. 44–5). Virgilia has few words to say in the tragedy but, occasionally, she draws out a gentleness from the hero that no one else does. Her last effort to change his mind is to echo Volumnia's vow to commit suicide if he does not withdraw from Rome.

Among the public encounters and ruthless actions of this tragedy, Virgilia's very presence exercises a counterpull on an audience's attention, an unfailing reminder of a trust and love that are ignored in the brutalities of war. Volumnia's presence has a similar power when it alone causes Coriolanus to change his intention to destroy Rome, a decision he had thought he would never recant. Both these women ensure that the thoughtless limitations of male heroism and self-promotion will be evident for all to see.

Death among Enemies

Coriolanus leaves Rome for 'a world elsewhere' without counting the consequences or planning any action. He seems to be driven more by instinctive frustration than any deliberate strategy. Putting on '*mean apparel*', more wretched than the 'gown of humility' he was forced to wear when asking for votes, he next appears in the Volscian city of Antium, '*disguised and muffled*' (IV.iv.0, S.D.). He is seeking out Aufidius, the enemy he had most wished to kill, and in two soliloquies he makes this purpose clear. Nowhere else does he speak so much of and for himself and yet an audience is not offered a direct entry into his mind: he gives no sign of uncertainty or growing conviction, speaking only of what he knows and has already decided:

> O world, thy slippery turns! Friends now fast sworn,
> Whose double bosoms seem to wear one heart,
> Whose hours, whose bed, whose meal and exercise
> Are still together, who twin as 'twere in love
> Unseparable, shall within this hour,
> On a dissension of a doit, break out
> To bitterest enmity. So fellest foes,
> Whose passions and whose plots have broke their sleep,
> To take the one the other, by some chance,
> Some trick not worth an egg, shall grow dear friends
> And interjoin their issues. So with me.
> My birthplace hate I, and my love's upon
> This enemy town. I'll enter. If he slay me,
> He does fair justice; if he give me way,
> I'll do his country service.   (IV.iv.12–26)

By suggesting that his proposed action is due to some 'trick not worth an egg', he might seem to belittle his intended treachery because he is ashamed of it, and yet 'So with me' can hardly convey a thought that much troubles him; indeed, the whole speech is too neatly phrased to be spoken as a struggle with a guilty conscience. The thought of being slain, however, is dealt with so briskly that his words may betray tense nerves and a narrowly focused attention.

Although Coriolanus does not speak of treachery, an audience is shown what a traitor may be when two spies meet secretly in a scene that immediately precedes his arrival at Antium and appears to have no other purpose but this. That he has placed his life in danger is also established in the prolonged and comically amazed reactions of the servants he encounters when he presents himself at Aufidius' house. Having lost all moral authority, he must rely entirely on his physical strength and the innate, personal authority that derives from that. Meeting Aufidius at the entry of his house, he acknowledges his hopeless situation and now, more specifically, offers his own 'revengeful services' to be exercised against Rome in 'mere spite' and with 'the spleen / Of all the under-fiends' (IV.v.79–93). Recognizing that what he says 'is true', Aufidius welcomes his enemy and, as Coriolanus had embraced Cominius on the field of battle (see above, p. 344), Aufidius now embraces him, making a similar, marital comparison:

> more dances my rapt heart
> Than when I first my wedded mistress saw
> Bestride my threshold.   (IV.v.117–19)

Military prowess and personal passion unite in the embrace and the long and engrained antagonism of two nations evaporates as if hard-fought campaigns were of no consequence. Calling him 'thou Mars', Aufidius offers half his commision and the leadership of his army so that Coriolanus can revenge himself on Rome. This meeting has broken down age-old convictions and both characters are now on a new footing to which an audience will have to adjust rapidly and revalue earlier events.

Before Coriolanus leaves with his former adversary, who is now his host, his only verbal response is 'You bless me, gods' (l. 136) which means that an audience is kept in doubt about the effect of his new bond with Aufidius. One of the Volscian serving-men is the first to give information:

> He is made on here within as if he were son and heir to Mars; set at upper end o' th' table, no question asked him by any of the senators but they stand bald before him. Our general himself makes a mistress of him, sanctifies himself with's hand, and turns up the white o' th' eye to his discourse. . . . He'll go, he says, and sowl the porter of Rome gates by th' ears. He will mow all down before him, . . .
>
> (IV.v.196–207)

The scene changes to Rome, where plebeians and tribunes are enjoying the fruits of the peace that Coriolanus had won by his fighting at Corioles, but that mood is soon shattered by news of the Volscian army approaching the city. Cominius gives an eyewitness account of Coriolanus leading these enemies 'like their god':

> they follow him
> Against us brats with no less confidence
> Than boys pursuing summer butterflies,
> Or butchers killing flies. (IV.vi.96–9)

More information comes from within the Volscian camp where a Lieutenant says that there must be some 'witchcraft in him' and Aufidius, in reply, admits that he 'bears himself more proudlier, / Even to my person, than I thought he would' (IV.vii.1–12). Resentment builds in Aufidius, although he admits that the new general:

> . . . bears all things fairly
> And shows good husbandry for the Volscian state,
> Fights dragon-like, and does achieve as soon
> As draw his sword. (ll. 21–4)

And still, even now, the traitorous Coriolanus is not seen on stage so that an audience can judge for itself. The action moves back to

Rome where Cominius reports his reception when he went to plead
for mercy:

> I urged our old acquaintance and the drops
> That we have bled together. 'Coriolanus'
> He would not answer to, forbade all names;
> He was a kind of nothing, titleless,
> Till he had forged himself a name o' th' fire
> Of burning Rome.   (V.i.10–14)

Besides heightening an audience's wish to know more, the delay
before Coriolanus re-enters the play demonstrates the effect of his
action on the whole city of Rome, his family and friends, senators
and tribunes, as well as the plebeians with their 'wives and children'.
By the time he does return to the stage, the consequences of his
treason are very evident while his own disregard of it may continue
to challenge an audience's understanding and risk losing its sympathy.

When at last the traitor does appear, closely watched by Aufidius,
he brusquely sends Menenius back to Rome and, in the following
scene, receives the deputation led by his mother. While she pleads
with him, he is silent and tries to turn away; he weeps and, at last,
relents and, making contact with her hand, relinquishes his revenge.
The consequences, he acknowledges, will prove 'most dangerously'
for him, perhaps 'most mortal', because he is about to go back to
Corioles with Aufidius. Once more, an audience does not hear the
making of his decision but it will understand its consequences rather
better than he; it has heard Aufidius declare his readiness to risk his
own life to break his rival's neck and so settle their 'account'
(IV.vii.24–6). From the moment he embraces Aufidius in Antium,
the hero of this tragedy has seldom been seen and, when present, has
been uncommunicative on crucial issues. An audience is left to make
its own judgement of Coriolanus, as he pursues his fierce revenge
and then experiences the tongue-tied suffering he has brought upon
himself in confrontation with his mother. 'O mother, mother! /
What have you done?' is perhaps the fullest expression of what he
has undergone. The narrative with its passions and confrontations is

at the centre of the experience that this tragedy offers, rather than the hero's developing awareness of his predicament and his own nature. The play moves on to show more consequences of his actions on the senators, citizens, and silent ladies. It is reported that the plebeians have turned on one of their tribunes:

> And hale him up and down, all swearing if
> The Roman ladies bring not comfort home
> They'll give him death by inches.   (V.iv.37–9)

When the threat to Rome is withdrawn, shouts, drums, and trumpets resound in the theatre, perhaps in Jacobean times shaking its wooden frame, but the action again moves on rapidly, this time to Corioles where Aufidius is the first to appear and, meeting with '*three or four Conspirators*', lays plans for killing Coriolanus.

Now the tragedy is soon over. When Coriolanus enters Corioles, bringing the spoils of war and peace with Rome, Aufidius denounces him to the Volscian Lords and a crowd of Commoners:

> . . . perfidiously
> He has betrayed your business, and given up,
> For certain drops of salt, your city, Rome –
> I say your city – to his wife and mother,
> Breaking his oath and resolution like
> A twist of rotten silk, never admitting
> Counsel o' th' war. But at his nurse's tears
> He whined and roared away your victory, . . .   (V.vi.93–100)

Coriolanus cannot remain silent at this:

Coriolanus.	Hear'st thou, Mars?
Aufidius.	Name not the god, thou boy of tears.
Coriolanus.	Ha?
Aufidius.	No more.
Coriolanus.	Measureless liar, thou has made my heart
	Too great for what contains it. 'Boy'? O slave! . . .

(ll. 102–5)

Disregarding much that an audience will have witnessed, he asserts
that this is 'the first time that ever / I was forced to scold' (ll. 106–7)
and immediately proceeds to remind Aufidius of the 'stripes' he has
'impressed' on him and calls everyone to a bloody fight: 'Cut me to
pieces, Volsces. Men and lads, / Stain all your edges on me.' The
insult of 'Boy' continues to wound his pride as he makes the worst
possible argument for reconciliation:

> If you have writ your annals true, 'tis there
> That, like an eagle in a dovecote, I
> Fluttered your Volscians in Corioles.
> Alone I did it, boy!   (ll. 114–17)

According to the Folio's speech-prefix, '*All People*' call out, remembering the son, daughter, cousin, or father he had killed, and
demand that he should be torn to pieces. He draws his sword,
wishing that he could slaughter 'six Aufidiuses or, more, his tribe',
and then, to cries of 'Kill, kill, kill, kill, kill him!', two of the
Conspirators strike him down. Since he wounds no one as he dies
and falls at once, he is probably killed from behind; ignomy is complete when '*Aufidius stands on him*' (Folio S.D.). In a *coup de théâtre*,
this tragic hero goes to his death shocked and helpless. He does not
reconsider past or future, but once more takes pride in his valour,
considering no other option but to fight against impossible odds,
and that he is unable to do.

An audience is given several cues for its response. A Lord who had
tried to stop the 'outrage' with 'The man is noble. . . Stand,
Audifius, / And trouble not the peace', now decries 'a deed whereat
valour will weep' (ll. 124–8, 133). Another Lord orders:

> Bear from hence his body,
> And mourn you for him. Let him be regarded
> As the most noble corpse that ever herald
> Did follow to his urn.   (ll. 142–5)

When Aufidius says he will justify what he has done to the Senate,
the Lord who had tried to stop the assassination intervenes again
with:

> His own impatience
> Takes from Aufidius a great part of the blame.
> Let's make the best of it.   (ll. 145–7)

Only Aufidius speaks further and he is now compliant – 'My rage is gone, / And I am struck with sorrow'; he asks for a drum to mark a stately funeral procession in which he will be one of the bearers:

> Though in this city he
> Hath widowed and unchilded many a one,
> Which to this hour bewail the injury,
> Yet he shall have a noble memory. Assist.

So the tragedy ends, not with reconciliation but assassination, not with forgiveness or reassessment, but outrage and mourning, not with looking forward, but a memory of what has passed. 'Rage' is soon spent and 'sorrow' strikes home; everyone is asked to 'make the best of it' and some are called to 'assist' in a funeral.

Tongue-tied Tragedy

'Let's make the best of it' is one in a series of speeches which use very ordinary words as the means of responding to extraordinary events. Neither the play's action nor the exceptional personal qualities of its hero are diminished by these devices – the excitements of the narrative and the hard energy of much of the writing will prevent that – but rather the relevance of chosen moments is enhanced by the use of familiar words that are often spoken by everyone, by the crowd that repeatedly comes onto the stage and by everyone who has gathered in a theatre to watch its performance.

Several of the most conspicuous uses of entirely ordinary speech occur after Coriolanus has been banished from Rome and the ladies return to be confronted by the Tribunes. Menenius' simple and familiar 'You'll sup with me?' offers a return to a healing normality but, as we have seen, Volumnia refuses the invitation. She then calls Virgilia to follow her:

> Come, let's go.
> Leave this faint puling and lament as I do,
> In anger, Juno-like. Come, come, come.   (IV.ii.54–6)

Although she likens herself to Jove's great queen, by four times repeating 'come' she also seems dependent on her daughter's company in a very ordinary way or, alternatively, concerned for her well-being. The Folio text directs both ladies to leave immediately so that Menenius remains on stage alone. He might be expected to soliloquize at length but all he has to say before he also leaves, is 'Fie, fie, fie!' The utmost simplicity of this repetitive speech shows that he is nonplussed and leaves onlookers to imagine the thoughts and feelings underlying it; helplessness, pity, reproof for the ladies, for Rome, or for Coriolanus, whatever the actor's performance may suggest. A moment's hesitation can accentuate any effect, a rapid and immediate exit suggest fear or personal anxiety. However played, this ordinary speech brings attention back to the situation in which the banishment of Coriolanus has left his friend and family, and Rome itself.

In much the same way, repeated silences draw attention to the pressures on individual persons and their tongue-tied helplessness. When young Martius 'kneels and holds up his hands for fellowship' alongside the ladies confronting the revengeful Coriolanus, Volumnia draws attention to the speechless boy who 'Does reason our petition with more strength / Than thou hast to deny't.' As if it has prompted her, the boy's silent pleading is followed by her own crucial decision to leave the stage and so brings about the more ominous silence shared between Volumnia and Coriolanus. Sometimes the repetition of very simple words, and not silence, shows that a speaker is conscious of the inadequacy of words, as when, almost comically, Volumnia greets her son's first, victorious return to Rome:

> I know not where to turn. O, welcome home!
> And welcome, general, and you're welcome all.   (II.i.177–8)

When Coriolanus relents and spares Rome, repetition of his first and simple verbal response – 'O mother, mother! / What have you done?' – helps to signal that this expresses his deepest feelings. It soon recurs with a slight, but meaningful variation – 'O my mother, mother, O!' – and then, once more, after he has said he will return with Aufidius to Corioles, this time significantly changed: 'O mother! Wife!' One of the thoughts lying behind these repetitions may be an acceptance of his own death which is eventually expressed with still greater simplicity. Having warned his mother that her victory may be most mortal to him, he speaks four simple words, 'But let it come' and then breaks off to speak to Aufidius (l. 190). These words are similar to those used by Hamlet in the far more explicit context of a discourse on destiny, responsibility, and death:

> There is a special providence in the fall of a sparrow . . . if it be not now, yet it will come – the readiness is all. Since no man owes of aught he leaves, what is't to leave betimes? Let be. (V.ii.211–18)

In the last Act of *Hamlet*, the prince has a clear sense of duty and fatality, expounds it carefully, and considers its outcome; in *Coriolanus*, the hero becomes almost a puppet, not manipulated by others until his very last moment but continuing to act as he did earlier, as if he had no other motive and could make no other decisions. In this later tragedy, an audience is likely to view the progress of the action and, especially, that of its last scene, as an inevitable progress towards catastrophe, a process that has political and personal consequences for the hero and those close to him and who, like him, have few words to express their private, inward thoughts. Ideals of military virtue and nobility have led Coriolanus towards slaughter and political violence, and, finally, to an ignominious death that brings no advantage to himself or anyone else. This tragedy seems to affirm the worth of nothing except the common and enduring bonds and demands of family, the on-going processes of life in which no person is alone.

16

Timon of Athens: Beyond Tragedy

In the 1623 Folio edition of Shakespeare's works, *The Life of Timon of Athens* is placed among the tragedies where it was a stop-gap when a manuscript of *Troilus and Cressida* was not available when the printers wanted it. Pointedly and uniquely, its title was not '*The Life and Death of Timon*', which would have matched those for *Richard III*, *Richard II*, and *King John*; nor was it '*The Tragedy of Timon*'. Neither would have served and yet the chosen title is also strange, since the time-span of the play is short. Perhaps it was the best that could be found for an unusual play, certainly more appropriate than 'Tragedy' in that the death of its hero is not shown and very little information is provided about its circumstances. It must have been written close in time to *King Lear* and *Coriolanus* with which it has incidents in common and speeches that echo or anticipate each other, yet it is very different from these and all other tragedies of the mid sixteen-hundreds, in tone and form, as well as characters, action, and argument.

In Act I, Timon represents the virtues of generosity and hospitality, as *Antony and Cleopatra* and *Coriolanus* provide exemplars of love and valour, but other personal qualities soon intrude on an audience's attention and obscure first impressions. Timon is also blind to the faults of others and recklessly prodigal; when all his wealth has been squandered, he is self-centred and unresponsive to offers of help and good advice. His eventual denunciations of the evils and self-serving of others are passionate with an anger that is unproductive of any change within himself beyond the growth of a corrosive hatred of his fellow men. For himself, he longs to be further impoverished and then to go away from all mankind to the salt sea and, before dying, carve himself an epitaph in stone. In the last scene, when a copy of that inscription is brought to Athens and read out to the assembled senators and soldiers, it becomes clear that the dying Timon had no thoughts of generosity or hospitality:

> Here lies a wretched corse, of wretched soul bereft;
> Seek not my name. A plague consume you wicked caitiffs left!
> Here lie I, Timon, who alive all living men did hate.
> Pass by, and curse thy fill; but pass, and stay not here thy gait.

Timon is neither tragedy nor comedy, but a moral parable, by turns satirical, passionate, argued, and spectacular. In Shakespeare's tragedies, a departure along these lines had been only faintly suggested in parts of *Lear*, *Macbeth*, and *Coriolanus*. Almost certainly, this play was an experiment that Shakespeare saw no reason to complete. The sole surviving text of the Folio has many features that make it unsuitable for performance: muddled entries, confusions, repetitions, and false trails in the plotting, passages that yield no sense, plenty of faulty versification, and some writing that is weaker in phrasing or syntax than almost anything in Shakespeare's other plays except those in texts that are obviously corrupt. Only self-contained episodes, some of them very short, seem to be fully or confidently accomplished. No record of a Jacobean performance survives and the infrequent modern productions have used heavily edited or adapted texts, often introducing a great deal of music, stage-effects, and topical stage-business. While we cannot say for sure that Shakespeare left the play unfinished because he was dissatisfied with what had been achieved, we do know that, with more plays to write, this one was to remain a one-off among all his other writings.

Timon of Athens' place in a study of Shakespeare's tragedies is not as a completed work but, mainly, as a demonstration that, during the decade in which he wrote seven major tragedies, his mind was seeking alternative forms of drama that did not concentrate so strongly on the death and consciousness of a tragic hero. *Timon* is like *Antony and Cleopatra* and *Coriolanus* in its concern with ideal qualities of mind and behaviour, but in other ways it is closer to three plays that were written in the same years, *All's Well that Ends Well*, *Measure for Measure*, and *Troilus and Cressida*, now often considered together as 'problem comedies'. These plays also develop abstract themes – the nature of nobility, personal integrity and public responsibility, war and lechery – but they do not concentrate on any one or two protagonists or a small group of privileged persons. They have plots that involve contrasted classes of society and give similar and almost equal attention to both masters and servants, notable personages and private citizens, Greeks and Trojans, in much the same way as the action of *Timon* brings its hero into contact with a wide range of less advantaged persons.

By telling the story of Timon's short journey from wealth to impoverishment and onwards towards death, while removing that death from the stage, Shakespeare had taken what proved to be a decisive step away from tragedy, even though, so far as we know, this realignment did not yield a completed alternative. The long, episodic narratives of *Pericles, Prince of Tyre* (1608–9) and the romance that the Folio calls *The Tragedy of Cymbeline* (1609–10) were to prove far more productive innovations. The varied action and frequent shifts of style of these plays are found again in the two later romance–comedies, *A Winter's Tale* and *The Tempest*, and in the history play, *Henry the Eighth*. A careful study of these plays, rather than of *Timon*, would provide a more credible view of the direction in which the writing of tragedies was leading Shakespeare.

Works Cited

Akrigg, G. P. V., *Shakespeare and the Earl of Southampton* (London: Hamish Hamilton, 1968).

Clark, Peter, *The English Alehouse: A Social History, 1200–1830* (London and New York: Longman, 1983).

Clark, Peter, 'The Alehouse and the Alternative Society', in Pennington, Donald and Thomas, Keith (eds), *Puritans and Revolutionaries* (Oxford: Oxford University Press, 1978).

Williams, Penry, *The Later Tudors: England 1547–1603* (Oxford: Oxford University Press, 1995).

Index